NOW IN MEXICO

Now In Mexico

by

HUDSON STRODE

New York

HARCOURT, BRACE AND COMPANY

"Now in Mexico you will find strange paradoxes abiding under the clearest sky."

I wish to express my thanks to *Holiday* and *Harper's Bazaar* for permission to use material that appeared as articles in these magazines. I am indebted to John Robertson and Orestes Cabutti for the use of photographs which appear over their names, and to the Mexican Tourist Association for permission to reproduce all of the other photographs in this book except those which I made

For

THÉRÈSE

Contents

FOREWORD   xiii

I. YUCATÁN   3

    1. Mérida   3
    2. Temples in a Wilderness   9

II. GEMS OF TOURIST TOWNS   22

    1. Cuernavaca   22
    2. A December Evening in Taxco   29
    3. Christmas at Acapulco   37

III. MEXICO CITY AND ITS ENVIRONS   47

    1. The Approach   47
    2. First Hours in the Capital   51
    3. Panorama in the Sun   57
    4. About the Zócalo   62
    5. Chapultepec   70
    6. Place of Flowers   75
    7. The Place of the Miracle   82
    8. The Place of the Gods   86
    9. Two Afternoons with Diego Rivera   88
    10. A Morning with Orozco   100
    11. Plaza de Toros   104
    12. The Days Pass Pleasantly   125

IV. BY MOTOR TO MICHOACÁN   136

    1. Market of Toluca   136
    2. The Road to Morelia   142
    3. The Clean City   146
    4. Church in the Afternoon   151
    5. Differences   155
    6. Quiroga   161
    7. Monster in the Corn Patch   164
    8. Uruapan for Lacquer   169

V. PÁTZCUARO   175

    1. The Lake   175
    2. Island of "Janitzio"   186

3. Workers in the Vineyard   191
4. The Jail Veranda and the Nun   195
5. Great-great-granddaughter of a Noble   206
6. Return by Tzintzuntzan   213

VI. TO PUEBLA   219

1. The Way of Brigands and Old Churches   219
2. City of the Angels   226

VII. OAXACA   232

1. The Route of the Three Volcanoes   232
2. Municipal Heart   235
3. Factory in a Garden   238
4. Private Bath and Historic Names   241
5. Corners in Antiquity   244
6. The Stirrup Servant   249
7. Within the Doors   256
8. Strange Fruit and Priceless Treasure   260

VIII. THE ISTHMUS OF TEHUANTEPEC   266

1. The Women of Juchitán   266
2. Ixtepec by Night and Day   282
3. And So to Bed in Tehuantepec   287
4. Food and Farewell   296

IX. SAN MIGUEL DE ALLENDE   303

1. Historic Pleasure Town   303
2. With the Artists   313
3. Bits of Talk and Music   320

X. QUERÉTARO   328

1. To the Glory of God and Man   328
2. Convents and an Execution   337
3. Sunday Shopping   345
4. A Cake and Departure   352

XI. POSTWAR   359

EPILOGUE   367

Illustrations

FACING PAGE

The domes and towers of San Miquel de Allende   112
Entrance to the harbor of Acapulco
The parish church at Taxco
A colonial doorway in Mexico City
Church and volcano
Bearing burdens in a weary land
The aqueduct to Queretaro
The peak of Orizaba
Primitive agriculture
On the road near Amecameca
The canals of Xochimilco
Mexican street scene
Rufino Tomayo and his wife
A church on the outskirts of Cholula
A lonely church on the road to Puebla
In the ancient village of Huegotzingo

All Taxco lies on hills   272
The maguey is the typical plant of Mexico
A village cross
Water carrier
Mariposa fish net and dugout canoe, Lake Patzcuaro
Temple sculptures
Cacti before the pyramidal temple
The famous giant Ahuehuete tree
Children played at its roots centuries before Cortes
Old man of Juchitan
A beauty of Juchitan
Diego Rivera in his garden museum
Chucho Solarzano with his son
Children of Lake Patzcuaro fishermen
Flower girl at Xochimilco
A pure-blooded Tarascan Indian boatman on Lake Patzcuaro

Foreword

IT WAS the aging widow of the famous romancer Sir Rider Haggard who gave me a special slant on Mexico, after I had twice visited the land myself. I was taken to see her at the family seat in Norfolk by her husband's nephew Admiral Sir Vernon Haggard. Old Lady Haggard was in her eighties, and so crippled with British rheumatism that she walked with two sticks. But if her legs were halting, her mind and her conversation were as sharp as her steel-gray eyes. Knowing that she had traveled with her storytelling husband over the face of the globe, I asked her what country was to her the most vivid in memory. For a moment she seemed to let the far-flung regions of her journeys whirl past in revolving panorama. Then she said, "Mexico."

Looking into space, she visibly began to recapture glimpses of the past. "We were there in the early nineties—in the time of Díaz. It remains as clear in retrospect as the white-and-blue atmosphere of the high plateau. To an Anglo-Saxon its ways are more astonishing than those of other lands more notoriously exotic. For often in the most everyday events you do not quite believe your eyes. Mexico is an eternal drama . . . the Indians unaware they are acting and making pictures every time they move . . . the Spaniards and mestizos rather consciously dramatizing themselves. I will give you an instance. On our walks along the streets we would often be fascinated by the extraordinary ladies at their iron-grilled windows. There they sat, enameled and bejeweled, exhibiting their hands—for all the citizens to see—on pastel satin pillows, pale yellow, mauve, or azure. Their pointed nails were an inch long—to prove that they were ladies of such essential decoration that they were as incapable as the Venus de Milo of doing anything useful with their fingers."

Lady Haggard gripped tightly the knobby handles of her sticks, as if to reassure herself that though racked by rheumatism she could still do things with her own octogenarian digits.

"The emphasis on façade! On what was shown to the world!" she went on remembering. "In the afternoons those ladies who did not sit before their windows with the satin cushions took the air in carriages that concealed their persons below the waist. Up and down the boulevards they drove, in full décolletage, with diamonds dangling from their ears, or woven in their dark hair or looped about their thickly powdered throats. The bodices of their gowns were of lace or silk or velvet, very rich and fancy. Never have I seen such lush beauties on parade. But the glamour went only waist-deep, as we found."

The old lady's lips drew together in a restrained smile. "My husband and I came upon a sorry sight in the suburbs. Two ladies of our acquaintance had been overturned in their carriage. There they stood by a roadside ditch among trailing moon flowers like some mythical creatures half this, half that. Above the waist full evening dress, jewels, and camellias. Below the waist—which the world could not see in the depth of the carriage—monk-brown flannel petticoats. On their feet they wore flapping red carpet slippers that might have belonged to their slaveys. We gave them a lift back to the city—and throughout the agonizing drive the hectic flush of their embarrassment showed crimson through their thick powder. The poor creatures were quite prominent in society, but never during the rest of the season while we remained in Mexico did they have the courage to venture out. It was a pity, for they were most amiable as well as extremely pretty, though they had hardly a sentence of really interesting conversation between them." Lady Haggard relaxed her grip on her sticks.

"Strange," she went on speculatively after a moment, "that a land so opulent and original in its natural beauty should have an upper middle class so easily beguiled by sham and show. But for all its pretensions and perversities, I remember Mexico with special affection. Parts of it seem like a fantastic land my imaginative husband might have made up for one of his wild tales. You hardly believe Mexico when you are there. You may laugh over it. You may suffer over it. But invariably it fascinates. And it stays in memory."

Luncheon was announced. But before Lady Haggard gathered herself together to rise, she turned to her nephew the Admiral who had never visited Mexico and continued her rumination for some moments.

"Mexico is a mural created by a collaboration between divinity and man. Deity is there in the brilliant sky, the volcanic cones, the fantastic vegetation. The Spanish builders provided churches and palaces and plazas worthy of the landscape. The Indians by their complexions, their costumes, their innate picturesqueness, lend themselves to artistic grouping."

She grasped her sticks and rose, and then stood still. "In retrospect," she said with a nod, turning toward me, "all Mexico, from the rock-studded deserts of the north to the flowery hot lands of the coast, is one vast mural never to be forgotten."

After the publication in 1944 of *Timeless Mexico,* a history on which I had spent three years' writing, I received many letters both from friends and from persons unknown to me who said in effect: "This is all very well, but we want to know something about Mexico besides history. We want to know more about the land and the people today. We would like to learn of places to go and things to do. We want to know why the alien corn of Mexico is so appealing to you." For some months I thought on the matter. And then I set to work to write another book on Mexico. Fortunately I had kept rather full notes of daily happenings.

This book is a selective recountal of various trips to different parts of the country made at intervals during the past eleven years. For the sake of variety and for emphasis, I have arbitrarily chosen from strings of weeks special days to write about. Sometimes on these trips I was alone; sometimes my wife accompanied me; sometimes I traveled with old friends, and sometimes with new friends. I have chosen to write of certain visits rather than others because the happenings seem better calculated to reflect the varied atmosphere and the diurnal drama of Mexico.

So this is not a tale of a continuous journey like *South by Thunderbird.* The record lies between 1935, when I first arrived on Mexican soil in a little six-passenger Sikorsky amphibian, and 1946, when I left by one of the great Stratoclippers. But the majority of the stories about places visited belong to the year 1943, though I may have seen those places also in '35 or '41 or '46. The persons mentioned throughout are real, and what they say in the book is what they said at the time.

In *Now in Mexico,* though my sympathies are not disguised, my attitude is one of friendly comment, not of criticism or crusade. My hopeful purpose is to give pleasure, as in *Timeless Mexico* it was to give information and interpret history. If the Courteous Reader misses this or that in the present volume, he may be able to find it in *Timeless Mexico,* for in a sense the two books complement each other, and I have endeavored to avoid repetition. I have made use of such selection and emphasis and implication as seem helpful in revealing the social seductions of Mexico's civilization and the contrasting merits of its scenery.

"The thing that strikes me," Will Rogers once remarked in speaking of Mexico, "is that we go away over to Europe and prowl all around hunting for odd and different things. And here they are at our very doorstep. I was all around Spain and Italy, Russia, and Switzerland, and Holland, and all of them, and there is more quaintness and difference to see here in Mexico than in the whole of Europe." In his shrewd and homespun way the man from Oklahoma merely spoke a pregnant truth. Our next-door neighbor to the south is more alien than any province of Europe. The strangeness and the beauty lie just across a river.

In a story by José Rubén Romero, a man goes up on a hill above a town to contemplate the landscape, "to fish for memories," he says, "with the landscape as my bait." I have the hope that this book may serve as bait for those who have visited Mexico either briefly or for a long sojourn, that references here and there may bring fresh to mind pictures that time has dimmed. For those who have never visited the fabulous land to the south with its storehouse of diverting scenes, I hope that this book may prove an apéritif to the traveler's feast. As Enobarbus said of the glittering Cleopatra, if one has failed to see Mexico, he has then left unseen a wonderful piece of work.

HUDSON STRODE

Cherokee Road
Tuscaloosa, Alabama
July 23, 1947

NOW IN MEXICO

I

Yucatán

The art of the tropics, like the civilization produced there, is always a total thing. To express itself it utilizes all forms and all rhythms. The primitive peoples of the cold and temperate zones call this barbarous, because the penury of their surroundings reflects itself in their judgment.

—JOSÉ VASCONCELOS

I. MÉRIDA

IT WAS MORE BY chance than design that I approached Mexico the first time by the Cortés way. On the second day of July 1935 I was in Havana, and a Sikorsky amphibian was scheduled for the Isle of Cozumel off the coast of Yucatán. From Cuba's chamois-colored capital we flew to the southwest—the direction in which Hernán Cortés had sailed with inordinate self-confidence more than four centuries ago. After the lush mosaic of sugar-cane and tobacco plantations, we flew over the Strait of Yucatán, where the indigo-blue was more intense than any blue the sky has ever known. At half-past one a dark speck that was Cozumel came into view. Soon we were circling above the vanished footprints of conquistadors, the tracks of their fabulous horses, the imprints of musket butts and lance stocks. The plane swerved inward and hovered over a purple lagoon, its verdant edges studded with white cranes. As the amphibian skimmed the water's surface, the birds rose into the air like holy men making ascensions, and disappeared over the plumes of the coconut palms.

We taxied to a rude wooden pier, where a tall, swarthy fellow with enormous black mustaches came to greet us. Adjusting the holster of the foot-long revolver that was strapped to his waist, he asked us courteously in a soft-spoken bass if we would not refresh ourselves with fresh pineapple and coffee. He led the way up the dirt path to the passenger hut, where refreshments had been prepared. A flattish mail sack lay sealed for air transport. In the place and the moment, the primitive and the contemporary mingled with easy harmony.

I took my coffee and my plate of sliced pineapple and went to sit on a rise of ground in the shade of a palm tree. As I listened for historical echoes in the sea-washed air, only an idyllic calm pervaded the island.

It was not Cortés who first discovered Yucatán, but Hernández Gonsalvo de Córdoba. He had sailed from Cuba exactly two years before the date of the great conquistador's epic departure. But Córdoba found the Indians of Yucatán unfriendly, and they killed and wounded so many Spaniards that the expedition returned without reward. The leader himself succumbed ten days after he reached Cuba.

A year and two months later, on April 6, 1518, Juan de Grijalva, "a hopeful, well-behaved young man," sailed for Yucatán and discovered this "Isle of Swallows." Grijalva came upon towns of stone-paved streets and houses of stone with grass roofs, and a tower, "large at base and small at top." Though this expedition also proved a failure as far as loot was concerned, it was Grijalva's report that fired Cortés's imagination and launched the fleet of little ships on the unsurpassed adventure.

The tenth of February was the auspicious day in 1519 on which the eleven small vessels of Cortés sailed into history. On board, as many schoolboys know, there were one hundred and nineteen sailors, five hundred and eight soldiers, a few hundred Indian slaves, and sixteen horses destined to their own special immortality. In the artillery there were ten small cannon and four field pieces called falconets. Among the fighting men, only thirteen were musketeers and thirty-two, crossbowmen.

When Cortés landed on Cozumel, he found a deserted village not far from the shore. All the natives had run into hasty hiding, but they had left behind a few golden trinkets. This little gold was the appetizer to the great gorging to follow. Out of respect to Christian theology, the native village idols were immediately laid low; and Cortés ordered his stonemasons to build an altar. Here he set up an image of the Virgin and left it for the Indians' speculation. But Cortés did not tarry long in Cozumel, for he felt magnetic forces drawing him to the greater lode in Mexico proper.

We on air-transport schedule tarried only long enough for the refueling of the plane and to let the pilot eat a bowl of sheep's brains cooked in black butter. From the lagoon we flew northward, leaving the Island of Swallows to its drowsy peace until the arrival of the next "thunderbird."

For almost two hours we flew over a solid jungle of trees, like a painted green-black sea stretching beneath us. Some of the trees were pine and some were sapote, which produce chicle, the essential ingredient for chewing gum and one of the major factors in Yucatán's economy. At four o'clock we sighted the multitude of whirling windmills that mark the city of Mérida. In the flashing of their silver blades they resembled great birds on ridgepoles twirling wings in some calisthenic ritual. But they did not rise and vanish like the cranes. They stuck to their job of catching the sea breeze and pumping water for the householders of Yucatán's bright capital.

Mérida was a Spanish town almost four decades before Captain John Smith was born in Devon, and seventy-eight years old before the *Mayflower* pilgrims sighted the rock they called Plymouth. Officially founded in 1542 by Don Francisco de Montejo, the city is in reality vastly older. Long before the Spaniards came it was the important Mayan town called Tihoo, for the sacred bird of the Mayas. The Christians razed the pagan city's austere symmetry and reset the blocks of stones after the Moorish fashion. The date 1542 merely marked the year of the Spanish rebuilding and rededication.

Mérida's landing-field was cut out of the same solid stone that furnished building material for the municipality. Though the co-pilot let down the amphibian's wheels by the cable crank, it was like landing in another lagoon, for water stood several inches deep. A torrential tropical rain had just preceded us. The streets were canals. The water sucked at the hubs of the automobile wheels, and boys on bicycles doused their feet on every downward stroke of the pedals.

The surface of Yucatán rests on a porous limestone formation resembling that of Bermuda, and a cloudburst is quickly absorbed. By the time we had covered the distance from the airport to the capital's main plaza the waters had subsided. Señoritas in bright-colored organdies and with flowers in their hair were taking their afternoon drive in *pulpitos,* the high narrow black buggies so called because their structure resembles a pulpit. "See, señor," said the dark-skinned

English-speaking chauffeur, "the rainbow has shattered to bits and fallen onto the carriages."

The first impression that Mérida gave was one of remarkable neatness and cleanliness, as if it had been washed daily by the heavens and dried by the sun. The rain had so deepened the azure and oleander and buttercup colors of the houses that they seemed freshly recalcimined for some fiesta.

The windmills at a distance had suggested pastoral Holland. The streets a foot deep in water a quarter-hour ago had recalled Venice. Now the Moorish-Spanish façades bespoke Seville. The Plaza Mayor, planted with the Indian laurels salvaged from the wreck of a Bombay cargo boat on its way to Cuba, reminded me of those other lovely laurels finally planted on Havana's Prado.

On the streets of Mérida modernity and the past and another very ancient past rub shoulders companionably. American motorcars and electric lights and easy-going traffic cops are imposed upon an emphatic Spanish colonial atmosphere and a population that is predominantly Mayan in feature and physique. For a city as old, as isolated, and as unvisited as Mérida has been until the last decade, its modern aspects are surprising. Yet progress has not interfered with that ineffable quality called atmosphere. The spiritual languages of diverse cultures blend in a chorus that is peculiarly agreeable—mild-voiced rather than exciting.

The dark-skinned people on the streets—except for occasional obvious scions of Spanish landlords and merchants—belong to the ancient past. In feature and color they are of the race that achieved the remarkable temple-building civilization between the seventh and twelfth centuries. Through expert anthropological researches and measurements, the Mayas of today can lay claim to twenty-five hundred years of continuous residence in the Yucatán Peninsula. From the scientific examinations of skeletons it is conceded that the majority of the present race has maintained its physical characteristics. For the most part, the Mayans are smallish people of relatively light skeletal setup. In aspect they are gentle, with kindly eyes and melancholy mouths. Their white-drill pajama suits and straw hats make their sun-beaten faces browner, their dark eyes blacker.

On Calle 59, the motorcar stopped at No. 495. Until recently the Hotel Itzá had been a private mansion large and handsome enough to be called a palace. Its owner, a Spaniard of purported highborn lineage, had become a tavern host. The vast double doors made for a coach-and-four opened onto a vestibule used as the lobby. Beyond an arcaded corridor a patio was so jungle-thick with orange trees and flowering shrubs that the fountain was almost obliterated by the tropical greenery. Three barefooted, white-suited mozos escorted me up the stairs and around the gallery, which was furnished with hammocks and wicker long chairs and huge Chinese jars. The walls were lined with cases of museum treasures, relics of Mayan, Aztec, and Spanish colonial culture. The rows of glass cases were interspersed with cabinets of stuffed tropical birds, rare insects resembling intricately carved jewels, and butterflies sparkling in death.

My room turned out to be a suite with ceilings twenty feet high and with a crystal chandelier that might have graced the Vatican. The hangings in the sitting-room were amber satin with gold-colored cords four inches thick. The chairs were high-backed and gilded, like those in palace scenes of 1890 dramas. In one corner of the bedroom, a bath had been partitioned off as a tribute to modernity. But there were no screens at the great windows. Yards and yards of white netting trailed from a ceiling hook over the bed, where "Katharine Hepburn slept" one of the brown boys informed me.

As I was unpacking my bags an ingratiating young man with rich olive skin and even white teeth announced himself. He had the engaging and assured air of one who expects to be liked at sight. His name was Enrique Valles, he said, with a natural smile, but one flashing like an Arab's. But he was called Henry, and he was to be my personal guide during my stay in Yucatán. He spoke good English, without an accent, for he had attended school in New York from the age of eight to fourteen. "Now we are quite poor," he said debonairly. "But my grandmother once owned one of the largest ranches in the country—that was twenty-five years ago. We had five years of drought, the cattle died to the last one, the crops failed five times. We were ruined. So was almost everyone else. Now we begin again." His smile was charming. "At what hour shall we start to do the town?"

The next morning a fine breeze from the Gulf of Mexico twenty-four miles away was whirling the multitude of windmills briskly for the service of its hundred thousand inhabitants. In Yucatán the rivers run underground and measureless to man, like those of Xanadu. The windmills sucked the water from subterranean streams to the surface. The average householder, unless he caught rain water in jars and barrels, had to depend upon the wind for his water supply, because until only a few years before there was no municipal water-supply system whatever.

"The name 'Yucatán,'" said Henry as we set off to the market, "means 'Land of Yucca or Henequen.' But we think of Yucatán as 'the land of the deer and the pheasant.' By the way, let me recommend venison for dinner, and ask them to serve it in white sauce with raisins and olives."

The market in Mexico is the social meeting-ground of the humble. This morning Mérida's market was a study in sepia and yellow and cream, with high lights in green and scarlet. Though thickly crowded, it was slow-rhythmed. There was no jostling, no loud talk, no melodramatic haggling, as in the souks of Tunis. Indian girls sat on low stools or on the ground motionless as idols, with their country wares spread out on spotless white cloths, their bare feet tucked decorously out of the way. One dove-eyed damsel had nothing to sell but four speckled guinea eggs and some little bundles of dried cornsilk tassels, "good for flavoring beef or broth," and little mounds of ground squash seed, "good for flavoring almost anything." The girls were all dressed in chaste white cotton, and looked demurely at the ground when Henry and I paused before them.

A toothless old woman smoking a brown cheroot sat before trays of unground spices, adding to the deeper sepia tones of the scene. On either side of her, men in vast sombreros sat before yellow and orange and green and speckled red pyramids of fruit: tamarinds, guavas, pomegranates, star apples, custard apples, papayas, and sweetsops. A wrinkled Korean in an undershirt and tan trousers offered to sell us a live brown squirrel, as he shared the banana he was eating with the little animal. A matron in chemise and mud-colored rebozo squatted in the shade before a pile of panama hats—"the finest hats are woven in pails of water in dark caves." An emaciated man in white pajamas dispensed baked banana leaves from a stack—"they are for wrapping tamales." A sad-faced boy looking like a poet stood behind a counter under a pavilion of unbleached domestic regarding the geometric patterns he had just formed of green string beans and tuberoses.

The bargaining was done quietly, in monosyllables and semi-whispers. Sometimes it was carried on with nods and signs, as if buyer and seller were gentle-mannered deaf-mutes.

Hammocks by the thousands were stacked in bales, coarse machine-made ones of sisal hemp for only five pesos, and beautiful handmade hammocks of linen for a bride's hope chest. "The poor spend a great part of their lives in hammocks," Henry said. "They are the one indispensable article of furniture in a peasant's hut. They are cheap and cool, and protect you from crawling insects."

As we moved among the kaleidoscope of buyers at the multicolored fish counters, I realized I was thirsty, and asked where we could get a drink of water. Henry's bright intelligent eyes darkened. "Let me warn you now, never to take a drink of water that any woman in Yucatán hands you." I looked at him quizzically. "Our women know a trick of preparing a glass of water that looks genuine, but it's *love water*. If a man drinks it, he falls in love with the woman, and becomes her slave. I know. I have a relative who is that kind of victim of his wife. My grandmother says it's absolutely true. And she knows the formula of preparing the water. No man does. It has something to do with the female's secrets. But it's deadly. . . . Of course, girls from the best families are not supposed ever to give you love water when you are calling. But never risk it, except in the very best society."

We stopped at the nearest bar and ordered bottled beer. With the beer, the barmaid brought us a little pottery bowl filled with odd-looking objects. "This is perfectly safe," Henry reassured me, laughing as I stared. "Appetizers—bits of fried pig's hide and crisp curlicues of pig's intestines."

2. TEMPLES IN A WILDERNESS

At four in the afternoon, pilgrims by Buick, we started for the Mecca of the ancient Mayas, Chichen Itzá. The road to the temples was paved with evil as well as good intentions—the worn places and the hazardous bumps were evidence of political rake-offs. The eighty miles of paving between Mérida and Chichen Itzá had been constructeu at great expense in 1928 and dedicated with exultation and high hopes. But soon the corrosion of graft or negligence showed up in the poor workmanship and the road became a symbol of inefficiency and the constant repairing the theme of derisive jokes.

The landscape of the flat limestone plains was not alluring. It had a dry and barren aspect, though the poverty of the inhabitants was mitigated by their wantlessness. The famed henequen plantations were hundreds of acres of dark spiny plants following hundreds of acres of the same thing, with only an occasional plastered hacienda fallen into disrepair. The henequen used for hemp fiber is cousin to that decorative shrub we in the United States call the century plant. But under the hot sun of Yucatán it may unfold its white waxen candelabra every five years, though in the actual production of henequen it is not allowed to bloom at all.

Some of the fields were immaculately groomed, but half of them appeared neglected or abandoned. In Mérida men had complained that the lands had gone to ruin because of the Government's expropriation and the parceling out of the estates among the peons. The former owners were bitter about the new revolutionary land division. The peasants, they said, cared for nothing but a hand-to-mouth existence, and would not work if they possessed beans and corn for the morrow. The radical Government has ruined not only the plantation-owners, they said, and the henequen industry, but the land itself; for it takes seven years' cultivation after initial planting before a new crop is marketable. And they had also ruined the peasant himself, they declared, for he had no initiative of his own and could only work under direction.

This reactionary complaining seemed to have some basis in fact, for to right and left of the road lay apparent proof of the allegation. But I recalled the exact opposite opinion of John Lloyd Stephens, when he wrote of his famous journey to the temples a century before: "The whole way lay through lands of waste and desolation, showing fatal effects of accumulation in hands of large proprietors."

When Stephens wrote, the trouble lay not only in the greed that made such a variance between the limited hierarchy of haves and the multitudes of have-nots, but in the vicious absentee-landlord convention which has cursed all Latin America since the white men took over.

The great prosperity that came to Yucatán four or five decades ago sprang from the Spanish-American War in 1898. The hemp used by the United States in twine rope, sackings, and especially as binders for the wheat shocks of our Midwest harvests, had previously been imported from the Philippines. When the supply was temporarily cut off by the war in the Pacific, United States importers turned to Yucatán for sisal. As the price more than doubled, the Yucatecan landlords became rich. Fortunately the state had an honest governor, Olegario Molina, who created an export tax on sisal and used the money for civic and state improvements. After fifteen years of unprecedented boom, an agent of President Venustiano Carranza was put in command of Yucatán and set about his political and economic "reforms."

Among other things he created a cartel of governmental control of sisal sales and boosted the price charged to the United States importers to such an unreasonable figure that they began to encourage other markets, and shortly were buying heavily not only from the Philippines again and from Cuba and the Bahamas, but from equatorial Africa. The sisal market in Yucatán tobogganed. And shortly the Government, which had artificially elevated the price, began to confiscate certain haciendas and tracts and to divide the land among the workers. But many of the Indians did not care to be bothered with larger responsibilities. So now there are weeds and waste where not many years ago there were fruition and prosperity— at least for some.

Villages of clustered huts made of earth, stones, and fodder-colored thatch broke the monotony of the way. Some houses were almost entirely concealed behind vicious cactus fences twice a man's height. Some were set close to the road's ditches and open-doored, with orange-brown children playing on the dirt floor and old women swinging gently in the hammocks. Along the road, groups of pajama-suited workmen were plodding homeward with rifles across their shoulders, and carrying gunny sacks as well as machetes. "In Yucatán," said Henry, "the farmers do not live on the farms. They live in villages and walk to their work. They always take their guns along in case food flies overhead." One little man grinned at us and patted his thick bag proudly as we passed him. "He's shot a wild turkey," Henry said. "The woods are full of them, and sometimes they cross the fields."

I wondered if Aldous Huxley had not been misled by mere appearances when he wrote of Yucatán in 1934: "As for the life of the laborers—that is poisoned . . . by the interminable village feuds and family vendettas which make it necessary for every man to go about armed to the teeth, ready at any moment to shoot or be shot." It was not for organized manslaughter they were so equipped, but for routine work and in hope of passing wild game.

The Indians of Yucatán today, Henry insisted, are as honest as they are mild-natured. When they are not friendly, they are merely apathetic. Even when drunk they do not become pugnacious, as the Yaquis do, but more docile and gentle. Those who can read the newspapers are shocked at the homicides and thefts of the ill-tempered, hotheaded folk of Mexico City and Chicago.

"Happiness is very cheap in the tropics," Henry went on, almost speculatively. "Perhaps that is why we have virtually no crime. We often had to fight in ancient days, but we did not like to. Mayas never glorified war or encouraged it by carving battle scenes on the temple walls. And the Mayas we are passing now live much like our ancestors. Corn to make tortillas and a place to sling a hammock—those are about the only necessaries of the people."

Henry's face suddenly lit up and he nodded for me to look down the road. A mile in front of us across the plain rose a pyramid, shimmering like mother-of-pearl mirage in the afternoon sun. Behind it and on both sides stretched the castellated jungle. When we drew nearer I saw that the pyramid rose dramatically from ground flat as a cow pasture. And here and there scrub cattle were cropping at the dry grass growing all about. No sacred cows ever chewed their cuds in more splendid shadows. For in every direction the eye might take, white temples rose, making a scene beyond compare in the lands north of Panamá. In all of Europe that lies above Italy and Greece there is no antique show to compare with this one in the heart of Yucatán.

The city of Chichen Itzá itself had died before Cortés was born. The jungle had already drawn a pall of concealing green over the consecrated place. On the Fourth of July in 1838, John Burke, an American engineer working on a henequen plantation half a day's walk to the south, had rediscovered the dead city. John Lloyd Stephens says that Burke was the first white man to behold the ruined temples after the collapse of Spanish domination in Mexico. When Burke, the engineer, and Stephens, the New York lawyer, looked on these stupendous relics, the fecund jungle had smothered the sacred city until only bits of its treasures were to be discerned. It was Stephens who told the world about the templed area which was then privately owned by a Spanish cattleman, ignorant of its significance. A century ago, when the feudal system was yet in rank flower, the whole of Yucatán was owned by less than a hundred Spanish families. And the once proud and defiant Mayas, who had valiantly kept the conquistadors at bay for sixteen years, had become so abject that the laborer crawled like a dog to kiss the hand of the alien overseer who had just finished lashing him. The plantation-owner would shrug and say of descendants of the temple-builders, "The Indians cannot hear except through their backs."

Now with the recent restorations and excavations of the Carnegie Institution and the Mexican Government, the architectural treasures of the city have been brought to light again, but its mystery is still to be fathomed. The hieroglyphs about the temple walls have yielded few of their secrets, and even on these scientists rarely come to accord. When the first Christians arrived, they not only burned the books, but made it a rigid practice to obliterate traditions, as well as memorials, wherever possible. Who the ancient Mayas were, whence they came and why, no one can say with absolute authority. A titled English anthropologist made a lifework of trying to prove that they were of the lost tribes of Israel. That they were an agricultural people, cultivating maize and beans and squash, we know, and that they had achieved an advanced civilization in some respects superior to European civilization at the same time in the Middle Ages is stoutly maintained. We know that after they had established their culture they were invaded and conquered by certain strong tribes from the north, and these mingled their ways and their religion with those of the defeated. The architecture of the Maya speaks for itself straight to the brain and heart of man today as something remarkable that only a developed people could have achieved.

We did not tarry now for either admiration or talk, for it was almost dinnertime. We drove on out of the clearing, and turned to the right into the woods. A half-mile farther we reached the grounds of Mayaland Lodge. As we drove up the winding road to the door of the hostelry, on this Fourth-of-July afternoon, I thought of John Burke's long holiday trek that other Fourth of July in 1838 which had ended in wonderment.

This hostelry sits unique and luxury-offering in the midst of a jungle, with temples and pyramids and ruined palaces for neighbors. Spread about an inclined garden, landscaped with subtle care for tropical naturalness, it splits into many parts: a long low central building, which is mostly enormous veranda and dining-room, and several white-stucco bungalows built in ancient Mayan style with overhanging roofs of fresh-scented thatch.

I was shown to the north room of Bungalow No. 1. The room was immaculate, with hand-carved modernistic-looking furniture embodying Mayan motifs, and yellow field flowers in brass bowls. I undressed quickly in the sweet odor of thatch that filled all the breathing-space between maroon-tiled floor and hay-green roof. I took a hot shower and a cold one, and then began a rubdown in a state of semi-intoxication and wonder. For out of the rectangular window, set chest-high, I gazed through an unprecise clearing in the trees upon the magnificent Temple of the Warriors. The great masonry platform of white stone with its superimposed temple and its colonnade of a thousand roofless columns gleamed against a screen of primeval verdure. As I watched, the illumination from the setting sun touched the temple with its alchemy and turned it into a mass of white gold. I stood leaning against the window frame, entranced, and let the evening air do the towel's function. Twilight is brief in the tropics. As the sun dropped swiftly, it sent up a last red flare that bathed the temple in rosy radiance and turned the pale-gold pillars to shafts of pink pearl. Quickly the transfiguration was over, and the temple became a blur of oyster-white in the dusk.

By the time I had dressed, the night creatures were tuning up for their accustomed summer evening's concert. In the dining-room I was seated at a small table across from the beautiful Norwegian-looking wife of a Yale law professor. We dined well on *pavo en pebre:* turkey breast cooked with sour oranges, almonds, onions, and tomatoes. For dessert we had green limes stuffed with shredded coconut and stewed in sugar until almost crystallized.

While coffee and liqueurs were being served, a distant low drum-beat captivated everybody's attention. It was a jungle sound that was unexpected. I thought of the Indians beating on turtle shells with deerhorns whom the Spaniards had heard before they were routed in their attempt at conquest in 1535. But the insistent sound came not from the forest, but from the little settlement half a mile away. We learned that a traveling marionette troupe was giving a "gala" per-formance—a love romance, a risqué farce, and a bullfight, all for the price of one admission. I offered to entertain at a box party. With the aid of one uncertain flashlight and a thousand vagrant fireflies, three of the guests, Henry, and I picked our way down the muddy road to the show. The playhouse turned out to be the side veranda of the general store. We were given choice seats, on cracker boxes on the front row—eight cents each.

The veranda was crowded beyond capacity. The overflow of spec-tators stood on the bare earth alongside the veranda like the ground-lings in Shakespeare's time. Between us and the improvised stage, three vari-aged infants of the master puppeteer and his lady lay sleeping on burlap sacks, like offerings to the Tragic Muse. The per-formance was illuminated by one acetylene torch, attached to a porch pillar and supplemented by a lighted taper held by the tousle-headed eight-year-old son of the showman.

This youngster also played the double drums between acts and handled one of the puppets in the final number, a burlesque bull-fight. When it came his time to work the strings, a smaller brother, aged six, was scheduled to take his place at the drums. But there was a halt in the procedure. The substitute had disappeared. The father, backstage, called his name in hoarse whispers. "Gonzalo!" The mother began to call aloud with anxiety, "Gonzalo! Gonzalo!" The audience grinned and began to take up the call: "Gonzalo, we want Gonzalo." Frogs croaked gutturally, as if calling Gonzalo. Men poked about the yard searching for the substitute drummer. And then he was discovered by one of the patrons, who rolled him out from a bundle of carpet like Cleopatra before Caesar, but semi-clothed and scowling. He had only sneaked into the pile to take a nap. Now like a zombi he was set up on his stool and handed his drumsticks, and the show went on. Amid shouts of glee from the audience, the puppet bull cavorted grotesquely, and finally, like a more original and manly Ferdinand, seized the sword from the matador, ran him through, and won the lady for himself.

The Indians laughed uproariously when the doomed bull turned the tables and conquered the conqueror. Here was a revolution in entertainment—an eight-penny puppet show in the very shadow of the pyramid where once human sacrifices had been enacted in gory earnest and maidens had passed in sacrificial procession on their way to be drowned in the Sacred Pool.

That night as I sank into a luxurious inner-spring mattress set in a bed carved with a stylized design of jaguars, the contrasts in time and history seemed no more than aspects of the same dream. The July air was fresh, and sweet with lemon blossoms and mimosa. Sleep came quickly.

At six everyone was awakened. By seven we were on our way to the temples. The natives know how to co-operate with the climate. The guides pay tribute to the sun by remaining in the shade from ten to four. In summer, the arranged hours for temple-visiting are seven to ten in the morning and four to six in the afternoon. So the tourist never suffers from the heat or is exhausted with a too-much-ness, though the temples of Chichen Itzá are scattered over a radius of two miles and the visitor must go on foot.

When I viewed the plain that was once the center of the holy city and saw the massive white structure luminous in the early morning light, I felt much as those Spanish soldiers did who rushed to tell Cortés that they saw house walls of pure silver.

In the center of the plain, the vast compound mass of El Castillo, the Temple of the Plumed Serpent, is built up solid from the ground seventy-five feet—a pyramid composed of nine receeding terraces, with a square pavilion on top. The summit is approached from the four directions of the compass by grand staircases of ninety-one steps each. At the foot of the stairs gigantic feathered snakes lie open-mouthed, with lashing tongues—to Mayan pilgrims an awe-inspiring warning of the world's great snare.

From the high pavilion of the temple there is a splendid sweep of panorama. The landscape is laid out much like a university spread over a hundred acres: some buildings in the open meadows, some half-concealed among the trees. Henry pointed out different tombs,

palaces, and pyramids, some audacious in austerity, some richly decorated with traceries and mosaics.

Toward whichever corner of the twelve-winded sky I looked there
was a work of art and beauty. In this direction stood the Temple of
the Tigers; in that, the House of the Dark Writing. The Temple of
the Warriors, which I had seen from my bathroom, lay at the northwest corner of the group of the Thousand Columns. In that direction was the rounded Caracol, or Observatory. The Red House was
back in the forest. Still farther south was the Nunnery, where the
virgins were housed in splendor before they were sacrificed in the
sacred *cenote*.

Exposed to the intense sun, the epigraphic structures stand mysterious, inscrutable, still to be deciphered. Before 1924, most of them
were half-buried under the blown dust of centuries. That is why they
had been so little known, so rarely visited. The Carnegie Institute,
under the inspired leadership of Dr. Sylvanus G. Morley and his
trained corps of archaeologists, ethnologists, and anthropologists, has
done a superb job of uncovering the grandeur of the past and repairing the ravages of nature. The breath-taking Temple of the
Warriors was nothing more than a broad sixty-foot-high hillock of
earth overgrown with trees when Dr. Morley guessed at its secret
and began to delve. Like John Lloyd Stephens in 1842, he found "a
strong and vigorous nature struggling for mastery over art, wrapping
the city in its suffocating embrace and burying it from sight."

From El Castillo we went to the Ball Court with small temples
set on the ramparts like royal watchtowers. The place was still in
the process of reconstruction. Massive stones lay about like gigantic
pieces to be fitted into a mammoth jigsaw puzzle. In this stadium
the Mayas had played a ball game called *tlachtli* or *pok-ta-pok*. It
was a game so strenuous, and often so mortal, that compared to it
college football is like a croquet game played in a vicarage garden.
For the spectators it combined the excitements of a football game,
a heavyweight championship fight, and a major Wall Street speculation. Rulers and warriors and priests bet themselves into a frenzy,
some even staking the bondage of their own offspring on the out-
come of a game. *Tlachtli* was a kind of basketball played with a
large solid rubber ball. The men played barefoot and naked, except
for loincloth and knee guards, and when they were thrown down

they crashed not into sod but against the stones of the floor. The goal was to propel the ball through a stone ring set vertically twenty feet high, and just barely large enough for a ball to go through. To touch the ball with hands or feet was against the rules. The players had to bunt it with their buttocks, their thighs, or their elbows.

As I stood beneath one of the stone rings and looked up and down the vast walled court, with Henry's promptings I recreated a game in progress, and marveled at the physical vigor of the early Indians. Their athletic prowess was as incredible as the fierce energy and patience that had erected these massive monuments without benefit of modern machinery, without iron or steel, without beasts of burden, without even a wheel. It was small wonder that a people whose ancestors took athletic games so strenuously could keep the mailed Spaniards sixteen years at bay.

At Chichen Itzá, among these temples, raged one of the most bloody of the conquistadors' battles "where Spaniards fought for their own lives—and the Indians to remain masters of their own soil." At last the Spaniards, almost defeated, exhausted, surrounded on three sides by Indians, tied a hungry dog to a clapper of a great bell, putting food before him, but just out of reach. While the dog agitated the clapper frantically, the Indians, thinking it an alarm bell, waited quietly for the attack. The Spaniards stealthily marched from the camp to the coast. All night the Indians waited for the attack that was to be their triumph and the final destruction of the white men. At dawn, when the bell continued to ring beyond all reason, they investigated, and found the Spaniards had escaped.

On the way north to the Sacred Well, Henry pointed out the fresh paw prints of a puma on the forest path. And a little farther on he showed me thousands of warrior ants who were constructing a military road for some conquest. "They are vicious fighters," Henry said, "and as cruel to their victims as the Spaniards were."

"Do the insects follow man, or does man imitate the insects?" I commented.

"*Quien sabe?*" Henry answered. "It does seem perversely unreasonable that with a superabundance of earth for any conceivable ant activity the creatures should need to kill their own kind. Yet is it more ridiculous for insects to wage war on their brothers than for mankind to do so? And the art-creating Mayas drowned their most desirable girls to the glory of some imagined god."

In the midst of the forest, the immense water hole, approximately one hundred and fifty feet in diameter, gaped sullenly in the shadows. The water was greenish black and as murky as a Gothic tale. Creepers and vines tangled about the trees, crouching at the rim of the well just above the slow-crumbling stratified walls of purplish gray and rusty black. The stagnant water reflected the pall of dark greenery draped about the rim. After a lapse of centuries, the sacrificial spot still exuded the appropriate sinister atmosphere.

We moved to the rock from which the priests tossed the virgins, who were doped to semiconsciousness and perfumed with incense of copal gum. From here too were hurled male slaves to serve the maidens after death. And pilgrims, come from hundreds of miles distance, would cast in their sacrificial offerings of golden vessels, jeweled bangles, household utensils, or whatever their hearts held dear. An intense silence enshrouded the desolate spot, broken only now and then by the laments of mourning doves and the faint echoes from archaeologists' reviving chisels.

The well, as a part of the expansive sacred city, has known strange ownership. Stephens had found the place in possession of the disinterested Spanish ranchman. A Yankee from Worcester, Massachusetts, named Edward Thompson bought the whole of Chichen Itzá in 1885. For thirty-nine years this extraordinary man was monarch of the most opulent strip of memorial in North America. In a seventeenth-century hacienda he lived like a feudal lord, with temples for next-door neighbors and with uncivilized Indians in the bush behind him. Several times he barely escaped death. Once he was wounded almost fatally when he stumbled into a trap of thorns poisoned with putrefied fox blood. Yet, undaunted, he remained, and fathered and reared seven children, and had the time of his life conducting amateur excavations. Don Eduardo grew into a legendary figure, as well as a highly respected padrone. Because he was fearless, he was reputed to be able to charm the savagery out of wild beasts, and he was known to win menacing enemies by strumming an old guitar.

When he began dredging the Sacred Pool, he brought up a quantity of skulls and skeletons, sacrificial knives, sandals, copper bells, hard-rubber dolls, jade figurines, balls of copal, and basins of pure gold. These relics he quietly shipped to the Peabody Museum at Harvard University. At last, in 1924, the Mexican Government, hearing a vastly exaggerated rumor of the value and magnitude of these objects—half a million dollars' worth was the alleged estimate—challenged Thompson's four decades' ownership, and virtually expelled him from the country. But Don Eduardo had paved the way for the Carnegie Institution's scientific interest in the work that had been his hobby. It was this tough, ingratiating, and romantic Yankee who made the Mexican Government aware of the value of forgotten Chichen Itzá. In 1935, though the ownership of the acres was in litigation and the Mexican Government held a lien on the property, by law the heirs of Edward Thompson still owned the hacienda, and temples beyond price. A neat commentary on the mutations of greatness and legal possession.

What treasure still lies sunk beneath the ooze at the bottom of the well no one knows. Someday the Mexican Government hopes to do a thorough job of dredging. In the meantime men enjoy their speculations.

The routine is back to the Mayaland Lodge by ten or ten-thirty, iced beer, some reading in Mayan history, an informal lecture by Henry, luncheon, and a two-hour siesta. Then off at four to another group of buildings. We saw the Temple of Dates, where Dr. Morley discovered on the underside of a lintel the date which corresponds to A.D. 452. At the threshold of the Nunnery, the plant called "queen's slipper" flourishes—a plant with slender stalks laden with transparent white petals that form a slipper. It looked as if it were the custom for some mythical race of little people to enter here in stocking feet.

In the Phallic Temple, obviously dedicated to phallic worship from all the hardy specimens wrought in stone, there was a musty smell of bats. Before the Temple of the Guards, ants piled up green leaves "to make mushrooms grow under them," said Henry, "for their communistic table." And so we went up and down endless steps, wound about terraces, paused before hieroglyphic writing, admired murals in red, blue, yellow, and black, looked at bright mosaics, noted a hundred stone representations of pumas, jaguars, feathered serpents, and more unmistakable phallic devices.

Again the sun turned the sky to flame and gold as it set behind a dense screen of branches. The tops of the buildings were fired with sunset tints.

"Look at these buildings now," said Henry. "You see how beautifully careful the architects were never to violate the principles of proportion and mass? And authorities say that in the handling of perspective, the Mayan surpassed all the ancient civilizations." We stood among the half-restored relics in an aura of rigid beauty. "It is difficult to penetrate the mystery," Henry went on, "for the Spanish priests destroyed our books and all the memorials possible of my people. Yet we today are the descendants of those who built these temples. Mayan peasants still strangle turkeys with ceremonial bark beer. Back in the forests to the south, Indians still use bows and arrows and hold to their pagan aboriginal way. And yet our forefathers created these temples, and their genius developed an accurate calendric system." He gestured vaguely toward the rounded tower of the Observatory. In his voice there were pride and wistfulness as he said: "Why do the Americans go to Egypt to see things? Why don't they come first to see what kind of neighbors they might have had if history had not conquered us?"

II

Gems of Tourist Towns

In all this incongruous, delightful mixture may there not be
perhaps the germ of a new world?
　　　　　　　　　　　　　　　　　—ERICO VERISSIMO

I. CUERNAVACA

"IF YOU GO TO live in the Indies," says an old Spanish proverb, "let it
be in sight of the volcanoes." I do not know what significance the
saying had for the emigrating Spaniard. But it is a wonderful thing
to abide with a view of a volcano, crowned with an immaculate
glory of snow, lit by the sun or the moon. Once for a whole year I
lived at Sorrento, where my single floor-to-ceiling window opened
on a prospect of Vesuvius, beyond a garden of lemons and guavas
and stretches of Bay of Naples blue. At Taormina one February
I took a room that gave on a grove of almonds, with a background
of Mount Etna glittering white against the Sicilian sky. For a
stretch of incomparable mornings I breakfasted at Arequipa in
Peru on the roof garden of Tia Bates's boardinghouse, with three
volcanoes—Pichu-Pichu, Chachani, and El Misti—to look up to over
the coffee. And in Arequipa the idea had occurred to me that volcanoes speak a special esthetic language of their own, as the sea does
to receptive sailors.

In Mexico City, from the heights of Chapultepec, from the terraced roof of the Reforma Hotel, from the athletic stadium, from the
top western tiers of seats at the bullring, and from scores of other
vantage points, one can gaze upon the neighboring volcanoes, Popocatepetl and Ixtacihuatl. The Warrior and the Sleeping Lady lie
shrouded in snow and perpetual beauty, impelling man to lift up
his eyes.

While I was doing some special research in the capital, I was off
on sudden invitation to drive to Acapulco for Christmas with an
Italian friend of mine who had lived in Mexico for twelve years.
With us on the journey was my friend's Swiss-born fiancée, half
English, half French by extraction, and her sixteen-year-old son by

her divorced Mexican husband. The Italian was affectionately called Jim by all his friends, though he bore the classical name of Orestes. The mother, who was hardly more than twice her son's age, was named Andrée, and the youth was called Max. Jim's wire-haired terrier bitch answered to the name of Petrouchka. There was quite an international flavor to our assembly, but it could not have been more harmonious had we all been brought up on the same food and customs in some provincial valley.

I had not met the mother and son until Jim brought his car to pick me up at my hotel. Max had the engaging address of young upper-class Mexicans, but with a soupçon of the mestizo distrust. He had a slim, sinewy, adolescent body, and a good-looking, small-featured, withholding face, with rich olive skin and light olive-colored eyes flaked with gold. Hardly any two persons in Mexico looked more unrelated than he and his mother; for she had spun-gold hair, large blue eyes, and a skin fairer than the complexion-soap advertisements. Her perfect English diction, learned in exclusive Swiss schools, her assured charm, and her inviolable amiability made her an excellent commentator as well as a delightful companion.

The volcanoes accompanied us on our journey to Cuernavaca, but they were not with us every minute. Again and again blue-gray palisades, like shifting screens, thrust between us and the volcanoes, as if to remind us that beauty cannot stay ever at a point of ecstasy, that it is evanescent even when always there, like desire when one is terribly in love. In Indian folklore, the volcanoes are said to be lovers, and he, Popo, is taller than she, as the male should be. Humboldt himself measured them in 1790 and found the Warrior to be seventeen thousand seven hundred feet above the sea, and two thousand feet taller than the Sleeping Lady. But even she was two thousand feet higher than "the most elevated summit in Europe."

The road to Cuernavaca is a continuous excitement of breathtaking delight. It scales heights, makes arcs and loops and sudden descents into luxuriant tropical valleys. Around jutting promontories looms the majesty of the volcanoes in the full splendor of the sun. The air of the Mexican plateau is so remarkably clear and thin that it brings them as close as if one had field-glass lenses to the eyes. There they lie immaculate against the backdrop of shimmering azure, and there they will remain, serene in perpetuity, as generations come and go, as cultures emerge, reach their peaks, decline, emerge afresh.

Dotting the mountainous slopes like eagles' aeries are villages set among the rocks. And far down below are the settlements of those who love valleys and things pastoral. Both kinds of villages seem to be cut off from all communication, as if they had been dropped there intact straight from a parachute. But at the 70-kilometer sign a road leaves the highway for Tepotzlán, breeding-place of revolutions, so near but so isolated, penned in by the stockade of mountains. Snuggling against a mountainside twenty-odd miles across the abyss of variegated rocks and flowers, the town was once as remote to most tourists as something in the dead center of South America. Robert Redfield wrote an excellent monograph on the place, which still speaks Aztec and which has never had a hotel, though it boasts an ancient temple to the god of pulque. Now throngs of tourists are making their own discoveries.

This road to Cuernavaca, which Stuart Chase declared was almost too noble for mere man to ride upon, was first laid out by Cortés along an old Indian trail. As Cortés retired to Cuernavaca from the fret and intrigue in the capital, so did the Emperor Maximilian in his three harassed years. His traveling carriage, built especially for the journey, was provided not only with lockers for provisions but with writing materials and a portable desk. When it swept around the curves drawn by twelve snow-white mules as exactly alike as matched pearls, and harnessed with turquoise-colored leather, it excited great wonder among the Indians. The coachman, the grooms, and the footmen were all dressed *charro*-fashion, in tight mouse-colored suits of chamois skin embroidered in silver, and they wore sweeping hats of white felt.

Today the President of Mexico and most of the Cabinet Ministers and foreign diplomats go to Cuernavaca for week ends and occasional holidays. But in these more democratic times the President's guard wears soldierly khaki, and the Ministers indulge in no more folderol than special-bodied Lincolns and Packards.

From a height we were plunged suddenly into the subtropical Valley of Cuernavaca, with a climate famous for its mild and salubrious qualities. Here the sun warmed, but did not sting. The sweet air fondled the fruit and breathed lightly upon the flowers. As I had remembered it from six years before, Cuernavaca was still a mellowed Spanish town set down in Mexican gardens, with modernization going little further than plumbing and refrigeration. Its fashionable-resort features were lost sight of under the colonial patina and the screen of bougainvillea, orchids, and palms. Popocatepetl, which had stalked us like a glorious specter, eluding and then appearing at unexpected places, came at last to rest framed between papaya trees in an American lady's garden. Here, with the aid of a Yucatán gentleman of ruined fortune and architectural bent, she had reconstructed a lovely house with a drawing-room minus its fourth wall. The volcano was the focal point of nature's priceless mural that filled the space of that fourth wall.

Farther down the same street, Cortés had built his palace so that his upper back gallery too gave on the lure of the volcano. Dwight Morrow, as a gift to the nation, commissioned Diego Rivera—for ten thousand dollars—to fill the wall space of the Cortés veranda with murals. Rivera did a superb job of painting, and mocked the conquistadors in their own Captain General's house. At one end of the murals is the Spaniard, Cortés; at the other is Zapata, the Mexican half-blood, with down-sweeping mustachios and his magnificent white horse. Somewhere between them in spirit is the pale Austrian Prince, with history linking the three in a chain of four centuries. These three men—the great conqueror, the imperial interloper, and the firebrand patriot—are the personages most closely associated with Cuernavaca, whose name is the Spanish corruption of an Aztec word meaning not "Cow Horn" but "By a Wooded Mountain."

Cortés and Maximilian found their greatest solace here. Zapata, brooding over the encroachments on the peasants' land and liberty, swept out by the crags of Tepotzlán like a whirlwind upon the drowsing town and took over the surrounding haciendas, burning and razing those that resisted. And all about the outskirts of the place and throughout the whole of the sugar state of Morelos are crumbled walls of ruined houses which Zapata in his patriotic zeal consigned to fire, as General Sherman did the columned mansions of the South in his march to the sea. Zapata broke forever a system begun by Cortés, who here cultivated the first sugar cane and set up the first sugar mill on the continent.

Zapata is Diego Rivera's favorite character in Mexican history—

the only one, he told me, he thoroughly approves of and salutes with whole heart. Zapata is the prime idol of many a revolutionary. But to the Creole landlords, Zapata spells one thing only—destruction, not only of their houses and fortunes, but of a way of life.

"I cannot burn a candle in my heart before the image of Zapata," Andrée said, looking at his painted figure. "I appreciate the man's intentions, but like most Mexicans, he let his zeal run away with him. My husband's uncle's hacienda lay about forty miles from here, growing both rice and sugar. Zapata sent a courteous message by a peasant soldier advising the family to clear out—tomorrow his troops would take over the place. They were allowed to take one mule and two horses, the horses for his wife and himself, the mule to carry away as much personal property as the beast's back would bear. The workers on the place gathered about my uncle to say good-bye. They were very sad, but they were powerless to defend the place against Zapata's troops. 'If we help you try to keep the hacienda, we too shall all be killed,' they said. As my uncle and aunt rode off, leading the laden mule, the army appeared in the distance.

"The house is gone now. They didn't destroy it all at once. They did it piecemeal. The first thing they did was to take their bayonets and stick holes in the polished floors to keep from slipping in their new shoes. Then they tore out the doors and used them for fuel. Then they ripped up the floors for fuel, and then the beams, until the house finally fell down about them. Once when my aunt had the temerity to return for some special souvenir of a dead daughter, she was received by the mistress of an officer, decked out in two of my aunt's dressing-gowns at once. In the courtyard, as she left two grisly-looking soldiers dismounted. They were using the damask vestments of a neighboring church for saddle blankets. My uncle had just bought ten thousand dollars' worth of machinery for cleaning rice. Zapata's men tore it up to make coins of the brass. The truth is there is a lot of the vandal in the Mexican. It is sickening to think of the waste and the devastation that has gone on in this country. Revolutions rarely take into account human nature." Andrée turned her back on the murals.

A mozo in a white pajama suit interrupted. It was a note for Jim, which resulted in our going for cocktails to a remarkable American household where seventeen dogs greeted us like a jubilant reception committee in the hallway. In the drawing-room a donkey stood by the radio listening rapt and moist-eyed to a sentimental rendition of *"La Paloma,"* a song that had been a favorite with the Empress Carlota three-quarters of a century ago. The mistress of the house was very proud of the she-ass's musical appreciation as well as her perfectly housebroken good manners. The donkey was named Blanche, after her mistress. Although the beast got along very well with the seventeen dogs, who treated her with all the respect of an honored kinswoman, the master and mistress felt she hadn't the proper companionship, so they were negotiating for a consort.

When we went to the patio for cocktails, Blanche accompanied us. She took her stance politely by her mistress's long chair; the mozo trickled a cocktail into her wide-open mouth. As she closed her eyes and a tremor ran along her donkey ears, master and mistress led the laughter. The seventeen dogs were not offered cocktails, but they each got a yolk-of-egg canapé. The monkey and the macaws, too, got titbits; but it was easy to see that the donkey was the household favorite, even with the servants. The conversation was almost exclusively of the menagerie. Though the patio itself was a charming and harmonious one of discreet taste and design, I hankered after a renewed acquaintance with the Borda Gardens; and since our time was short, I slipped away.

The Borda Gardens are not extensive like those of Tivoli or Hampton Court or Versailles. But that special area of earth has doubtless been trod upon by as many famous men and women as any single garden spot in the Western Hemisphere. Important foreigners who visit Mexico spend at least a half-hour in its cool arcades. Before it was a formal garden, Cortés wandered on this site from his place across the way. And Carlota and Maximilian loved this spot best of all Mexican territory, and took the Borda house for a summer palace. Dwight Morrow bought a home within a three-minute walk.

The gardens were the inspiration of a Frenchman Joseph Le Borde, who in the first quarter of the eighteenth century came as a sixteen-year-old youth, seeking adventure and riches, like Cortés. He did mining in Tlalpujahua, Zacatecas, and Taxco, and amassed a fortune of forty million pesos. As a thank offering to God he built a church near a silver mine at Taxco; and as a gift to himself, he created this garden at Cuernavaca. In time he became known as José de la Borda, and lived to enjoy his wealth until his eightieth year.

In its pattern and design, its walks and stonework, the garden still shows the formal French conception, overlaid with a Spanish influence. But the latitude put the imprint of Mexico upon it. Luxuriant abundance overwhelmed symmetry, unpruned beauty spilled and splattered upon the stones in blossoming branches and shadows. The result of this marriage of Mexican verdure with Spanish-French design is one of the most evocative small gardens in the two hemispheres.

Unlike most gardens in France, the Borda is rarely on a level. It descends a ravine, arranges itself on various stages. It is broken with stone benches and summer pavilions, with romantic fountains, and brooding rectangular pools where aquatic plants make pale reflections in the dark waters. The mangoes and the laurels have long since grown disdainful of clippers and pruning hooks, and collaborate to weave canopies pricked with bits of azure sky or the platinum of moonlight. The air is perfumed with mango, rose, and jasmine, and the acrid scent of bark and ancient roots. Fruits can be identified by their odors on dark nights, and one can lead a companion by scent down an alley of lemons or figs or guavas or cherimoyas.

Because of the density of foliage there is little bright flower color, except along the edges of the gallery. The colors are somber—deep rich green running to greenish black, with stone and marble weathered like yellowed parchment, with here and there a tinge of rust or bronze and spots of waxy white of magnolias or japonicas. It is a garden made for meditation, a garden for a Byron to brood in self-consciously, or for a Poe to conjure up fantastic tales. Even tourists, as they climb up and down the various levels photographing cascades and fountains, mute their voices and move cautiously.

No other personalities except Carlota and her futile husband seem to have left echoes of themselves in the garden. If you see in imagination a woman with her silken skirts spread swanlike on the stairs, it is Carlota. You can picture her stooping to feed the ducks, or netting spotted butterflies, or leaning back against a laurel tree, holding hands with her youngish husband in the dappled moonlight. In these precincts, she and Maximilian enacted an idyllic interlude in their unhappy tragicomedy which a violent ending turned into real tragedy.

The Emperor liked to work in the airy portion of the house's long gallery, where a table was placed for him. The gallery was spaced with faience jars filled with flowering plants. Orchids climbed the walls. And bright-colored fish swam in crystal globes, beneath cages of songbirds. Here twenty-three of the gay young bloods of Cuernavaca, who created among themselves the exclusive Cocks' Club as a voluntary guard of honor, would come to ask the Emperor's commands. They wore uniforms of black trousers and blue blouses. In their hats they wore a black feather, and on their breasts was embroidered a golden cock.

Now the "summer palace" is turned into a hotel; and those who can afford the price of a beer, if not luncheon, can be served on the terrace beside the coffee trees and stroll at will about the gardens once reserved for a new-created Court. What was Maximilian's bedroom is now the bar. When I first visited the Borda Hotel in 1935, on either side of the French piano reputed to be Carlota's, like signposts to mark the change from the nineteenth century to the twentieth, stood two enormous brass spittoons. On my return at the end of 1941, the spittoons were gone—so apparently the generation of gentlemen who spit in drawing-rooms had passed. But Carlota's piano was also gone—probably to save it from total destruction by tourists who cared more for pounding jazz than for an unhappy lady's memory.

Many who once loved Cuernavaca resent its becoming a tourist town. But it was ever a place to be enjoyed. Doubtless it will long continue to be a refuge for escapists or those in need of rest or relaxing play. And the Borda Gardens, still breathing a haunting atmosphere, will remain a rendezvous for romantics.

2. A DECEMBER EVENING IN TAXCO

From Cuernavaca to Taxco the road runs through the heart of Mexico's sugar bowl before it begins to climb into the savage beauty of mountainous Guerrero. The December landscape was exalted with all the radiance of the sun. The cane was in seed and tossing its ethereal plumes proudly. The plain looked as if massed with a green-armored soldiery wearing aigrettes in their casques. Nopal cacti were festooned with morning-glories, the electric-blue color of incandescent globes used in Christmas decorations. Front yards of humble peasant houses were aflame with red carnations, spice pinks, and poinsettias. Some settlements were bathed in a cherry-colored glow from the heavy shade of royal poinciana trees. Without holly or mistletoe, subtropical nature had decorated the Christmas season lavishly in its own way.

To the left rose the stacks of a huge co-operative sugar mill established for the benefit of the peasants at considerable cost to the Government. Farther on, Indians at their task of road-mending invariably paused in their work to admire Petrouchka, who kept up a constant waving out the window with her front paws, as if she were doing a water race. The men rarely noticed us, it was always the dog; and they saluted Petrouchka respectfully, with smiles and rough affection.

Jumper-suited men with wide flopping hats were laboring in the rice paddies. Along the twisting highway, children trotted beside burros bearing bales of dry brush. A man sitting astride his flop-eared ass came from the opposite direction, with his woman walking demurely behind him. I was reminded of the chivalrous American who stopped a similar couple in a similar situation, to demand why the woman did not ride. "But, señor," explained the surprised man ingratiatingly, but with simplest logic, "my wife does not own a burro."

We slowed down to a stop where a group of Indians stripped to the waist were busy at a critical stretch of road-mending. Their torsos of copper, sculptured by the sun and hard labor, were strong and supple. The men smiled as we passed—showing their white teeth, which continual corn-meal cakes kept polished and gleaming. The hands that gripped the work implements were small and delicately molded, and the feet in the open sandals were small too. But these fellows could carry loads on their backs that would stagger a husky stevedore.

Every sharp curve in the climbing road seemed to echo a plea for the most expert driving.

"The ravines of Mexico are a feast to the eye, but a calamity to agriculture," Ezequiel Padilla, the Foreign Minister, had pointed out to me in conversation only the day before. And here, as I looked at the resentful, arid soil of some mountainsides laid out in cultivated rows with what must have been superhuman labor and danger to life and limb, my admiration for the Mexican peasants was profound. I marveled how anything besides an eagle could ever get to such inaccessible places. A man cultivating his mountain slope was leaning at an extraordinary angle to keep from hurtling to jagged death. Surely in all the world there could be no greater outlays of human energy and pluck for such scanty returns.

No wonder the revolutionaries had chorused "Liberty and Land," "Land and Water." Where men had the courage to try to wrest subsistence from a grudging mountainside, what might they not do in irrigated land or in coastal swamps that had been drained? One thing was as clear as the silhouette of the man and his ox pressing against the mountain just under its rim: The Indian in Mexico will endure. In a race that can almost make bread out of stones the life force is so compulsive that no matter how tribulations stalk a fellow, his kind will survive. There is an indestructibility in the Indian make-up that attests to the good human material the Reform had to work with. The hopelessness which D. H. Lawrence said everyone who visited Mexico went away with did not seem hopeless at all this day in late December. I saluted with humility the plowing Indian's persistent will to live.

After the stretch of gray rock monotones, the road seemed to writhe with sinuosities. Then suddenly, around a palisade, the twin towers of Taxco's famous church appeared, in the first flush of sunset, and there across the barranca the Hotel Borda sat atop a silver mine in full operation. Spread upon the fawn-pink flanks of the Sierra Madre, Taxco is like a town in a fairy tale. It is the nonpareil of mining camps and trading posts. The viceregal flavor of the place has been preserved by a wise law which ensures it against the opportunism of modernity. The National Department of Colonial Monuments has decreed that no structure can be erected, no reparations begun, until Federal sanction has been stamped on the plans. New buildings, additions, gates, walls, doors, balconies, must harmonize with the architecture that existed in colonial days. No colors that "cry out" may be applied to house walls or railings. If one of the sienna tiles from a house roof is broken, it is replaced by another

made by the same eighteenth-century process, because the tilemakers
of Taxco have learned no new way.

The colors of Taxco vary by the changing lights from dawn to
sunset, but the patina and an iridescence are always there. The predominant tones are oyster-white, amber, soft amethyst, and olive,
with the round of cerulean blue in the tiled dome of the great church.
But after he has left ask anyone what is the color of Taxco, and he
is just as apt to say "Opal," or "Rust," or "Chamois." The profusion
of flowers and blossoming vines, tumbling over pastel-shaded walls
and spilling out of patio gateways, blurs the color impression.

Directions are blurred, too, in Taxco; none is exact. There is no
east, west, south, or north. There is up or down or around or behind
or above. The houses spill over the mountainside, one man's front
door seeming to open on another man's roof. The cascading roads
paved with small cobblestones stop their daring gambols at the plaza,
where the market wares are spread under the glossy foliage of Indian
laurel trees.

The church "which Borda gave to God because God gave to
Borda" is memorable and distinctive viewed from any angle—from
any hillside, straight up from the plaza, or from the gallery bar across
the square directly opposite the portals. The town describes a kind
of semicircle around the church, arranged by nature something like
the balconies of an opera house, where from every position one has a
view of the center of the stage. With its lyrical twin towers, its richly
ornate façade, and its heavily gilded altars, the church is an excellent
example of Mexican Churrigueresque. But the outside is far more
pleasing than the inside, where in a frenzy to pour out gratitude,
Borda's decorators lost their sense of proportion and taste.

You are told that the mortar that holds the bricks together was
mixed with Spanish wine instead of water, and that the bricks themselves were tempered with powdered silver. The legend is most likely
false, but there is a mellowness of old wine in the atmosphere of
Taxco, and from a distance a haze sometimes lies upon the town like
a protective tissue of silver gauze.

Remarking the graceful houses, the trails of orchids, the waves of
magenta bougainvillea, it is hard to realize that Taxco was and still
is a mining town. Yet you have only to look into the side of the hill
under the Hotel Borda across the ravine to see the activity of mining.

All night the work goes on, the hillside in shaded illumination, the sound of cables winding slowly. Silver was discovered in the Taxco district over four hundred years ago—in 1522, the year after the conquest. From here, the first silver mined under the conquistadors was sent back to Spain.

Much of the precious metal that is extracted from the local earth is locally processed and turned into beautiful silver handicraft work at William Spratling's famous atelier, a football's throw from the plaza. A dozen years or so ago this enterprising American expatriate found out what the natives remembered of their ancient skill. He taught them what he knew; he learned more as he went along. With a distinctive talent for design, he creates new models, and the Indian boys work them by hand in their own way. The final product is the nearest rival on this continent to the modern silverware of the Danish Georg Jensen and the exquisite creations of the Swedish Baron Fleming. At Spratling's showrooms one buys not only objects made by native silversmiths with .980 fine silver from the Taxco mines, but woodwork with woods from the hot country, serapes of pure wool spun and woven in the shop, and tin hammered in the best Mexican tradition and finish.

The four of us, Jim, Andrée, Max, and I, sat on the gallery of the bar overhanging the twilit plaza and relaxed from the whirling drive. Andrée does not drink anything alcoholic, so she and Max sipped orangeades while Jim and I had a couple of tequilas, taken straight with the lime-and-salt formula. I like tequila—it is a downright, clean drink, to the point, like Danish schnapps. We watched the easeful loafing in the square. Swarthy men in white pajama suits and wide sombreros, and women with their dregs-of-wine-colored rebozos wrapped about their heads, idled on the benches or leaned against the laurel trees. The band was not playing, there was no wail of a jukebox, no blatant talk-talk of radio. In their infinite wisdom the authorities of Taxco do not permit radios to be owned except by special dispensation. So the noise about the plaza was only a soft blur of conversation, the murmuring of pigeons on the flagstones, a guitar plucked on a balcony, the muted grind of machinery at the mine, the tinkling of donkey feet on the cobblestones as a burro train returned from another mine in the higher mountains.

Although Taxco is a place where its five thousand inhabitants really work, it is called the Fiesta Town, because its people are also much given to play. Its citizens seem gayer in spirit than those in most Mexican towns. The soft-voiced, nubile girls, and the deep-bosomed women, who wash and slap-dry their clothes in the open public washing-stalls, do not suffer from male neglect when evening comes. Much time is consumed in the pursuit of love-making in Taxco. Romance lies in wait at the foot of any street, on the next bench under the laurels.

In the last decade, besides being a prime tourist attraction, Taxco has become a rendezvous for serious artists—Mexican, American, European—with the usual hangers-on of the Muses. A few of them, as sometimes happens in the best artistic circles, had come trailing lavender wisps of gossip. I had noticed young Max staring quizzically, with a faint contemptuous sneer on his lips, as men came and went on the gallery or in the bar. And then he blurted out suddenly, catching his mother's arm, "Mama, I think that one's a fairy."

With the most casual savoir-faire, his mother said, "Do you? Why?" and turned her head to look at a fattish dark young man in a beret. "You're right, Max, they say he is," she said coolly. "I know him—he comes from a prominent Mexican family. He is supposed to have a dash of Negro in him, too."

A little later Max indicated a pale British-looking chap at another table. "I think that pasty-faced fellow over there may be a 'forty-one.'"

The mother looked again. "Um-m—I don't know—you can't always be sure. Don't be suspicious."

"Forty-one?" I said.

"There was a party going on in Mexico," Max said. "The police raided the place and nabbed forty-one of them."

"Since then," Jim said, "'forty-one' has become the refined name for that sort. No man in the city dares say 'I'm forty-one' on his forty-first birthday, because of the kidding. He smiles and says, like the French street numbers, 'I'm forty-*bis*.'"

As we started to the Borda for dinner, down a winding cobbled street came a procession of lighted candles and voices chanting *Ave Marias*. Four children preceded, carrying a decorated litter in which lay images of the Virgin, Joseph, and an angel. Young folk were going to a *posada*—the eighth and next to the last of the Christmas season. Before a closed doorway farther on, other persons were lined up two by two, and through a gateway we saw guests already arrived and standing in a patio with lighted candles.

All over Mexico, in every strata of society, *posadas* were in progress—they had been going on since December sixteenth. For more than two centuries, the *posada* has been a Mexican custom, shared by rich and poor. Literally, the word means an inn. It symbolizes the search of Joseph and Mary for a night's lodging when they went from Nazareth to Bethlehem to be inscribed for the new Roman taxation decreed by Augustus Caesar for all the dependencies. The little town of Bethlehem was so crowded with people come for the same purpose that the pair could find no house in which to lay their heads, and so they wandered for nine nights and finally took shelter in a stable just in time for the infant Jesus to be born.

When the *posada* guests arrive, the electric lights are extinguished. With lighted candles in their hands the guests march to a closed door and beg in song to be admitted. Keepers behind the door or from an upper balcony refuse admittance, in song. Then the Josephs and Marys sing their weariness and the discomforts of the cold night. At last Mary reveals her identity as the Queen of Heaven. The door is ostentatiously unlocked, the guests file laughingly through, and pause to kiss a doll that represents the newborn Jesus reposing on a bed of flowers. Then they gather in a circle about a *piñata,* an earthenware jar, which is suspended from the ceiling. An honored female guest is chosen to break the *piñata* with a wand, whereupon fruit and candies and toys spill over the floor, and the guests squeal surprised delight as they scramble and grab. If the hosts are poor, there is no more to the party. If they are rich and in the city, there may follow a ball and a supper at home or at the country club—and instead of fruit, corsages of orchids and boutonnières of gardenias cascade from the *piñata*. The custom and performance of the nine *posadas* Madame Calderón de la Barca found "extremely pretty" back in 1841, when she came as the wife of the first Spanish Ambassador. She was a bit perplexed, however, as foreigners are today, by "the curious mixture of religion and amusement." But foreign residents in Mexico have learned to follow the custom; and they too give *posadas,* as well as attend them.

After dinner that evening, we sat long into the night on the hotel's open terrace enjoying dolce far niente. Some towns seem more open than others to the stars, and Taxco is one where stars assume especial brilliance. The December heavens were as thick with them as Danish beech forests are with white anemones in May. We watched the lights in the houses across the barranca gradually go out one by one. The day-shift miners, the silversmiths, the washerwomen, the mule-drivers, the merchants, went to bed, all except those invited to the two private dances that had hired the town musicians.

The faint reverberation from the mine machinery came like the lulling pound of sea waves. "Do you remember," Jim said, "those revolutionary lines of Cruz that inspired Rivera's murals at the Secretariat of Education? They go something like this:

> " 'Comrade miner,
> Bent low by the weight of earth,
> When your hand extracts the metals
> Fashion them into daggers,
> And you will then see
> That all the bright metals are for you.' "

"But," Andrée added, "blessedly all of our latest revolutions have been fought out on paper, and innocents on both sides have been spared."

In the peace of Taxco we had forgotten for some hours the stupendous strife in the outer world. A clock struck midnight. We got up from the long chairs to go to bed. It was the morning of Christmas Eve—the period of special observance of goodwill in the Christian world. A distant cock crowed and another answered, and another, like eerie echoes running up the hills. From somewhere in the near flowering shrubs a Mexican mockingbird began a flutelike trilling. Across the barranca came the music of a *corriendo el gallo.* Local troubadours were serenading under some señorita's balcony. It is called "the serenade of the cock" because it takes place after first cockcrow. There were no artificial lights anywhere now. But the illumination from the multitudes of stars bathed the twin-towered church in silver radiance with a chiaroscuro of star shadow that accentuated the misty outlines. The peace of the hour was perfect.

3. CHRISTMAS AT ACAPULCO

To get to Acapulco by car we crossed thirteen mountain ridges of savage beauty. But the approach by airplane perhaps does the town more justice than that by the motor highway. From the air you see it at once—an exquisite fantasy in miniature set against the Pacific's liquid sapphire. By the road it unfolds in foam-flecked beaches, in green hills, in pastel daubs of stucco walls, in jutting rocks and fearsome precipices, in tile roofs with grasses idling in the breeze, in white and pea-green sails, in spiraling ribbons of roads, in wharves and piers with drying nets like spider webs in silver-gilt. It is a labyrinth of steps and stairs, with tangles of coral vines and tidal waves of bougainvillea. Except for rims of bay beach and a grassy flat just large enough for a landing field, Acapulco is all up and down, like Taxco.

Here the earth upheaved to form a haphazard but tightly landlocked harbor. Some of it rushed into cliffs and stark promontories. Some of it spread out in the shape of a bird's wing. There it circled gently like a curve of the new moon to form white-gold bathing-beaches. The typography of Acapulco is the most exciting of any western port from Alaska to the tip of Chile.

From the simple plaza, with its undistinguished church, radiate the streets of the humble every-day-of-the-year folks. The heights above the ocean and the edges about the bay have been taken by the well-to-do for their seasonal villas. Spread out on different levels, the man-built town climbs and twists. Villas like varicolored stairsteps ascend the hills. Some houses seem to crouch in pockets between boulders. Others defy the laws of gravity and tempt destruction by partially hanging over a precipice.

Out in the blue bay the fishing smacks of those who catch fish to live mingle neighborly with the pleasure yachts of those who fish for sport. Over the still lagoons pass the shadows of the red-and-silver passenger planes on four-a-day schedules. And at any unpremeditated hour glide the shadows of flamingos, just as those of their ancestors did a thousand years ago.

Near where the yacht-club pier now stands, silver from Taxco mines was loaded on boats for Manila and Hong Kong in the seventeenth and eighteenth centuries. Fabrics and spices and porcelains of the East were unloaded to grace the viceregal houses of Spanish officials and the haciendas of Creole landlords. There at the corner of the plaza where the modernistic Hotel La Marina stands, muleteers of the caravans guzzled and diced between trips. After Mexican independence the traffic from the East ceased, and there was little intercourse between the port and the capital. The royal highway fell into disrepair.

Today Acapulco is like a town that has been awakened from a century-long siesta. A dozen years ago there was scarcely a tourist. "Only yesterday" did ex-President Cárdenas complete the automobile highway. Now distance has been telescoped. The weeks by mule pack have been rubbed out. Eight hours by expert driving from Mexico City, or one and a half by plane. Now that Acapulco has been rediscovered, it has already superseded many favorite resort towns. Some of the international set that flocked to Cannes and Antibes began drifting to Acapulco in 1939, adding a dash of ultra-sophistication to the ingredients that make the atmosphere of the little seaport. The breath of society gossip permeates the hour of the apéritif. A well-known Continental countess had just taken a house for the season and frightfully upset her aristocratic British male secretary by bringing in a Cuban prize fighter to make a *ménage à trois*.

When we arrived on the afternoon of Christmas Eve, we drove straight to the brand-new La Riviera Hotel on a hill overlooking the bay. It was a charming layout, mostly roof garden and terrace, and each room was a cottage with bath and private veranda. Along with tea we took a quinine capsule as precaution against malaria.

On the sheltered beach, men and women of various nationalities and complexions were still taking the declining sun and splashing in the water. Umbrellas made red, blue, and yellow polka dots on the creamy beach. Here nerves were soothed or excited, love was made, children grew strong, refugees found solace, discordant city rhythms were stilled, the escapist believed in escape for an hour at least.

"For the fisherman there are swordfish and sailfish and marlin and giant rays in the ocean," Jim said. "For the hunters there are deer and mountain cat, and in the marshy regions of the Laguna a plenitude of mallard in season and alligators at all times."

After a swim, we went for a highball to the Mirador bar, hewn in the side of a precipice that rises sheer above the Pacific. It was like a tiny theater, with booths for opera boxes. The first evening show is a performance of the sunset's color organ, with the waves pounding out a magnificent accompaniment on the rocks a hundred and fifty feet below. When darkness fell, we had dinner at La Riviera and then drove through the town.

Down hills and up hills came processions of party folk going to *posadas,* bearing candles and chanting litanies. The folk of Acapulco who were not invited to a *posada* were taking their fun where they found it. In the poorer sections, the bodegas and *burdels* were crowded with men listening to the wail of jukeboxes—the *traga-diezes,* "swallow-dimes," as the Mexicans had aptly named them.

Sitting in darkened doorways with guitars across their knees, men "made ballads blossom with their cultivating fingers," feeding their hopes with song; girls, half hidden, half reluctant, listened from behind iron-grilled windows. In the plaza, a romantic-eyed dock worker, leaning against a laurel tree, turned himself into a human mockingbird and drew an admiring throng as he imitated the lament of the mourning dove, the harsh mew of the sea gull, the calls of scores of songsters.

At half-past eleven the crowds from the plaza began pouring into the lighted cathedral like moths seeking candle flames. At midnight the *misa del gallo,* the mass of the cock, was celebrated with all the pomp and ceremony within the local ecclesiastical scope. And then the people went home to suppers of lamb and wine. Some went to parties that lasted until dawn and some drank themselves to sleep in the *pulquerías* along the wharves. But no one looked in his stocking on Christmas morning; for in Mexico the right time to give presents is on January sixth, the day when the Wise Men brought gifts to the Christ Child. On Twelfthnight the children of this land without chimneys would put their huaraches out upon the balconies or in the patios, so that the Wise Men—not Santa Claus—could fill them with goodies as they passed.

✦

On Christmas morning we took breakfast at Los Flamingos. The hotel stretched its modern architecture along the rim of an orange and slate-blue precipice more than three hundred and fifty feet above the Pacific. It was as extensive as a transcontinental streamliner. Every room and suite had an ocean view with railed terrace and long chairs. The dining-room had no outside walls, only a high-beamed roof; and one portion of it disposed even of roof, for those who liked to tan while they ate, or to chat with the yellow-and-blue macaws moored in papaya trees.

Out in the ocean, a whale was spouting, and sometimes enormous fish that looked no larger than anchovies from our great height leaped high out of the water. The view cried out for a temple. But the magnificence of the seascape did not subdue the appetite, and we all ate heartily of pancakes.

Ten miles along the coast, northwest of the modernity of Los Flamingos, the scene changes dramatically. Bamboo huts at the jungle's edge might make you think you had been transported to Africa. We had motored here after breakfast, and now we were spending Christmas morning relaxing in grass hammocks under a loggia of palm thatch, with the Pacific stretching before us to China. The four of us lay in a kind of charmed silence as the symphony of the pounding sea poured out its music and the walls of waves broke into spray like lemon petals. Never, even in midocean, had a sea seemed more vast to me. The eye beheld nothing but an infinity of indigo under the lacquered bowl of heaven. It was like resting at the edges of Nirvana.

As minutes and then quarter-hours passed, familiarity muted the boom of the sea, and my breath came and went with more profound and even rhythms. Imperceptibly, I glanced at my companions on the left and the right. Jim—with his prominent, highbred Italian nose making a fine subject for a mummy's profile—was as motionless as a figure on a sarcophagus. Andrée lay like a supple statue, her gentle breathing stirring the azure silk of her open-throated blouse. Though young Max was beyond my range of vision, he too was as still as if asleep.

The row of hammocks stretched on and on, until there were thirty of them for hire. But we four had the beach to ourselves. On

Christmas morning, other folk did something else besides commune with seascapes and drowse in hammocks.

A dog barked without conviction. I turned and saw figures emerging from the clustering palm trees and bamboo shacks across the flat stretches of sand behind us. In their van came a dusky lad with a gleaming machete in his hand and bag of fresh coconuts on his back. He looked like a shepherd boy descended from a Del Sarto canvas, and walked with an air of manly self-sufficiency, as if he had always got on well with the world's people. He spread his coconuts on the thatch-shaded sand by us, ran his hand through his black ringlets, and began dexterously whacking through the hard fibrous casing of a nut.

Though I had not realized I was thirsty, no cup of nectar could have been more welcome than the cool refreshing draught of coconut water. As we quaffed the green-white liquid in the tropical noon, it seemed better than any Christmas eggnog.

Three little women had followed the boy across the sands, each with a basket over an arm. They were all very thin and light-cinnamon in color, and of indeterminate ages; but two of them were not too old for childbearing, for they carried a baby apiece in their free arm. They looked strangely akin to nomadic desert women I had known in Algeria, but little like the stolid Indian squaws of the West. Behind them came a ragtag assortment of girls and boys. And bringing up the rear at a respectful distance were three ribby, woeful-looking little dogs of a sickly yellow-brown color.

"What do the women want?" I asked.

"To sell you fish," Jim said.

"That *they* have cooked in *those* shacks?" I said, with a *norteamericano* emphasis of dismay. And then before he could answer, the fried fish aroma reached me, mingled with the fragrance of cut green limes. The diminutive women shyly took their stands between the heads of our four hammocks. The two with the babies laid them in the shade of the loggia, and immediately little girls squatted to tend them. The jet-eyed babies did not blink or complain. I saw why people said the most resigned expression on earth is that of an Indian baby.

The odor became more beguiling as one of the women thrust her basket closer under my nose. An earthenware platter was piled with golden-brown fried fish hardly larger than silver dollars. A saucer of sweet green limes cut in quarters lay beside the piled fish. Warnings against Mexican unsanitary methods vanished in a single deep inhalation. I decided to try *one*. I took it gingerly and squeezed lime juice plentifully, somewhat like a disinfectant. When I bit into the morsel and got a good taste, my expression of delight made them all laugh, even the little women. "What do you call them?" I asked enthusiastically, smacking my lips and reaching for another.

"Mojarra," Jim said, with his mouth full. "They come from the lagoon."

"They are better than pompano at Antoine's or the fillet of sole at Marguery's," I said, and reached for another and another.

The three thrown-away-looking curs hovered on the edges of the party dejected and without illusion. Petrouchka seemed uncertain that they belonged to the dog species. "Why don't you feed your skeletons?" Jim asked the boy with the machete.

"There's hardly enough for us to eat." The boy smiled enchantingly. "But they like fishbones," he added.

I called one of the pitiful creatures and prepared a fish for him, properly, with lime juice. The children giggled. The cur took it hesitantly, unbelieving, as if such fare wasn't for the likes of him. Then his eyes bulged with surprise and delight as mine must have done.

"What do you call the dog?" I asked the boy.

"Almirante."

"Admiral. That's a fine name," I said. "How did you ever think of it for this specimen?" The boy shrugged and smiled. "And what is this one named?" I pointed as an even more emaciated cur, with pale bloodshot eyes, crept forward humbly. *"Brisa."* Breeze. An almost poetic gift for nomenclature, or was it irony? Breeze looked as if the faintest stir of wind would blow him from the face of the earth. "And this one?" I asked as the third and most poor-relationy of them all sneaked up for a morsel. The fancy had been quickly spent, or even as a puppy he had not been worth study, for he was merely called Second Breeze.

"You will notice," Jim said, "that all dogs at the seashores in Mexico look as if they are made of bamboo with a bit of skin stretched over the rods. They say it's because the constant diet of fishbones hurts their intestines so they can't digest properly."

I began to bite the flesh from the bones of the fish and give the dogs only the meat. The children exchanged looks of astonished glee, as if I had been a Punch and Judy show. When we had cleaned out one platterful, the dogs and I, and Andrée and Jim and Max had had all they wanted from another, I settled the bill. For all the fish and limes, the charge was something like twenty cents without tip. Living comes cheap in the tropics ten miles from Acapulco.

The women and the smaller children dispersed across the hot noonday sands. The boy who had come first remained out of curiosity or because he liked our company. Max asked his name. "Natividad, at your service." *Natividad*—the Nativity—the Spanish word for Christmas. "Why?" asked Max.

"Because today I am ten years old."

Natividad was the handsomest child I had seen in Mexico, and he looked different. He was quicker to smile than pure Indian children and less shy. "It's the touch of Negro blood in him," Andrée said. In the midst of the poverty about him, he had a well-nourished look and a lively, intelligent expression.

Max asked about his school. Ten years old and he had never had a day's schooling. "It's a pity," we said, "a shame."

"Oh, I don't know," he said cavalierly. "Life and experience will teach me all I need to know."

Natividad's mother, the parent with the Negro strain, could not read or write. But the father, who seemed to have as much Spanish as Indian blood, could. Yet he was apparently not perturbed by his children's lack of education. He himself ran a leased motorboat and took men fishing in the lagoon or acted as a guide on alligator hunts. For that sort of work book learning was not essential.

The house of Natividad's parents was one of a little cluster of huts under the coconut palms. It had one enclosed bedroom with bamboo walls, but living-room and kitchen and nursery were al fresco, covered only by a roof of piled palm leaves. But the dwelling was not dirty. Though a cock and some hens were privileged to stroll about like relatives, the hard-packed dirt floor of the loggia was cleanly swept. The bath was twenty feet away—a screen of cut bamboo under a mango tree in a space hardly larger than an ordinary bathtub, with a great earthenware jar to dip water from and sloosh over the bathers' standing body. There was no visible toilet. The family evidently took to the reeds behind the house at the edge of the lagoon.

Here, as Jim pointed out, little in the manner of living had changed since before the Conquest. Under a shelter of palmetto leaves families were born, lived, and died. They still slept on straw mats, with sometimes hammocks for the babies—like the one Natividad's naked baby brother was sleeping in now. The wife still hand-clapped her flat tortillas—as Natividad's mother was doing now. Her earthenware vessels were similar to those of her ancestors.

The famous "damned wantlessness" which a German peddler once bewailed in the Indians came to mind. These Pacific Coast houses, built of bamboo and palm leaves, cost no more than fifteen dollars. These folks and their neighbors drew fish from the lagoon behind and the ocean before them, shook nuts from coco palms, raised little patches of squash and peppers and tomatoes, picked the wild limes— and knew naught of keeping up appearances. The climate made the scantiest of cotton clothing desirable. The charcoal brazier or the one-burner oil stove set on a table was all that was needed for the family cooking. Except during the periods of hard rains, the straw mats were as good for sleeping as mattresses. Daily living was simple indeed. I thought of the café-society set in Acapulco, striving to relieve the tedium of aimlessness.

"After the strain of city business," Jim said, "these simple rhythms have peculiar charm."

We were going to a village thirty miles through a jungle. Jim wanted to arrange about a hunt for some New York friends a fortnight hence, and there we would pick up a pot-luck Christmas dinner.

Tropical foliage never ceases to be exciting to me, but it was strange to be driving at Christmas among towering palms, gigantic ferns, and ropy lianas with tight blossoms like green belts studded with pearls and amethysts. Some of the wilderness had been turned to cultivation, and there were hundreds of hectares of coconut palms planted in wide-spaced rows, making arcades of a thousand slim and leaning columns. The dark earth on which the trees stood was smooth, like a carpet of black velvet, and their plumes rushed together high in the air to form a fretted ceiling of silver-green. Along watery sheets of marshland white egrets preened and paraded, their delicate crests shimmering like coronets of diamonds in the gold-flecked sunlight. The birds would stamp their images on the waxy green water, and stand as if enchanted with their own reflections. Then when Jim would sound his horn, they would stir the air into an ecstasy with sudden winged flights.

It was half-past two when we emerged from the green tropical wilderness into the yellow adobe town of Coyuca, "Place of Coyotes." At the street-corner hotel we ordered Christmas dinner.

In the patio, around which the eight rooms for let were ranged, a mozo brought us a tin basin, a jug of water, and one clean towel. We made our ablutions, all using the same towel, while black hens, like cloistered nuns murmuring prayers, uttered contented gutturals as they picked insects from the shrubbery. In one corner, next to Room No. 5 and diagonally across the patio from the kitchen, was the W.C., three-holed and windowless, in perpetual gloom except when the door was left ajar. Its vault was considerably in need of spring-cleaning, but such a momentous event would necessitate the closing of the inn for a day, since the only entrances and exits were through the kitchen and the two double doors of the dining-room-office-parlor on the street front.

Despite the W.C. and the gorging on mojarras, we ate well. There was no turkey or plum pudding, but we had a substantial meal, with minestrone, fish, eggs à la rancho, tomatoes, fresh-baked bread, papaya, and cold beer. I learned that in remote places in Mexico one can get food that is not swimming in grease or stewed with chili.

When we got back to Acapulco, we drove to Bill Spratling's new villa by the sea for cocktails. He had acquired the house and the trim yacht moored in the bay with profits from his famous silversmithy in Taxco. We knew the place was within an arrow's flight of Lord Morley's new house, but we couldn't find it. We passed it, we were redirected to it, we passed it again. At last there on the roadside appeared Spratling himself, bronzed and hospitable, scouting for us with a highball glass in his hand.

His house was down, not up. Even its roof was ambushed in greenery. We descended steep winding stairs through towering shrubs and arrived at the doorstep. It was a spreading house of a warm color between oleander and brick dust. But though it had cost a pretty penny and used up great quantities of tile and stucco, it was no more a regular house than Natividad's home had been a real house. The sophisticated folk had copied the primitive. Rather it was one vast loggia with pillars and balustrades and long chairs and inviting hammocks. Spratling's home seemed to rise straight from the water. There were no walls, only a cool tiled floor and a spreading roof. Yet it was as private from the road and neighbors as if it were encased in windowless masonry ten feet thick. And then one discovered, far down the loggia at the corners, flats of walls with doors. A kitchen tried to efface itself by pressing into the rock of the precipice. A bedroom dropped off another corner, and crouched until it was almost in the water and spray peeped in the long window without glass. The whole villa seemed planned to minimize such things as cooking and sleeping.

And as if the superlative view out of the open veranda-drawing-room-dining-room were not enough, at the southwest corner there was a mirador ascended by winding stairs. Here aloft, stretched out in long chairs, the men had highballs and Andrée and Max drank orange juice while the sun went down behind a promontory. All our eyes were magnetized to the islands across the inlet, which the unearthly rose-violet glow from the setting sun had turned into heaps of carved amethyst set in silver. "I see now," Andrée said to Spratling, "where you get inspiration for some of your workshop creations."

Just before the blackout of night descended, we drove once more around the sea edges of Acapulco to our hotel. The incandescent lights came out in dots and clusters like signals to the sky. Then the stars began to release their cryptic answers. The lone protective gunboat in the harbor displayed its own pale geometry of illumination.

When I lifted my eyes to the heights again, their fantastic and memorable silhouettes were effacing themselves in camouflage against the night sky. They seemed to be saying, "In any case, we shall be here a long time after you and the houses are gone."

III

Mexico City and Its Environs

On no other spot in America did Spain lavish the same jealous
affection as on the Valley of Anáhuac, whose veil of mystery
Hernán Cortés rent asunder with his daring lance.

—GERMÁN ARCINIEGAS

1. THE APPROACH

FROM THE OUTER WORLD, the capital of Mexico has many approaches.
Each offers its own advantages, novelties, excitements. A popular
way is by Gulf steamer and Vera Cruz; or one may come in at
Acapulco on the Pacific coast. Trains and airplanes from the south
pass beyond the Guatemalan border at a tropical river town. An excellent air service comes direct from Los Angeles. A railway line
comes down from El Paso, another, from Nogales. A most convenient way is by stratosphere clipper from New Orleans to Mérida,
where one changes for the Mexico City plane. The great majority of
Americans, however, enter by the international bridge at Laredo.
Some drive the Pan American Highway. Others continue by train
in Pullmans they have boarded in Chicago or St. Louis or San Antonio. The train trip via Laredo has its special compensations, and is
to be recommended.

Within an eleven-year period between 1935 and 1946 I entered and
departed from Mexico by various routes. In 1943, when Thérèse
went with me, we took the train trip from Laredo, because I wanted
her to get the first impact of Mexico's alien atmosphere from the
mountain and desert landscape beyond Monterrey.

Luckily, the railways have arranged the schedule so that the best
tourist train arrives at Nuevo Laredo across the border in the middle
of the night, and the visitor does not get the repellent impression that
the Mexican border town offers. He misses hours of flat, profitless
scenery. When he awakes at six or eight or ten and raises the Pull-
man-berth shade, he looks upon such a strange, stark world that it
stirs some atavistic wonder.

The scene is like a stage set representing a time before mankind was evolved. From the desert plain the mountains rise abruptly, barren, unmitigated, the color of lead. No vestige of vegetation, no trickle of water, relieves the impression of stretching desolation. The mountains stand like stupendous monoliths of dull marble, monuments to a kingly race of mythological beasts. The scene has no kinship with prose; it is an awesome poem. The forbidding grandeur has a sublimity that makes one think of Milton.

At breakfast Thérèse said: "I have the feeling that nothing in Mexico will surpass the mountains as I saw them when I woke. It's like traveling through a region older than the Book of Genesis."

As the morning advanced, the sky became an intense and vibrant blue, but the mountains did not lose their out-of-the-worldness. Living men did not belong in this landscape. Yet, here and there, human beings had dug up hunks of gray earth and baked them into bricks under the sun and made themselves habitations in the wilderness. Still, the little square adobe huts with flat roofs did not break the impression of the uninhabitableness of the land, even though some of them had been adorned with tin cans nailed to front walls in which scraggly geraniums bloomed.

Before one of the huts, which lay close to the tracks, a nondescript mud-colored woman in raglike garments stood turning a kitchen meat-grinder, which had been attached to the wall like a pencil-sharpener. She was grinding corn kernels for the tortillas in a most unorthodox manner. How came she by such an implement of modern civilization in this prehistoric area?

Along the banks of a dry river bed, where scrub mesquite and clumps of green-brown grass grew, bony sand-colored cattle loomed up like specters of their kind. Then a flock of goats appeared, accompanied by an old goatherd, who did not bother to turn to remark the passing train. Miles beyond, three women came stalking across the desert, their dingy black rebozos muffling them to the eyes like Mohammedan women on the edges of the Sahara. In the distance appeared the faded salmon-pink walls of a tiny village to make one wonder how and why human beings would choose such a spot in which to live out their earthly days.

In the two hundred and seventy-five miles between Monterrey, which we had passed in the night, and San Luis Potosí, which we reached after dark, Saltillo and Vanegas are the only two stops. The region has been described by another traveler as "dry and sterile, monotonous with cacti, aloes, and yucca—yucca, aloes, and cacti, with infrequent towns and ranches." And it is the monotony that impresses many travelers far more than the strange beauty of the formation and mass of the mountains. Hour after hour the shadows of great rocks in a weary land pass, until there is a near-surfeit of sterile beauty, and one would prefer to cherish the first impact of the scene in memory rather than have it in continued actuality.

The station called Saltillo briefly broke the monotony. In the station garden red roses bloomed, and calla lilies, and pink geraniums. Large, cool, and juicy tangerines could be bought for ten cents a dozen, and passengers from every coach rushed to buy some. The sky above was bright, cloudless blue. "Look, oh, look at our beautiful Mexican sky!" a Mexican girl cried out in ecstasy. She had been visiting in Chicago. "Chicago has no sky—just a gray rag across the heavens."

After Saltillo, with its irrigated grapes and grainfields and orange groves, the slope steadily rose as the train wound in and out of other fantastic mountains. The landscape became the color of dust and silver-green. The spiny *xotols* stood like battalions of soldiers deployed on the mountainsides and bristling with weapons. Mouse-colored burros picked their way among stones, and the faces of the men riding them were lost in the shadows of enormous sombreros. Then again nothing but mountain and desert and cacti, mile after mile.

At the station called Vanegas crowds of dusky children, short-legged women, and withered old men clustered about the passengers. Most of them had something to sell: blouses in drawnwork, pink coconut candy, or tiny opals, wrapped invariably in black paper. Little boys offered toys and figurines made ingeniously of cornhusks, the favorite being Don Quixote in armor on horseback. Some venders were persistent, but none showed ill temper when they lost a sale.

Some who had nothing to sell held by the hand an idiot child to whom they pointed dolefully. Others indicated sores on their own neck or arms. A stary-eyed girl led a quavering old blind man, who was hatless in the bright sun to make his infirmity more patent.

These dark-skinned, undersized people obviously relished the games of barter or begging. But a few looked so authentically poverty-stricken and ill-nourished that they made one wish them out of the world and their misery.

"What chance have these poor creatures?" Thérèse said at dinner to the jolly, sleek mestizo waiter.

"Oh, plenty. Look at me!" He patted his broad chest, and pointed out the window. "I came from right out there near the antimony mines. I came from just as poor a family as those people at Vanegas selling things. My mother brought up ten children right here after my father left her a widow—ten children, with the oldest only eleven. She did washing for the people at the mines. And all ten of us are alive and doing well. I do the best, because I live in San Antonio, and have a nice house and a family there. Of course you have to be resourceful and have a little ambition, but you can get on, if you look out for yourself."

In the late afternoon, like slow-action chameleons the mountains took on a blue tinge from the sky, and a bluish haze hovered over the dust-dry plain. The whole landscape assumed a timeless, out-of-the-world quality, which the sight of stations and adobe huts and the talk of electrification and social custom could not diminish. As dusk fell and a few stars appeared, the alien landscape was beautiful and a little awful.

In a spreading plain of cacti, we crossed the imaginary line called Tropic of Cancer. Just before complete darkness we reached a valley village with trees and a small twin-towered church. But San Luis Potosí, a busy city of seventy thousand population in the center of a large mining district, was only a station called out in the night. Those splendid places farther on, San Miguel de Allende and Querétaro, were reached in dead hours beyond midnight.

On the second morning, Mexico looked like another earth. Broad valleys were in cultivation. Boys and men were plowing with oxen. In a wheat field an Indian was reaping with a hand sickle, slashing with swift, energetic strokes, not with the more measured rhythms of European reapers accustomed to wheat.

A maze of tin cans was attached to the walls of the peasant houses, and from them poured out cascades of bright-colored blossoms.

Where there were windows, songbirds perched in wicker cages. Brown children tumbled about, plump, half-naked, happy.

A silver lake was an oblong mirror flat on green grass. Beyond it, blue mountains with snow rose thousands of feet above the high plateau into the unbelievably blue sky. Billowy white clouds drifted lazily among the distant mountain peaks, lingered over a near-by hacienda where the great house was going to wrack and ruin in the new social order.

More and more gardens and vineyards and orchards broke the stretches of cornfields, where the land was so rich it was only scratch-plowed with a stick. And at little streams, willow-bordered, women knelt companionably to do the family wash.

The land between Querétaro and Mexico City was to be lived in, for rain blessed the region. And rain was that essential ingredient which had been absent in the north-central district. This land of the high plateau looked so opulent that the entrance into the capital itself was shocking by contrast.

On the northern outskirts of Mexico City lay a poverty more dreadful than that of the adobe huts in the barren desert. Here it was not the natural uncontested poverty of simple, primitive living, but something degrading. Derelicts existed in the squalor of pigsties, and somehow one knew that the appalling conditions were created by human minds aware of their own shame. Stones and pieces of scrap iron held down odd strips of rusty corrugated iron forming the roofs of haphazard hovels. Perhaps it is well that the traveler enters through something like a hobo jungle, so that he senses some of the sad truth that lies at the heart of Mexico.

2. FIRST HOURS IN THE CAPITAL

Of all cities I have seen in the world, Mexico is the most difficult to describe. The aura of Florence, Rio de Janeiro, Bogotá, Copenhagen, even London or Paris, is pronounced. But Mexico eludes composite impression.

On its high plateau, rimmed by blue porphyry mountains on three sides, with a drained lake bed as large as itself to the immediate east, the city sprawls in lopsided dimensions, its lowest paving stone almost a mile and a half nearer heaven than the topmost tips of New York skyscrapers.

The oldest capital in the Western Hemisphere, Mexico is the only world capital that can boast of the sight of two snow-crowned volcanoes. The first Spaniards who arrived declared the city the Aztecs had created to be "the fairest on earth." Certainly today there is no metropolis in the North American continent that holds such interest and beauty, that has so much to show, as Mexico City, if one takes it exhibit by exhibit, from environs that extend south to the gardens of Xochimilco and north to the temples of Teotihuacán.

Mexico is a Spanish city erected on an Indian foundation. It is a city of fresh flowers and dubious elegance. It is gracious and grasping, pseudo-smart and draggle-tailed, proud and superficial, pretentious and priceless, magnificent and unjust. Its sunny squares are shadowed by dark memories, its people are troubled with confused aspirations. Its Indian inheritance is its plus and its minus.

Though antiquity has left a glamorous patina in scores of districts, there is yet an indescribable feeling of impermanence about this city of short breath and quick heartbeat, as if the reclaimed land on which it is built might dissolve into ooze, or as if a volcano might conceivably be born straight out of a plaza pavement, like the monstrous Paricutín, which disgorged in a peasant's corn patch in 1943.

The effect of the city on strangers is as unaccountable as an uninitiate's reaction to a bullfight. Some go into an ecstasy; others speak mainly of the defects and mention bowel trouble. But whatever its glories, its fakes, its fascination, not to see Mexico "would greatly discredit your travels."

The driver of the taxi we took at the station was a sardonic, smoldering-eyed fellow who seemed half-reluctant to give up what he was doing to accept us as fares. He was finishing a sketch in oils, and the picture was quite wet. Two dry paintings stood on the seat beside him. He explained that since he had to make a living by chauffeuring, he carried his avocation about with him and in the waits he practiced his art. The paintings were crude but arresting, rather startling in design and color; but of the man's honest intention there was small doubt. He had felt his subject passionately, though he lacked the skill of execution.

I mentioned Diego Rivera. The chauffeur cast me a melancholy and disparaging look. "We have many painters in Mexico better than Diego Rivera," he replied laconically. After he had negotiated an intersection where cars seemed to come from six instead of two directions, he spoke again. "I should not be afraid to paint on a wall side by side with Diego Rivera."

"Really?"

"*En verdad*," he answered with conviction. "Rivera may have his ideas, but I also have mine." He blew his motor horn loudly.

I turned to Thérèse. "You will find considerable independence of thought in Mexico," I said, with a grimace to suit the moment.

"It is obvious," she said.

"When I was here a fortnight after Pearl Harbor," I said, "the manager of a tourist office was astounded to discover that his window decorator had filled the windows with pictures of Japan, and all over the walls were gay posters suggesting that vacationists see the East Indies now.—Pro-Japanese? Anti-American?—Not at all. Merely independence of thought. The limitations of time and space and the restrictions of war have as little meaning in their calculations as comfort."

But at the Reforma Hotel we found order and comfort and most amiable service. I had stayed there before long enough to know several of the twelve bellboys by name, as well as Tony Pérez, the engaging young manager, who had started his own career as a bellboy at the Ritz. Isidro, No. 10, and Fernando, No. 5, were the ones who looked after us with efficiency and solicitude, with as much personal interest as if we had grown up together in the same neighborhood in the same town.

Our Italian friend Jim had asked us to dine with him and his fiancée Andrée our first evening. We did the most conventional thing one does in Mexico City: we went to the Ritz bar at half-past seven for cocktails and nibbled on fried pumpkin seed with our Martinis.

For many foreigners and many Mexicans the Ritz bar symbolizes respite after a strenuous day in the mart, the museum, or the motor. For some, it is a hunting ground. It is a pleasant bar, in no special style, but it has tone. And the whole western wall is of glass for the world in the lobby to see through. It was raining, and the bar was just comfortably filled. We noted the fresh coolness of the room;

the imperceptible suavity of the waiters; the pleasant sound of the cocktail shaker in dexterous hands; the flash of glasses, with pale-colored liquids, like birds rising from the low round table tops to the mouths; the movements of silken legs, and silken toes peeping from slits in the thirty-dollar shoes.

Hanging over the bar among four American college boys was a thickset show-off, the son of a former Mexican President, who had aspirations to be both boxing champion and a state governor. Along the wall sat the blond and cherubic young Swedish Minister with his stunning wife. With them was the tall young Swedish manager of the Erickson Telephone Company. And at the next table sat the silver-haired, Siegfried-looking Axel Wenner-Gren, the multimillionaire manufacturer of Electrolux, and his rather bizarre spouse from Kansas. At a corner table sat four swarthy Mexicans who looked like politicians very much on the make. There were a half-dozen wall tables filled with American women, each sharing a single escort. In one corner sat the handsome Semitic-looking nephew of the great patriot Francisco Madero, with his fragile date dressed in gray chiffon and platinum fox.

This evening the Ritz bar held a half-dozen Mexican gallants paying well-bred attention to well-dressed American women. One of them was quite charming, and disarmingly un-self-conscious. He bore the distinguished name of Cervantes. He worked a few hours a week receiving the rentals from his wife's business property. He remained in the bar from seven to nine—virtually year in, year out. But like Cinderella, he kept an eye on the time. At nine he vanished to go home to sup with his wife, who never appeared in the cocktail lounge. He had told me all this about himself two years before. I told Thérèse now.

"To many of the young aristocrats of ruined houses," Andrée said, "there seems to be only one career open—to marry an heiress who will support him in the manner that a descendant of ancient family should be supported."

One could see that Cervantes made a good cavalier servente for the two hours he served—for he was tall and masculinely built, with handsome features and fair hair. There was no malice or meanness in him—and the cotton wool of life in which he had wrapped himself had not made him stuffy. Instead he was debonair, and as radiant as a youth setting out for a summer camp. The only responsibility he had ever accepted was to brighten his corner, wherever he was. And from seven to nine in the evening that corner was the Ritz cocktail lounge. The succession of American husbands who bought the drinks seemed to like Cervantes, and he was most polite to them. The current American wife with the English accent smiled a bit smugly on the whole assembly as she sat between the mate who bought her Paris frocks and the "sublimate" who gave her evenings an appearance of intrigue.

"The girls of the old aristocracy," Andrée was saying, "have been more adaptable than their brothers since the Revolution. The girls got positions or made the best of reduced circumstances. The men who had never worked could not adjust themselves. Now, three decades after the fall of Díaz, many of the men still can't take it. Some of them become gigolos—until they marry rich women. The less aggressive hang about Sanborn's waiting for someone to buy them a cup of coffee.

"Do you see that rather good-looking but pinched-faced man alone at the table by the door?" Andrée went on. "He is a relative of De la Torre, who was Díaz's son-in-law. When the end of the Díaz regime came, and people were rushing into hiding or exile, Señor de la Torre dressed himself in his best and walked the entire way to Vera Cruz, over the mountains, like the conquistadors. He had rarely had his little feet on the ground except when going to mount his horse or enter his carriage. But he made it, and got a freighter to New York. There, however, he did not know how to get bread, and when he died, his refined flesh was laid away in the potter's field."

"I'll bet you," said Jim, who was remarking the female tourists, "that a big percentage of the American women you see here are divorced and enjoying alimony. It's incomprehensible how the American men let the women who won't live with them run around making whoopee on alimony. In Mexico there is no law for alimony, which is a shame and a pity. In the United States you protect women too much—here we protect them too little."

We lingered an hour and a half over two rounds of cocktails and little dishes of pumpkin seed. We knew when nine o'clock approached, for Cervantes glanced at his wrist watch and nodded to it obediently at five minutes to nine. Then he rose and made his adieus to his lady friend, her husband, and persons of his acquaintance here and there. He bowed to our table in passing. Andrée and I bowed in return.

"He goes through life an aimless, no-good darling," Andrée said, "well-built in the mold of a man. But he's pure decoration, a modern museum piece."

Jim checked by his watch. "Yes, just nine. Shall we go? Though everyone comes to the Ritz for cocktails, it's rare that anyone eats here."

At a Hungarian restaurant a couple of blocks away, we dined on excellent roast duck, and talked until eleven.

After the soup, Andrée and Jim each confessed to having had a nerve-racking day. They had both been victims of the *mordida*—the bite. They explained to Thérèse the modus operandi of this old Mexican custom whereby a governmental official from the tax department lines his pockets. Andrée, who was divorced from a Mexican without alimony and had had to support herself and her son, had become the manager of a new smart shop dealing in beautiful hand-woven woolens. The shop had been opened only a few weeks, and this afternoon an official had come to "inspect." He examined the books, made several vague, unjust accusations, and waited for cash to be passed over to him. When Andrée pretended unawareness of the *mordida,* he began gathering up some bolts of the most expensive stuff in the shop. She quickly explained that the cash had been deposited at noon. They opened their safe and let him look. It contained one hundred pesos in change. "That will be satisfactory," he said, and accepted the hundred pesos. Laying by his bolts of cloth, he then became perfectly charming, raved over the shop—"what a lovely décor, what beautiful things"—and departed. "If we had refused the bribe," Andrée said, "he might have condemned and closed the shop."

Jim had had a similar experience. His place of business—it was an international concern—was only two blocks from Andrée's. Jim had settled for 1600 pesos. But he was so relieved it wasn't 4000 pesos the officer demanded that his nerve strain had turned to elation. After the officer had pocketed his bite, he embraced Jim Mexican-fashion, complimented him on his business, his staff, the goodwill he created abroad for Mexico. "If ever I can be of help," he exclaimed, "just call on me!" Jim said, "I am always at your service, sir." Then they embraced again, and patted each other's backs.

"It's perfectly ridiculous," Jim said, breaking a Viennese roll and putting unsalted butter on it. "But that is the way Mexico works!"

Thérèse felt a sense of outrage at such bald-faced thieving.

But Jim said with a shrug: "Oh well, it's really not much compared to graft and trickery in the States. In America, graft is often on such a vast scale that the very amount clothes it in a kind of dignity. Here, it's done on such a small scale that it's contemptible, and no one respects it."

He pulled two thin strips of rubber out of his pocket and laid them on the table. "This, for instance, the rubber of my windshield wipers. They are pretty essential on rainy nights like this. And though I am paying a boy to watch my car, I did not dare leave these. I've had dozens stolen. Kids steal them and sell them for a few centavos. You can hear curses up and down the street on rainy nights after concerts when men who don't have chauffeurs come out and find their windshield-wiper rubbers gone."

It was still raining when we went out and found the car, fitted in the rubbers, and drove to the hotel through the wet and glistening streets. Tomorrow morning, Jim assured Thérèse, the sun would be shining on the city. "Take breakfast on the roof," he suggested.

3. PANORAMA IN THE SUN

The next morning the sun shone with a radiance that seemed extraordinary until we realized that virtually all mornings in Mexico have a special glory. On the Reforma roof garden we had breakfast under a striped umbrella, where we could look out and across the flower-bordered parapet to the snow-crowned volcanoes with the fantastic Aztec names. Popocatepetl and Ixtacihuatl looked like two distant temples designed by competing celestial architects in entirely different styles.

Lying halfway between the Gulf of Mexico and the Pacific, the city graces the center of a high plateau, ringed off from enemies by a protective rim of castellated mountains. High and cool under a tropical sky, with measured seasonal rains and with good quality of volcanic-ash soil for growing things, the place is endowed with a munificence of natural elements to attract man. The wandering bands of Aztecs had discovered its potentialities when they settled here on the lake islands in 1325.

The city now spreads over almost thirty square miles. Growth has been rapid since the turn of the century. In 1900, according to that excellent volume *The World Almanac,* Mexico City had a population of 329,000. By 1943, it had increased to 1,754,000. In that year there were, then, slightly more than five persons to each person in 1900.

For the last two decades Mexico had been in a fever of reconstruction and modernization, following the alarums and disruptions of civil factions struggling for domination. Crassness has naturally accompanied some of the intensity of building, but you do not notice the flaws in the panorama from a high roof garden. From an upper view the city retains a certain majesty, with its flowering avenues, its old palaces, its churches, and its modern office buildings. But down on the level, you are as acutely conscious of the jostling of brash newness with antiquity as you are of the cross-purposes of its crossed Indian and Spanish population.

At the roof's edge between the flowering shrubs, we speculated on the city as Cortés had first seen it, when it was called Tenochtitlán, "Place of the Fruit of Nopal Cactus." Its proportions and originality made the conquistadors speechless with admiration. The first soldiers beheld a plaza "so well placed, so symmetrical and large, and so crowded with people," that they declared they had never seen anything like it. Then it was a city much like Venice in the multiplicity of its canals. But the canals are all filled up now—many of them with the ruins of Tenochtitlán.

From the hotel roof we could discern approximately the three great causeways that led from Montezuma's main island to the mainland beyond the lakes. The one by which Cortés made his heralded entrance to the city has now become the boulevard to Coyoacán. One is the street to Guadalupe and its celebrated shrine. The third, the Tacuba Road, is the one by which Cortés made his bloody retreat that Sad Night of June 30, 1520. Where Lieutenant Alvarado did his famous leap over the canal from which the bridge had been torn, motorcars now whirled on paving stones.

Cortés saw the wisdom in the Aztec's plan, and in much of his municipal design he followed it when he began rebuilding the city. He ordered the construction of the cathedral on the spot where the great pagan temple had stood. He used the very stones of the destroyed teocalli for the foundations of the cathedral. And for the public buildings and the dwellings of the conquering Spaniards, the mellow *tezontle* was used, a porous traprock composed of volcanic ash and silica. *Tezontle* comes in shades of soft rose and mulberry, and it is strong and earthquake-resistant. Walls erected of *tezontle* stand today as steadfast and solid as when Cortés builded.

Thérèse pushed some dwarf sunflowers aside and looked far over and beyond the parapet. She recalled what a historian had said of the fall of the Aztecs. "Here is the one example in history," he had written "of a culture ended by violent death. It was not starved, suppressed, or thwarted, but murdered in the full glory of its unfolding, destroyed like a sunflower whose head is struck off by one passing."

"But the energy of Cortés," I put in, "was so terrific that within three years of the demolition a new Spanish city had arisen out of the fire." On December 17, 1523, the great Charles V bestowed upon Mexico the grand title of "City, most loyal, distinguished, and imperial."

The Spaniards, like the Aztecs, were a race of builders who knew how to make the most of stone. It was their way, as it was the Aztecs', to erect first their temples and their buildings of state. Though the Indian pyramids are gone, spires and towers and domes of churches stand out in all directions above the city's rooftops, emphasizing the aspiration and the fantasy that went into the city's construction. And the Spaniards provided far better breathing-space for city dwellers than have the Anglo-Saxon Americans. Parks and promenades and little plazas are scattered plentifully about the municipal geography. As the city expanded, it gathered in, like garlands, picturesque old communities and new residential sections called *colonias,* and left green areas between and among them.

When we had looked our fill from the roof, we made another conventional move. We took a taxi and drove east along the Paseo de la Reforma, which runs two miles from Chapultepec to the splendid equestrian statue of Charles IV. The widening and beautifying of the Paseo was an inspiration of the Empress Carlota. Shaded by eucalyptus trees, interspersed with statued gloriettes that make green islands in the white thoroughfare, and with little flowering plazas breaking the lines of handsome houses, it is one of the world's finest boulevards. At the "Little Horse," the Paseo makes a diagonal cut, and becomes the Avenida Juárez.

The "Little Horse" is what citizens affectionately call the statue, ignoring the figure of the Spanish King who sits astride the fine animal. It was the first excellent bronze statue to be made in the New World. Baron von Humboldt put it second among the world's equestrian statues. The order granting permission for its creation was given in 1795, but it was not unveiled until the end of 1803. The sculptor was Manuel Tolsa, the director of sculpture in the Art Academy of San Carlos. Horse and rider are cast in one piece, and the whole thing weighs twenty-nine tons. At first it adorned the Zócalo facing the cathedral. But after independence from Spain, to protect it from the passions of the mob it was encased in a blue wooden globe, later moved to the semiseclusion of a courtyard in the university, and then finally to the most prominent intersection in the capital.

Once a residential district, Avenida Juárez is now given over to smart shops and office buildings. It smells of candied fruits, French perfumes, and tooled leather goods, and when it parallels the green shade of the Alameda, it smells of bark and flowers too. Beyond the open space before the pretentious Palace of Fine Arts, it narrows and becomes the Avenida Madero. Until the last three decades this street was known as the Calle San Francisco. Though through the three centuries of colonial rule San Francisco had been Mexico's best-known street, it had been blocked by a convent garden. Juárez's Reform Laws of 1859 had cut through many conventual buildings and grounds in Mexico, continuing or widening streets; and part of what is now Avenida Madero had been sliced off from the garden of the Convent of San Francisco.

Next to the Lady Baltimore Restaurant stands the entrance to this ancient Church of San Francisco, founded in 1524 by the first friars Cortés brought over from Spain. Though today it is lost or hidden behind some of the busiest shops in Mexico, the Church and Convent of San Francisco, with its eleven chapels and three hundred cells, was once the largest ecclesiastical structure in Mexico, touching on four streets. Now it is clipped and bound in by crowding commercial houses; only a slight trace of its former glory remains. But the relic is beautiful, and its shadows breathe an aura of history. Cortés supplied the land and the gold for the original church, as well as for the buildings where the friars resided. The land had been originally used by Montezuma for a botanical garden and a zoo. Much of the stone in the Christian construction was salvaged from the debris of pagan temples. For decades this was the religious center of New Spain, and here the famous Fray Pedro de Gante established the first Indian school to teach the natives Holy Writ and Spanish ways.

Approximately in the same spot where Cortés confessed his sins, penitents today were kneeling for absolution. Cortés's mortal remains lay in this San Francisco church for a hundred and sixty-five years and were then mysteriously moved. Here on October 27, 1821, *Te Deums* were sung to celebrate the independence of Mexico from Spain which Agustín de Iturbide had maneuvered. And here, after his fall, exile, and execution, Iturbide's embalmed body rested in state for three days in the late October of 1838.

Across the street from the entrance to the Church of San Francisco is the imposing House of Tiles, which gives on three streets. Now its patio is a restaurant, and its former drawing-rooms display drugs and hammered silver for sale.

On the same side of the street as the Church of San Francisco, at No. 17 Madero, rises the beautiful Iturbide Palace, with its richly carved façade of pink *tezontle*. It has the distinction of being the only colonial building that reached a height of four stories. In 1780, it was built by the Marquesa de San Mateo de Valparaiso, whose one-time importance in the social order is marked by the magnificent carved door with the coat of arms of the Royal Crown. The wily hero Iturbide came here to live after he had had himself crowned Emperor in 1822. Now the seignorial mansion has been taken over for shops and offices, like the other massive houses with the fine façades.

In the next block is the American Book Store, and across the street is the Pan American Airways office. Farther along come the Ritz Hotel and the National City Bank of New York. The past and the present rub shoulders almost every foot of the way, just as on the sidewalks dark workmen in dirty white pajama suits mingle with

men in well-tailored business suits. Lottery-ticket venders hold up
scrolls of thin green paper with the alert insistence of messengers
from Augustus Caesar bearing mandates for the populace to read.
Before a modernistic bank building liveried chauffeurs open the
doors of American motorcars and self-important citizens step im-
portantly to the sidewalk. Beggars of both conventional and original
categories indicate specific handicaps or specific lacks. Before a
photo-supply building, near the curb with cars passing within a
foot of his body, a man stripped to the waist lies on a bed of nails
and urges passers-by to jump on his chest. Another fellow a few
yards away puts on a rival attraction by swallowing flame. Flung
coins ring out on the concrete, and attendant boys dash among the
speeding motors to retrieve the contributions.

Against the walls of buildings Indians from the country sit placidly
eating their lunches or doing some needlework. They have never
taken the city seriously, not even though they now wear huaraches
or shoes when they come to town. Women pass in black flowing
skirts that skim the pavement, their dark faces shadowed by black
rebozos and their expressions grim with memories. In and out the
perfume and jewelry shops go the tourists of both sexes. And private
cars and taxis flow in a thick stream into the Zócalo, along with
Indians bearing huge bundles and leading offspring.

Down this single short and narrow thoroughfare, which has the
honor of having been named first after the beloved Saint Francis,
and now after Mexico's beloved patriot Francisco I. Madero, one
can get a fair first impression of the city's tenor, even though it is
Mexico's most important upper-class business street. The cosmopolite and the native, the Spanish and the Indian influence, antiquity
and modernity, merge to form a strangely rich mosaic. Breathing
history and tradition block after block, the street is yet restive and
impermanent. But elegant or mongrel, it is unflaggingly interesting.

4. ABOUT THE ZÓCALO

We came out into the great square known as the Zócalo, officially
called the Plaza Mayor de la Constitución. This spot of earth has
preserved its prestige from the time of Montezuma's ancestors,
through the Spanish colonial period, down to today. Though it is

no longer the geographical center of the city, since the growth has been steadily westward, the Zócalo is yet the city's heart. From it all the trams and busses radiate, and to it ten streets converge.

On the stage of this plaza more dramatic history has been enacted than anywhere else in the Western Hemisphere. These were the most sacred precincts of the Aztec hierarchy. Where the great cathedral of Mexico now dominates the square, the awesome pagan temples stood. There upon the high altars the revolting human sacrifices were performed wholesale, the beating hearts were ripped from the living victims by the slaughtering priests and eaten while hot. We are told by the conquistadors of a temple with a gaping serpent's mouth in stone for a door; of a tower of a hundred and thirty thousand human skulls; of the monstrous idols "in whose service five thousand priests chanted day and night"; of gigantic staircases, and consecrated fountains; of the birds kept for sacrifice; of the cages for captured warriors waiting to go under the obsidian knives. Here were seminaries for priests, squares for religious dancing, and a special house for the Emperor's devotions.

After the capitulation of Tenochtitlán, Cortés ordered the sacred pyramids to be razed, the idols broken into chunks. On the ruins of the war god's temple he had laid the foundations of the cathedral. Mexico's cathedral is both the oldest and the largest church in the continent. It dates from 1525, though the first structure was torn down; the present one was begun in 1568. Consecrated in 1667, it was still being built in 1813. Considering the generations of architects and builders who were employed, and the combined use of Doric, Ionian, and Corinthian features, the exterior has achieved a remarkable harmony.

The cathedral is not breath-taking or inspiring, but it is impressive in its mass, and by moonlight it takes on an aura of majesty and beauty. Its façade of gray sandstone and white marble is divided by heavy buttresses and broken by three grand portals. The twin towers rise impressively more than two hundred feet above the pavement, and they are furnished with a galaxy of varisized, varitoned bells. The largest bell, cast in 1792, weighs twenty-seven thousand pounds, and required thirty days to raise it to its position in the west tower. These cathedral bells have rung for many national joys and sorrows since 1792, for many crises in the careers of history-making men.

Attached to the cathedral on the east is the Sagrario, which is really a complete church. Done in an entirely different style, it is an excellent example of eighteenth-century Mexican Churrigueresque. Its mellow rose façade is quite charming, and adds considerably to the beauty of the plaza.

The interior of the cathedral is far less harmonious than the exterior. It is loaded with so much expensive bad taste that the really good things are lost in the mass of conglomerate vulgarity. There are few corners to remember with pleasure, and one carries away a depressing impression of dank gloom, heavy carved gilt, crimson plush, green malachite pillars, teak-wood confessionals, dust-streaked statues, and a wooden floor that billows like an enridged sea and proves a sounding board for flapping huaraches, guides' voices, bumping knees, Latin exhortations, and mutterings from the confessionals.

At right angles to the cathedral, comprising the entire east side of the plaza and extending for six hundred and seventy-five feet, is the National Palace. Built of gray stone and rose *tezontle,* three stories high, with three monumental entrances, it is rather splendid in its breadth and symmetry. Over the central doorway, high up in the third story, hangs the Liberty Bell from the little parish church of Dolores, which Father Hidalgo rang on the morning of September 16, 1810 when he uttered his famous cry for independence. The building covers some three city blocks and contains a dozen courtyards. It is the seat of the chief offices of the Government, including those of the President and the Ministries of Finance and Defense, and it also houses the National Museum.

When Cortés came, the new palace of Montezuma sprawled over the site. The Europeans were much amazed at the hundred parlors, the baths, the inner gardens, the feather-mosaic hangings, the chafing dishes, the cotton tapestries, the ornaments in silver and gold.

Cortés built his own house here, partly for his residence and partly for governmental offices. It stood until 1692, when it was badly damaged by fire in the Indian riots; it was rebuilt in 1720. Today the palace is a tourist attraction partly because of the Diego Rivera frescoes on the walls of the great staircase in the central patio. Crowded with hundreds of figures, the themes range from the legend of the god Quetzalcoatl to a malicious satire on contemporary social problems. These wall paintings are among Rivera's most notable works, and are not to be missed in any case; but the more Mexican history one knows, the more interesting they become.

On the west side of the Zócalo, across the acres of paving, flower-beds, and palm trees, stand the Arcades of the Tradesmen. They date back to 1524, when the newly established colonial government granted permission to the merchants to erect a portico over the broad sidewalk as a protection against the weather. In viceregal days, the great columned arcades were much frequented at night by young blades who used them as political clubs and rendezvous for romance. Now they are like a cheap bazaar, crowded with hundreds of stalls and counters, offering anything from poison-green rayon panties to plaster saints.

On the same side of the street, to the north of the arcades and facing the west side of the cathedral, is the National Pawnshop. Here stood the residence of Montezuma's father, where Cortés and his men were domiciled when they were reluctantly received in Tenochtitlán. The pawnshop was established in 1775 by Pedro Romero de Terreros, Conde de Regla, who had made a fortune in mining. It was a kind of philanthropical institution for the benefit of humble citizens in financial distress. Today it is a branch of the Federal Districts Public Charity, and a moderate rate of interest is charged on loans.

On the southwest corner of the Zócalo stands the Municipal Palace, dating from 1532. It had been the residence of the commander in chief of the Aztec city before Cortés set up the first city hall. Some of the best of the Aztec manuscripts are preserved in its upper story. Humboldt confessed that he loved to pore over the hieroglyphs written on agave paper and stag skins, "sixty-five feet long, and folded here and there in the form of a romb." At the southeastern corner of the Zócalo, where the fruit market is, the Aztecs played their athletic games and the first Spanish bullfights took place. And just beyond is the new Department of Justice with the flaming Orozco murals.

All about the great square we looked with double vision, beholding the diurnal drama with contemporary eyes and catching visions of the past with the mind's eye, remembering ironically that until 1933 pensions were paid to descendants of Montezuma, because

Cortés had promised the fallen Emperor on his deathbed that he would "take care of his children."

On the way to the National Museum we paused at the corner of what are now Calles Moneda and Licenciado Verdad before the place where the first printing establishment in the New World was set up in 1534. When I began calculating some comparative dates, the stones of the corner building took on more significance. The printed word and its implications of a transplanted culture went forth from this spot thirteen years before Cervantes was born, twenty years before Shakespeare. Elizabeth of England was only a year-old baby, and the Pilgrims' first sight of Plymouth Rock eighty-six years in the future. And yet how slowly had Mexico moved. For three centuries little had been done to make the mass of Mexicans capable of reading the printed word. José Vasconcelos had had the vision and the plan in the 1920's. In 1934, Cárdenas began an intensive program of building Federal schools. Jaime Torres Bodet, who became Minister of Education in 1944, was to inaugurate a campaign purposed to wipe out illiteracy.

We moved along the halls and patios of the National Museum, taking in at glances the authenticity of the pre-conquest sculptures. But the savage idols grinning with cold malevolence were revolting to Thérèse. She passed by the sacrificial stone as if she did not care to take it and its horrendous history into her consciousness. She vastly preferred the stark unfeeling mountains of the northern desert to the ferocious carvings motivated by fear or hate. But the huge Aztec Calendar Stone with its carved geometrical symbols, astronomical and sacred to the ancient Indian, impressed her greatly. She stood before its cryptic circumference for some time, and said, "Now that should have a room or a special alcove to itself."

From the Hall of Monoliths we walked through the sections of the Arte Industrial Retrospectivo. The magnificent Monte Albán treasures, which had been removed to their native state of Oaxaca, Thérèse would have loved. All we saw now of special interest— largely because of their historical association—was the state carriage of Maximilian, an elaborate golden affair created in Milan, and an old-fashioned somber vehicle that Benito Juárez used.

The sun was hot on the streets when we walked down Calle Moneda back to the Zócalo to find a taxi. One P.M. is not a flattering time of day to Mexico. To cross the Zócalo now at the lunch hour was hazardous. Ramshackle busses in broad rows a dozen deep jumped the gun on green lights like nervous horses at a race. Pedestrians scurried like field mice to reach the frail sanctuary of little safety islands where thirty would huddle on a space built to accommodate ten. The horns of the busses blasted the air with brazen din; the horns of the taxis answered the giants in manly defiance. All over the city the iron curtains of shop fronts were being rung down to the pavement with bangs and screechings—an old Spanish custom against thieves during the siesta. The lunch hour was on, and until three o'clock there would be no more commerce withindoors.

Scores of full taxis tore past, often suddenly changing their course in the thickest of traffic. Pedestrians dodged with the trained alacrity of bullfighters escaping piercing death by an inch's margin. Not in any high-keyed city in the United States is there such flurried bedlam of traffic in the rush hours.

Thérèse would not budge to venture across the agitated square. Would we have to stand here until night fell and dispelled the fevered flux? Oh well, then we too might echo Fanny Calderón: "We returned home by moonlight, the most flattering medium through which Mexico can be viewed; with its broad and silent streets, and splendid old buildings, whose decay and abandonment are softened by the silvery light."

It was by moonlight eight years before that I had first seen the Zócalo, and it was magnificent with its noble proportions and dominant colors of dusty rose and gray. I remembered how suddenly I had felt strangely light in the head, and knew I could not be that much affected by the beauty. My Mexican companion had looked concerned for a moment, and then laughed. "It's the altitude. Let's ride back—we've walked enough." But we continued walking. The sensation passed. And I had never felt the discomfort of the altitude again in my numerous visits to the capital. It was as if the inoculation in the moonlight on my first arrival had rendered me immune.

While I was recounting my experience to Thérèse, a taxi with *Libre* on the printed card on the windshield appeared at our side, and a driver with the kind eyes of a rescuing angel invited our patronage.

I said, "Sanborn's," and added significantly in Spanish, "We are *not* in a hurry."

We sat back, and I relaxed. No matter how pressing or treacherous the waves of traffic, it is well to have confidence in your Mexican driver and his alert responses. He seems guided through perils by some incredible sixth sense, and he can squeeze between cars with only a fraction of an inch to spare on either side.

Because of the one-way streets, our driver had to follow a round-about and oblique course, but he did it with deftness and assurance. When we drew up before Sanborn's in a space that seemed utterly unnegotiable, Thérèse breathed again, and took an all-embracing look at the façade of blue-and-white tile before she descended to the sidewalk.

For all its changes in usage and ownership La Casa de los Azulejos has retained its original architectural distinction in the heart of a business section. It is one of the rare houses in Mexico whose exterior is completely covered with Puebla tiles; and the battlemented roof, with its rows of niches for holy figures, seems peculiarly uncommercial in aspect. The house was built in the seventeenth century by the son of Rodrigo de Vivero, whom the King of Spain created Count of the Valley of Orizaba because of his success in establishing trade relations between Mexico and the Orient. When the son, Luis de Vivero, seemed destined to be merely an extravagant profligate, his father rebuked him with the proverbial remark, "My son, you will never build a house of tiles." The son mended his ways, worked hard, and on inheriting the old place that had originally belonged to his grandfather, rebuilt it and covered it completely with glazed tiles, blue-and-white like the sky and the clouds.

In its centuries, the place has been owned and occupied by many noted Mexican families, among them the Suárezes, of the same blood as that Catalina Suárez, Cortés's first wife, who died so mysteriously immediately after her arrival in New Spain. In the time of Carlota, the house belonged to a Suárez who was one of the Empress's chamberlains. In the rule of Díaz, the mansion was transformed into the fashionable Jockey Club. After the 1910 revolution, it became temporary headquarters for a labor union.

In 1904, a few doors away from the House of Tiles, two young Americans, Walter and Frank Sanborn, opened the first soda fountain in Mexico. They provided a piano and a pianist, whose specialty was Viennese waltzes. The elite took to the commercial novelty, and ladies who rarely entered shops stepped out of the most elegant carriages in the capital to refresh themselves at Sanborn's with those amazing concoctions called ice-cream sodas. With the vogue of the soda fountain, Walter Sanborn, who held a degree in pharmacy, set up a prescription department so arranged that persons had to pass the tempting beverages and piles of sandwiches to reach it. The success of the American sandwich plunged the brothers into the restaurant business, and they acquired an adjoining patio for a tearoom. Tea at Sanborn's became fashionable with the diplomatic corps, and even old Dictator Díaz and his glamorous wife Carmelita often came to join friends there.

The brothers shortly became agents for nationally advertised British and American drug products, and later started their own drug-manufacturing plant, which soon outstripped their retail trade. After the end of World War I, to meet the public demand for a restaurant that served good American food the Sanborns took over the beautiful colonial mansion, La Casa de los Azulejos. Over the enormous patio they spread a roof of glass, and turned it into the most popular restaurant south of New Orleans. To the drug business was added a fur shop, an imported-perfume department, and a silver shop, which has even a larger custom with local residents than with tourists. Sanborn's is a tribute to the ingenuity of two American boys who tried a new business venture in old Mexico and succeeded far beyond their dreams.

Two highly significant personal factors in the success had been Fred Davis, who came from Illinois thirty years ago, and Señora Rovzar, the Mexican widow of a Dutchman and a goddaughter of Señora Díaz. Davis, an art connoisseur, was director of the silver and jewelry departments and the chief inspirer of many of the attractive features of Sanborn's. Señora Rovzar gave information and advice. Her unusual charm and sympathetic understanding of humanity was partly responsible for that quality which had made Sanborn's a center for tourist and social Mexico.

Sanborn's cooks are too busy to spend two days over a dish of sauce as those at Antoine's in New Orleans used to do before the war. The restaurant serves good, tasty American food attractively in a vast high-vaulted room that is a combination of conservatory and palace courtyard. The place has one drawback: its popularity. It is patronized by as many Mexican business and professional men as American tourists. And from twelve to half-past two the tables are all occupied. It is not a place for lingering, except at teatime. We were lucky to secure a table promptly, and we enjoyed an excellent mixed grill and an avocado salad.

5. CHAPULTEPEC

Late that afternoon, when the rain was over, Jim came to take us for a drive. And Thérèse found something in the city to win her heart completely: Chapultepec Park, with its thousand-year-old ahuehuete trees. These ancient cypresses, noble in girth and majestic in height, were standing long before the migrating Aztecs first reached the isolated hill of rock called Chapultepec that rises like an island in an emerald sea. The trees are the only living things—unless one includes an active volcano—that had witnessed the upsurging glory of the Aztec kingdom and its obliteration by the white conquistadors. Montezuma II and his forefathers had used the woods for a hunting and recreation ground before Cortés appeared. In the adjoining meadows the young monarch had his fishponds. On the hilltop had stood his summer palace, with his harem of dark-eyed damsels.

The forest is a fairy-tale woods, with broad curving drives cut in the 1860's by the Austrian Maximilian. Great branches meet high above to form green arcades, cathedral-cool. Violets and creeping myrtle make casual patterns on the dark-green carpet of the ground. Enchanting vistas fill one with a desire to wander off in several directions at once. Bridle paths trail among great clumps of rain-fresh fern. Footpaths meander to leafy dells and pergolas. Flowers and vines that love only the tropics mingle with shrubs and blossoms of temperate zones. From some of the trees, festoons of hoary Spanish moss hang like magic nets to catch the wind.

But there was no wind now, following the June shower of mid-afternoon. Except for muted bird song, there was only a hallowed silence under the windless trees. I thought of the gabble-gabble and movement in the cathedral service, amid the gilt and red plush and stale incense; and I thought of the simple admonition, "Be still, and know that I am God." This forest, where the silence itself was eloquent, seemed created for communion with whatever one believed divinity to be. The great swollen tree roots formed natural stalls for meditation. The air was clean, and sweet with the faintly aromatic smell of leaves. Prayers breathed here might well reach Heaven more directly than those said in a cluttered, man-made church.

We stood still in the greenwood hush, and looked up to the great height of the forest ceiling, where a silver-blue light sifted through the green tracery.

After a little, Jim said quietly, "It's nice—to get away here from the dirty devices of the world."

That said the thing quite aptly, I thought, for the forest could be a spiritual bath to wash away rancor, or a healing poultice to draw the fever from a fret.

The great naturalist Baron von Humboldt loved to come to these haunts to muse. The Empress Carlota would steal away from her ladies deep into the forest, alone on foot, when the pensive mood was on her; or ride a white mule with a string of little bells about his neck when she felt joyous.

I was glad Thérèse first saw Chapultepec unadulterated, without people; for she loved woods and absence from the modern madding crowd beyond most things in life. This afternoon, the rain had driven the scant weekday visitors home or to the shelter of the spreading café near the entrance gates. I had seen the park first on a Sunday, when the world and his wife and all their fruitful issue come to make merry or relax from the weekly grind. These trees, walks, ferns, the blue sky above, the lakes and little streams of the meadow-land, which had once been reserved for the most highly privileged only, now belonged to each man, each woman, each child. And that was good. Some came for games, others merely for an orgy of doing nothing. Sweethearts took as discreet advantage of leafy retreats as did the meditative. Some citizens occupied their hours with the classics provided in the deep stone bookshelves between the poly-chrome seats around the Cervantes fountain. There in the presence of sculptured images of the immortal knight and his squire, one could sit for an afternoon reading Plato or Poe, Dante or Tolstoi, as well as Cervantes; for the classics were all in Spanish. And to stimu-late the pursuit of culture, around the base of the memorial ran the opening line of *Don Quixote:* "In a certain place in La Mancha, whose name I do not care to recall—" Apparently the books were regarded as sacrosanct; for without benefit of librarian or rule, no volume was ever stolen, none left out in the weather to spoil.

The Mexican populace displays its most admirable side in its behavior in Chapultepec Park. The crowds are always well behaved. They row in the little boats, play on the sports fields, eat their lunches, sprawl to take the sun on grass studded with "golden buttons," all in seemly fashion. And they scrupulously clean up their litter, as if the very eyes of the saints were on them. Few people have a more magnificent natural landscape to live up to than the citizens of the capital. And in this venerable, ghost-thronged spot, they seem determined, at least for a few hours, to make themselves—in the phrase of Plato—"worthy of the cosmos."

But human beings are human beings, whatever respect they reveal for public benefits; and it was very pleasant for an hour or so to have great stretches of woods all to ourselves, even while thinking how we would like to bring everyone we were fond of to see Chapultepec Park.

Chapultepec itself, "Grasshopper Hill" in its Aztec meaning, is a mass of porphyritic rock that rises like a natural fortress at the eastern edge of the forest and the western terminus of the boulevard called the Paseo de la Reforma. Its summit is two hundred feet above the Zócalo, which lies three and a half miles to the east. From the springs beneath the hill went the drinking water to the citizens of ancient Tenochtitlán, and the destruction of the aqueduct by Cortés was significant in the capital's miserable fall.

The present palace that crowns the summit dates from 1783. It was begun, with the King's sanction, by the forty-seventh Viceroy, Don Matías de Gálvez, as the summer residence of Spain's high representative. The building was never entirely finished and only briefly was it inhabited by viceroys. In 1840 it was used as a branch of the Military College, where young officers were trained for the Mexican army. Shortly before the war between Mexico and the United States the hill was strongly fortified. On September 13, 1847, the American forces began the bombardment of Chapultepec, which was mainly defended by teen-age cadets. The lads put up a valiant fight until there was only a handful left, and rather than surrender to the invading gringos, some of the last survivors wrapped themselves in Mexican banners and leaped over the parapet to death and immortality.

The great gate at the entrance of the steep winding drive that leads up to the castle is embossed with the profile medallions of some of these youthful heroes.

When Maximilian and Carlota came to Mexico in 1864 on their ill-starred adventure, the young Empress refused to abide in the dreary National Palace, where she was attacked by bedbugs on her first imperial night. So the Emperor ordered the remodeling of the Chapultepec palace. The gardens, the miradors, the winding stairs, the loggias, the intimate patios, were all the inspiration of the young royal pair, and it was they who had the forest cleared of unsightly underbrush and laid out with roads and walks. From the balustraded terraces of the palace one can view in all its spacious sweep that other great monument to the Austrian and his Belgian wife—the Paseo de la Reforma. Carlota had the old dirt road that leads into the city transformed into a boulevard planted with a double row of eucalyptus trees, and spaced with gloriettes.

Though since Maximilian a series of Mexican Presidents have used the palace as their White House, including Díaz in his thirty-odd years' rule, it is the imperial couple whose presences are felt in the place today. The furnishings reveal the varied tastes of people who have lived within the walls and the tastes of kingly givers of gifts from China to France. But the most attractive things go back to the time of Maximilian and Carlota: the Sèvres vases, the pink-and-gold brocade walls, the petit-point chairs, the silver épergnes, the crystal chandeliers. Chief executives of Mexico made Chapultepec their home during office until 1934, when Lázaro Cárdenas refused to move into such undemocratic quarters, and turned the palace into a state museum.

The terraces afford superb views of the spreading city, and beyond the dry lake bed of Texcoco to the encircling mountains and the volcanoes blanketed with snow. From approximately this same spot Montezuma had gazed many a time at his canalled capital, surrounded by lakes bearing the pirogues of paddling Indians. Here he had been borne in his jewel-encrusted litter after dinner to smoke tobacco treated with amber, and to feast his eye on the great temple of the pagan god Huitzilopochtli washed with the colors of sunset.

Maximilian and Carlota had gazed many an evening from this terrace into the surrounding beauty, and into the future so inexplicably mingled with dreams and dark forebodings. We looked long at the pattern of the hillside garden laid out by Carlota, and then we drove down the winding road again, out the gates and along the northern side of the park. There was no doubt about it: Hyde Park and Central Park were not to be compared with Chapultepec. And though the Bois de Boulogne has great charm, it lacks the ancient cypresses with their silvery mantles of moss to give it a quality of wonder.

"This," said Jim, with a wave of the hand, "is a symbol of what was Mexico. Now I take you to something hideous that Mexico bids fair to become."

Thérèse saw at close hand how the city had spread into *colonias,* residential clusters. Haciendas that were once considered far out in the country had been transformed, or were being transformed, into subdivisions. Those houses built before 1940 were on the whole pleasant enough; but many of those erected since 1940 were in the most offensive bad taste—pretentious, showy, dripping with gimcracks, studded with abortive turrets, and splashed with violent-colored glass. The style seemed to be bastard Near East tinctured with phony Hollywood.

"What a terrible waste of plaster and workmen's hours," Thérèse said. "These houses have the look of having been erected with money got by swindle or graft."

"Some were built by Syrian merchants," Jim said, "some by rich war refugees who wanted to do something quickly with their salvaged cash, some by Mexicans who had enriched themselves through political chicanery."

"What Mexico City needs above all," I said, "is a façade committee like that of Stockholm or Helsinki, where a man must submit his plans before he builds, and where no one is allowed to rear an architectural horror on a whim."

Instead of the rise of the proletariat in Mexico, about which so many words have been printed, the most palpable evidence proclaims the rise of a crass new-rich class. Here, one could not help feeling, was patent testimony of the decline of an age where a creeping decay had set in, and was shortly to be exaggerated by a conscienceless inflation.

But looking at these flamboyant houses so obviously built for vulgar display, and thinking of the crass persons who occupied them,

I recalled with a smile what Madame Calderón de la Barca had written a century before: "The Marquesa de San Román and her contemporaries are fast fading away, the last records of the days of Viceroyalty. In their place a new race have started up, whose manners and appearance have little of the *vieille cour* about them; chiefly, it is said, wives of military men, sprung from the hotbeds of the revolutions, as ignorant and full of pretension as parvenus who have risen by chance and not by merit must be."

Jim, who had come from an upper-class family of lawyers in North Italy, found much that was painful to him in the immediate modern civilization. In Italy his people had not been rich, but they knew dignity and charm in their living. They had a large house in the country, with lovely gardens and servants—"that was as it *used* to be," he emphasized—when he left a dozen years before. "Now here," he said, "though I make a good salary, you might say I live like a rat in a hole." (We had found his four-room bachelor apartment quite comfortable, in excellent taste, in a row of one-story houses on a quiet street.) "But to live as I do is better than to live as men do in New York. Think of existing in a high building, in a box, say No. 123— to have your love there, your children, your dreams—in a little divided box No. 123—what a life for a sentient being!"

His seriousness of tone made modern urban life sound peculiarly wrong and unnatural. Thérèse told him that in Alabama we had fled to a plot of twenty acres of woodland and built a house in the middle of it.

"Ah, yes," Jim said, "but that is to be wise."

6. PLACE OF FLOWERS

Within easy walking distance from the southeast corner of Zócalo is La Merced Market. Fronting Calle Carranza, it occupies a part of what was once the extensive gardens of the Convent of Mercy. Formerly the Viga Canal, which brought the boatloads of fresh vegetables and flowers from Xochimilco, came to the edges of the market. In viceregal days, and well past the middle of the nineteenth century, the promenade called La Viga was one of the city's chief attractions and a rendezvous for the haut monde. Now the district about La Merced has fallen into draggletailed estate. Though the building itself occupies only a city block, the market spreads out into the neighboring streets, where former proud buildings are little more than slums, and where two-peso prostitutes can afford to pay the meager rent of apartments. The busy bazaar still has sight-seeing appeal, though it is by no means so attractive or so orderly as when Baron von Humboldt found the stalls divided by flower patterns, the produce displayed in hanging boxes or arranged in pyramids and rectangles.

For a second reading, Thérèse had brought along a copy of the Calderón de la Barca letters written a century ago. Before we set out to the Merced Market, Thérèse read from "Letter the Twelfth" about the once fashionable drive called the Viga:

The Viga is one of the most beautiful promenades imaginable. . . . Which rank of society shows the most taste in their mode of enjoyment must be left to the scientific to determine; the Indians with their flower garlands and guitars, lying in their canoes, and dancing and singing, after their own fashion, as they glide along the water, inhaling the balmy breezes; or the ladies, who, shut up in their close carriages, promenade along in full dress and silence for a given space of time, acknowledging by a gentle movement of their fan, the salutations of their fair friends, from the recesses of their coaches, and seeming to dread lest the air of heaven should visit them too roughly.

Yet enter the Viga about five o'clock, when freshly watered, and the soldiers have taken their stand to prevent disturbances, and two long lines of carriages are to be seen going and returning, as far as the eye can reach, and hundreds of gay plebeians are assembled on the sidewalks, with flowers and fruit and *dulces* for sale, and innumerable equestrians in picturesque dresses, and with spirited horses fill up the interval between the carriages, and the canoes are covering the canal; and could you only shut your eyes to the one disagreeable feature in the picture, the number of *leperos* in the exercise of their vocation, you would believe that Mexico must be the most flourishing, most enjoyable and most peaceful place in the world, and moreover the wealthiest; not a republic certainly, for there is no well-dressed people; hardly a connecting link between the blankets and the satins, the poppies and the diamonds.

The contrast between Mexico's rich and poor, which had so impressed Madame Calderón de la Barca in 1842, was continually impressing Thérèse in 1943. But there was even a sharper contrast between the neighborhood itself as it was now and what it had been a century before.

Today La Merced is crowded at all hours. Even ladies sometimes go shopping here, with their maids or footmen carrying large market baskets. Besides fresh vegetables, one may expect to find anything for sale from ocean fish to lace, from penny writing tablets to honey-colored cocker spaniels, from plowshares to needles, from hand saws and sombreros to tripe and coconut candy.

To some the market is a carnival; to some, a livelihood; to some, a thesis in folkways. However one takes it, it is a colorful kaleidoscope, and the smell of mortality is strong. The atmosphere is redolent of unwashed skin, tropical fruits, dogs, boiling grease, butcher's meat, sun-hot leather, rusting metal, heliotrope, and unchanged infants. The earthiness of the market is that of the city, and not the clean, creative earthiness of the country.

Thérèse did not care to poke about long in the depths of La Merced. So we took a *libre* to two flower markets, which delighted her with the almost overwhelming profusion of beauty and scent. On the north side of the Alameda, between the ancient churches of San Juan de Dios and Santa Vera Cruz, was a market that sold only cut flowers. But a still better one was directly south on the narrow, picturesque street called Dolores, in the Chinese district. Stall followed stall, with great tubs and jars of almost every variety of blossom. The flower-sellers were mere brownish blobs against shimmering color spectrums. Hundreds of thousands of gladioli in infinite variety and shade; truckloads of carnations, filling the atmosphere with their spicy sweetness; Mariposa lilies, looking like clusterings of delicate white butterflies and smelling too good for this world. Thérèse passed up the orchids and sweet peas, and bought two dozen long-stemmed yellow roses for sixty cents. The marvelous abundance and cheapness of the flowers, she thought, ranked high among the delights of Mexico.

Besides the great open flower markets, florist shops behind glass dot the city. In the high, cool atmosphere of the capital there is no need of refrigeration to keep the blossoms fresh. Hothouses are unnecessary in any season. Flowers naturally respond to the soil and sunlight and atmosphere of Mexico. And it is in the Mexican heritage to love and cultivate flowers. From the time they met Montezuma's taxgatherers, who came into Cempoalla carrying roses, the hard-boiled Spanish conquerors never ceased to wonder at the Indians' love of flowers. Whenever the Indians brought gifts of corn meal or game to Cortés's troops, they always accompanied them with bouquets. And when the soldiers entered friendly towns, they and their horses were hung with garlands. To the Indians it was a most natural courtesy. Today, everyone in Mexico sends flowers to someone.

When we returned to the hotel, there was a box of orchids for Thérèse and a note from a gentleman I had known on a previous visit. He deplored the fact that a slight case of pneumonia had prevented him from calling to meet my wife, and the flowers were an earnest of a forthcoming visit.

To see the flowers of Mexico in their most picturesque and original setting one goes to Xochimilco, where there are islands solid with them and canoes loaded with blossoms for sale flit about like dragonflies. We asked Jim and Andrée to go with us on the next day to the floating gardens. I had been there twice before in past years, with Mexican friends, and the last time in the month of December I remembered buying an enormous bunch of long-stemmed white violets, literally hundreds of them, for a dime.

Xochimilco—the name means "Place of Flowers"—is as unique in its way as Venice. There is nothing quite like it elsewhere in the Western Hemisphere. It is a maze of canals and islands, popularly called floating gardens. For the tourist it is the prime attraction in the environs of the capital. The town lies fourteen miles to the south, and any one of the three roads that lead to it holds historic interest and beauty.

Xochimilco is emphatically Indian and Aztec. The citizens have owned their land since long before the arrival of Cortés. Property cannot be sold, unless death wipes out a family. Many of the islands have stayed in the same family for centuries. The descendants of warriors who fought fiercely to retain their land against Cortés are now flower-sellers.

The islands are supposed to have been originally floating rafts of wicker that in time took root. As a matter of cold fact, it is doubtful if they ever drifted. From the citizens of Xochimilco, Montezuma demanded his tribute in cut flowers, and boats freighted with blos-

soms glided every day out of the various small canals into the Viga
Canal that went to Tenochtitlán. Now the Viga has its terminus at
Jamaica Station some miles south of the Zócalo, and flowers and
vegetables are sold there in the great open market.

Xochimilco was a pleasure resort for the Aztec nobility. Today
all classes go there for diversion. The humblest citizen can afford to
hire a boat for an hour and bring joy to his black-eyed brood. The
Mexican rich do not scorn occasional outings at Xochimilco, and it
is an excursion sure to please their foreign guests.

Before you come to the gardens themselves, there is the town,
with a memorable little sixteenth-century church, dedicated to San
Bernardino, and the stone cottages of the villagers who own the
islands. Near the water's edge, where you take a boat, venders of
handicraft work have set up their movable establishments. Many
merchants are peripatetic, bearing their goods in trays strapped to
their shoulders, or across their arms; the drawnwork, the embroidered hand-woven bags, the mats woven of reeds, the wire-embossed
leather riding crops.

At the beginning of the main canal, flower boats are lined up
for custom. Flat-bottomed and half-covered with canvas awnings,
the boats are equipped with short-legged chairs, which can be moved
into the sun or under the awning, and a table for those who bring
picnic lunches or buy their meal en route. At each end is a floral
arch, with the boat's name designed in pansies, daisies, rosebuds, or
sunflowers, according to the owner's fancy. Most of them are named
after women, a wife or a sweetheart: *Carmen, Juanita, Dolores;* but
some are called names like *Viva el Amor* to attract courting couples.
You choose your boat according to name, to appearance, or to the
simpatico quality of the fellow who is to scull you. We chose an
engaging lad in his teens, whose boat's name signified *My Delight
Is to Sail,* and was formed of blue cornflowers and tuberoses. The
gondoliers are also the gardeners, the sowers, and the gatherers. One
day they till and another day they punt, so that by using different
sets of muscles their physiques have been evenly and agreeably developed.

After we poled off from the shore out into one of the larger canals,
we trailed slowly between islands bordered with spear-slim willows
and Lombardy poplars. The level of the opulent earth rises some six

feet above the dark-green water. Out of the rich black loam grow acres of blossoms to feed the soul and acres of vegetables to nourish the body. An island of pink carnations is followed by one of white gladioli, and another of mixed sweet peas; then an island of egg-plant, and an island of corn and squash. When we turned off into a very narrow canal, hardly broader than a ditch, we floated between banks of violets. Back in a larger canal, the spaced willows thrust their foreshortened reflections across the mirrored surface and merge with the lily pads and the delicate fresh-water algae.

"In Venice," said Jim, "your gondola passes down canyons of dark masonry. Here you float between walls of calla lilies and campaniles of silver poplars. But these canals do business, like the Rialto."

Everyone was not drifting for sheer pleasure. Scores were paddling or punting for good commercial reasons. Stringed orchestras floated, and marimba bands. To the tune of flutes and plucked guitars you could make your watery progress; for musicians would grapple their outfit to a pleasure boat for a price. Floating photographers plied their trade in the main canals, so that you could carry home documentary reminders of the day's occasion. Floating restaurants might be no more than a fat Indian woman squatting in her canoe broiling chickens over a brazier. Barmaids with flowing black hair bound with garlands would come alongside to dispense cold beer from tubs of ice. But the flower-sellers far outnumbered all other business folk. They were of both sexes and all ages; and as they sat in the center of their canoes, deep in blossoms, they appeared to be some mythological creatures half human, half bouquet. An oldish man in white pajamas looked like a convalescent warmed by a crazy quilt of pansies. One dark-skinned girl in a yellow dress, half-buried in white gladioli, resembled a honeybee in a bower.

A lovely lass with great black eyes and a wistful smile came paddling by, her canoe laden with corsages and old-fashioned finger bouquets set in valentine lace paper. *"Por favor, señorita!"* I called her closer. Andrée selected a corsage of tuberoses that had been dyed pink and yellow and woven into a design among lace flowers. Thérèse chose one of forget-me-nots and small gardenias. The flower girl asked only a peso each. That was for the labor of creation. The flowers in them could have been bought for two pennies. From another canoe Thérèse and Andrée got great bunches of lavender sweet peas neatly tied with raffia, so that the bouquet could be carried swinging from a crooked finger.

For a couple of hours we floated leisurely, remarking the color and the scents from the island gardens, the color and the attitudes of the holiday-makers. Family parties with half a dozen children ate their midday meal at the boat tables. A group of obviously upper-crust Mexicans bought sweet corn roasted over a canoe brazier. Lovers sat holding hands, oblivious to the passing glances or the scenery. Everyone seemed friendly; each boatload, glad for the other boatload's happiness. One middle-aged American sat in lonely state, with full and empty beer bottles on the floor beside his chair; but even he hospitably handed over a bottle of beer to an old Indian paddling an empty canoe.

When the next beer boat passed us, we called to the proprietor and got four bottles of cold "Monterrey." The woman paddled good-naturedly beside us until we returned the empty bottles.

But we did not eat anything from the floating restaurants. "There is probably typhoid in the canal water," Andrée said, "and they wash the dishes and utensils in it." Nor did we stop for lunch at any of the large shore restaurants, where the fish is good and there are music and a dance floor.

We decided to return to the city for luncheon at the restaurant called Unos, Dos, Tres, near the American Embassy. On the way back we stopped at the Jamaica terminus of the Viga Canal, where at the great open market Jim and Andrée bought their next days' supply of vegetables: cauliflower and leeks, cucumbers and little green beans. And Andrée went to a dozen stalls of gladioli until she found exactly the shade of shrimp-pink that would go with the shrimp-pink lampshade in her modern apartment.

At Unos, Dos, Tres, in the patio under the trees, we enjoyed breast of wild turkey, with a *mole* of avocado, tomato chili, and little shrimps poured thickly over it. The restaurant was owned by a Dane, and we said, you see even here how the Danes deserve their world reputation for good eating. The restaurant is one of the most agreeable places to dine in on the continent. There are glassed-in verandas with tables, and lounges where one can take shelter from summer showers. The rain began to fall in the patio just as we finished dessert, so we had coffee and liqueurs in the modern lounge, and lingered listening to the stringed orchestra until the rain stopped. "Mexico," Thérèse said, "can be such a pleasant place for simple indulgence."

7. THE PLACE OF THE MIRACLE

One day I took Thérèse to Guadalupe to see what is perhaps the most famous length of cloth in the hemisphere. The suburb was formerly called Guadalupe Hidalgo for the revolutionary priest who started off to war to win freedom from Spain with little more than a banner of the Virgin for his artillery. Today it is officially called Villa Madero, but everyone still calls it Guadalupe. In the violent feud between Church and State during the rule of President Calles, the Government began changing names of towns to minimize the Catholic influence. Guadalupe was rechristened Colonia Gustavo A. Madero, after the murdered brother of the martyred President Francisco I. Madero.

The town lies only a fifteen-minute motor ride north from the Zócalo, and just four blocks off the Pan American Highway. Behind and above, rises the hill of Tepeyac, the scene of Mexico's foremost miracle. Ordinarily the place has a population of eleven thousand, but on the feast day of Our Lady of Guadalupe, December 12, tens of thousands of pilgrims come from all over the Republic, some trudging hundreds of miles on foot.

The crowds take over the church and the town, and civil authorities helplessly give up any attempt at regulation. Every hour the church is filled to suffocation. Minor as well as major statues get kissed all over in frenzied devotion. The pilgrims sleep and eat in the streets, most of them having brought their sacks of food with them.

In viceregal days, the little municipality was far more important than it is today. In the eighteenth century new viceroys arriving from Spain assumed office in Guadalupe. When the war between Mexico and the United States ended, the pact of peace known in history as the Treaty of Guadalupe was signed here. On the morning of June 11, 1864, preceded by five hundred horsemen, came tenscore carriages bearing "the best in beauty, knowledge, and social position of the capital of the Empire," to welcome Maximilian and Carlota, and to witness their blessing by the Archbishop.

The eighteenth-century church does not add up to much architec-turally, but when Indians pass through the portals beneath the star-shaped window set in blue and yellow tiles, they know an ecstasy that no other spot in the Republic could give them. At every hour of an ordinary day, some penitent is kneeling before the cloth on which is limned the image of a Virgin. It hangs before the high altar in a glass case, and the colors have a remarkable freshness after four centuries. Who has touched it up recently, or how many times it has been restored, if ever, no one can say. And no one can know what early sixteenth-century priest conceived the original marvel, or who painted the picture. Innumerable intelligent Catholics through-out four centuries have chosen to accept the miracle as authentic. Prelates who have publicly doubted or denied the direct hand of Heaven have suffered exile for their ill-advised lack of tact. The skeptical among the laity merely shrug, but they do not smirk.

The well-known story goes back to the year 1531, only a decade after Cortés and the Spaniards had become masters of the proud Aztecs. The hero of the incident is an unlettered, middle-aged Indian, who had recently been converted and christened Juan Diego—John James. On a Sunday, December ninth, the man was on his way from his village to Tlaltelolco to attend mass. As he was crossing the barren hill called Tepeyac, he was surprised to hear strange music in the air. Then an opalescent radiance, like light from the throne of Heaven, almost dazzled him. In the center of the light he beheld a lovely lady, who spoke softly and called him "my son." She told him that she was the Mother of Christ, and instructed him to inform the Bishop that she desired a church erected to her on the spot where she stood.

Rapt with the wonder of his vision, Juan Diego sought the Bishop —the famous Juan de Zumárraga, who burned the priceless Aztec manuscripts in the market place of Tlaltelolco. The skeptical Bishop smiled at the Indian's fanciful tale, and sent him about his business. On the next day, however, the Virgin again appeared to Juan Diego. She told him to return to the Bishop and relate his story with stronger emphasis. This time Zumárraga demanded that the lady send him a sign of her identity. But Juan Diego, now considerably perturbed, stayed at home on Monday.

On Tuesday, the twelfth, he was forced to return to the town to

get help for his dying uncle. Now he chose a different route. But
for the third time the Virgin appeared before him. She told him his
uncle was already healed, and that he must go to the top of the hill,
gather the roses he would find growing out of the rocks, and take
them to the Bishop. To his amazement Juan Diego found blooming
roses where nothing had ever grown before. He wrapped the roses
in his *tilma* and bore them to the Bishop.

When he opened his mantle in the Bishop's presence, and the roses
spilled out, Juan Diego was as wonder-struck as God's vicar; for the
image of the Virgin was imprinted on the rectangle of cloth. News
of the miracle spread, and both Spaniards and Indians made hasty
pilgrimages to see the figure painted by divine hands. Juan Diego
was to tell his story hundreds of times; for when the shrine was built
the next year, he became the custodian of his own, now sacred, *tilma*.

Rome would give no credence whatever to the miracle; but a century later, in 1663, Pope Alexander III did order an investigation.
Finally on May 25, 1754, two centuries and twenty-three years after
the vision of Juan Diego, a papal bull gave official recognition to the
miracle of Guadalupe. But the Indians had not waited for Rome's
sanction. They had immediately taken the Guadalupe Virgin as
their own special patroness.

Today the picture is protected with such thick glass that it is impossible to tell how it was produced. The mantle, six feet by two,
is of some coarse fabric. According to the Abbé Clavigero, the cloth
is woven of the bark of the palm called *ixotl*. The figure stands on
a crescent moon. The face is conventionally sweet, the complexion
deep-cream rather than white or Indian brown. The dress is rose-
colored, flecked with gold, and gathered by a violet belt. The cloak
is light-green and studded with stars. A distinctive feature of the
painting is the golden rays that diverge from the picture in all directions. Faintly suggesting the style of Murillo, the painting is no
great work of art, but it has perhaps been viewed by more indi-
viduals than any other picture in Latin America.

Nothing could have been calculated to hasten the spread of the
Catholic faith like the appearance of the *morena* Madonna to Juan
Diego. It gave the Indians a deity who was all gentleness and for-
giveness to take the place of Tonantzin, the virgin goddess of earth
and corn, as well as all their blood-lusty Aztec gods. That the

vision came to an Indian of humble estate was important and significant. Had Cortés himself or any other Spaniard beheld the
divine apparition, the event would not have impressed the masses.
Some commentators have suggested that the whole affair was a
shrewd maneuver of the Bishop to win souls, and get willing laborers
to build churches and convents. But whatever the truth, the comfort the Virgin of Guadalupe has been to millions of heavy-hearted
Indians in the four centuries since her appearance should wipe out
any duplicity on the books of Heaven. And she has exerted more
influence for good on the Indian than any other ecclesiastical factor.
It was the balm of her tenderness and compassion that brought con-
verts to something beyond lip service, because the Christian Virgin
has never been associated with punishment, has never demanded a
sacrifice. For the bleeding Christ the Indians have pity; for God,
awe; but for the Virgin of Guadalupe, they have love, and it is to
her they say their prayers.

In the neighborhood of the church there is always activity: photographers and beggars ply their trade; people squat over *carbón*
stoves cooking corncakes; supplicants crawl up the hill to the Chapel
of the Well. One of the domes of the chapel rises above the well dug
where a spring arose at the spot on which the Virgin appeared to
Juan Diego. This well is supposed to have curative value. Empty
whisky bottles lie about conveniently, in which believers can carry
away the blessed water. Or they can purchase mud balls to use as
salves and plasters. The commercialism at Guadalupe is not so offensive as that at Lourdes, but it is in evidence up and down the hill.

Atop the summit is a rich man's cemetery, where the graves had
to be cut in solid rock. On the tombs are the coats of arms of old
Spanish families. The remains of the famous General Santa Anna
lie here. "Strange," Thérèse commented, "that so many powerful,
well-to-do Spaniards wanted to be as close as possible to the Indian's
Virgin in death."

We turned from the white mausoleums and looked across the
Valley of Anáhuac to the snow-covered volcanoes, immaculate
against the blue expanse of the sky. The atmosphere was intensely
clear. In their glory, the volcanoes seemed themselves like perpetual
miracles.

As we came down the steps, a handsome mestiza, obviously of

good class, was mounting on her knees. She bore in one hand a revolver, and in the other a silver bullet her family had had cast in gratitude to the Virgin. On the afternoon before she was to be married, for some secret reason, she had taken her brother-in-law's pistol, pointed it at her heart, and pulled the trigger. The bullet lodged in the barrel. Now recovered from a nervous breakdown following the attempted suicide, she was on her way to express gratitude for her preservation. It was, of course, the Virgin of Guadalupe who had held back the bullet. Behind the girl, mounting slowly, came three female members of her family dressed in black.

Farther down, we passed an Indian woman ascending and weeping quietly. Castigating cactus spines were stuck like a pendent necklace into the bleeding flesh of her chest. It was incredible to us how she could think she was pleasing the compassionate Lady of Guadalupe by torturing herself.

8. THE PLACE OF THE GODS

Fifteen miles north of Villa Madero lie the grandiose remains of Teotihuacán, "The Place of the Gods." This sacred city of the Toltecs had been abandoned to ruin long before the migrating Aztecs came into the region. But the ruins stand as massive monuments to a great primitive race whose culture provokes compelling speculation.

The ancient city was laid out geometrically, eight square miles in extent. Once the waters of Lake Texcoco lapped at its eastern boundaries. To the north rises the extinct volcano Cerdo Gordo, which in its fiery heyday spit up the stone out of which the temples of Teotihuacán were constructed. The two great pyramidal temples lying half a mile apart are known as the Temple of the Sun and the Temple of the Moon. The larger Sun Temple is a truncated pyramid built of blocks of volcanic stone, with five receding terraces rising from the plain to a height of two hundred and sixteen feet. This massive pile, which is greater than any pyramid in Egypt, has been excavated and restored. The smaller Temple of the Moon has not yet been restored, nor have the lesser pyramids that are supposed to have been erected in honor of the planets. The wide street between the two temples is called the Highway of the Dead, because the mounds on either side resemble graves.

In the Temple of Quetzalcoatl, about a mile to the side of the Temple of the Sun, the carved and cryptic decorations are in a remarkable state of preservation. The chief motif is the feathered serpent, which writhes up and down the staircases in sculptured stone, its stylized vicious head repeated in high relief in tier after tier of masonry. The serpent that could fly was the symbol of the good Quetzalcoatl, the most gracious and beneficent of all the Indian gods. For those who have their own ideas about snakes and what they represent, it is hard to accept the winged serpent as the god of life. Mr. Waldo Frank tells us that his traits were "sun, wind, music, love, joy, justice." As one remarks the grinning malicious face with bared fangs, the long, scaly phallic body, one might concede the sun and the wind, and even music of a barbaric, hissing kind. But what is there in the malignant eye or mouth to suggest love or joy or justice?

Standing in the gray-green quadrangular courtyard looking up to the terraced altar of one preserved side of masonry, a spectator may recreate in fancy what grand ceremonials he pleases, what categories of savage splendor, what strange sacrifices. The mysteries and the riddles will never be solved. But Teotihuacán will long stand as one of the most treasured archaeological zones of the New World. And unborn generations of Indian children may perhaps be peddling tiny clay masks and figurines, carved and baked by their parents, as veritable relics dug from the once sacrosanct soil.

On my first visit to Teotihuacán, partly to please the youthful venders, I had purchased more than a fistful of sour-visaged masks, obsidian arrow points, and one small head in jadite that may possibly have been centuries old, as the urchin swore repeatedly with bated breath. The jadite was smooth and cool and felt good to the touch. It was skillfully carved, too, and the expression was somewhat impish and slightly mocking, not malevolent, but just amused at the pointless phenomena of life that had been, that was, and was to be.

Today, we were not to be blandished into buying. Nor did we have any desire to climb the high steep stairs of the great pyramid. We could see the distant volcanoes quite as well from the ground as could the ancient peoples, who had presumably chosen this plain for their sacred city with the view of the volcanoes as a guiding factor.

Thérèse glanced ruefully at a glaring and cruel-eyed lump of baked clay which a kid was insisting was an Aztec god. "It is good," she said, "that the Indians now have their Guadalupe Virgin."

As we drove away I took one last look back to the massive memorials of the vanished Toltecs, and I thought of Nezahualcoyotl, the poet king of Texcoco who died just before the conquest of Cortés. "Rejoice in the green freshness of thy spring," he had written, "for the day will come when thou shalt sigh for these joys in vain; when the scepter shall pass from thy hands, thy servants shall wander desolate in thy courts, thy sons, and the sons of thy nobles, shall drink the dregs of distress, and all the pomp of thy victories and triumphs shall live only in their recollection. Yet the remembrance of the just shall not pass away from the nations, and the good thou hast done shall ever be held in honor."

9. TWO AFTERNOONS WITH DIEGO RIVERA

Diego Rivera told me he much preferred the Toltec ruins of Teotihuacán to those of the later more graceful Maya ruins of Chichen Itzá and Uxmal. The more primitive, the more massive, the better for Diego Rivera, for these are qualities that accord with his own nature. Physically he is enormous, and temperamentally a part of him is attuned to elemental forces. And for all his shrewd sense of showmanship, for all the complicated sinuosities of his mind, and in spite of his implicit genius, he seems yet a rather simple person when you meet him.

"Diego is just a big overgrown boy, so natural, so genuine, so sweet. My husband and I love him very much." The lady who passed this judgment was an American from Texas who had married a Mexican who had lived with Rivera in Paris when they were young men in art school. It was her husband who first took me to see his old roommate at the studio in Villa Obregón.

Rivera had chosen to build his studio home in one of Mexico's loveliest suburbs close by the famous San Angel Inn, which was formerly a seventeenth-century Carmelite Convent. There he and his wife, Frieda Kahlo, have twin studios. Diego's is painted in intense Prussian blue, Frieda's is a turgid crimson—both colors of high saturation and low brilliance. The houses are erected on stilts, with only upper stories—the lower floors have no walls whatever, just concrete square columns and open spaces. The studios are joined by a concrete bridge high in the air, like the Bridge of Sighs. They are functionalist in the extreme, boldly modern, smacking of New Russia, and defiant in their cleavage from the mellow and gracious architecture of the neighborhood.

Persons are as divided in opinion over the studios as they are over bullfights. Some find them practical and cute, others find them atrocious. But it is what the artists themselves like, the removal to an upper-story privacy, with excellent light for painting.

It was in late July of 1935 that I first saw Diego Rivera in the flesh. He was at the height of his fame, still in the publicity dazzle of the Radio City controversy, which resulted in the destruction of his murals because he insisted on deifying Lenin and Communism on capitalistic walls. But this day he was not high up on a scaffold sweating fourteen hours at a stretch, expressing his terrific indignation against social injustice in emphatic lines and strong colors. He was in his studio painting the portrait of a breath-takingly beautiful blonde. Clad in a brassière and shorts of water-green silk with white polka dots, she half-reclined in a small beach chair, her pearly flesh radiant in the coppery glow not of the sun, but of an open-faced electric heater little larger than an imperial dinner plate. Behind her, ranged against the wall, stood sightless stone idols, some whole, some maimed, like a bodyguard of zombies honoring a living goddess of beauty. On the floor in front of these images excavated from an unreckoned past were strewn odd feet and arms and broken heads, suggesting heroic sacrifices and fanatical tributes.

At our entry—another Mexican was with Rivera's old school friend and me—the lady's luminous gray eyes dilated as if in surprise, her lips parted ever so faintly, and she made a charming gesture of half-covering one brassière-concealed breast and with the other hand she touched her golden hair. She was as exquisite a piece of flesh as I ever remember looking upon.

I heard three gasps and a kind of restrained throat rattle behind me. The second Mexican had gone pale at the sight of the refulgent body. He turned from the door and stepped back out on the little stoop at the top of the stairs, pressed his hand over his solar plexus, and gulped air to get control of his emotion. While he was recovering from the surprise and impact of beauty in the raw, I turned back to be presented to Diego Rivera.

My impression was of a huge man with bulging sorrowful eyes, a man shy in manner, gentle in movement, and kindly in nature. I liked him from the first look at his homely face and the first touch of his large sensuous hand. With all his homeliness and his casual sloppiness—even with all his buttons buttoned and his brown shirt tucked in, he gave the impression of being doubtfully buttoned—he possessed an odd sort of attractiveness.

But though I looked him straight in the face, I saw him only vaguely. The corner of my eye held the vision of the half-reclining figure. When I was presented to the model, she looked up with an appealing, deprecating expression that said do-please-forgive-me-for-catching-me-this-way-but-I-am-having-my-portrait-painted. Raising an expensively manicured hand smelling subtly of the Rue de la Paix, she offered it in such a way that I knew she was accustomed to having her hand kissed by gentlemen. But I refrained, and she remained demurely inert until the other Mexican, recovered sufficiently to face the glory, re-entered. Then she glanced toward a robe of pale green which lay on the couch. Rivera set aside his palette of oil patties, retrieved the garment, and threw it about her exquisite shoulders as she rose from the beach chair. Slipping her feet into silver-studded sandals of green leather, she made her excuses and disappeared into a room at the back. Then Rivera clicked off the electric heater that had both simulated the effect of sunshine on a beach and warmed the lady's bare flesh in the studio coolness.

We stood for some moments before the almost completed portrait on the easel, murmuring admiration but thinking more of the breathing model than the replica. The portrait was rather lovely in its way. But though beautiful women might be Rivera's forte in real life, they are not his best subjects in painting. He is better with men and animals and children, with people in mass, better depicting injustice, violence, hatred, greed. He needs something stronger for his talents than mere cultivated and desirable female loveliness. And this immediate subject was a pampered parasite, an American girl brought up since childhood in Paris in the luxury of what is called the society world. She had recently married a wealthy Mexican playboy whose grandfather had been a famous name in Mexico. What had she to contribute to Rivera's scheme of a communisitc society?

Obviously he was not satirizing her or making fun of her sweet dependency, though in his practical ideology she would be broken straightway like a butterfly on the wheel. Certainly she was something I had not expected to find in the Rivera studio. Was this the beginning of a change in him, I wondered, or was it merely a temporary surcease from castigating the rich and dealing with violence and mockery? Perhaps it only revealed his manly susceptibility. Diego was then only one year from fifty. Perhaps he really needed the money. He had built the studios with Rockefeller gold, and now it was all used up.

In 1935 Diego Rivera found himself without more walls to paint. The controversy over the Radio City murals had brought him extraordinary publicity, but no new commissions in the United States with fat capitalistic checks. He had reproduced the destroyed mural in Mexico's Palace of Fine Arts at a smallish fee. And just now the revolutionary government had no more work for him. Cárdenas had become President, the lot of the Indian was being daily improved, the landlords were being divested of most of their land, and the Revolution seemed to be doing just fine. It needed no propaganda at the moment. So here was the Number One revolutionary artist out of a job, and painting the bourgeoisie for pretty pennies.

Rivera and a dozen other fellow artists had reached their high reputations on the upward swirl of the Revolution which had begun with Madero in 1910. Rivera had been twenty-four at the time. But he was no mere convert. He had become a radical about the age of five, and at eight he had renounced the Church. Much of his radicalism he had imbibed from his black-bearded father, an advanced thinker who was making his living as a country schoolteacher in Guanajuato when Diego was born in 1886.

While the lady of the portrait was dressing I managed to get the artist to talk to me about himself. In his blood stream, he told me, there is a mixture of Tarascan Indian, Spanish, and Portuguese Jew.

"There is a sizable percentage of Jew in the mestizo Mexicans," he said in his soft-toned voice, "far more than most people know.

That is why we are so clever at trade, why we can beat the Yankee at bargaining." His eyes narrowed shrewdly. "Did you ever hear of a Yankee really getting the better of a Mexican in a trade?" he said with a grin. "It's the Jewish blood in us."

Rivera had been born on the feast of the Conception of the Virgin, December eighth, the elder of twins; and he had been named after his father Diego and the Virgin Mary and several deceased members of his family. At the insistence of his mother, who claimed some connection with an ancient nobleman, he was christened with a name longer than most crown princes: Diego Maria de la Concepción Juan Nepomuceno Estanislao de la Rivera y Barrientos Acosta y Rodríguez. As soon as he could assert himself in spoken language he shortened his name to Diego Rivera.

Proving a prodigy, he began to draw before he ceased nursing at his mother's breast. Remarkably understanding parents allowed him to cover the walls with his baby studies in colored crayon. At the tender age of eleven the tough-minded child was enrolled at the Academy of Fine Arts in Mexico City. Here he became influenced by the caustic revolutionary drawings of José Guadalupe Posada. His nature soon revolted from the rigidity of the Academy and he left the school to paint as he chose. At twenty, with a scholarship he sailed for Europe, where he stayed for several years and missed the shooting phases of the Revolution.

Of the old masters it was Goya in Spain who most attracted him. In France he was inspired by Picasso and Cézanne and the more extreme French experimentalists. With the radical in art he also took seriously to the radical in social ideology, and he became a passionate devotee of Karl Marx. On his return to Mexico after 1920, full of the revolutionary spirit in politics, he was immediately recognized as a maestro in painting. A liberal government had taken over during his European sojourns, and when José Vasconcelos became Minister of Education under President Obregón, Rivera and other artists got salaries to express their true genius on the inner walls of public buildings. Art in Mexico became a vehicle for social propaganda. Diego Rivera was given commissions to fill many square yards of wall space with his frescoes.

During the decade of 1920 to 1930 Rivera worked with prodigious energy, making sensational propaganda for the socialist cause and everlasting fame for himself. He put onto walls in the tremendous ABC letter language of paint ideologies that the French and Russians put into books and pamphlets. He wrote messages in color that the illiterate could read and respond to. He reinterpreted Mexican history, and the worker and the peasant saw themselves depicted as noble beings who could do no wrong, but who were shamefully mistreated. His reputation spread abroad, and at the beginning of the 1930's Diego Rivera was probably the best-known name among living Mexicans.

As he talked very simply and soft-voiced in answer to my questions, I regarded the two-hundred-and-fifty-pound mass of flesh beside me and recalled Peggy Bacon's impression of the man. She had found him "a gentle heavy sea lion, with naïvely separated teeth, smooth Latin manners, and high-minded but crafty integrity." I kept looking from him to the primitive thick-lipped idols—and I could easily see why they had such fascination for him. His own face and his obesity would lend itself quite naturally to primitive sculpture with its penchant for distortion.

On Rivera's return from Paris in 1921 he had looked at ancient Mexican art with new eyes, he told me, as he led me over to his collection of figures that had been plowed up recently by Indians in their fields or that had lain in corners of huts for years. He bought everything good he could lay hands on in the western provinces of Michoacán, Jalisco, Nayarit, and Colima. Some rare small statues the artist got for a few pesos apiece.

Casually Rivera picked up a head from among a pile of fragments and asked me to guess its age. I bent to remark the face and then glanced up quickly and caught a wily, dead-pan expression on Rivera's face. We both grinned. I was not fooled. A sculptor friend had carved the head of Rivera in the primitive manner.

Many of the images were Tarascan, with a good sense of humor and caricature. Distortion often seemed to have been made a criterion, as when this hunchback bore a hump larger than his torso, or that grinning youth was overshadowed by his own phallus. Some of this ancient quality of distortion, I thought, Rivera has put into his own mordant satire on the vertical walls of courtyards and staircases.

When the lady of the portrait came out in a smart afternoon attire of gray and yellow, it was obvious that she was dressed by the best Parisian couturières. Her seven slim diamond and yellow sapphire bracelets were doubtless specially designed. She and I had just begun to speak of Paris—I knew several of her friends—when a discreet but arresting knock came at the outer door.

Diego went to answer it. His wife, Frieda, had crossed the bridge between the studios. Standing in the doorway with her black hair parted in the middle, drawn tight, and braided high, she was strikingly handsome. Her eyes flashed under the heavy eyebrows that met above her nose, her nostrils flared, and she held her small head high and imperiously on a splendid column of neck. Her blouse was embroidered muslin, her flowing cotton skirt brightly Mexican in color.

"Frieda has made Diego an excellent wife," their old friend had told me on the way to call. "She looks after him well—even goes to market with her basket on her arm just like a woman of the people to select the proper vegetables for him. They have had some rocky times, and they have just been through a crisis and she almost left him. But I believe she will stick with him to the end. She's twenty-three years younger, you know."

He had told me, too, that Frieda had been a tempestuous problem child—a tomboy full of tricks, a personal revolutionary who was the despair of her teachers. She was the kind of girl who refused to play with females and joined boys' gangs, and admired the pistol-toting gals of the Golden West. She had had the distinction of being expelled from the National Preparatory School by Lombardo Toledano, who was then the director. While in this school she decided she wanted to have a child by Diego Rivera. At nineteen she married him. But entirely on her own she has achieved a reputation as a painter.

Though she was vibrantly attractive, Frieda Kahlo spoke hardly a word. I thought she had the tense, alert attitude of a female on the watch. I may have imagined it, but the impression remained even after the model was gone and we were having a cup of tea. Perhaps it was because the alluring scent of the lady still lingered in the atmosphere. At any rate, Frieda made a gesture of opening a large window to let the late-afternoon breeze blow through the room.

As the breeze stirred her thin muslin blouse, I thought of her as a flame—one which no circumstance short of death itself could ever put out. She gave the impression, too, of a prima donna who scorned to act the role, who would hold her part of the stage in silence by merely being. Diego, with his bulk and genius, impressed one by the charm and wit of his talk. As he told tall tales in a soft and sympathetic voice I thought how there was no trace of pomposity about him, nothing of affectation. He would smile boyishly. Frieda listened with a detached air, half critical, half approving. We all enjoyed ourselves very much.

That evening at dinner with a Mexican bank manager—formerly a noted socialist—and a famous Mexican poet I told them of some of the amazing things I had learned about Mexico from Rivera. The men exchanged glances.

"Ah, yes, Diego is a wonderful talker," said the banker. "In a couple of hours he is able to construct an entire new history of Mexico."

"Listening to him is like reading a novel of Jules Verne," the poet said. "His talk is a metaphysical impossibility of synchronization."

The next time I saw Diego Rivera was on a winter's afternoon just before the New Year of 1942, not at his studio in Villa Obregón, but at his house in Coyoacán, that most charming of all the charming suburbs that lie about the city. With his extraordinary acumen, Hernán Cortés divined the quality of the place, and chose it for his residence. But before his time it had been a favored resort with Aztec princes. Here in August 1521 the Spanish Government established itself, for it was the Captain General's idea to make it the viceregal capital instead of the ruined city of Tenochtitlán. The conqueror built himself a little palace on the plaza. Today the Cortés coat of arms is set above the main entrance of the town hall, known as the Casa de Cortés. Now Coyoacán drowses in an aura of colonial mansions and old gardens, with moss-stained stone walls brilliant with bougainvillea. It is a mellow, unspoiled town, a place of peace and bird song, with none of the crass newness that tinctures parts of the capital.

The Rivera house at Calle Londres 127 is surrounded by a great stone wall that has been painted the same striking Prussian blue of the artist's studio in Villa Obregón. I was let in the heavy gate by a mozo who might also have been a guard. Within the gate, the house lay to the left and the garden to the right. Dominating the garden, and directly opposite the slightly elevated front patio of the house, was a strange structure built of steep masonry stairs, and roofed something in the manner of an Oriental shrine. It suggested a miniature Toltec god house. Here a small forest of figures had been set up: gods and goddesses of ancient Indian tribes, and replicas of mere human beings in stone and clay. These were the unearthed treasure Diego Rivera had been collecting for years, some of which I had seen lining his studio walls in 1935. Now they had been brought together in convocation in a private museum set up in the family garden.

The place really belonged to Diego's wife, who had inherited it from her father, a German Jewish photographer who had married a Mexican. There was the orange tree that had been planted the day Frieda Kahlo was born. And in the branches of that tree she had first received the forty-year-old painter, when as a teen-age girl she had enticed him to call to give an opinion of her own painting. When he had helped her down from the tree their romance had begun.

The orange tree, now in fruit, stood looking like any worthy old orange tree. But the camellia bushes filling the spaces between the walks of the patio looked strange indeed—for they were growing fluffy cotton instead of the blossoms of their species, Pink Perfection. I was remarking them with some bewilderment when the artist appeared at my side, looking me over with casual shrewdness and a kind of sly smile. He gave me his soft, sensuous right hand somewhat limply, and then he said: "December nights are treacherous. So we wrap the buds and blossoms in cotton batting."

I stood there in the space between the exhibit of primitive idols and the camellias so lovingly protected, and looked at the bulk of the man beside me. He had aged, and he wore glasses now. The large sad eyes were sadder, and a bit watery. The boyish quality which he had still possessed at forty-nine was not evident. But the greatness was there in the aura, and the kindness showed through the Indian caution.

"Will you come inside now, or would you like to see the gods?" We climbed the twelve steep stairs, and I looked at the relics. Of course the setting and the owner made them the more interesting, but it was undoubtedly the finest private collection of primitive sculpture in Mexico. I remarked dwarfs, convivial laborers, a seated nude, a vain lady, some ballplayers, as well as the malignant representatives of deity. When I expressed a special interest in a Tarascan figure done by a sculptor with a sense of satire that communicated its good-natured malice through the centuries, Diego Rivera seemed pleased, because it was one of his favorites.

In the small sitting-room with two doors opening out on the patio, I took the chair the artist indicated for me facing the pavilion, and he sat with his back to the light. A half-grown black tomcat emerged from the shadows and leaped into Rivera's lap. His name was Nero.

I refrained from smoking, and Rivera was grateful, for smoke stung his eyes. He had had a disturbing time lately with the right eye. He confessed that he was not in prime health, and he was forced to live on a diet of vegetables cooked without salt. In weight he had not lost much, but there was a tiredness about him. Now at fifty-five he seemed mourning something lost. Was it the failure of the Revolution to measure up to his hopes? Was it his interest in women? Was it because Trotsky, for whom he had made considerable sacrifices and been thrown out of the Communist party, had renounced him before his assassination?

"Trotsky and I had our quarrel right in this room," he said quietly. "In the very chair you are sitting in he was sitting when he broke our friendship. 'Diego,' he said to me, 'you and I shall never again be friends. You are worse than Stalin.'"

Quietly Rivera sat stroking the black cat, telling me of the quarrel. He spoke of his extraordinary admiration for Trotsky—"the greatest man of our time"—of all he had done for Trotsky, of how he had secured permission from President Cárdenas for Trotsky's entrance to Mexico in 1936 when he had been forced out of Norway and no other country in the world would give him asylum. He had arrived on a December day to be the guests of the Riveras in this, Frieda's house, together with Madame Trotsky, secretaries, and a bodyguard.

"Trotsky had the greatest brain of his generation. He defeated the armies of the fourteen nations, built the Russian railways, and planned the Five Year Plan."

For half an hour Rivera spoke of his relationship with and his feeling for Trotsky. Here Trotsky had stayed, sitting in the next room at his desk, writing his vindictive life of Stalin, a revolver at his elbow. The Riveras did not intrude often on his privacy; they had moved to their studios in Villa Obregón. At night floodlights played on the villa and guards stood duty. If reporters were admitted, they were frisked for weapons. Trotsky got his exercise by walking to the edge of the garden to feed his rabbits in his plus-fours, with a pink tie under his little salt-and-pepper goat's beard.

"And then"—Rivera made a kind of summation—"in a brief few minutes our friendship was ended. Trotsky hated me. Do you know why? I told him I did not believe that a classless society, which we both desired, would rid the world of war. For one classless society in one part of the world, I said, would have things so much less in abundance than another classless society more blessed by climate and natural resources that the have-nots might eventually make war to get some of the good things the more fortunate had. Trotsky leaned forward with dismay and controlled fury. 'Do you really believe that?' he said between his teeth. I said I did, and repeated it: that even a classless society would not ensure world peace. Even world Communism would not bring about the millennium.

"Trotsky's expression turned to loathing, as if I had been a poisonous snake. He sat very still and white-faced for some moments—in that very chair you are sitting in now. At last he said, 'Then, Diego, you are even worse than Stalin. We shall never be friends again.' He rose and left the room."

The cat must have felt the flow of adrenalin which the unhappy memory induced in Rivera's cosmos; for suddenly it sprang from its master's lap and tore out into the garden.

"Trotsky moved from this house, and never spoke to me again. They tried to kill him several times—but—"

"They?"

"The Stalinists here in Mexico. And they tried to kill me. Finally, in spite of all precautions Trotsky was murdered—you know the story of the pale young man with the Alpine pike concealed under his raincoat."

"And you still liked Trotsky all the time?"

"I still regard him as the greatest mind I have ever come in contact with."

"What about Stalin?"

Rivera looked off for a moment, wiped at his bad right eye, and then let his weighted gaze come to rest slowly on me again.

"Do you know, I rather like him personally. But his politics I hate."

"You do feel sure it was the long arm of Uncle Joe that really got Trotsky?"

The artist studied my face for a moment, as if he were going to draw me. Then he smiled an odd smile that was not at all cryptic. "What do you think?" He excused himself, took a small vial from a shelf, and put some drops in his eye.

When he sat down again, I found him quite ready to talk about anything except his own art. Politics, the failure of the Revolution to accomplish its aims, the oil situation, Russia, Mexico's most famous men, were subjects congenial to him. In the two hours we talked Rivera finished off most of the Mexican heroes, leaving none that he admired wholeheartedly but Zapata. Of Americans he really admired only Thomas Jefferson, "and, a little bit, Franklin Roosevelt."

"Conditions in Mexico today are no better than they were under Díaz," he said. "The former peons have become peons to the local politicians and the state banks. They are worse off than when under landlords or the Catholic Church. The farmer is always in debt to the Agrarian Bank. The land in fact does not belong to the peasant, and the peasant is merely the slave of the Agrarian Bank."

No, the Revolution had not turned out as he had hoped. And in his resentment Diego Rivera, the socialist and anticleric, had renounced Cárdenas, the undoubted friend of the common man, and in the 1940 election had voted against Cárdenas's liberal candidate, Avila Camacho, and supported the reactionary, church-endorsed candidate, Almazán.

Such a turn astonished me, and I did not attempt to conceal my astonishment. I got no satisfactory explanation, and I could not help feeling that there was some personal pique involved, and considerable political confusion. He had not voted *for* Almazán, he insisted, but in protest against the party in power. "When you deal with bandits," he said, making a wide ellipsis, "you cannot act like a gentleman."

The telephone rang. It was Paulette Goddard. Rivera was to paint her portrait.

The evening paper was brought in, with headlines proclaiming the prodigious numbers killed within a week of war. I spoke of the grim effect on society of human beings killing human beings.

"But there can be a wonderful satisfaction in killing a man," Rivera said, smiling as benignly as if he were standing godfather at a christening.

The telephone rang again. His wife had not come in yet, and she was calling to say that she would be later still. She was at some artist tea, doing the family honors, since he himself rarely went out nowadays.

Dusk had come swiftly, and in a few minutes it would be black night. It was time for me to leave. As I rose to go I thought how strange it was that this huge, swarthy fellow, without a redeeming physical feature, could so inspire tenderness and wishes for his happiness in so many persons.

Rivera excused himself and returned with a wide sombrero and an old tweed topcoat. He said he would take me back to Mexico City in his car. The car turned out to be a station wagon with a chauffeur. As we drove through the blossom-scented evening, I thought that for all his famed controversies at home and abroad, Diego Rivera seemed remarkably simpatico to be with.

10. A MORNING WITH OROZCO

Two days after my second visit with Diego Rivera in Coyoacán, I was taken on New Year's morning to call on José Clemente Orozco. Mexico's other great-name artist had just built a new house on a city street within walking distance of the Hotel Reforma. It was as yet only partially furnished, and some of the plastering was still to be done.

I was taken by a young German-American from Ohio named Pfriem, who was studying art on a scholarship, and who was one of the few privileged to observe Orozco at work. For unlike Rivera, who did not seem to mind being surrounded by a vast audience while painting, Orozco demanded to work in private. But somehow young Pfriem had won him, and now there was a bond between the husky blond student and the maestro. Pfriem addressed him always as "Maestro," and spoke the word reverently.

A servant took us up to the north front room on the third floor. The studio ceiling was high, and a vast window occupied the space of almost the entire front wall. There was also a skylight in the roof and another window high in the south wall, where the light was subdued by a cream-colored silk shade. I had never seen a studio with so much clear bright light; but Orozco needed all he could get, for he was almost blind in one eye and he looked at the world through a thick lens with his medium-good eye.

The room was furnished only with an easel, three straight chairs, and a table, where the clean brushes were arranged neatly in precise rows with the tubes of pigment laid out in proper order. The walls were without hangings or pictures. But along the floor with their faces to the wall stood nine or ten recently completed canvases.

When Orozco came in I saw he was slight in build and just under medium height, quite swarthy in complexion, and minus a left hand and wrist. When a child, while playing in the streets with some gunpowder he almost blew himself into eternity. He had a way, like Chucho Solárzano, the bullfighter, of cocking his head slightly to the side and turning his right ear toward the speaker, for he was deaf in the left ear. But Chucho's impairment was due to a crashing bull's horn, while Orozco's resulted from his childish experiment.

There seemed to be little in common between Mexico's two foremost painters except genius, dark complexions, and weak eyes. Unlike Diego Rivera, who knew from babyhood that he would be an artist, José Clemente Orozco did not begin to study painting until he was twenty-six. Born in the state of Jalisco in 1883, he was educated to be an agricultural engineer. Then he studied architecture and mathematics and architectural drawing. In 1909, in secret he began to teach himself to paint; and six years later, in 1915, he exhibited his original sketches of the capital's underworld. The painter's rare ability was recognized at once, though, as one critic said, Orozco had departed completely from the artist's usual procedure and had developed "clandestinely and heretically." His independence was marked from the first. And he has continued to stand alone, untrammeled by politics, but passionate in his personal condemnation of the evils of society and almost violent in his compassion. Whereas Rivera squandered much of his creative fire in political wrangles and personal squabbles, Orozco put all his energies into painting.

While he talked in the bright clarity of his studio, he casually gave me a private showing of his recent months' creative output, bringing out one canvas at a time, setting it up on the easel, and then standing back and regarding it intently.

The pictures varied from figures in action to stark landscapes of forbidding volcanic rock. Done in dark and livid colors, some of them were like tragic poems of desolation. One represented a kneeling, supplicating beggar with arms outstretched and palms spread as if to receive the nail points of a crucifixion, and huddled by his side in a murky doorway was the shadowy figure of a miserable old woman. Persons like these, Orozco seemed to be saying, went through daily crucifixions—while Christ died on Calvary but once, these wretches were crucified again and again, year in and year out.

"You don't paint from models?" I said.

"I paint from models always."

"But surely you did not paint these from models here in your studio. They are figures that could not be posed."

Orozco smiled. "Ah no, of course not. But I see figures and scenes on the street, and I come home and paint. First I see, and then I record my impression of what I saw. I do not make abstractions in my mind. For me to paint, it is necessary to see."

So Orozco painted according to what was in his heart after he beheld misery on the streets. I looked again at the colors, mold-green, skeleton-gray, excrement-brown, the red of dried blood. Because there was a kind of sublimity in the work that came from passionate conviction, there was nothing repellent. It was his conviction that made the impact of his work so convincing. What he displayed on the canvases was dynamic and emotional because his ideas had been fused in spiritual experience.

As before when I had stood before Orozco's spreading murals in public buildings, now in the studio I thought again how Orozco in his painting says the unsayable, as great poets do in their verse. The explanation or meaning of his work cannot be put into words. His pictures must be felt, their spirit divined, like the writings of religious mystics.

When we had sat down in the straight stiff chairs in a corner of the room and were smoking cigarettes, I asked Orozco why it was that the best talent in Mexican painting seemed to turn to murals.

"But mural painting is in the blood, in the tradition," he said. "Latins have always liked to cover their walls with figures. It is so in Spain and in Italy. When the talented Mexicans grow to maturity they take to the walls. I painted as a child, but just like all little boys, for I had no thought then of making a career of painting. But when the Government made it easy for the development of mural painting here, it was natural to turn to walls. Because they gave us the walls to paint on, it made easy the expression of the Revolution. The Revolution put vitality and force into the subject matter. But the Revolution did not make us mural painters."

"We don't hear very much of the Spanish muralist of today, do we?" I said. "The modern Mexican artists seem to have over-shadowed him."

"There are many excellent muralists in Spain, but they are less known because Spaniards have always scorned to make propaganda for their art. A painter must go to Paris or to New York to become publicized and be made famous and get large prices for his work. Publicity is important in the price of a man's work. We in Mexico have benefited by publicity, but we had to paint some pictures in the United States and had to have Americans write about us before we were well known. Propaganda has made the price of my pictures advance manyfold—the true value being ever the same. All the publicity Diego so easily gets reflects on Mexican modern art in general." The maestro smiled with an amused sense of satisfaction. "It has had considerable commercial value for me."

So the great Orozco, who did nothing to create publicity himself, was quite aware of the value of propaganda.

"Tell me," I said, in an effort to sound out his political views, "which of the important Presidents since Díaz has been the best for Mexico?"

The dark eyes behind the thick lenses took on a judicial expression, washed clean of prejudice. He named them slowly, as I had them in mind: "Madero, Carranza, Obregón, Calles, Cárdenas, Avila Camacho." Then he said: "None of these six have been bad; all have been good, each in his own way. Each did something necessary for the good of Mexico at the time. They made mistakes, but each has been good on the whole. Cárdenas, of course, very good."

"And Díaz?"

"Díaz, too, had his qualities, and for the period he lived in his virtues were greater than his limitations."

For the artist who sees so profoundly the human tragedy and the peculiar misery of his own fellow countrymen, Orozco certainly had a temperate and reasoned judgment. Grief, wretchedness, despair, the pangs of poverty, Orozco noted and painted with zealous passion. But he never let his own mind become tainted, and he kept his personal emotions in leash. By his revolutionary depiction of stalking greed, or rank indifference to human suffering, Orozco has stirred men to legislation and reform—as an artist, not as a political-party man.

"To quote a great man," he said, "nothing in the whole range of mental poison corrodes like political-party spirit. I myself only ask whether a thing is right or wrong, not whether it be good for one party or another."

We spoke of the war and the United States declaration of war following Pearl Harbor. To the young man from Ohio he said: "You should find a way not to go into this strife as a fighter. A true artist is not a good fighting man. They could use you in the camouflaging department."

The young man said hopefully: "They might use me here in Mexico for camouflage against a Japanese attack."

Orozco replied with a grin: "I think it might be more useful if you would go and camouflage San Francisco."

11. PLAZA DE TOROS

I took Thérèse to see other famous murals besides those of Diego Rivera at the National Palace, which she had seen on her first morning in Mexico. At the National Secretariat of Education we beheld plane after plane depicting the nobility of workers and peasants, and the scoundrelly ways of exploiters. In the auditorium of the National University, Creation seems to be Rivera's theme, with the arts and sciences as man made use of them. In the Palace of Fine Arts is a copy of the destroyed panel of Rockefeller Center, in which Rivera makes his subject "Man at the Crossroads," the conflict between capitalism and socialism, where all the good forces of nature, science,

and industry are portrayed as destructure when used by capitalism
for private gain.

At the University of Mexico we saw striking murals by Siqueiros,
Montenegro, and Charlot; but we were much more impressed by the
Orozco frescoes covering the walls of three floors around the first
patio of the National Preparatory School, making use of the general
theme "Revolution, Justice, Liberty, Church," and those of the stair-
way depicting the compassion of the early Franciscans. At Sanborn's
Restaurant Orozco has done a symbolic staircase panel which might
mean many things; it is called "Omniscience." In the Palace of Fine
Arts he has pointed up the dangers of false leaders of revolution, and
the general chaos of the world in modern times. In the Ministry of
Justice he accuses the world of its blind and awful injustices, and
has covered three far-spreading walls with flaming indictments.

It was interesting to compare Rivera's range of showmanship, his
grandiloquence, slyness, malice, and terrific vitality, with Orozco's
imagination, poetic passion and even greater violence. But Orozco
does not press socialistic doctrines into his work except by implication. Rivera's propaganda is definitely political. His murals often cry
out for strife. Orozco's dramatize the ghastliness of war, at the same
time eloquently expressing the tragic and human aspect of Mexico's
social struggles.

Thérèse was impressed with the sweep and passion of modern
Mexican art, the strong colors and the pictorial excitement. But after
looking long at her sixth or seventh series of murals, she remarked
thoughtfully: "There is something so satisfying about a clean white
wall or a surface of mellow gray stone. I should think an artist would
consider a long time before he could bring himself to impose scenes
of hate and horror on its quiet satisfactions. I grant that many of
these murals are tremendously moving, and a few are even beautiful,
and they definitely have a distinctive new flavor. I would not have
missed them, but I cannot look at more. From the pre-Cortés days
Mexico has had too much blood and death."

"It is not only from the Indian human sacrifices," I said, "that
Mexican painters have inherited a strange affinity with death, but
from Spanish poetry, and the Spanish bullfight."

"Well," she said with conviction, "enough of violence and in-
humanity and bloodshed have been depicted by these Mexican paint-

ers to last for eternity. I think they would do better to renounce their culture of death and appreciate the blessings of their wonderful land. And how can a nation come to any lasting good when its people go to a bullfight every Sunday afternoon? That is bound to have a brutalizing effect on the public. The best men of Mexico, men like Madero, loathed bullfights. Cárdenas knows it is evil, and hates it."

I gave her the usual line about the tragic significance of the bullfight, the Aristotelean "catharsis," the mob purgation. I spoke of the pageantry, the marvelous display of skill and grace, the spectacle of supercourage, the beauty and costliness of the matador's costume. She was not in the least impressed.

Then I told her about the gentleness of a young bullfighter I had met just after a fight on one of my former Mexican journeys. His name also happened to be Rivera. He was only nineteen, and he had the face of a mystic, with great dark eyes and a most innocent and sweet expression. He displayed breath-taking bravery, and missed death several times by barely an inch. Finally he killed his bull with extraordinary grace, and accepted the thundering applause with humility. And when I was introduced to him ten minutes after the killing, except for a cigarette between his slender fingers and a streak of blood on the silver silk of his sleeve he might have served as a model for an artist depicting an emissary from Heaven.

Thérèse was still not even faintly convinced by my attempt to give evidence for the defense. But the next Sunday afternoon she found herself where neither she nor I had dreamed she would ever be—in a box at the bullfight.

The Casasúses had invited us to Sunday dinner with Nathan Milstein the violinist, who had just concluded an engagement of four concerts. When we accepted we did not know that our hosts always took their Sunday guests to the bullfight, and that they maintained a box at the Plaza de Toros just as families in New York maintain boxes at the Metropolitan Opera.

The party of seven was as cosmopolitan as they come, even in Mexico. The host was of Spanish blood and educated at Princeton, his very blonde wife was pure Swedish in heritage but born in Minnesota, and called "Toots" by her friends. Milstein was Russian

Jewish. His publicity manager was a beauteous English woman, statuesque, yet Madonnalike. Then, besides Thérèse and me from Alabama, there was a dark little mestizo as lively as a monkey, a passionate aficionado who was yet terrified of motorcars when they went more than thirty miles an hour.

The Casasús house is remarkable in that the rooms are on different levels, and to reach the bedrooms upstairs one has to traverse a mezzanine that is a mirrored bar with little glass tables and all the latest fixings. Stairs circulated from the drawing-room to the bar, and other stairs curled to the bedrooms and baths still farther up. The style of architecture was hardly Spanish, and it certainly was not Swedish, though the furniture was something of each; but the pictures on the walls of dressing-rooms and baths were lushly French, and the color schemes were emphasized by the tints of the perfumes and lotions and salt crystals gleaming through the glass of their quart and half-gallon containers. It was a house built for fun and entertainment, and it all seemed in tune with the rippling laughter of the young gold-haired hostess out of Sweden via Minnesota into old Mexico.

The excellent menu was Swedish here, Spanish there, and again Mexican in a special piquancy. Through the open French windows the sun poured a cascade of golden atoms over the damask of the table. Milstein, who had had a splendid success with his concerts at the National Theater, was in relaxed mood and full of gay talk. The little Mexican was sprightly and amusing. The hostess's laughter bubbled like the sparkling wine. But with the coffee came the bombshell for Thérèse. "I'm afraid we must swallow this quickly," Toots said, "for in this land of unpunctuality one is never late for a bullfight."

I saw the look of consternation that came over Thérèse's face. "You mean," she faltered, "we are going to a bullfight?" She could not quite believe what she had heard too clearly.

The hostess laughed as happily as an excited child going to its second circus. "Of course. We never miss a Sunday. We have a box— all year. We always take our Sunday-dinner guests to the bullfight." She dashed away up the winding stairs to fetch a scarf. The Englishwoman looked almost as consternated as Thérèse.

But the others did not notice their expressions. Señor Casasús was telling Milstein not to be disappointed if we did not get a tiptop performance this afternoon. "You know we have the two seasons: the formal, November to March, and the semiprofessional, the *novilladas,* April to October. You'll get the same colorful atmosphere, but you won't see the stars, the three-thousand-dollar-an-afternoon chaps. But, do you know, sometimes a *novillero* can be astonishingly good."

"No Chucho Solárzano this afternoon?" I said. I was showing off my bowing acquaintance with the sport. A Mexican friend of mine and the famous Chucho had married sisters. Chucho was one of the few bullring stars who went in the best society. Almost all the famous matadors were definitely of the people, as humble in origin as stableboys. Though they were idolized by the public and took on the graces of the boulevards, most matadors were never invited into the best homes, and never could dance with the ladies who threw them flowers.

"No Chucho this afternoon," said the host, "no big names at all. But we'll get something good out of one of the six runs. It's not once in a year that an entire *corrida* is a flop. Sometimes, though, it happens with the experts. I saw one last winter. You know the President's brother, Maximino Avila Camacho, is the impresario of the bullfights." He turned towards Thérèse and the Englishwoman, who were standing speechless and very still. "He is there as master of ceremonies of the most rigid protocol ever devised. Well, he made history last December twenty-eighth, when the thing was the worst flop I have ever seen. It was just one of those days. It took the stars— no, Chucho was not there—eight and nine thrusts each, to kill their bulls. The audience hissed and booed, and finally started hurling cushions."

"And they began yelling for the bull to kill the man," the dark little Mexican put in gleefully.

"Maximino felt that the audience had been cheated, and after six sorry fights far from standard he donated a valuable bull at his own expense and demanded a *novillero,* an apprentice, to fight the bull. But the members of the bullfighters' union howled indignantly that this could not be, since the ceremony had not taken place at which the man had passed from *novillero* to professional. He had not been presented with the sword with all the ceremonial rights. The union said, 'It cannot be done—this *novillero* cannot fight.' Maximino said, 'Is that so?' Then, being the President's brother and one of the richest men in Mexico, he broke the traditions of centuries: He had his chosen *novillero* fight the donated bull then and there in the formal season. The fight came off brilliantly; the novice killed his bull at the first stroke."

"Oh," cried the little Mexican in an ecstasy of remembrance, "it was magnificent!"

"The day was saved, the spectators got their money's worth. Maximino got a lot of publicity and popularity out of his gesture."

Thérèse was very tense, but outwardly calm. I gave her a cigarette, and lit it for her with my back to the others. "What do you want to do about it?" I said sotto voce. "You don't really have to go. I could take you back to the hotel now."

But we were going seven in the Casasús car. The Plaza de Toros was much nearer than the Reforma Hotel, which lay two miles in the opposite direction. There was never a taxi to be had in the residential district between three and four of a Sunday afternoon. It was now on the verge of four, and Señora Casasús came circling down the stairs, hatless and twirling a yellow scarf in the air. So in the midst of the gaiety of rushed departure Thérèse murmured, "Maybe it won't be so terrible." With the resignation of one entering a tumbrel for the guillotine, she took her place in the back with Milstein and the other two women. "You may like the crowd and the pageantry," I whispered, "and you can leave after the first fight if it's unbearable."

As I got into the front seat with the little man and our host, who was driving, I muttered that I doubted whether my wife could sit through a bullfight, but my words were drowned by the hostess's calling out gaily, "Step on it, Mario!"

Thérèse steeled herself in fatalistic silence during the mad drive to be on time. But the little Mexican between me and our host turned pale through his dark pigments. He pressed on the floor boards, called on the Blessed Mother of God and a whole series of saints, screamed warnings, swore at Casasús, swore so help him *Jesucristo* he would never ride with his friend again. Finally he covered his eyes with both his clenched little fists and gurgled in his throat. No one paid any attention either to him or to Milstein, who had also suggested slower speed, as we brushed cars and coattails and dashed like jagged lightning through the traffic. Señora Casasús, who was sitting far forward on the crowded back seat, laughed delightedly and cheered her husband's skill. Just as the little Mexican seemed about to heave the gorge, we stopped with a brake-screeching flourish.

Pushing through the hurrying remnants of the crowd under the shadows of the great iron girders, we arrived at the wooden door of the box, which was only three or four steps above the flat concrete. In the dimness of the low-ceilinged bottom-row box, with hardly more than a rectanglar slit for seeing, I saw at once that this was the wrong way for Thérèse to be introduced to a bullfight. The tried advice was invariably: "One who doubts his reaction should see his first bullfight from a top gallery seat; there will be the crowd and all the spectacle and less of the painful detail." Here hardly anything was to be seen but the sand of the arena and the barricade. Whatever there would be of bloody action would be in intense focus. None of the crowd in the *sombra* above us could be seen, and the tiers of cheap seats facing the sun across the arena seemed very far away.

The seats were not armed chairs, but two wooden benches, one behind the other on a foot-higher elevation. To be less prominent if overcome by emotion, Thérèse and the Englishwoman were put on the back bench with our host and the shaken little man. Toots, breathless with the delight at having "made it," sat on the front bench between Milstein and me.

In the two-minute interval before the trumpet sounded, Casasús gave abbreviated pointers to his lady guests. I heard him quote Pliny to the effect that Julius Caesar had introduced bullfighting into Rome in the first century B.C.—probably from Thessaly. But in the Peninsula, old carvings showed that the sport was known to Spain long before the Romans or the Goths. The present technique and etiquette of the bullfight, he said, had developed in the eighteenth century. From fighting on horseback with lance and cloak, fighters had got to the ground with banderilla, muleta, and sword. A *veronica*, he explained, was a graceful pass a torero—the bullfighter on foot— made with a cape, and it was so called after Saint Veronica, who once wiped the face of the Saviour with a cloth. The cape played an important part in tricking the bull by making him feel foolish when his horns struck nothing; it was used to tire him, sometimes to weaken his attacks by stopping him short, or by changing his course abruptly.

"The wrist is peculiarly important—" Señor Casasús broke off at the sound of the trumpet. The twenty thousand-odd spectators quieted as a horseman in sixteenth-century regalia rode across the ring to the box of Maximino Avila Camacho, the master of ceremonies. His box was almost directly across the ring from us. The man bowed, the impresario gave permission for the fight, the band played. Out of the gates came the three matadors in gay-colored silk, with elegant capes draped over their left arms, and marched together toward the Avila Camacho box. Behind came the banderilleros and the picadors and the lesser functionaries. The host explained how each matador—the man who actually killed the bull—had a caudrillo of about six men working at his direction, the banderilleros to play the bull on foot with their capes and to place the banderillas, and the picadors, who remained mounted.

When the entrance march was finished the matadors tossed their parade capes to friends, who spread them out to decorate the walls of the stands, and then they retired along the red fence that surrounded the arena. "The parade capes of the stars are often superb, and cost thousands of dollars," Señora Casasús informed her lady guests over her shoulder. "But the men use just cerise and yellow percale for the actual fighting."

A horseman rode up to the impresario and Maximino tossed him a key. He caught it deftly and the crowd gave him a friendly cheer. The man wheeled his horse and dashed to unlock the door of the toril, where the first bull to be slaughtered was waiting.

An intense hush fell upon the crowd. Maximino signaled with his handkerchief. The trumpet sounded again, the door opened. For a moment, nothing. And then a glossy black bull bolted from the darkened enclosure into the fierce glare of afternoon. He stopped short in bewilderment, with the thousands of enemy eyes looking down upon him. He did not know that he had one friend at least in the audience—Thérèse was on his side.

The small barb which had been thrust in the bull's right shoulder at his entrance, to anger him, showed the colors of his breeding ranch. "Think," said Milstein, "four or five years of the most expert care and expensive rearing—all for this last quarter-hour in the

beast's life." The violinist had been to a bullfight before and knew
something of the ritual, but he was still uncertain just how to feel
and think about it all.

"I don't like the looks of that bull," said Toots, staring with a practiced eye. "He looks *mansa* to me—tame. I hope the other five are
better."

Thérèse learned to her horror that there were six bulls to be killed
by the three different matadors—she had imagined there would be
only one.

"Look," said Señor Casasús, being the perfect host, "the banderilleros are trailing their capes before the bull so that the matador can
judge which eye he uses most and which horn is his favorite one for
hooking."

The bull would charge. The men would rise on their toes, suck in
their breath, make graceful arcs, and the horns would just miss their
chests as the bull lunged at the cape. This part of the performance
was not so bad. Thérèse and the Englishwoman relaxed a bit.

The first bullfighter was not impressive-looking. He was below
middle height and I judged him to be close to thirty-five, whereas
the other two *noverillos* were probably only a year or two past twenty
—the proper age for *noverillos*. The first man made some routine
passes with his cape, and twice seemingly showed his disdain for
danger. But I felt he was not in good form, and imagined him to be
a has-been or one who had never quite made the grade. When he
signaled for the picadors and they came out mounted on their nags,
I heard Thérèse's quick intake of breath. "But see," I said consol-
ingly, "the horses are padded. They wear mattresses, or something
like those contraptions baseball catchers use to protect their fronts.
You won't see any entrails spilled on the ground, as in the past
generation of bullfighting."

"Protective padding for horses," said the Englishwoman, "was at
the instigation of the English-born Queen of Spain, Alfonso's wife;
but it was not made law until Primo de Rivera became Dictator."

"In San Sebastián," I said, "I heard that the Queen used opera
glasses with the lens painted black, so that she could not see a thing."

Unfortunately one picador guided his horse right in front of our
box—and out of his unbandaged left eye the poor creature showed
its terror. It had evidently been used in the arena before, and sur-

A VIEW OF DOMES AND TOWERS OF SAN MIQUEL DE ALLENDE FROM UPPER LEVELS
ON THE HILLSIDE TOWER.

ENTRANCE TO THE HARBOR AT ACAPULCO ON THE PACIFIC.

CABUTTI

A VIEW OF THE PARISH CHURCH AT TAXCO REVEALING ONE OF ITS ORNATE TOWERS.

MAGNIFICENT COLONIAL DOORWAYS ABOUND IN MEXICO. THIS FORMER RESIDENCE ON
AVENIDA MADERO IN THE CAPITAL IS NOW A COMMERCIAL HOUSE.

SUN HIGHLIGHTS A CHURCH TOWER AND THE SNOW ON A VOLCANO.

BEARING BURDENS IN A WEARY LAND.

STRODE

THE EIGHTEENTH CENTURY ACQUEDUCT WHICH BROUGHT FRESH WATER FROM THE MOUNTAINS TO QUERETARO REMAINS SPECTACULAR UNDER ALL SUNS AND MOONS.

HUGO BREHME

THE PEAK OF ORIZABA FROM A COUNTRY ROAD.

PRIMITIVE METHODS OF AGRICULTURE OFTEN ENHANCE THE PICTURESQUENESS OF A SCENE.

MAX

ON THE ROAD NEAR AMECAMECA.

FOR CENTURIES GARDENERS HAVE PADDLED THEIR BOATS TO AND FROM
WORK ON THE CANALS OF XOCHIMILCO.

THE OX AND THE ASS, THE BIG HAT, THE BUNDLE OF PRODUCE AND THE CHURCH
ARE TYPICAL OF A THOUSAND SCENES IN MEXICO.

RUFINO TOMAYO, THE ARTIST, AND HIS WIFE WATCH THE ARRIVAL OF A BURRO TRAIN
BEARING STONES FOR THE BUILDING OF THEIR HOME IN SAN MIQUEL DE ALLENDE.

STRODE

CHURCHES ARE DOMINANT AND MEMORABLE IN THE MEXICAN LANDSCAPE. HERE IS ONE AT
THE EDGE OF CHOLULA, A SMALL TOWN FAMOUS FOR ITS COLLECTION OF CHURCHES.

STRODE

A LONELY CHURCH ON THE ROAD TO PUEBLA.

INDIANS SIT WITH THEIR BACKS TO THE SUN IN THE CASUAL MARKET
OF THE ANCIENT VILLAGE OF HUEGOTZINGO.

vived, and knew what was coming to it again. But the fattish picador sat there half-grinning, his face radiant with stupidity. The bull charged. The picador aimed his long *pica* at the bull's shoulder. As the steel point of the lance went in, the pain and surprise made the bull attack the horse savagely, trying to toss horse and rider, but not able to get his horn through the quilted padding. "Close your eyes," I warned Thérèse over my shoulder, "or just look at your lap, and it won't be so bad."

The picador jabbed again, and this time his *pica* went too low down on the side near the ribs, and blood spouted. Both of the Casa-súses and the little Mexican had risen and were yelling warnings and imprecations at the picador. "Idiot! Imbecile! You'll ruin the bull!" At the next charge, horse and rider toppled over and banged into the wooden barricade a few feet in front of us; the picador's flat hat with the pompon flew over the barrier and dropped in the passageway. Despite the heavy protective armor under the chamois skin of his right leg, the plump picador climbed over the barricade to safety. The miserable horse took the powerful horn thrusts. The matador and the banderilleros waved their capes frantically trying to attract the attention of the bull from his victim.

"Get him away," screamed Toots, "get him away!" Then, turning to me indignantly, "The bull will wear himself out on the horse and have no eagerness to attack." To the Englishwoman she said over her shoulder: "The picador and pic are not to injure the bull severely, but to weaken him. That fool pic stuck him too deep and not in the right place. There's too much blood."

Thérèse's head was bent and her eyes shut, but I knew she had seen the thick red blood streaming from the bull's black hide.

The men got the bull in the center of the ring again. Attendants coaxed the terrified and injured horse to its feet. It was such an object of weak and shivering despair that it almost sank when the picador remounted. I knew it would die from internal injuries soon after it had left the ring, if it was not mercifully dispatched with a sharp knife.

During the second bout with the horses I said to Thérèse: "Just keep your eyes entirely shut. I'll tell you when to look." Then at last I said: "That's all with the horses. Now this next part requires great skill, and you can look." But I did not look back at her. I knew she was trembling with indignation and pity.

A banderillero came forward without a cape to face the bull. In his hand he held the two shafts with the sharp, harpoonlike barbs, but festooned with carnival-like ribbons. The banderillero called the bull's attention, and as the animal charged he ran to meet him as gaily as a bridegroom on his way to bed. As the bull reached him, the man rose on his toes, placed the banderillas deftly in the bull's shoulders, and swerved gracefully away from the horns of death. The bull, maddened with new pain and dazed at missing his prey, tossed the fore part of his body from side to side in an effort to shake out the intruding pain. Then he pawed the sand and bellowed in frustrated rage.

Not being an aficionado, the most exciting part of the bullfight to me is the placing of the banderillas—and in that last moment when the torero leaps with such swift grace from grazing death I involuntarily tense every muscle in my body and hold my breath. It is a natural reflex with me, for the excitement is almost painful. I have been told, however, that it is not really one of the best moments in a fight.

When the second banderillero came out to place his darts, I was too lost in my own excitement to pay any attention to Thérèse. The feat this time proved still more thrilling, for a horn tip caught in the embroidery of the man's jacket and ripped it. Toots let herself go and screamed and grabbed me by the thigh. The crowd yelled. Milstein stood up and sank back weakly. The banderillero tore off the ripped embroidery and tossed it aside, and walked away casually with his back to the bull, as if his own life were no more than a bagatelle or a strip of lace to be thrown away for the pleasure of the crowd. The spectators let loose thundering applause.

Thérèse opened her eyes only after the applause had spent its fury, and she saw nothing but the tormented beast trying in his pain to shake the beribboned shafts from his shoulders.

"But the people are enjoying it!" she said in horror.

"The man was very brave," I said.

And then the bull, seeking some sort of protection, came trotting over to the place where he had encountered his first horse and had his little moment of victory. I was afraid that would happen. I knew about the *querencia*—how a bull would find a place in the ring where he felt more comfortable, and would always try to return to it. Often the area about the door from which he entered was the chosen *querencia,* or home. Señor Casasús was explaining the psychology to Milstein, and saying how difficult it was sometimes to stir the bull from his preferred spot.

So now the dart-stuck beast came and stood in front of our nose and eyes, his rump almost against the red fence. He was bleeding more than I had ever seen a bull bleed, and the sleek blackness of his coat made the blood redder and more bloody-looking. As he swayed a little in pain from side to side the four gaily-colored banderillas waved like mocking fairy wands. There were still two more darts to be placed. The matador and the banderilleros twirled their capes and moved enticingly before him, but the bull stood there resolutely, as if he was onto their tricks and knew now he could not possibly win.

Toots said contemptuously: *"Mansa, mansa.* I told you that bull was tame from the first. He's got no spirit at all." The little Mexican, now completely recovered from his fright in the motorcar, stood up and made a gesture something like fist-shaking, both at the bull and at the *torero,* and cried, *"Cobarde!* Coward!"

Thérèse with her eyes wide-open was saying quietly, more like a prayer: "Oh, can't this be stopped? How can they go on torturing the animal? Why don't they kill him quickly?"

I hoped they wouldn't have to jab firecrackers into the bull's rump to get him out of his *querencia.* But finally he tossed his head at the challenge of three capes and dashed back out into the open. The third banderillero placed his shafts, and the second act of the drama was over.

Now came the last act, when the bull and the matador faced each other alone. It is called euphemistically "the moment of truth." The odds are overwhelmingly in favor of the man, though many a matador in the past has been gored and killed in the very last minute of the fight.

Before he went out for the finish, the matador paused in front of us to speak to one of his assistants. He did not look at all like the confident hero who is to conquer. He was sweating profusely, and great damp areas had appeared under his armpits. There was a dark scowl of uncertainty on his face as he was ceremoniously handed his muleta and the sword.

"That red piece of serge on the stick is called the muleta," Señor Casasús said to the Englishwoman. "With it the matador controls the bull, gets him into position for the kill."

But the bull would not be controlled. Though the fierceness had gone out of him, he was not hypnotized by the movement of the red serge, as he should have been according to the rules, and he would not get his front feet close together or his head properly lowered.

The crowd began shouting criticisms and advice, as bettors do at football games when they are about to lose their bets. Finally the matador dubiously made the attempt and lunged. The sword went in no more than eight inches. The bull jerked his head up and tossed the sword into the air. It fell behind him. Completely disarmed, the matador now stood at the bull's mercy as two banderilleros, waving their capes, appeared like guardian angels. One banderillero dashed out with an extra sword and handed it to the humiliated matador, who aimed again and struck. He missed a vulnerable spot, but retrieved his sword. He made five more attempts, wounding the bull and drawing more blood, but not hitting a vital spot. Casasús and the little Mexican stood up and yelled recriminations. At last the bull, bleeding profusely like a many-spouted fountain, trotted meekly back to his *querencia* just in front of us. His force was gone. He had no desire to charge, he wanted only to escape from the bedevilment and ease his wounds. But he still had enough strength left to run his horn into a man's inwards and kill his tormentor.

The matador now had to come our way again, to the hissing of the crowd. There was a confused desperation in the man's expression—a paralyzing fear of failure. The muttering hostility of the crowd was like his hearing the death warrant of his career. As the first cushion hurtled through the air from the seats above, the man stood for a moment, blue lips drawn tight, his body trembling. This was his own little personal tragedy, and in his prosaic way he may have been feeling a little of what Othello felt when he began to murmur the valediction to his career, ending on the moving line, "Othello's occupation's gone." Perhaps he was only thinking, "No more contracts, and how can I feed my family?"

Thérèse was softly crying. I felt it. And as the cushions began to land like thudding insults on the sand, I knew pity for the man's humiliation moved her—as well as the torture of the bull. She, who had rather the bull had killed a man than that men should torture a bull, was now on the side of the man against the hooting crowd.

Toots was furious at both bull and man. *"Mansa, mansa,"* she kept repeating contemptuously. "I told you from the first he was *mansa.*" The bull was certainly tame now; as the blood flowed, his spirit ebbed with it.

"How can they," Thérèse cried out in anger, "expect the bull to fight when he can hardly stand!" It was true. The beast was heaving mightily, and white ropes of saliva were dangling from his open mouth, through which he was struggling for enough breath to keep from falling. "Why, he is literally dying there before our eyes!"

The two utterly defeated, the man and the bull, were close together now—seemingly in strange partnership. The man, holding the mortal weapon, looked as though he would not greatly care if the beast should pierce his own heart with the long curved horn. The bravery which he had lacked and yet had made an effort to simulate was now born out of desperation. He had only a few seconds left of allotted time to finish the job. If he failed now, the bull would be driven outside to be slaughtered, and the man be completely disgraced. He walked directly toward the horns, attempting no skillful use of his muleta. The heaving bull, looking as if he had learned at last what was expected of him, docilely lowered his head, like an actor in a tragedy welcoming a dagger thrust. The matador sank the sword to the hilt between vertebrae and shoulder blades and stepped back—not in triumph, but in sour indifference. He watched the beast drop to its knees and pause there for a moment, the bullish eyes widening with the taste of death that came with a rush of blood out through the gaping mouth. Then the eyes snapped shut and the beast toppled over on his side. The gore made a crimson-lacquered platter for his black head to rest upon while his carcass stretched stiffly on the damask of the sand.

Amid hisses and boos, the white-faced matador, unscathed in body but lacerated in spirit, took one last glance at his vanquished victim, and made a swift ironic summation of the double defeat. Then he turned, and without a bow toward the impresario's box or in any direction, came to the opening in the *barrera* and stood with his face to the wall while four frisky little mules, jingling with bells, trotted in to drag off the dead bull. Attendants ran out to smooth the spot of death and sprinkle clean dry sand to make ready for the next fight.

When I turned to Thérèse I knew I had to take her home. She looked utterly stricken. She was trembling, and I saw she was trying to control herself to prevent her crying out her indignation at her fellow human beings.

Señor Casasús, not dreaming of her anger at us in the box too, but sensing her distress, turned to her and said very gently, "Are you suffering too much, madame?" He kissed her hand to show his sympathy.

I was grateful for his solicitude and so was she; for it dissolved her indignation into a sort of resigned compassion, and saved her from telling us what she thought of us and the world in general. She was able now to make her apologies properly and leave quietly.

"I thought," she said, struggling to restrain the tears, "perhaps it might not be so dreadful. But it's so very much worse than I ever dreamed."

"I'm sorry your first bullfight had to be such a flop," said Señora Casasús. "It was really about as bad as I ever saw, and I've seen hundreds." She smiled understandingly and sweetly at Thérèse; for she had seen other women and other men who could not take it. "That man was an absolute idiot. No courage, and no style at all."

"Poor man," Thérèse said, "he looked as miserable as the bull."

I asked the Englishwoman if she would like to come too. She glanced towards Milstein hesitantly and then said: "No, I think I might stay on. You see, I keep my eyes closed most of the time."

Señor Casasús came with us to find a taxi. Thérèse insisted that I return. "We can't hurt our host's feelings too much," she said. "I'll be all right in a little while."

I thought she wanted to be alone for a bit, and I said, "I'll stay for a couple more and then I'll make my excuses."

Señor Casasús stopped a taxi cruising by. I said "Hotel Reforma" to the driver. Thérèse thanked Señor Casasús again for his hospitality, and said she was sorry to have been a nuisance. She appreciated his solicitude. When the car drove off we returned to our seats just as the second bull—a reddish one this time—charged into the arena.

"Now that bull I believe has *sentido,*" Toots said. "You will see he is no *mansa,* he has intelligence, and he is full of fight. You will see."

"And that matador is very, very beautiful," the Englishwoman said, more to cheer herself up than to give expression to any enthusiasm.

The young bullfighter was considerably taller than the average. He was slim, as a torero should be, with very narrow hips and splendid shoulders. He looked to be in his early twenties. The crowd took to him at once, for he moved with as much assurance as grace. When he came our way to speak to an attendant, we could see that he was strikingly handsome, with a profile and a neck for sculpture. In any costume he might have created admiration, but in his bullfighting suit he cut quite a figure. His backer must have sunk several thousand pesos in it. It was of coral-colored silk, the fabric patterned subtly in rectangular lozenges with silver threads, so that a silvery blush like that on Malaga grapes moved over the surface of the pink stuff as the man walked. And he walked lithely, like a puma; but there was no suggestion of arrogance in his demeanor, and none of the angel-faced innocence of that youthful fighter named Rivera whom I had once met. As the torero turned his head to glance at someone in the stands above us, he reminded me of Jim Burt, a friend from Opelika, Alabama, who had been a groomsman at our wedding, and who in his law-school days was considered the handsomest young man in the state. In my mind I began calling the fellow Jim, and during the fight I would say, "Bravo, Jim!" and "Look out, for God's sake, Jim!"

For some moments the torero watched the bull being played by the banderilleros with their capes. He watched intently, appraising the beast's temper and reactions. Then he himself ran forward a little toward the bull, and stopped and profiled as the bull charged the cape. With great deftness he made a lovely and exciting *veronica.* Then, pivoting on the balls of his feet, he passed the bull out of the cape and faced him for the next charge. Now he brought the bull so close to his body that it looked as though the horns were caressing the man's indrawn narrow waist when the beast flashed by. The crowd cheered lustily as the torero walked calmly away with his back to the bull, like a man who bears a charmed life.

"What a wrist! Oh, what a wrist he has!" Toots said in ecstasy.

"There's magic in that wrist," Milstein said, unconsciously glancing at his own that wielded the bow.

In his next moves the torero swung the cape still lower and lower with measured grace, and the horns and the flanks of the enraged bull brushed him, as if to whisk away the dust the charge had stirred up from the sand.

It was exciting, and it was beautiful—a symphony in rhythm and grace and skill and bravery. The crowd gasped in fear and admiration. All of us in the box except the Englishwoman became vocative. She kept her dignity, though her eyes were wide-staring with the wonder of it all. I regretted much that Thérèse could not have seen this part, and then nothing else.

All the following episodes of this fight were infinitely better than those of the first one. The picadors were more skillful. They did not wound the bull too deeply. The animal tired himself trying vainly to sink his long sharp horns into the mattress and to lift the horse.

The banderilleros performed well, and the humps of muscles on the bull's neck would rise with his fury each time they approached him. The matador himself tried his hand at placing the last pair of banderillas. It was thrilling to see him court death and defy it in the same movement. His leap to safety was a thing of such grace and lightness that I thought of Nijinsky in his prime. The crowd cheered lustily. Here and there a corsage began to drop from the stands onto the sandy edges of the arena.

The matador stood for a moment in the center of the ring, smiling with visible pleasure. "I told you," Señor Casasús said leaning forward, "sometimes the *novilleros* put on the finest shows of all. They have not been gored yet, and they take wilder chances."

"He jests at scars that never felt a wound," the Englishwoman beside him murmured vaguely.

"This fellow will make a great fighter," Toots said enthusiastically in my ear. "He is *muy hombre*."

"*If* he lives," said the little Mexican from behind. "If he *lives!*"

The excitement became more intense with the third act, when the bareheaded matador and the bull faced each other for the last bout. Doubtless some of the force had gone from the bull, but he had lost none of his spirit or his rage. He stood there panting, his legs apart, his shoulders bristling with banderillas and his eyes baleful with vengeance.

"It will be difficult," Toots said tensely, straining forward. "The bull has not been weakened enough. The fellow doesn't seem to know what he is up against."

As the matador began moving forward slowly on his flat shoes, like a dancer, Milstein observed whimsically, "He holds that heart-shaped piece of serge as if it were a valentine for Ferdinand."

"Watch his left hand," Casasús said to the Englishwoman. "You know it is a good left hand that really defeats the bull. He plays him and controls him with that left hand holding the muleta. The sword in the right only gives the death stroke."

Suddenly my heart stopped beating. There was a rush like a whirlwind in the arena, and for a moment the man and beast were as one—or the man at the center of a wheel. In the pass with the muleta he turned completely in a circle and let the scarlet serge wind about his body just beside the bull's horns, with the bull whirling round after the loose end of the cloth. Toots screamed, and clutched my arm.

"My God, what a *molinete!*" gasped the little Mexican.

I felt cold perspiration on my forehead, and then a mighty pounding in my chest as my heart started beating again. This time the matador backed away, unwinding the muleta as he moved. "What the hell, Jim!" I said weakly. "What the hell!"

"The man will be killed!" said Milstein, his face white now, and strained.

In the pause before the matador made ready for the finish, in the silence of the breathing spell, the Englishwoman said quietly: "Why does he do it? Why does the young man, so handsomely equipped for living, deliberately face imminent violent death?"

I did not wait for the local experts to reply. I said quickly: "A bullfighter loves the thrill of tempting death and conquering it. One torero told a friend of mine that there was no passion yet conceived to compare with its satisfactions."

"Perhaps," said Milstein in a hushed voice, "that is the reason some say bullfighters make unsatisfactory lovers, that their sweethearts are often jealous of their profession."

"Quite so. A woman may perceive that she can never give a torero by moonlight what he gets here in the glare of afternoon."

Toots looked at me in surprise at my observation, as Casasús said "Now!" in a loud whisper.

The matador had profiled, and his whole manner had changed. There was no smile, no bravura. He was ready for serious business, for the solemnity that is supposed to go with "the moment of truth." He stood poised for a moment with his muleta low in his left hand and crossed in front of him, his left shoulder toward the bull, the sword in his right hand pointed and held across his body, the tip of the sword dipping slightly down.

"His height is in his favor for the fatal spot," Toots whispered hoarsely as the matador took two backward steps and then started forward on a run. In a flash the streak of silvery coral that was the man was leaning against the bull's head between the horns, the sword sunk almost to the hilt into the bull's body. The man pressed his body loverlike, and the blade disappeared completely. Then he leaped clear just as the great head chopped upward and the horns slashed at the woundless air.

The crowd caught its breath. The bull staggered, made a frail feint at plunging, sank suddenly to his right front knee, and then dropped on the sand and rolled over dead, his legs ignominiously in the air.

A mighty tumult was let loose. The crowd was on its feet screaming. All of us in the box except Milstein's publicity manager were on our feet, too. The band started playing the "Diana" feverishly— off key. Men's hats began flying out into the arena like great black and brown birds in panic. They crashed into each other and into tossed bouquets. Thousands of handkerchiefs were being waved with frenzied emphasis, and thousands of pairs of eyes were turned to the official box. Maximino came to the front of his box and waved an outsized handkerchief in answer to the public's demand. A banderillero rushed out, sliced off an ear of the dead bull, and ran to present it to the young killer. The matador accepted it, bowed his thanks, and made a quick grand tour of the arena, holding the ear up and out for the crowd to see the token of honor. As he passed our box, smiling his thanks, we all beat our palms together in enthu-

siastic applause, and Casasús and the little Mexican shouted con-
gratulations.

"There's no public adulation that can touch what a good bullfighter gets," Toots said. She turned back to the Englishwoman.
"You wondered why he became a fighter? See!" She made a gesture
of indicating the general wild enthusiasm. "What could satisfy male
vanity beyond this? He is a hero to the public; he makes good
money; women will throw themselves at him. What might he have
been—a groom? a chauffeur? a shop assistant? a bricklayer? perhaps a gigolo? Here he dares for sport and for the big rewards."

"Yes, yes, I see. And he *is* very beautiful."

The bull had been dragged out. The "wise-monkeys" were sweeping the sand smooth to prepare the field for the next exhibition.

With sudden resolution, I stood up. I felt the climax of the afternoon had been reached, that none of the four fights to follow could
conceivably surpass this one, that this *novillero* could hardly equal
his own performance. I had seen something brilliant and magnificent in its way—the sort of thing that comes from a mating of
natural genius and good luck, as well as from painstaking practice.

I explained how I felt, and reminded them truthfully that we were
going to the Villaseñor's house for tea, that they were sending their
car for us and I did not want to chance keeping the chauffeur waiting. I said how marvelous the last performance had been and I did
not think there could be such excitement in any of the fights to
follow.

It turned out I was wrong about no greater excitement, but I was
not to know that until some hours later, when Señora Casasús tele-
phoned the news. In his second fight the young *novillero* we had
admired had not had the luck to match his superbravery. He had
had to fight a cowardly bull who was completely unpredictable. In
the kill, the bull's horns had ripped the coral-silk thigh to the bone,
making a long ugly gash to the groin. The man would doubtless
not die, unless gangrene set in; but if he ever fought again he might
never do it with the same fearless rapture of the first fight this afternoon.

In the taxi returning to the hotel, still feeling wrought up and
a bit weak in the legs, I did a little ruminating on the whys and

wherefores of different attitudes to bullfights, and of my own reaction.

Some persons are passionately pro-bullfight—like the Texas girl married to my Mexican friend who had first taken me to meet Diego Rivera. Since coming to Mexico she had missed only one bullfight, she told me, the one that occurred the very day her first child was born. The Sunday before and the Sunday after that event she had gone to the bullring. Her second child was born on a Tuesday; so, despite doctor, nurse, and family remonstrances, she had been right there in her accustomed first-row seat the Sunday after the delivery, and had felt no ill effects whatever. She had even carried a bouquet of pink roses and thrown it to a torero. She spoke of bullfighting with a kind of devoted fervor, like a fanatical patriotism. She seemed to feel as much compulsion and obligation to go to a bullfight every Sunday as a good Catholic does to attend mass. This girl understood and loved horses, too, for she grew up on a horse-breeding ranch in Texas, and was said to be an excellent horsewoman. But a bullfight gave her more pleasure than anything on earth. Her Mexican husband confessed to me he shared only a portion of his wife's enthusiasm.

I had talked with hundreds of persons as violent in their passion against bullfighting as this American girl was for it. I had talked with scores of Mexicans, including General Cárdenas, who looks upon bullfighting as brutal and degrading and who thinks it gives an unwholesome taint to the commonwealth. And more than half of these persons who hated bullfights held humble positions, such as those of waiters, chauffeurs, and mechanics. Once a Mexican bootblack shook his head sorrowfully, when I told him I was going to a bullfight, and said, "I don't see how a man has a heart in him to look at a thing like that."

Thinking now in the taxi, I had to declare myself with the antis, though I also confessed frankly that to me a bullfight is the most exciting spectacle in the world. I am fully and painfully conscious of its cruelty, but I see its drama. Yet, while I know that knowledge of the technique of any art increases the quality of one's appreciation, I have little desire to learn more. I have attended only three bullfights in my life. Though I have been in Mexico, in Lima, and in San Sebastián in the proper seasons when famous matadors were advertised, I made no effort to go, and rather avoided invitations. Yet I am not absolutely cured; and in the future, if a special occasion arises I may attend another bullfight.

But I do not feel "very fine," as Ernest Hemingway says he does, when a bullfight is going on, though I feel mightily excited. And when it is over I feel wrought up to the point of weakness in the leg muscles and a gone feeling in the pit of my stomach. But I certainly cannot say I experience any emotional or spiritual catharsis. The feeling I have is very different from what it is after witnessing a splendid performance of *Hamlet* or listening to a perfect rendition of the *Seventh Symphony* of Sibelius. And though I am much moved at a torero's exhibition of audacious bravery, I do not find a bullfight ennobling. It is something more akin to indulging a rich vice. I see no reason to disagree with Madame Calderón, the Spanish ambassador's wife, who wrote in 1842: "It cannot be good to accustom a people to such bloody sights."

12. THE DAYS PASS PLEASANTLY

The enrichment of a sojourn in the capital does not demand climactic excitements like the bullfights. And the days pass pleasantly whether you are idling or spending the time in half vacation and half work, as I always was.

On Sundays you stroll leisurely up the Paseo de la Reforma under luxuriant trees, remarking the neatness of the lawns and little private gardens. You note the homes of the long well-to-do and the recent rich, in three architectural styles: the colonial, the Díaz, the modern; but you cannot always discern who lives in which. There are gravel walks for horseback riders, and stone seats for pedestrians, and historic statues in bronze and marble, medium good and medium bad. Nurses are out with their eager-eyed charges, and balloon venders with such voluminous clusters of bright red and yellow globes that they look as if a strong wind might carry them high above the tall trees.

Sleek thoroughbreds bear *charros* to the park. The *charros* are men who enjoy horseback riding. They are the gentlemen cowboys, who keep up the honorable tradition of sportsmanship of tricks with the lasso. They like to ride and like to be seen riding in all the pride-

ful glory of their marvelous hats, their skin-tight fawn-colored
breeches embroidered in silver, and their saddles and bridles that
are often works of art in themselves.

You go often to watch the *charros* cavort in the field before the
entrance of Chapultepec Park, just as you go once to see the ceremony of the changing of the guard before Buckingham Palace in
London or the Amalienborg in Copenhagen. And you hear some of
the riders, as they mount for a daring stunt, still breathe the traditional prayer of the *charro:* "In the name of God, who is all-powerful,
who will defend me from harm, I mount."

To sit on a park bench in Mexico is to be assured of some sort of
show. To walk in almost any direction is to run into some quaint
custom or some unfamiliar modus operandi, like that of a man dexterously mowing a lawn by hand with a sharpened tomato-can top.

Almost anywhere you may find the past evidenced in the daily
routine of the present. Some families still maintain private chapels
in their homes, with altarpieces of gold and holy images carved in
Spain three centuries ago. There are successful businessmen who do
not take insurance on their warehouses or their coastal merchant
ships, but pray to a wooden image of Saint Anthony in the corner
of the household chapel for protection and bestow the amounts of
the insurance premiums on charities in the name of the guardian
saint.

We sniffed musty ancient libraries and visited the convent where
Marina's son by Cortés endured torture, and the Hospital of Jesus
at No. 53 Calle Piño Suárez, founded by Cortés. And after hours of
poking here and there into history we might drop into the La
Cucaracha cocktail lounge to drink a martini and to nibble pumpkin
seed toasted like almonds. Here invariably we would meet someone
we knew from somewhere.

After a morning shopping for leather or silver or tin, we would
sometimes lunch at the charming old San Angel Inn in the suburbs,
and for an apéritif wander through the gardens and cloisters of
what had been a convent, where heliotrope climbs to the second
story and growing gillyflowers perfume the tables around the patio.

In Coyoacán and Villa Obregón we dined with Mexicans who live
very naturally and without ostentation in what is called the old
manner. We ate from such silver services and porcelains as are not

often to be seen outside of museums, and drank from wineglasses to inspire lyricism. We sat in rooms in which each piece of tapestry and each cabinet and chest excited special admiration. We got at least a flavor of the elegance in which some of the viceregal families had lived before 1821 and Independence, when most of the wealthy Spaniards returned to Europe, taking with them their plate, their brocades, their mirrors, and their rugs.

We were taken to call on the widow of the martyred Francisco I. Madero by his nephew Guilliermo Madero. We sat in chairs of cream-and-orange cowhide with legs and arms of curving bull's horns in a little drawing-room dominated by a three-quarters-length life-sized oil portrait of the patriot. Señora Madero, in the middle seventies, a sweet, birdlike little woman, had a passion for singing birds, and our talk was almost drowned by the volume of bird song that flowed in from the patio, where seventy-six bird cages hung along the galleries.

Culture is evidenced in Mexico by her intellectuals. One Mexican we visited had a remarkable collection of Wedgwood in black and white, and a rare shelf of first editions of Milton and Thomas Gray and Blake. A Cabinet Minister with whom we lunched was a profound lover of Shakespeare and had all the Shakespearean recordings made by John Gielgud, Maurice Evans, and Orson Welles. We dined with another Mexican who was also a sincere admirer of Shakespeare and who could quote from *Titus Andronicus* as well as his favorite *Hamlet*.

While the old aristocracy of Mexico is dwindling fast and taking to strange or humble professions, a few families have managed to cling to a kind of French Victorian magnificence. At luncheon with the Marquesa de Mohernando, who had a cook famous all over Mexico, we met some of the aristocratic Amors. There is scarcely any family in Mexico who was once more wealthy than the Amors. They could hardly count the extent of their holdings, which included towns and villages. The land expropriations under Calles wiped away their possessions. Now Nasco Amor and his wife have become de-luxe guides—to persons of special recommendation. And Inés Amor, the lovely, fragile-looking sister, runs a distinguished art gallery, where she sells the work of the leading Mexican artists.

The Spanish-born son of the Marquesa, who had the inimitable manners of a well-bred cosmopolite educated in England, had just gone into the Venetian-blind business. The Mexican-born Marquesa, a charming, intelligent, level-headed woman, was not Spanish at all. Her mother was from a titled French family, her father an Irish-American named Thomas Braniff, who helped construct the first Mexican railway from Vera Cruz to Mexico City and who was known as the Mexican Midas. It was he who, driving himself in a double-seated buggy and with a passport made out to him in his capacity as Superintendent of Construction for the Mexican Railway, rescued the departing Empress Carlota and secretly conveyed her from Córdoba to Vera Cruz, where she sailed on her futile mission to Napoleon III which ended in her madness.

The Mexican dinner hour has the spice of uncertainty. The Marquesa, accustomed to cosmopolitan ways, calls the midday meal "luncheon" and sets it for half-past one. But generally when you dine with Mexicans it is dinner at two, as in Savannah. Those who hold government positions sometimes cannot get away from their offices until three or later.

Once I was asked to dine at two o'clock with Miguel Alemán, then Minister of Interior, and to meet him at the Secretariat on Calle Bucareli at half-past one. The halls and anterooms of the busy Ministry were jammed. (Some petitioners sit there day after day, some stand, some bring their food and eat it half-surreptitiously.) I was received by one of Miguel Alemán's advisers, a short, stocky, blond Doctor of Laws and a former history professor, who was going to dine with us. He was an interesting fellow, who had been an admirer and friend of Edna St. Vincent Millay when she was girlishly burning her candle at both ends. He wanted to talk of her, but I turned the conversation to the Minister. I had been taken to see him once before in his offices and I had been impressed by both his ability and his charm. I had seen for myself why they said, "Alemán takes the crowd with his manners."

Now I asked some questions about his early days. Born in 1903 in a small agricultural village in the State of Vera Cruz, Miguel Alemán was the son of a small farmer who became a general under Obregón. He had received his primary education at the knee of his mother, a bright little woman with an infectious gaiety. As a lad he delivered milk at dawn to the town of Orizaba, whistling in all weathers as he went on muleback. He grew up wiry, sturdy, and self-reliant, with the inherited ability of his mother to see nothing but the silver linings to the clouds. "His seems to be a kind of glandular optimism," said the historian.

After a sketchy education at Orizaba, Alemán came to Mexico City when he was nineteen to study law and earn his living at the same time. At twenty-five he received his degree, and he quickly made a name for himself defending labor unions and individual workers. At thirty-two he ran for the Mexican Senate from Vera Cruz and won; and when the new Governor of Vera Cruz was murdered shortly afterward, Miguel Alemán was chosen without opposition to fill his place.

Young as he was, he proved he had an extraordinary flair for unifying various factions, and he alleviated the troubles with the Church. He furthered all the right things: education, roads, public health. Without any special gift of eloquence, or any passionate ideology, Alemán, through his innate common sense and goodwill toward man, brought about reforms in his native state.

His accomplishments, his genial vigor, and his persuasiveness made him the logical choice as the man to manage Avila Camacho's presidential campaign in 1940. And he was rewarded for his success by being asked to head the Cabinet as Secretario de Gobernación (Secretary of the Interior). So at thirty-seven Miguel Alemán found himself in a position something like that of heir apparent. It was a good bet in 1943 that he would be the government party's candidate for President in 1946.

While we were talking, a dashingly romantic-looking young man with a complexion darker than an Arab's came in and bowed and said the Minister was ready—we were to meet him at the secret elevator. This was Alemán's debonair chauffeur, noted for being the handsomest chauffeur in diplomatic circles, and noted too, like his boss, for his smile and his small mustache.

It was like running a gauntlet. The Minister was already in the dim-lit elevator. Down it came into a passageway where the automobile stood. The chauffeur had preceded us and got the motor running. "Quick, quick!" said the historian. We hurled ourselves into the car as those petitioners in the know about the Minister's private way pressed forward. One white-bearded old man laid both hands on the open window frame and started his tale of woe. Alemán smiled sympathetically. *"Mañana,"* he said soothingly. The car glided slowly off. *"Mañana,"* the old man repeated vaguely, and removed his hands. *"Mañana!"* he called as we drove out of the shadowed passageway into the bright streets. Alemán smiled with relief. "And now that we have once more escaped—"

We sat down to dinner in his home a little after three. Señora Alemán said she never knew whether dinner was to be served at two or three or four or even five. She sighed with whimsical resignation. "We heat it up, heat it up, heat it up, at intervals all during the afternoon."

Miguel Alemán laughed and said: "It takes strong stomachs to survive in Mexico. I can stand anything, because I did not die as a child. Nature makes her selections among us when we are young and those who reach maturity generally have stomachs that long delays, overfeeding, or even famine cannot destroy. In Mexico to survive one must possess two things: patience and a cast-iron stomach."

Most high government officials take time out for a siesta before returning to their offices at six to stay until nine, ten, or eleven, depending. But Alemán himself is not given to the custom of siesta. He generally spends the leisure spell playing with his children. When we went for coffee into the Minister's study, his little boy, Miguel Junior, insisted on showing me his toy motion-picture machine. So the room was darkened, and we witnessed some jumpy flashes of Franklin D. Roosevelt and Winston Churchill framing the Atlantic Charter on the high seas.

When you dine with Americans living in Mexico, it is dinner at seven or eight. But when I dined with the parents-in-law of Chucho Solárzano the bullfighter, we sat down to dinner at half-past ten. It was not a party, not even black tie, but just a family Mexican dinner from which we rose to move into the drawing-room for coffee and liqueurs at a quarter to midnight. I had been invited by Chucho's brother-in-law—a Mexican friend of mine named John Robertson, who had a Scotch great-grandfather—especially to meet the bullfighter. Thérèse could not come because she had an engagement with Patricia Minnegerode for a concert. And Chucho and his wife suddenly had to go to another matador's birthday party, and so they came to the Reforma to pick me up for cocktails, since they could not be at home for dinner.

Chucho's young wife was quite glamorous in her platinum fur scarf and diamond pendent earrings, and the bullfighter was just a slim handsome young man of thirty-two in a well-tailored gray-flannel suit. I had been told by some Mexicans that Chucho "spends all his time drinking coffee in the Madrilena Café, dressed like Seville and speaking Spanish slang," but I could not discern the faintest trace of upstage importance in his manner. He had a soft way of talking, and he would cock his head attentively with the right ear slightly forward because of a bull's-horn injury which impaired his hearing in his left ear.

Though his wife looked as fresh as the dawn with very little make-up, she said her husband's profession was a great strain on her. She feared for him too much, she said, and all men who fought bulls long enough got seriously maimed if they weren't killed. Chucho's luck had been so marvelous, she had begged him to quit while he was still whole. She said she had got his promise to retire on his thirty-third birthday. The coming season was to be his last, and she hoped then to breathe easy the rest of her life. She confessed she was terribly afraid before a fight, though she said Chucho seemed to have no fear. But Chucho's sister-in-law, Señora Robertson, told me later at dinner that although the bullfighter had absolutely no fear before a fight he sometimes had dreadful nightmares after one. "He dreams," she said, "that all the bulls he has ever killed have ganged up on him and are chasing him across a plain."

Robertson thought I should visit a bull-breeding hacienda, and Chucho knew a colorful one in Michoacán, his native state, where the owner still lived in the old style with footmen in eighteenth-century livery and with candles for illumination. It was a four hours' drive from the capital, and he would take me himself and we would spend two nights.

"Four hours!" Robertson said laconically. "It's a good six hours' drive. Four hours—with Chucho driving at eighty miles an hour. A drive with him at the wheel is about as thrilling as confronting an enraged bull yourself."

"I'll hold it to sixty over the mountains," Chucho said, with a conciliatory smile. And we set a date depending on the convenience of the hacendado.

The Robertsons and the Solárzanos and another daughter and her husband were all living with the girls' parents in the old Spanish fashion. But John Robertson had just bought a little house, and he and his wife were this day in the process of moving. After the cocktails we drove to pick up his wife at the new place. And there we found the father-in-law, Señor Pesado, a benign, silver-haired gentleman with a pink-and-white complexion like the Palmolive ads. He was sitting by some upended bedsprings and a small radio, taking a lesson in English over the radio. He seemed quite pleased at his ingenuity in utilizing the bedsprings as a transmitter.

This innocent-looking man had shrewdly interpreted the revolutionary handwriting on the wall three decades ago. He had sold his thousands of acres of rural patrimony and reinvested in city property. Now he was richer than his ancestors.

The family place, a mile away in another part of the city, covered an entire block. It had a solid ten-foot wall surrounding what had once been a manor house. A mozo responded to the honking of the motor horn and swung back the great copper-studded gates. We drove into a flagstoned courtyard that looked medieval by the moonlight. The house lay between the court and a garden with towering ancient trees and a menagerie and deer that begged cigarettes off you and swallowed them whole with relish.

In the drawing-room a fancy pink-and-white birthday cake with one pink candle sat on a center table—tomorrow was little Chucho's first birthday. But most unhappily the child was ill with a sore throat and the festivities would have to be minimized. While Señora Pesado, his grandmother, was showing me a photograph of the baby seated on the floor surrounded by huge dogs, a door opened and a pack of Great Danes came bounding in and sliding on the rugs. They looked as large as the Hound of the Baskervilles, and made straight for me with a mighty sniffing. Before I could recover from the surprise another canine pack broke in. These were Dalmatians, and one was a pretty bitch with five puppies. I began to count—altogether, including the puppies, there were twenty-three dogs of the two breeds. They all belonged to the eldest sister, who had married a dentist. She had a wonderful way with them; she would speak in a low voice and they would respond and do tricks. When she told them to go and lie against the wall, they went in unquestioned obedience. Even the Dalmatian puppies seemed to know they must mind their mistress. They lay end to end alongside their spirited mother and looked peculiarly "cute" in their self-conscious docility.

Before dinner we wandered about among the flowering shrubs of the moonlit garden and gave the deer cigarettes and at the menagerie paid our compliments to the monkeys behind bars and the bright-feathered birds behind wire.

Each member of the family had his or her special pets. But the father's pet was obviously the absent bullfighter. The host wanted to talk of nothing else, though he did bring out some volumes of poems of his father, the poet José Joaquín Pesado, whose portrait hangs in the Biblioteca Nacional. (The father had been one of those rare combinations, a poet with a sense of real estate.)

"I think our father would have passed away with disappointment if my sister had not married Chucho," Robertson's wife whispered. "You will have to see his color films of Chucho in action. They are his hobby and his passion."

The host had already set up the machine and the screen, and was delving into his boxes of films. He was all for showing the pictures now and postponing dinner, but at my deliberate look of consternation (I was exceedingly hungry and the clock was on the verge of striking half-past ten) Robertson suggested that we wait until after dinner.

The twenty-three dogs trooped into the dining-room with us and spread themselves decoratively all about the green carpet like cast-iron statues on an 1890 lawn. Two of the Great Danes, still sniffing desultorily at me, took places directly behind my chair. Three Indian women—not in maid's uniforms—served the dinner, which went through six courses. Since Robertson and I were the only ones who seemed hungry, I had a sneaking idea that the other five members of the family had had snacks before dinner. But I recalled that many Mexicans never took anything after three o'clock except a cup of chocolate.

After dinner, in the drawing-room we had an hour of Chucho in the thrilling action of actual fights. Now and again the father-in-law would make an adulatory comment in a gentle, barely audible voice. They were excellent pictures, in good color, and cut to show only the most dangerous and exciting phases. I lost track of the number of bulls killed. The father-in-law would doubtless have gone on through many more rolls of film, or even repeated the whole show at my request, but Robertson suggested that I might like to see some of Chucho's costumes. The host was delighted. He turned on the lights, called servants, and gave orders. Then he himself disappeared to help. The dogs, who had dropped off to sleep all over the darkened drawing-room, roused at the excitement in the atmosphere and rushed this way and that with deafening barks to ascertain what was up. Their mistress gave stern commands, got them quiet, and then sent them trooping to bed upstairs in the dog-training apartments.

When the stage was properly set, we returned to the dining-room, and there spread out on the long polished mahogany of the table that could seat twenty-four lay seven exquisite costumes. They lay like seven sleeping matadors—seven Chuchos in repose in seven different colors. Some were suits made of special woven silks that cost a hundred dollars a yard. All were elegantly embroidered in silver or gold thread. The colors were pastel: silvery canary, soft amethyst, turquoise-blue, a dusty apricot, apple-green, white with silver trimmings, cream woven with gold.

The host would touch a shoulder lovingly and then he would say, "Chucho wore this one when—" And his eyes would light with a kind of triumph as he recalled the special feat. And then he would point to a place that had been expertly mended and shake his head sadly. "See! Ah, here he had a close call indeed!"

A great clock struck the hour of one. I began the overture to departure. I took a last glance at the beauty of color, design, and fabric that lay stretched along the table top and regretted that Thérèse had not seen the costumes. What a deal of delicate and exquisite fancy, I thought, what devoted labor, and what expense went into the creation of suits for Sunday slaughter.

As John Robertson drove out of the moonlit courtyard, I said to him by way of thanks: "Where on earth besides Mexico might one have such a delightful evening—en famille and so different at the same time?"

And where is the moonlight more luminous, I thought, than in this capital set on a balcony of mountains? At the late hour, without benefit of the harsh illumination of electric bulbs, the city street became evocative like a mise en scène for a masquerade. Moonlight caressed the crenelation of old walls, turned time-weathered towers to ivory, emphasized the solemnity of solid cupolas, and made a lovely glitter on the porcelain domes. Whatever was glaring by sunlight, whatever was shoddy, was dissolved in flattering shadow.

IV

By Motor to Michoacán

They might have been a joyous race: God put them in a garden, like the first couple. But four hundred years of slavery have dulled for them the very glory of their sun and their fruits; it has made the clay on their roads hard beneath their feet, yet it is as soft as fruit pulp.

—GABRIELA MISTRAL

I. MARKET OF TOLUCA

THOUGH AIRPLANES AND TRAINS and busses go to Morelia on regular schedules, the most rewarding way of travel is by motorcar. When four share the expense, the price is not extravagant. Two men we had met on the train from Laredo had arranged to go with us. One was Dr. Charles Hoagland of the Rockefeller Institute, a specialist in tropical diseases. The other was Jess Wagus, a young Spanish instructor in an Iowa college, who had done considerable study of various tribes of American Indians. Of Polish and Scottish extraction, he spoke excellent Spanish. He wore a pince-nez, and had such an infectious laugh that he sometimes set the stolid-faced Indians to smiling broadly. Both men proved easy to travel with. They were amiable and possessed a lively sense of humor, besides being full of odds and ends of interesting information.

Our chauffeur was named Señor Sánchez. He was a tiny little man with dark Indian skin and delicate Spanish features. Besides being a steadfast driver of the Buick 8 we had engaged, Señor Sánchez proved to be a gentle philosopher without illusions. He observed life as it passed and was faintly amused by it. If his heart was touched by abuses, he shrugged, with brief comment, and looked the other way. Though he was anything but a chatterbox, he had a certain wit, as well as discretion. We all became fond of Señor Sánchez.

We had chosen Friday to begin our journey because Friday is the market day of Toluca, the capital of the State of Mexico. The morning was bright with June sun and the air as fresh as if cooled by the snowy crowns of near volcanoes. The road from Mexico to Morelia is a series of ascents and descents, and as sinuous as the revolutionary movement that began in 1810. It is also as exciting in panoramic beauty as it is varied in contour. From the road that clung leechlike to the mountain flanks, the pattern and design of the terraced farms below looked more like scenes in some stylized Grant Wood painting than something man had actually done with nature.

Wagus, who came from the fine farming districts of Iowa, was voluble with admiration as he remarked the orderly swirls of cultivated rows set in beautiful and fantastic oblongs this way and that to get the full advantage of variegated slopes. Leaning forward, he grabbed my shoulder enthusiastically with one hand and adjusted his pince-nez with the other. "Talk about your contour farming! Boy! Those Indians have got it, haven't they? You'd never get an American Indian worked up to doing that."

"One of the greatest virtues of the Mexican Indian is patience," I remarked to Señor Sánchez, by way of drawing him out. I was sitting beside him on the front seat, and Thérèse sat between the doctor and the teacher.

Señor Sánchez smiled dryly. "In Mexico, señor, patience is more a necessity than a virtue."

"I have a friend who has a little money and who asked me to look into his buying a small ranch somewhere in Mexico. What would you think of the idea?"

Señor Sánchez considered briefly. "I think, señor, it is better to visit than to invest in Mexico." With a slow smile, he added, "The foreigner who invests capital here now and expects a quick turnover is going to be sadly disappointed. Wherever private capital is invested there are apt to be headaches. When American gentlemen traveling alone ask a waggish chauffeur friend of mine about investing in Mexico, he says, 'Señor, as a friend I would advise you not to put your money in but one thing in Mexico—I would buy nothing but a señorita for a week, and even then you should exercise the maximum caution.'"

I laughed and passed the advice to the back seat.

The highway began to climb sharply into the wooded mountains, and just past nineteen miles we had already reached the highest spot in the road between Mexico City and Los Angeles. It is called La

Cima, "The Summit." As we began to descend, the first persons we passed were a couple of pedestrian charcoal-burners. I thought of the lines:

> Even the mountain trees
> Have their allotted goal,
> For some were born for saints
> Whilst others serve for coal.

The carving of holy images had been one of the popular handicrafts since the arrival of the friars in Cortés's times. And charcoal for cooking the daily bread in the shape of tortillas went back into the mists of Mexican prehistory. These trees in their metamorphoses had significant roles in forming the culture of the race, helping to nourish both body and soul. And the people we began to meet on the road some ten miles beyond La Cima were going to the Friday market of Toluca to minister to their spiritual and emotional as well as their material needs.

For all his taciturnity and innate melancholy, the Mexican Indian is gregarious. His temperament cries out for human companionship. Almost never does the countryman live in an isolated hut. He prefers the village, and since time immemorial Indians have lived in clusters, for better protection and sociability. But even the village does not satisfy his gregarious instinct, and he goes to the nearest big town on feast or market days. He will trudge a dozen miles to get to a market. For a special fiesta he will trot twoscore miles or more if necessary.

"The Indian loses the sense of his own misery in a crowd," Señor Sánchez was saying. "He goes to sell his wares in the market to live. But he would rather go to market and not sell his wares than stay at home and sell them at twice their value. Often week after week he will bring the same trifles and spread them on the sidewalks for sale. It is an excuse to be with his fellows in the midst of movement."

The road leading into Toluca became thickly dotted with Indians. Some rode on burros, some led burros laden with produce in baskets. Some drove goats and turkeys before them. Some bore sacks on their backs or trays on their heads. Women, wrapped about the head with pigeon-blue rebozos, bore babies on their backs, held toddlers by one hand, and used the other to carry foodstuff or some handicraft work. As Mrs. Dwight Morrow once said, "A really capable Indian woman can balance a baby, a load of wood, a hen, a bunch of flowers, and a live pig on her shoulder."

The narrow streets and lanes leading into the market place of Toluca were crammed with Indians, their dark skin glistening like copper or bronze in the bright sun, their varicolored serapes looking like a mass of palette colors smeared together. In the rude open plaza outside the covered market the crowd milled about. A kind of liquefaction of Indian talk in Otomi, Aztec, and Matlaltzinca, mingling with the Spanish, created a strange droning noise. A jackass brayed, a fettered turkeycock gobbled, an offended dog yelped, a church bell clanged stridently. On the narrow sidewalks, merchandise was spread so haphazardly that in order to pass pedestrians had to press against the wall or leap the display. We negotiated an island-like exhibit of cans of sewing-machine oil, suckling pigs, squash flowers, and old empty bottles. A man kneeling beside a nanny goat impeded our progress. He was not milking her. He was not her owner. He was a prospective purchaser, and he was squeezing the root of her tail to test her fatness and succulence for eating.

Wrinkled old women were squatting over charcoal braziers cooking tortillas, or black beans, or pink coconut candy. Mothers sitting on the curb were nursing dark-eyed infants. There was the fresh smell of animal dung and the stale smell of human urine mingling with the odors of carnations and heliotrope from the flower stalls. Here was the real Indian by the thousands: the Indian in the raw, barefooted, ragged, dirty. No lay figures, these, which some commentators are wont to use as mere decoration for the Mexican scene, untouched by the human values of striving and suffering, of longing and failure.

"They say the Indian enjoys savoring life, while the American enjoys crowding it," Dr. Hoagland commented as our way was blocked by a recalcitrant, haltered calf, "but the Indian seems to enjoy crowding it on market day."

"Ah," replied Señor Sánchez, "but at least the Indian is not in a hurry."

As we looked upon the milling and gaping mass, I thought of Blasco-Ibañez, who had visited Mexico in 1924 after Madero, Huerta, Carranza, Zapata, Villa, and Obregón had each in his hour held out golden promises to the masses and for which scores of thousands had let themselves be slaughtered in civil strife. "If there is any group that has won my sympathy," the novelist had written, "it is the Mexican people, the eternal victim of a tragicomedy that never ends, the poor slaves whom all pretend to redeem, and whose lot has remained unchanged for centuries, the everlasting dupe whom redeemers shower with fine phrases, never telling him the truth, because the truth is frequently cruel." It was only too easy to feel indignation and pity as Blasco-Ibañez had felt it. But as I looked deeper into the kaleidoscope of dark ignorant faces, half-stirred to awareness, I felt it in my heart to have some sympathy for the redeemers too.

Thérèse was looking stricken at the thought of this dark seething going on forever. She seemed overcome with that sense of hopelessness which D. H. Lawrence said eventually attacks everyone who loves Mexico.

"It's strange that the hardness of life doesn't deter them from hanging onto it," she said. "How can the Government ever do the right thing for so many? And if you stir the poor Indians too violently with discontent, you might only succeed in embittering them. I'm afraid it will be a long and difficult process."

"Yes, madam," said Señor Sánchez quietly, "it will be a long and difficult process." He shrugged, as if he could not speculate on how it would come out. Then, noting an expression of distress on Thérèse's face, he added gently: "Sometimes you have to balconize your thinking in Mexico. We often do."

"Balconize?"

"Bring your thoughts up from the street to the balcony and see above the sordidness."

"I remember an editorial in the old *Life,* when I was in high school," Dr. Hoagland said. "It suggested that asking the Mexicans to elect a President by constitutional methods was like asking the infant class to select a teacher."

As we worked our way slowly through the mass I recalled something Vasco de Quiroga had written to the Council of the Indies in 1531: "There are so many Indians here that they are like the stars of the sky and drops of water in the sea without number. Their manner of living is chaos and confusion." The Bishop, who had done so much to bring order into his own diocese of Michoacán by

encouraging handicrafts in the various villages, might have been disappointed in the progress made in four centuries if he made a cursory
expedition to Toluca today.

Besides the humble sidewalk displays in Toluca there are lanes,
like the souks of Tunis, where only serapes are sold, or woven baskets, or hand-carved leather goods, or drawnwork embroidery. Business is competitively cutthroat and haggling goes on, but the bargaining is not nearly so prolonged or so sociable a process as among the
Mohammedans. The Toluca marketmen reach their bottom price in
three or four sallies rather than ten to twenty, and then an adamant
expression comes over their faces that means "No further talk is
necessary—take it or leave it."

In the arcades of the great market proper you can buy anything
from lacquer ware to dried sheep's hides, from orchids to chitter-
lings, from oil paintings to fish. The numerous handicraft villages
within a thirty-mile radius send their wares co-operatively or individually to Toluca to meet the demands of the tourists from Mexico
City, who come because prices here are considerably less than they
are in the capital. The toys, the pottery, the blankets, the baskets, the
crude jewelry, are largely made by the citizens of the state.

Thérèse made two purchases—a hat for summer gardening and
an oblong basket to hold her knitting. Both objects were beautifully
wrought of fine-textured straw. The basket was the purplish color
of muscadines, with Aztec profiles and tropical birds done in medallions of reddish yellow and blue-green. The great brimmed hat
was of aquamarine and cream color, and its shape faintly suggested
China. "More subtle than a peacock's spread tail," Dr. Hoagland
remarked as he twirled it about in appraisal. But in all the blocks and
blocks of market these were the only two objects that Thérèse was
eager to buy. An hour's wandering was quite enough for us, though
we ran into American tourists who planned to spend the day and
who were indiscriminately filling up whole backs of touring cars
with variegated and tawdry junk.

The Indians were spending their centavos as freely as the Americans were spending their pesos. If they themselves made a sidewalk
sale, they would soon leave the money at another's shop.

"The Indian does not like to keep money," Wagus said. "He believes in spending it quickly to be rid of the responsibility of keeping it. Right, Señor Sánchez?"

"Right, señor. No one ever heard of an Indian miser in Mexico. Some of the peons even used to take pride in being deeply in debt— the bigger the sum of the debt, the more important a man felt. Once the Indian saved money chiefly for a wedding by the priest. Now that only civil marriages are legal, he will save only for four things —a gun, a horse, a big sombrero, and a sewing machine. These objects give him a sense of prestige in his community."

We did not tarry in the town of Toluca. Although it is the state capital and has a population estimated at almost fifty thousand, there is little of significant interest besides the market. The aura of the town is not attractive.

2. THE ROAD TO MORELIA

As we drove away from the swarming humanity into the green countryside, fresh with the rains of June, the world was again well-ordered, placid, charming. The fertile lands were in orderly cultivation; cattle grazed on nourishing grasses. However, a metamorphosis in social and economic structure had come within the last two decades. The great days of the hacienda were irrevocably gone. The houses and barns still stood, if in disrepair, but the immediate acreage that often went with the hacienda had shrunk from thousands of hectares to some two hundred.

The tables had been neatly turned. Less than three decades ago the law and custom of feudal times still held sway on the haciendas. All the laws were for protection of the hacendado. Peon and tenant were dependent on the word and the whim of the master. The overseer might be a villainous petty tyrant. Often his job was to keep the peons working as hard as possible on rations that merely held body and soul together, so that the master and his sons might indulge in luxury or in vice in Paris or Madrid or Mexico City, according to inclination.

Now from being like children in a reformatory school, some of these peons suddenly became their own bosses, and were faced with the problem of using their own minds, the first of their people to do so in over four hundred years. These Indians, so long "condemned to obscurity and peace of mind" as one commentator put it almost nostalgically, were thrust into the sociological limelight and invited to think for themselves. Former peons now held title to the expropriated land, and the better of them seemed to realize that they were on trial before the world in their endeavor to succeed at being their own masters. In the green valleys edged with far-off mountain peaks that look like extinct volcanoes, Indians were plowing with white oxen, leisurely turning the dark opulent earth over the weeds. Behind the ox and the plowman came teen-age boys with hoes working fast and furiously hilling up the stalks of young corn.

Each quarter-mile there was an hacienda house, looking forlorn and beginning to disintegrate. But every vista was picturesque, whether there was a great house somewhere in the composition or merely a cluster of thatched huts. One little white church in the distance looked like an objet d'art carved in ivory and set on chartreuse velvet. The horn-yoked oxen, the white-suited plowmen, the little boys with enormous hats, the women kneeling at the clear streams washing clothes, made charming, unfamiliar pictures, at once intimate and cosmic.

"The black-and-white cattle look like those we knew in Denmark," Thérèse said, "and like storybook animals at the same time." And from an eminence in the road, twenty-four cows, some standing, some reclining in a fenced square of pasturage, did look for all the world like carved chessmen in ivory and ebony waiting for some player god to make a move.

Again and again we discovered and pointed out to one another striking compositions for a painter. I recalled that Frederick Remington, the Western artist, had been fascinated by both the unfamiliarity and the panorama in the days before good roads and motorcars. Once he wrote:

There lies the hacienda, gray and silent on the great plain, with the mountain standing guard against intruders, and over it the great blue dome of sky, untroubled by clouds, except little flecks of vapor, which stand, lost in immensity, burning bright like opals, as though discouraged from seeking the mountains or the sea from whence they came. The marvelous color of the country beckons to the painters; its simple natural life entrances the blond barbarian, with his fevered brain; and the gaudy *vaquero* and his trappings and his pony are the actors on this noble stage. But one must be appreciative of it all, or he will find a week of rain, and a week of stage and a week of horseback all too far for one to travel to see a shadow across the moon.

When a chill misty rain did begin to fall, instead of picnicking idyllically out of doors, we stopped at a village corner café and ordered coffee to go with our boxed lunch. We had taken Jim Cabutti's advice and had the lunches prepared by Super-Sandwiches, a private family incorporated who made a business of putting up lunches for Pan-American Airways. It was an excellent lunch, with plentiful pieces of fried breast of chicken. But the local coffee was bitter, and so strong it would have borne up an egg.

To get to the Señoras' place on the other side of the patio, Thérèse had to leap mounds of trash and dirt as well as rain puddles. But the patio was filled with flowers and bird song, and the toilet was modern and austerely clean and superior to what she might have found in a French village. Madame Calderón de la Barca had written in one of her delectable letters: "Dirtiness is certainly one of the greatest drawbacks to human felicity in this beautiful country." But even in the midst of dirt, flowers generally abound, and here there were cages of *sinsontli,* the Mexican mocking-bird, to lift the thought from sordid earth and help one balconize his thinking.

Before beginning to climb the mountains again, we came into the tropical valley of Túxpam, where mangoes, oranges, and bananas grow and small coffee plantations spread themselves over the gentle hills. Then came twenty miles of wild scenery, the car swinging like a sailor's hammock as the road curved about the mountains. At El Mirador de Mil Cumbres we paused for a view of the thousand peaks. But the thickening mist veiled the stupendous panorama and made the obviously spectacular more like a vision of another planet. The extinct volcanoes piled up one behind another, apparently without base or origin. They were like ghostly promontories floating in air. A grayness silvered everything into a monotone of peaks and precipices that seemed to be and not to be. The windows of the Buick became moving magic casements as we gazed on these faery lands forlorn. And then a waterfall came leaping down a gigantic rocky stair, recalling Norway above the Arctic Circle and a corner in the actual world of man. The misty mountain woods gradually turned into trees of distinguishable species: spruce, larch, cedar, oak, white pine, a local tree called beefwood, and finally the shrub known as American hawthorn.

The State of Michoacán, which we had entered many miles back, is one of the most gracious and varied of all the states in Mexico. It is blessed with good climate and abundant natural resources. Fine horses and golden wheat flourish, and men who make history. Michoacán has produced or nurtured five among the foremost names in Mexico: Quiroga, Hidalgo, Morelos, Iturbide, Cárdenas. The last three were born there. Bishop Vasco de Quiroga, who died in 1563, spent the last and most productive portion of his ninety-five years' span in the territory. Father Hidalgo was educated in Morelia at the College of San Nicolás founded by Quiroga, and in his time he became its rector and there taught José María Morelos the doctrine of the integrity of the individual thinking man. Morelia, too, was the home of Melchor Ocampo, the intellectual revolutionary who stood at Juárez's right hand and formulated the famous laws of the Reform—a statesman soldier who gave his life for the cause of democracy. Lázaro Cárdenas, by all odds the greatest living Mexican, was born in the village of Jiquilpán, northwest of Morelia on the road to Guadalajara.

Was there something in the atmosphere of this high-lying land that bred qualities of greatness? The Tarascan Indians of Michoacán have traits that make their qualities outstanding among other tribes. From prehistoric times there has been a tradition of culture among the Tarascans. They are a proud, independent, and self-reliant people. There are no beggars among them, as one finds them in nuisance quantities in Puebla. And though they have never been aggressive, with that itch to conquest that plagued the Aztecs, they have been fierce enough fighters in their own defense. The mighty Aztecs could not subdue them. The post-Cortés Spaniards did it only by trickery after they had beguiled the last Tarascan king, Caltzontzin, into accepting the blessings of Christian baptism, and later put him to incredible torture and death.

Perhaps it was this incident of treachery and cruelty that has made the Tarascans wary of foreigners. It is hard to get strangers to agree on their qualities. Some find them aloof to the point of insolence. Others find them amiable. But whether they are engaging or coldly indifferent often depends on how they are handled; and they seem hypersensitive to judging character and disposition. They are illusive and often taciturn. Yet when they give their friendship, it is with loyal devotion. They seem to possess a kind of inner serenity as well as insight, a contentment within their breasts that is impervious to rebuff. The men are strongly knit in physique, rugged without being tough, and the bony structure of their faces has distinction.

There is a sense of endurance about the Tarascans, and they are dependable, like Basques. Although new cottages were being built everywhere now, generations have lived in the same little stone huts, changing the old thatch for fresh with the decades. It almost seems as if they have absorbed into their marrow the emotionlessness of centuries. But they have most memorable smiles. From several Tarascans I have known in their own habitat and far afield, I believe I prefer the Tarascans to all other tribes.

3. THE CLEAN CITY

It was still raining softly when we passed through the forested National Park of Atzimba, ninety-nine hundred feet above sea level. Here white waterfalls gave emphasis to the dark ravines. As we began to descend into the valley of Morelia, the rain ceased. Soon sunshine spread in profusion over the fertile farms, and then the pink towers of the cathedral gleamed like twin lighthouses to welcome the voyager with a double welcome.

The first impression of Morelia is as pleasing to strangers in the 1940's as it was in the 1820's. "I was much struck on entering Valladolid [Morelia]," wrote the British Captain George Francis Lyons in 1826, "by the width and airy appearance of its streets, the goodness of the houses, and its magnificent cathedral. The city of Valladolid pleased me more than any I had hitherto seen. It has indeed but one principal street; but this is broad, clean, and cheerful; so that a stranger escapes all the filth, misery, and crowds, with which most other Mexican towns abound."

The ruins of an architecturally pleasing aqueduct run parallel with the highway entering Morelia; and where the road has been filled in and built up, the height of the noble arches diminishes until one end vanishes completely into the earth as if into the past itself, while the other one is left standing and terminated, as a memorial and as a contrast to the modern waterworks system. No longer are the picturesque water-carriers a numerous body gathering about the deposits of the aqueducts to fill their great globular jars and to carry them off, poised on their backs and supported from their heads by a strap. But an air of grace still lingers in the town that in colonial days was a seat of Spanish aristocracy. The spiritual past mingles agreeably with the material amenities of modernity.

In 1931, more than a century after the English officer's visit, Harry Carr of California, on a road-commission inspection tour, wrote very much like him: "Morelia is the cleanest city I have ever seen. It is absolutely spotless. It has one long magnificent street, which once seen will be never forgotten."

What Mr. Carr said in 1931 might be written by a grateful journalist in 1947. But the atmosphere of the crowd is considerably changed from the time of Captain Lyon's sojourn in 1826 when he wrote:

As it was Sunday all the gay people were in their best clothes, and rambling in the public walks, amongst which, clumsy heavy carriages were rolling, laden with ladies in court-dresses and plumes of feathers. All were smoking and eating alternately, between their puffs of genuine Orizaba, cakes and painted sugar-plums. . . . Here pulque, the juice of the tuna, and fiery *mescal,* were selling in great quantities, to the evident bewilderment of some of the gentlemen sportsmen, of whom many were lying drunk and asleep upon the benches, while others were sitting or rolling about with their eyes starting from the sockets, and in a happy state of uncertainty as to whether they should sleep or quarrel.

Today the ladies of Morelia neither wear Court dresses on the streets nor smoke cigars, and there are no sportsmen sprawling soddenly on the plaza benches. But Morelia is still the cleanest-looking city in all Mexico. Its one extensive street with splendid seventeenth- and eighteenth-century mansions interspersed with old churches makes a charming evocation of the past. The mellowed façades, the arched gateways, the cobblestoned courtyards, the fountained patios bright with blossoms, stir the imagination. But no longer do fine folk roll out of the gateways in their liveried coaches. For even in 1826, at the time of Captain Lyons's visit, the so-called great days of Mexico's aristocracy were waning. Many of the prominent families had departed for Spain after the Independence of 1821 rather than give up their royalist allegiance, just as many of the best American families moved to Canada after 1776. And during the preceding decade, from 1811 to 1821, wealthy Spaniards had been departing for Spain, taking with them the cream of their household goods, and even their finest carriages, along with their jewels and coffers full of gold pieces.

As Señor Sánchez drove us up and down and around slowly to give us a coup d'œil, we felt that Morelia, like much of the rest of Mexico, is still emerging from its feudal hangover. The atmosphere of the town today, though unflurried, is dramatically in flux with the new social order. The citizens on the street are as mixed in their minds as they are mestizo in their complexions. The Revolution that in the last two decades finished forever the age of the hacienda has also given a mortal blow to the tradition of the town mansion. New tenants occupy most of the houses, which have been turned into apartments, or have been bought up by politicians, or have become business offices or municipal and state agencies. However much the outside appearance remains unchanged, the heart of the dwelling is quite different. The white grandees and their highborn wives of a century and a half ago have been supplanted by mestizos whose tastes and codes are different.

In the new vaunted age of the common man, with all its needful benefits for the masses, there was obviously a discompensation of mediocrity. The fountained mansion of what was once called the aristocracy was now the tomb of a dead social order. And while only a very small percentage of thoughtful people would recall the old days and its attendant evils if they could, a number of new middle-class folk seem to wonder just what they are to aspire to as a way of life.

As we passed along some especially charming façades, my thought went to Mrs. O'Shaughnessy, the wife of the American chargé d'affaires, who lived in Mexico through the bloody strife of 1914.

She reminded her fellow countrymen of a debt that Mexico and the hemisphere owed to Spain, one which Americans often try to discount or ignore:

The seed of Spanish civilization implanted in this marvelous land has produced a fluorescence so magnetic, so magical, that the dullest feel its charm. All that has been done for Mexico the Spaniards did, despite their cruelties, their greeds, and their passions. We, of the north, have used it only as a quarry, leaving no monuments to God nor testaments to man in place of the treasure that we have piled on departing ship or train. Now we seem to be handing back to Indians very like those the Spaniards found, the fruits of a great civilization, for them to trample in the dust.

But the masses are by no means trampling anything in the dust now. They are merely enjoying the visible and tangible evidence that they are no longer forgotten in a social scheme that once put its whole influence on keeping privileges for the privileged. Señor Sánchez pointed out a stately building which once housed the dread Inquisition and where suspected heretics writhed in agony. The implements of torture have been removed and gymnastic equipment substituted. It is now an industrial school for waifs and orphaned sons of soldiers. Boys are taught useful crafts and trades, from cabinet-work and typesetting to airplane-repairing. Lads once hounded by houseless poverty into becoming sneak thieves have been taught not to fear.

The former seminary for priests, an excellent specimen of dignified colonial architecture, is now the governor's mansion. Another handsome building near the market has been taken over by the Workers' Federation, and the walls are decorated with frescoes by young Mexican muralists. With such a superfluity of churches, Cárdenas had one in disrepair turned into a public library. The Bishop's palace that once made a rich setting for a solitary man has now become a hostelry to house a hundred guests.

We stopped at the Bishop's palace, which gives on the Plaza Mayor. The hotel is called El Virrey de Mendoza in honor of the first viceroy, the man who had ably laid the foundations of colonial Mexico, which was to last for almost three centuries—from 1535 to 1821. There is an air of faded magnificence and dignity about the place. Out of the faintly musty lobby that had once been the great courtyard, the wide stone staircase rises, evocative and gracious. It seems to have been designed to make the most of a prelate's stately tread or the velvet sweep of a lady's train. The staircase does not begin or end architecturally where one would expect a staircase to begin and end, and it winds leisurely, as if hurry were the most unseemly thing in the world. It disappears and again appears, and is punctuated with resting-stages where fragrant shrub-shaded nooks invite meditation or a lover's rendezvous. Leisure is subtly suggested, too, by alcoves or small antechambers that pause before the bedrooms, in which other alcoves have been converted into bathrooms.

In our room the furniture carried out the colonial style in good reproduction. The afternoon sunlight, sifting through the blinds, high-lighted the Rembrandt tones, rich brown, dull red, and blackish yellow. In an alcove a great swelling bed with a modern innerspring mattress and a monogrammed cover invited restful sleep or luxurious dalliance. The two high wide windows set off in little alcoves of their own were reached by two steps, and on either side within each alcove were fixed seats where one could watch a bit of the world go by as if from an opera box.

From the colonial dignity of the window seat I watched the passing of a youthful military band, playing with spirit but not brazenly. And then, as I stared at the flashily modernistic new hotel across the way, I saw a flashy sports-model car drive up and a flashy slick-haired young man help a flashy peroxided blonde out, with all the sensual exuberance of their mission revealed in their gestures. I thought how much more vulgar and blatant sin could be today than when the Bishop of Valladolid lived in the palace that was now a hotel. I could not entirely subscribe to Burke's idea of "vice gaining more of evil by losing half its grossness." Yet one might "sin with a high hand" in the Old Testament phrase and still not be so ostentatiously offensive.

I turned back to the dignified proportions of the room and remarked that they had once been even more generous before the hotel management had cut them down somewhat for utilitarian economy. But the people had had to pay through the nose for the spaciousness of the Bishop's heyday. The first British Minister to Mexico, Henry George Ward, is our authority for the fact that in the 1820's "throughout the Bishopric of Valladolid the marriage fees vary from seventeen to twenty-two dollars," and this in a period when a cottage could be built for four dollars and the daily wages of a laborer did not exceed twenty-four cents a day. "Twenty-two dollars," says Mr. Ward, "is a sum which exceeds half their yearly earnings in a country where Feast and Fast days reduce the number of *dias utiles* (on which labour is permitted) to about one hundred and seventy-five." Of course, many an Indian got around the ruinous rates of marriage by cohabiting with his intended wife until she became pregnant, when the parish priest had to marry the couple without fee. Some more pious souls, however, feeling impelled to compensate the Church according to its decree, turned to larceny to pay God.

In time the reformers changed all that, invalidated ecclesiastical marriage, and made the civil ceremony the only one that holds legality. The standard of living for the higher clergy began to slide. And as the power and pomp of the bishops diminished with their receding revenues, no longer did the ignorant and simple prostrate themselves to lip the paving stones where episcopal feet had trod.

But religion that endured persecution and bootlegging under Calles was obviously enjoying a resurgence in 1943 under Manuel Avila Camacho. In the afternoon of a weekday in late June services were being conducted in five churches of Morelia, all within a few minutes' walk of the Virrey de Mendoza. Hoagland was not feeling very well, so he retired to his room while Thérèse and Wagus and I looked in at several churches and attended a service at the cathedral.

4. CHURCH IN THE AFTERNOON

The cathedral of Morelia is one of the handsomest and most harmonious in all Mexico. Nobly proportioned, with dominating twin towers, it is chalky-pink in color, being built of the native stone called trachyte. Set spaciously to the east of the great plaza, it is protected by a lofty wrought-iron fence that adds to the general effect. The early Spaniards, who had a sense of eternality unknown to the British settlers in North America, began the cathedral in 1640, when the Pilgrim Fathers were still getting themselves acclimated to the rigors of Massachusetts winters. It was a century and four years in construction. And when completed it stood a fine example of the plateresque style.

Where the interiors of other Mexican churches are often over-loaded and cluttered like the famous cathedral of Puebla, the cathedral of Morelia is extraordinarily clarifying and thought-releasing. It has cohesion and focus, and a kind of pure dignity. Though the solid-silver balustrade of the choir has been removed, and also the silver statues and the gold of the high altar, there is an atmosphere of restrained elegance. The recent modern decoration holds more a suggestion of Swedish taste in color than one of the ornate Hispano-American. The colors are all pastel—soft pink, silvery gray, delicate azure. Even the spare gold leaf is almost as pale as white gold. The gory representations of Christ's agony that disfigure so many Mexican chapels are here honored in the breach rather than the observance. Even the lesser images seemed to have been purified and stripped of gaudy ornamentation. Bleeding hearts, like lugubrious valentines, do not besmirch the walls and shriek "Suffer, suffer, suffer!" There is little to distract the spiritual thought from direct contact with Heaven.

In the center of the back open space, before the parallel rows of pews begin, an aged man is kneeling. He has laid his big straw hat on the pavement before him, and his long white hair reaches to the pink-wool shawl about his shoulders. His widespread arms are up-lifted, with palms turned in adoration and humility toward the distant high altar. From the expression on his face, he has already entered the Kingdom of Heaven, through his simple faith. Indian women with pigeon-blue rebozos over their heads come in pairs or singly, and kneel here and there, fixing their eyes on some illumi-nated place of emphasis, their lips moving inaudibly.

A chubby, big-eyed baby, crawling on the floor toward one of the sainted alcoves to gratify some infant curiosity, pauses in its progress and makes a great puddle on the floor. The baby proceeds, and then turns to regard its achievement in some dismay, as if it had a vague sense of misdemeanor. Then it crawls forward and stops again and, like Lot's wife, seems impelled to sneak a look at the dark disaster. After a debate with itself and a furtive glance to right and left, like a criminal lured to the scene of his crime, it crawls slowly back and tests the liquid with a fat little finger and then starts guiltily to scurry away again. A woman suddenly emerges from the shadow of a great stone pillar and swoops down like a silent Nemesis and bears the culprit off to some spotless portion of the church. The baby does not cry out or whimper. It seems to be holding its breath. But its eyes bulge with mingled emotions.

As the cathedral bell peals a final call to worship, the pews fill, and the overflow kneels in the open space at the back. A dozen or so little girls in their communion veils sit in the first row with a jumpy air of self-importance. Professional men and businessmen who have closed their offices are on their knees, side by side with the Indians from the country who have come for a last blessing before returning to their mountain or valley villages.

This Mexican equality before the face of Deity much impressed another Englishman named William Bullock, who visited Mexico in the 1820's. "In the Mexican churches," he wrote, "we do not meet with that distinction, so universal with us, of pews and seats. Here on the same floor the poorest Indians and the highest personages in the land mix indiscriminately in their prayers to that being to whom earthly distinctions are unknown."

Though the Bishop of Michoacán ceased living in the grand manner fourscore years ago, and though all the expensive pageantry of a church wedding will not make a marriage legal, the Roman Catholic religion is obviously deeply ingrained in the Mexican populace. No matter what the social legislators and Communists and Masons may say, religion has a hold on the Mexican. The rich and colorful ritual of the Church still gives joy and release to the Indians. Even if it is no more than an opiate to the people, as the Marxists insist, religion apparently does them no harm unless it degenerates into fanaticism. Watching the congregation at its devotions, I thought of George Santayana's reasoned attitude toward the Church in which he was brought up. "Catholicism," he says in his autobiography, "is the most human of religions, if taken humanly; it is paganism spiritually transformed and made metaphysical. It corresponds most adequately to the various exigencies of moral life, with just the needed dose of wisdom, sublimity, and illusion."

The tone of the organ was sweet and soft. And the priest's Spanish was as unharsh and gentle-spoken as his Latin. He did not scold, as many pastors do, nor exhort. His manner was in harmony with

the ambient of the architecture and the decoration. And when the
people left the church many of them looked as a people should look
when it leaves a church; that is, as if they had "left their sorrows on
the sacrificial altars."

I thought of the difference between Catholics and Protestants
coming from church, as Santayana had so shrewdly made the comparison.

When Catholics leave church they do so by the south door, into the
glare of the marketplace, where their eye is at once attracted by the wares
displayed in the booths, by the flower stalls with their bright awnings, by
the fountain with its baroque Tritons blowing the spray into the air, and
the children laughing and playing round it . . . and if they cast back a
look at all, it is to admire its antique architecture. . . .

Protestants, on the contrary, leave the church by the north door, into
the damp solitude of a green churchyard, amid yews and weeping willows
and overgrown mounds, and fallen illegible gravestones. They feel a terrible chill; the few weedy flowers that may struggle through the long grass
do not console them; it was far brighter and warmer and more decent
inside.

It was not because we had not been brought up Catholics that we
did not leave with the crowd by the south door (which in Morelia
actually faces the north). And we could not leave by the north door,
because what it symbolized was unsympathetic to us in any land.
But because we were both cheered and a little saddened at the same
time by what might be called Mexico's new social order, we slipped
out a side door, literally and figuratively.

The only persons who did not seem to leave the church more joy-
fully than when they entered were the very few who by the cut of
their clothes and the unreconciled expression on their refined faces
still held allegiance to the aristocratic tradition. They left as they had
entered, as if trying to make themselves invisible, and passed along
the street like shades returned to a familiar scene that had become
out of focus. The gentlefolk did not pause in the inviting plaza as
we did, but turned corners quickly to slip away from the sun-bright
avenue into the security of whatever shabby-genteel lodgings and
consoling lares and penates they were able to maintain after the
social table-turning.

5. DIFFERENCES

Like the cathedral and the long clean avenue of colonial houses, the central plaza of Morelia is most satisfying. At first glance, except for occasional motorcars, Captain Lyons would find the place more or less as he saw it in 1826. "The plaza," he wrote, "is remarkable as having broad piazzas on three of its sides, and the fine cathedral isolated from all other buildings bounding it on the east. A crowded market is held here, and the venders display their goods, as is the general custom, beneath the shade of rude mat umbrellas."

The palm-leaf umbrellas have now become écru-colored awnings, and the booths of the venders extend down lesser streets to the south until they reach the permanent roofed market several blocks away. Though the physical aspects look much the same after twelve decades, the psychic atmosphere is considerably changed. Class distinctions have been drastically leveled. All the people seem adequately clothed. There are no rags, no beggars. But in some of the booths, where there is a conglomeration of trashy knickknacks and Japanese gewgaws, the shopkeepers' faces look as artificial as the tinsel they sell.

"For the most part," Thérèse observed, "the Indians at Toluca sell their own handicrafts and look genuine."

Here many of the Indians looked oddly phony. And some of the mestizos strutted with an unwholesome bravado, as if they were coming to learn the price of gadgets, but losing the sense of values.

"It's not fitting for young girls to wear those cheap artificial flowers when the stalls abound in fresh blossoms," I said.

Looking at the Indians standing about the plaza and the booths of the al-fresco market in 1943, and vaguely measuring how far they had come in a century and twenty-two years of Mexican independence, I remarked to Thérèse and Wagus that though the Spaniard in Mexico exploited the Indians in the most shameful and sometimes savage manner, he at least did not kill them off until they became a negligible unit, as we did in the United States. He did not push them back by force or trickery into reservations, as we did. He did not attempt to exterminate whole tribes, as did the Spaniards in Argentina. He set up his European culture in the midst of them and worked them into the extraordinary fabric that is Mexico today. He intermarried with them, which the white American did only in the rarest instances. Yet Spain and Mexico never really mingled harmoniously except in architecture and in art. The social structure was wrought in a welter of rivalry, mutual contempt, and distrust, not only between whites and Indians, and whites and mestizos, and mestizos and Indians, but of whites among themselves, those born in Spain and those born in Mexico. During his mission to Mexico, Mr. Ward was considerably surprised at the intensity of class feeling. In 1829, he wrote:

It became, at last, a passion, which induced them to prefer the ties of native country to the blood. The son, who had the misfortune to be born of a Creole mother, was considered as an inferior, in the house of his own father, to the European bookkeeper or clerk, for whom the daughter, if there were one, and a large share of the fortune, were reserved. *"Eres Criollo, y basta!"*—(You are a Creole, and that is enough!)—was a common phrase amongst the Spaniards when angry with their children; and was thought to express all the contempt that it is in the power of language to convey. It was a term of ignominy, a term of reproach, until time taught those, to whom it was applied, to use it rather as an honourable distinction, and to oppose it to that of Gachupín, as designating the party of those infatuated men, who imagined that the circumstances of having been born in the arid plains of Castille, or La Mancha, gave them a moral, and intellectual superiority, over all the inhabitants of the New World.

In 1943 a Spaniard was still called a *gachupín,* with a contemptuous curl of the lip, but few enough *gachupíns* pass through Morelia's plaza now. And Spaniards are no longer given eminence in what is called "society" because of their Continental birth. But the Spaniards still are prominent in business even if they are not much in evidence on the streets. They are the moneylenders openly or through agents, and often the leading manufacturers and merchants, both wholesale and retail. And to them belong some of the best grocery shops. They have more enterprise and initiative than the average Mexican. And though the Mexicans dislike them, they are pleased to have the Spanish immigrants come because, as they say, "they lighten our nation's complexion."

It seemed strange to us, as we sat in the plaza commenting and speculating on the social fabric, that this beautifully preserved city should have been the nurse of such potent revolutionary forces. Here the most tearing physical and ideological contentions have taken place. Only a few paces between streets separated the birthplaces of Morelia's two most famous sons, José María Morelos and the Emperor Agustín de Iturbide. The latter was born in his Spanish father's fine town house, into well-to-do comfort and high provincial social position. The former, a mestizo with a purported strain of Negro blood, was dropped by his peasant mother behind a stranger's door, without benefit of midwife or a manger's straw. The country carpenter Manuel Morelos had brought his spouse to market that last day of September 1765, and in the street her time of childbearing came upon her so suddenly that she was carried into the nearest house and laid on the stone pavement behind a door, where the event was quickly over. The very spot is marked today, and commemorated with trumpeting words—"Not only the cradle of liberty for Mexico but for the whole world." The boast is not the utter hyperbole it might seem, for when Morelos rose to power and issued his radical manifesto for the uplifting of the common man, he was a half-century in advance of Marx and more than a century in advance of Lenin.

Iturbide's silver-spoon birth came also in late September, but eighteen years after that of Morelos, when José María was a husky peon mule-driver. These two home-town boys, who did the most to bring about the independence from Spain, became mortal rivals, and in the first years of the rebellion Iturbide fought against Morelos for Spain more violently than he later fought for Mexico's independence. At twenty-five Morelos left his job as farm laborer to study for the priesthood, where he was instructed by Father Hidalgo, the priest whose *Grito de Dolores* in 1810 launched the fight for freedom. At the age of fifteen, young Iturbide considered his own education completed and became a second lieutenant in a regiment of provincial infantry. Subsequently both men developed remarkable military genius. Morelos became the commander in chief of the rebel forces, while the younger man as colonel brought about his townsman's final ruin and temporarily saved Mexico for the Spanish Crown.

It is one of history's little ironies that Iturbide, who was chiefly responsible for strangling Mexico's independence under the leadership of the fighting priests, should himself have won that independence less than a decade later. On September 27, 1821, on his thirty-eighth birthday, mounted on a prancing black horse, Iturbide made his triumphant entry into Mexico City as the strong man who had severed Mexico forever from the rule of Spain. In 1822, by scheming to get himself "consecrated and crowned" as Emperor Agustín I, he became historically the first native-born ruler of Mexico since Cuauhtémoc, the noble nephew of Montezuma II. But his pretentious glory was short-lived. Within a year the imperial dynasty he had founded crumbled before jeering mockery, and he was forced into exile. On his return from abroad without permission in July of 1824, this hero of Mexican independence was summarily riddled with bullets by an executioner's squad. Before he had reached his forty-first birthday the earthly blaze of the meteoric Iturbide was completely extinguished.

For some years the mortal remains of the two rival liberators who fought for such opposed motives and ideals—one for the common man, one for the privileged—reposed under the same roof in the cathedral of Mexico City. Much later, the dust of Morelos was accorded extraordinary honor and removed to the vault in the Monument of Independence. But soon after the shooting of the whilom Emperor, the name of the city of his birth was changed from Valladolid to Morelia in honor of the one-time mule-driver.

At first dusk the Indians who live at a distance begin to pack up their unsold goods and their meager purchases in preparation for the trot home. They find it less tiring to trot than to walk. We watched one family start off. The father was first in line, with a great bulging bag on his back. The mother next took her place, with a baby secured in her rebozo, papoose-fashion, and with a brace of submissive hens dangling from each hand. A grandmother stood next with a bright woven basket in the crook of an arm. A yearling boy with a smaller sack like his father's came next, and then two girls who broke the single file and ran together, carrying some stalks of flowers. As they moved off their silhouettes against the background of church wall made a living frieze of singular charm. Though another drizzle had just begun, they seemed undaunted, and jogtrotted rhythmically, with masklike half-grins upon their faces.

"They can trot like that for twenty miles," said Señor Sánchez, who had joined us, "and never seem to tire."

"Have they flashlights?" Wagus asked.

"They can find their way in the dark like cats."

"They look happy enough," Thérèse said. "Much happier than the poor Indians at Toluca."

"Ah, that was this morning!" said Señor Sánchez. "By now at Toluca perhaps they too have had enough pulque to make them forget their troubles. They say a husband and a wife make compacts that one stays sober enough to guide the other home. Husbands and wives never get tipsy at the same time."

From the shelter of a projecting balcony we watched the family's orderly trotting as they took to the middle of the street. There was something so timeless and so harmonious in the movement of the file. And then a man in a cart said something that halted the leader. Each runner stopped precisely in his tracks, like the mechanical figures that appear to mark the hours in certain old medieval clock towers. The brief colloquy ended, the trotting was resumed—with exact intervals between the runners.

The peace of the street was suddenly broken by shrieks of laughter and finger-pointing. Two white men and two white women jumped out of a touring car before it quite came to a standstill. They were dressed in outlandish cowboy and cowgirl outfits, with garish blouses of orange and blue satin, boots and spurs, and Texan ten-gallon hats. They wore big imitation revolvers hanging from belts about their waists. Both women were plump, and heavily painted, and they were hilarious at the sight of the Indian family serenely trotting to their home in the country. Other Indians among the booths paused to look up in some amazement at such fantastic and obviously counterfeit attire. They exchanged looks with each other and shook their heads. Amusement and contempt mingled in their expression. Some muttered the word "gringo," as if it were a synonym for craziness.

The fatter of the women began to imitate the Indian trot. The other three fell in line, more in high spirits than in ridicule. Then the taller of the men caught sight of us in the shelter of a doorway and shouted, "Hey, look! There's some real white folks!" The burlesque trotting halted. The women, out of breath and giggling, adjusted their cowgirl hats, and the shorter fellow with a friendly grin yelled across the street, "What do you folks think of this funny dump?"

Like the protecting waters that rushed back into the Red Sea, a slow-moving motortruck loaded with donkeys blocked the way a moment. Under Señor Sánchez's expert guidance we made the sanctuary of one of the ubiquitous little churches and escaped the genial overtures of our fellow countrymen.

That evening during dinner it was almost a relief to see that it was not only Americans who sometimes make unsavory public displays of themselves. Having noted all through the day the natural good behavior of Mexican children, how they obeyed and seemed content with whatever they had, we were treated to a case of tantrums by the four-year-old son of the *gachupín* hotel proprietor. When the boy was served something that did not appeal to his Spanish palate, he created a terrific scene, throwing himself melodramatically on his back on the floor and shaking his heels in defiant fury at his nurse and his embarrassed mother. Evidently he had much less respect for his Creole mother than he did for his Spanish father, for when the latter appeared and merely glared at the brat, the kicks and shrieks subsided instantly. Arising promptly and climbing up into his chair, the muchacho hung his head over his plate and began to eat his porridge or his spinach like a chastened lamb. Being male and half-Spanish, he might defy mestizo nurse and white Creole mother. But before a European-born father—well, he knew differences at the age of four, even in a land where "equality" is pregnant with emphasis.

Dr. Hoagland was suffering from Mexican pains in his stomach and had stayed in bed supping on orange juice, but he insisted he did not yet want a doctor. He was in some doubt as to the skill and judgment of the provincial physician. Assuring us that he would be feeling fit in the morning, he urged us to go out for the evening. But there was no night life in Morelia, and we certainly were not eager for more entertainment that day. However, we strolled across the

side street to the modernistic hotel and there amid the chromium
and red leather and black-glass table tops, all looking strictly un-
Spanish, we sipped Cointreau. The atmosphere was not congenial,
though it was in no sense rowdy. A few groups were sitting about
apparently trying to create an impression of sophistication to match
the pseudo-smart décor. We soon left and took a turn about the
thick-leaved plaza under the stars, which had come out in fresh
luminosity after the rain. The wandering Venus, which the ancient
Tarascans worshiped as a goddess, far outdid the fixed stars in brilliance. And by starlight the cathedral's pink towers were even more
lovely and more mellow than by sunlight.

The air was fresh and cool. The venders had folded their tents and
departed. Citizens, still sitting on the benches, talked in subdued
tones, as if it were a tradition to talk softly at night in this plaza.
When the cathedral bell struck ten full and silvery strokes, we got
up and strolled back to the former Bishop's palace, enjoying a kind
of nostalgic pleasure in ascending the gracious stairs.

6. QUIROGA

Between Morelia and Quiroga, the towns named after two unorthodox priests, the red land is rich and rolling—soil worth a man's
taking root in and calling it home with pride as well as affection.
Along with the ageless activities of plowing and sowing, new cottages were being built to afford a better protection against wind and
weather, and with more space in which to raise a family. They were
plain and simple houses, functional in design, but not unattractive,
and they looked as if in time they too could sink their roots deep into
the soil. The obvious sense of indomitable stability about them recalled Spengler's line, "The peasant's dwelling is the great symbol
of settledness."

These countryfolk were earth-bound in the good sense. As Spengler said, "He who digs and ploughs is seeking not to plunder, but
alter nature. To plant implies not to take something, but to produce
something." And those who had never been peons, but have lived on
the land of their forefathers continuously, have remained essentially
untouched by history. One felt that they have a mystic communion
with the soil, and if they were transported to another part of the

Republic, they could still speak to the earth under any regime or
ideology.

Quiroga, which bears the name of that extraordinary Spanish
Bishop whose influence extended from Morelia all around the lake
of Pátzcuaro, is merely a village in which time has stood still. But it
possesses a charming little plaza with a pleasing church at the far end
and two parallel rows of colonnaded one-story buildings on the sides.
Benches are set at intervals under clipped trees, but except for one
lone figure walking the promenade as in a distorted dream, the plaza
was deserted in these morning hours. The figure was an old man,
ragged and dirty, halt in the limbs and half-blind and bleary-eyed
with syphilis—a legacy from the Spaniards, along with the memorable architecture. With the jerks and contortions of a grotesque
mechanical figure he made a groping progress about the square, like
a mute town crier warning citizens of the wages of sin. But the
youngsters spinning tops on the street at the open end of the plaza
paid the old man no heed whatever, though they paused in their play
to ogle a young nubile girl bearing a water jar on her shapely head.

The only thing memorable about Quiroga besides that tarnished
jewel of a plaza was a troop of long-eared donkeys laden with heaps
of lacquer-ware jars and bowls all tied loosely in bales of rope net.
With the midmorning sun shining full upon the train, a myriad
colors flashed—emerald, ruby, turquoise, topaz. The little mouse-
colored beasts looked as if they might be chattels of some Ali Baba
and forty thieving confederates who were moving their gem-
encrusted treasures from one mountain cave to another. But when
the donkey train came closer, the wares proved to be of small value.
This batch had been turned out with more thought given to tourist
sale than to pride of workmanship. The better pieces of lacquer were
to be found in Uruapan, where we were bound, and where Quiroga's
mortal career had ended.

All the territory beyond Quiroga is associated with the memory of
the Bishop who saw the necessity of hand-in-hand co-operation of
the Indians' spiritual redemption with material benefits. The poverty
and misery of the Indians had made an incisive impression on
Quiroga's heart—"some going naked through the market place,"
he wrote, "looking for something to eat which the swine have left."

Born in Spain in 1470 of a distinguished and well-to-do family, educated to be a lawyer, Quiroga came to Mexico when he was sixty. He came not as a priest, but as a high official of government, an *oidor*. The missionary zeal struck him after he beheld the crying needs of the Indians. He spent his generous salary on them, establishing a hospital for them near Mexico City. He studied their aptitudes, as well as their problems, and sought by a kind of instinctive psychotherapy of his own devising to bring them out of the terrible shock and dismay wrought by the Conquest and the wrenching-away from their pagan worship. Six months after his arrival he wrote: "There is no way of putting them in order or promoting good Christian life, eliminating drunkenness, idolatry, and other evils, unless they can be placed together in well-ordered communities." It was his idea that no one had the right to superfluous goods so long as others lacked bare necessities.

An opportunity came to put his mildly socialistic ideas into practice among the Tarascans of Michoacán, who were in a most disorganized state after the incomparable stupidities and cruelties of Nuño de Guzmán. Within a fifty-mile circuit about Lake Pátzcuaro numerous villages were established or rearranged in Quiroga's way. As the center of his communities Quiroga erected a house for the sick and a chapel. Then he built a series of dwellings, each large enough to accommodate some ten families. The hours for co-operative labor in the fields were six. The other hours were the Indians' own for agriculture or handicrafts, so that those who were markedly skillful or diligent should receive some extra reward for their labor.

With a natural sense of economics, Quiroga arranged matters so that each village made a specialty of one or two handicrafts. One village specialized in woven blankets, another in metal goods. One village was taught to fashion holy images out of maize paste. Another made chocolate-frothers, which were sold in the capital. Paracho became famous for its musical instruments, Uruapan for its lacquer. Today good guitars come from Paracho and some of the best lacquer ware in the hemisphere comes from Uruapan. The pottery Quiroga established at Camanja continues to do business after four centuries.

The Emperor was highly impressed with Quiroga's great success in pacifying the Indian not with the sword, but with good deeds and understanding. When it was decided to establish Michoacán as a diocese, and the Emperor was casting about for a worthy bishop, the administrator Quiroga kept coming to his mind. Finally he did a most extraordinary thing: He presented to the Pope the name of a layman for the Bishop of Michoacán. And the far-seeing Pope gave his blessing to the choice. Quiroga, who had never been a priest or even studied theology, was ordained and consecrated a bishop on a December day in 1538.

The famous Archbishop Zumárraga, who presided at the ceremony, was so well pleased with the choice that he wrote the Spanish monarch complimenting him on his "stroke of good judgment" in appointing this man who "adds luster to us prelates in this country." He reminded His Majesty that Quiroga had spent his entire salary in providing hospitals for his Christian Indians and family dwellings and flocks to sustain them. "When he has become the pastor, one can believe that he will do even greater things for his sheep, although I do not know of any other who has equaled him in this land. . . . He has put us bishops, and particularly the friars, to shame."

In the years between 1539 and 1543 Quiroga built many schools of various categories, and encouraged the exchange of language study between Spanish and Tarascan youths. In his work of stabilizing the Indians and making them prosperous, he was accused by jealous enemies of not doing his churchly duties in ordaining, baptizing, conforming. But he could prove to his enemies that he had traveled on muleback some six hundred leagues, holding communion services and baptizing, with only one chaplain and one page to assist him. In his ninety-fifth year he was still going on periodic inspection tours, bestowing spiritual and material blessings as he went.

7. MONSTER IN THE CORN PATCH

The little town that immortalized Quiroga's name lies at a crossroads. The highway goes straight on to Guadalajara, Mexico's second largest city. The road to the left goes to Pátzcuaro and Uruapan. But Uruapan can also be reached most agreeably by first taking the highway and then at Carapán circling over the mountains. We took the long way.

From an eminence in the road we got our first real view of the lake called Pátzcuaro, which means in Tarascan "Place of Delights." Serenely it stretched farther than we could see, holding within its thirty-mile circumference a steadfast yet ever changing loveliness. Sometimes it was said to be like a slab of aquamarine, sometimes it was a soft blue like turquoise, sometimes it was milky jade. This morning it was more like an opal, reflecting in its depths floating canopies of pink-tinted clouds, green masses of mountain foliage, the blue-gray flanks of pendent rocks. And as we curved on the road this way and that, now higher, now lower, mauve shadows shifted like gigantic water lilies.

Señor Sánchez stopped the car and we stood on the edge of a cliff to gaze. Pátzcuaro lies nearer to the sun than any navigable lake in Mexico—six thousand seven hundred and seventeen feet above its watery neighbor the Pacific, which lapped the coast less than a hundred and fifty miles away. We wondered if it was its high situation that gave the lake and its environs such special flavor and distinction. Here was no wild and luxuriant beauty like that of Brazil's magnificent hothouse. The situation was too high for nature to adorn with a prodigal hand. The mountains did not tumble and spill over each other. There was no too-muchness of anything. Beauty was restrained, cool, selective. The views in twelve directions were as clear-cut as Japanese prints, with more color. But they were not colors to be reproduced in lush oils or in dusty pastels. They were something suggesting hard crayon or some Hindu colored ink. In its clarity of outline against the pure cerulean blue of the sky, in some ineffable quality of composition, it was different from any other scene on the continent. And it touched some response in the soul rather than in the senses.

The road keeps more or less in sight of the lake for some ten miles before plunging into another series of mountains and fertile valleys. At length a projecting side of a mountain came like a thrust screen between the lake and us, and we were not to see it again until we had completed a sixty-mile circuit.

After Quiroga, whichever road you take north or west, it is as if you have vaguely crossed the frontier into another land. There are rude pagodalike gateways before all the huts, to cheer the roadway. Whereas the typical Mexican house is flat-roofed, here, whether houses are of bamboo or wattle or stone, the roofs are thatched, and the steep roof lines have an Oriental sweep. Even the wide flat hats of the men add to the illusion; the brims do not curve upward and the crowns are more or less flattened. Some of the men in the villages looked like a sturdy breed of Nipponese—with good shoulders and stout straight necks.

"It's Japanese," Wagus said.

"It's Chinese," Thérèse said.

"I know," said Dr. Hoagland, "the houses are like those outside Manila."

"Well, not to make a bad pun," Wagus said, "whatever the inspiration, the region certainly has a Mongolian slant."

"It is like this," Señor Sánchez said, "from here to the Pacific— we are not much more than a hundred and fifty miles from the ocean. Many believe than the Chinese and the Japs were here before the Spaniards."

We counted off villages like beads on a chaplet and then somewhere after Carapán we went over the mountains and passed Paracho, where the famous guitars are made and the folk songs are composed, and soon came upon a region like nothing else we had ever seen. The road was begrimed with black dust. The hillside trees stood stripped of foliage, stark and naked as gray skeletons. The ash-colored land looked like something accursed.

If a state-maintained road had not run through forbidding barrenness, one could have imagined himself back in the graveyard of some prehistoric age. If the fossil remains of Scelidotheriums and Megatheriums had strewn the wasteland, it would have seemed quite natural, and in harmony with the scenic composition. When we passed through a gap in the mountains we saw the monster whose poisonous breath had wrought the desolation. There rose the volcanic cone of Paricutín, making a magnificent and terrible silhouette against the ethereal blue of the sky. Its gray-black smoke ascended heavenward, four miles straight into the windless air. The fuming vapors were like a gigantic obelisk erected to some god of the underworld.

The terrestrial globe's youngest volcano was in late June of 1943 just four months old. A humble cornpatch in the little valley called Cuityúzero was the scene of its birth on February 20, 1943. The sole witness to the first worldly breath it drew was a peasant named

Dionisio Pulido. At the time he was engaged in the most peaceful of ancient occupations: sowing seed in fresh-made furrows. A puzzling wisp of smoke rose at his feet like some genie from a bottle mouth. In bewilderment Dionisio attempted to stamp out the unnatural smoke with his sandaled feet and then tried to beat it out with his palm-straw hat. To his astonishment, the trail of smoke widened swiftly, and with a groan like a god in pain the surface of the earth opened before him. Flames, rocks, and ashes spewed forth.

In terror, Dionisio fled for his life. Soon the citizens of the neighboring village of Paricutín were mumbling prayers, snatching up possessions, and fleeing from the radius of hurtling red-hot stones. The volcano grew with incredible celerity. Out of the bowels of the earth it drew up the crude materials to make itself into a hillock, then into a hill, and then into a mountain. And in the process, its poisonous breath blasted the growing things on the earth's surface. Trees, which cannot uproot themselves and run like man and beast, stood twisting in agony as they were gradually singed to death by peppering hot cinders or stripped of their outer bark like chained martyrs flayed alive. Within five days a whole square mile of land was drowned in liquid lava that cooled into porous rock. When the prevailing winds were from the northwest, dust particles reached Mexico City, almost two hundred miles away.

Geologists, meteorologists, and scientists of various categories were drawn to Paricutín as if it were a lodestone whose influence reached around the globe. Photographs were taken of the baby volcano's progress day by day, week by week, month by month. It was a monstrous growth. Within a year the cone was to reach almost twelve hundred feet above the surface of the high plateau. Several hundred square miles of agricultural lands were to be depopulated, except for intrepid Indians who found temporary livelihood by guiding tourists on burroback up the stony mountain paths to get a closer view of the flame-spitting wonder.

Here in our own time was happening an event that Humboldt might have happily given a few last years of his ninety-year life to have witnessed. And while an early view of Paricutín would not have measured up to what he considered the crowning glory of his adventurous career—the climbing of Ecuador's Chimborazo—it undoubtedly would have much excited and elated him.

I asked Señor Sánchez to stop the car while I took pictures of the great smoke column. On the roadside I stooped to pick up a handful of the black volcanic dust. It was almost as fine as talcum powder. I could imagine an Indian mother without benefit of white powder being tempted to use it to soothe a baby's chafed bottom. It seemed strange to be holding a handful of stuff that had come from thirty miles within the earth, through basalt and granite and the shallow sedimentary layers just under the earth's surface. Dr. Hoagland reminded me that the earth's crust floats thinly on a mass of boiling liquid rock—four thousand miles of molten lava to the center of the globe, held within bounds by what amounts to a film of skin. And the thin skin is as thick as it is only because the process of cooling has been going on for some two billion years, if the scientists are right. In comparison to the fiery furnace within the globe, the outer crust beneath men's feet is no more than the fuzzy skin of a peach compared to the entire inside of fruit pulp and stone.

Such scientific reflection makes all life seem extraordinarily unstable and precarious. What does this little world of man really add up to in the overwhelming face of a universe of millions of other suns and their enchained planets and earthy satellites? And yet how phenomenal it is that mankind had ever evolved at all. How really marvelous it is that man has already achieved the control he has over what are called the forces of nature. But whatever man may come to learn of Truth, the sum of his knowledge can never be more remarkable than the fact that man possesses the faculty of appreciating Beauty. A strange concomitant of being earth-bound, with a compulsion to survive, is that mystical awareness of a poetry in nature's wondrous mutations.

While men came from afar to marvel at the volcano, Dionisio Pulido grieved more for the loss of his sustaining corn than he felt elated by the discovery that immortalized his humble name. When the first strangers stood rapt in awful admiration before the infernal spectacle, the peasant turned his back on the monster and beat his breast and sobbed: "Oh, my cornfield, my poor cornfield!"

As we drove on and the landscape slowly changed from skeleton gray and black to vital green, Hoagland recalled that scientists have proclaimed the earth's crust to be thinner along the rim of the Pacific from San Francisco to lower Chile. Doubtless that is the reason for

Mexico's possessing more extinct volcanoes than any other equal area in the world. And it is these infinite volcanic peaks that give the land its picturesque difference. Is it also possible that living a trifle nearer to the inner ball of molten fire has an influence on the Mexicans themselves, and set off the rending upheavals of their history? Is it this that makes the average Indian, whose disposition is seemingly so placid, capable of an outburst that could turn him into a demon? Is there something more to the matter than coincidence?

8. URUAPAN FOR LACQUER

As we approached Uruapan the rain-fresh summer greenness lifted the heart. I took such long, deep, and audible breaths as we reached the town limits that Señor Sánchez cut his shrewd little eyes at me to see what the deep intakes signified. I was breathing merely because I enjoyed it. There was so much splendid health to be pulled down out of this fresh, life-giving air. There was no dust in the atmosphere, for the wind from the volcano was not in this direction today. But there was music in the air, the kind of music water makes tumbling over rocks in cascades. It was the little River Cupatitzio, whose name in Tarascan means "Singing Waters." And where it flows, swirling, leaping, bubbling at the very entrance to the town, the municipality has made public gardens out of the wild, luxuriant tangle of ferns and trees and abundant tropical flowers. We left our car parked outside the narrow-streeted town, with three school-boys for watchers, and walked into the town, whose Indian name means Where Flowers Abound.

Encompassed by green mountains in every direction under the twelve-winded sky, Uruapan lies in a valley at an altitude of fifty-five hundred feet. It is one of the oldest Spanish towns in Mexico, having been founded in 1533, exactly four centuries before Franklin D. Roosevelt's first inauguration. It is a trade center for an extensive area, and its markets are full of merchandise. Tourists come for the ride, because of the charm of the semitropical scenery, or to buy lacquer ware. The earth of the district holds natural pigments in the orange, red, yellow, and bluish clay. The texture and the quality of certain native woods are especially suitable for carving wall plaques, trays, bowls. The climate and temperature are an aid. The essential oil comes from an indigenous vegetable bean called *chia*. And Providence has bestowed upon the region a lowly worm whose peculiar chemistry gives the lacquer hardness and makes it waterproof.

The Spaniards were amazed and delighted with the lacquer they found on their arrival in Mexico. The gift of design and drawing and the method of rubbing in pigments are precious inheritances that go back beyond the chronicles of time. Many believe the process was introduced by Chinese, who probably came to Mexico a thousand years before the Spaniards. Certainly the best lacquer comes from this Pacific-coast state of Michoacán, where the Chinese are said to have landed. And the technical method of preparing lacquer is very similar to that in China today.

The lacquer industry of Uruapan was strongly encouraged by Quiroga, who came on countless visits to urge the beauty of individual workmanship and to help in the marketing of the products. Though the energetic Bishop may have suggested the use of more varied colors, there was nothing he or any Spaniard could add to the native process. But from the more simple bateas and trays, the Indians were induced to use lacquer on jewel boxes, chests, and small trunks.

To give more employment to clever Indians, almost four centuries after Quiroga President Cárdenas turned over an old chapel in the heart of the city to the municipality as a co-operative where the wares might be made and marketed. But the work here is not of the assured quality found in some of the private ateliers, for prepared dyes and linseed oil are often substituted for the essential ingredients of the region.

Señor Sánchez knew where the best work was done, and so after luncheon at the hotel we set out for the place, which lay up a hilly cobbled side street beyond the plaza. Roses and carnations bloomed in the public square—pink and red and white and yellow and black. Full-blown blackish blossoms grew on the same plant with pink or yellow buds. I had never seen black roses and black carnations before. But it was the volcanic dust that had begrimed the blossoms. The green grass, too, was black in patches. Black dust was thick in gutters, and a thin layer lay upon some unswept sidewalks. The houses of faded yellow and rust color, like those of Venice, were still streaked with marks of the monster. Uruapan was too far from

Paracutín for real danger, but close enough for the drifting ashes to send the citizens to their knees to ask for divine protection. After the recent rains it seemed as if the volcano had merely breathed a deeper patina upon the mellow aspect of the town.

At a most unpretentious doorway, Señor Sánchez bade us enter a poorly lit shop, where lacquered pieces were displayed in racks. A courteous young man received us and ushered us past an old woman nodding in a rustic armchair and looking like a tribal goddess in a semitrance.

Back in the patio, under the columned piazza, three Indian women sat on low stools, working pigment into cutout designs with the tips of their fingers. About the skirts of one young enough still to bear children, two tots played on the brick pavement. The women apparently were used to being looked at while they worked, for they smiled amiably at us. One was working on a great round platter almost as broad as an automobile wheel, and black as her own hair. She was rubbing a waxy orange yellow into a luxuriant spray of orchids. The second woman was doing a plate of vermilion across which cream-colored birds flew. The third was intent on a white tray strewn with delicate blue wild flowers. Here perfection of artistry was obviously still the goal. Here workers took joy in creating little works of art, and each piece bore some manifestation of the spirit of the one who made it, whether an ancient pattern was followed or an entirely new design was created.

"The object is decorated by what is known as incrustation," Señor Sánchez was saying. (I had read about the process in Frances Toor's book *Mexican Popular Arts*.) "The background, which may be black or white or cream, is lacquered on and dried. The design is cut with a pointed instrument of fine steel. One color is rubbed in bit by bit, and allowed to dry before the next one is applied."

Watching the first woman rhythmically rubbing the tips of her fingers over a tiny area as if having tender affection for it, I thought of an American factory worker. This woman was enjoying a complete absence of tension and hurry. "It is not good for Indians to hurry," Señor Sánchez continued. "They do not express themselves well when they make haste. The Indian craftsman likes to give to each piece of work his personal touch. I think the Mexican

is much more of an individualist than the American. Mass production is antipathetical to the Mexican temperament."

Thérèse called our attention to the little girls by their mother's
side. They had got over their shyness at the strangers' appearance
and returned to their childish pursuit. They had made some mud
cakes and were rubbing into them some waste colored clays their
mother had discarded. "They begin their apprenticeship early,"
Thérèse remarked to Señor Sánchez.

"Almost from their weaning, señora."

"And here the al-fresco factory is also its own nursery school," she
said. "The children can run and play in the garden when they get
tired of lacquering mud pies."

In the showroom Hoagland asked if they had any specimens of
lacquer in which powdered gold or silver had been used, such as he
had seen at a friend's house in Puebla. The young man said they
could not get the silver and gold any more. But Thérèse bought a
magnificent batea in which the flower stems and leaves had been
worked with a green that might have been of powdered jade. The
design was of some stylized flowers that looked like the tropical
angel trumpets, and the tiny veins in the petals and leaves were as
scrupulously drawn as if intended for an illustration in an authori-
tative botanical work. There were so many tempting pieces that
after we had got three for our own house, we began seeing others
as presents for friends. And as the young man waited on us and
named the prices, we selected ten platters and trays with ease.

The old woman who owned the shop paid little attention to us,
though she had risen from her chair and stood behind a counter in
a kind of dark temperamental cloud of her own creation. Her gray-
ing hair swirled about her disharmonious face as if she did not give
a hang what her hair looked like. She was a handsome old woman
and must have been a beauty in her day. When she spoke, her husky
words were scarcely articulate. She had been drinking. Despite her
sullen befuddlement, her sultry eyes were bright, if indifferent, and
her whole manner was dominant. We were sure the neighbors paid
her great deference. Drunk or sober, she could look any man chal-
lengingly in the eye, if she had a mind to.

Her son was so much lighter in complexion than she that we
imagined his father to be a white man. He was as gentle as he was

courteous in manner, and somewhat embarrassed at his mother's inebriation. The mother did not seem to think very much of him. Perhaps he did not have enough iron in his cosmos for her taste. The old woman had seemed quite unconcerned about our purchases until I offered the son lower than the asking price for the eleventh and twelfth pieces. He appealed to her, speaking very softly. The old woman roused herself and glanced over what we had bought. When she realized that we had selected all pieces of the very first quality, she glanced at us shrewdly, as if we were more worthy of her respect. Noting her change of attitude, I attempted to win a still higher opinion. I began to bargain with her for the lot. Scowling darkly at my offers, and mumbling thickly to herself, she yet seemed to regard us as of considerably firmer fiber than she had first surmised.

At last she made a sweeping, imperious gesture, and told her son to let me have the lot at the price I suggested. Her face even lighted up to such an extent that in a less self-willed countenance the expression would have flowered into a smile. While her son rushed out to get change down the street, she began looking Wagus and Hoagland and me up and down in turn, through half-closed lids, as an Amazon might perfunctorily examine foreign sailors.

When the young man returned, his mother handed out the correct change without even seeming to deign to calculate. I pocketed it casually in an empty coat pocket without looking at it. I knew it would be right. The old woman almost smiled, and then began grumbling about all the old newspapers she would have to give up to the wrapping. Newspapers were very scarce and hard to get, she complained while her son and Señor Sánchez did the wrapping. When I began to speak admiringly of a thirteenth platter, she scowled blackly, and defiantly clutched a few sheets of newspaper to her bosom, as if she'd be damned if she would sell us anything else—unless we took it unwrapped.

The pride of Uruapan, besides lacquer ware, is the public gardens just outside the town near the place we had parked the car. They are tangles of wild beauty on different levels, with winding walks and fern-bordered steps descending to the rapids and the river. The three mannersome schoolboys who had been the car-watchers accompanied us, like apprentice guides learning to make themselves ingratiating to tourists. They pointed out the coffee trees and pungent-scented shrubs and strange trees which we had never seen before, all growing profusely among gigantic ferns. The madcap river darted this way and that, hurling itself against silver-gray boulders that looked like porpoises leaping upstream. It was fresh and lovely in the gardens of Uruapan. "A fine place," as Wagus said, glancing into the cool glades, "for love-making to the singing of the river."

V

Pátzcuaro

The only hard facts one learns to see are the facts of feeling.
They are more solid than any statistics.

—HAVELOCK ELLIS

I. THE LAKE

THE ROAD FROM Uruapan to Pátzcuaro again suggested bits of China
set in fertile highlands. There were the pagoda gateways and steep
thatched roofs. Hats like those coolie rickshaw boys wear mingled
with the more conventional Mexican sombrero. The little boys and
girls looked particularly well nourished and lively, and might easily
have been first cousins of Chinese or Japanese children. The sparkling
weather was crisp and warm at the same time—sky-blue and sun-
gold weather—and the young crops were green and fresh.

Suddenly clouds appeared out of nowhere and a soft rain began
to fall, just the right kind of rain for tender growing things. One
gets to expecting rains on summer afternoons in Mexico. Often they
are merely brief showers and cause little interruption in a program.
As we approached Pátzcuaro, the rain became a fine mist that made
a gauzy veil over the landscape. Because it was already late afternoon, we did not go into the town, but stopped at the hotel on the
lake, where we had reservations. The hostelry was appropriately
named the Vasco de Quiroga. It was new and architecturally pleasing, built to look like a spreading Spanish manor house. Part of it
was one story, part of it two, with a pleasant patio and colonnades
and inner galleries and a staircase almost as spacious and easy to
climb as that of the Virrey de Mendoza. The architect had utilized
some of the best features of the old Bishop's palace at Morelia.

Our room lay on the broad outer gallery that faced the lake. The
new flower garden and an orange grove belonging to General Cárdenas followed the slope down to the lake shore. Pátzcuaro, which
had been the summer home of Tarascan kings before the Spaniards
came, was Cárdenas's favorite spot in Mexico. Here he had built the

house to which he retired when his term of Presidency was over in December, 1940. Among his lime and orange trees he had intended to spend whatever period of private time the public would permit him. But he had had less than a year of privacy, because the Government called him back into service as Secretary of War after the attack on Pearl Harbor.

The gallery of the hotel was long and wide and edged with an interesting balustrade of wood, painted a dull henna color. We paused to gaze on the lake. There was no sunset to illumine the scene, and the mist had turned the hills into a platinum monotone. The little islands looked like coins of oxidized silver. The sky seemed to hang very low over the gray silk sheet of lake. In color the sky had a faint green tinge of absinthe dropped in water. Far off in the middle left distance, on an eminence of an island, stood a bold white monument—the figure of a robed man with uplifted arm. It was a stylized reproduction of the revolutionary priest José María Morelos. Even in the dim light of a misty afternoon it looked strangely incongruous. At the extreme left of the scene, just barely within range, rose the funereal plume of Paracutín, its billowing menace turned to mere decorative beauty.

Since we had been indulging all day in the emotions of seeing unfamiliar sights, we decided to take a brief siesta before dinner. When we got up to dress, the atmosphere had grown so chilly there seemed a touch of Scotland in the air. Thérèse wore her tweed coat for comfort and I warmed myself with a whisky and soda in the bar, where Hoagland and Wagus joined us. Wagus had some news. "We have just missed Ann Sheridan—she was here last week with many sweaters and all her 'umph.' By the way, they have reserved her table for us in the dining-room."

The table for four was set by a great open fireplace crackling with cheering logs. The dinner was served by girls in native costume. The fish was something to rave about. It was the famed *pescada blanca,* the white fish in which the lake abounds. Served with slices of green lime it is to my taste unsurpassed by that of any other fish. One could get too much of salmon and too much pompano, but there was nothing surfeiting in the flavor of *pescada blanca*. Nature had blessed the region in filling the lake's thirty-mile circumference with food fit for gods and in bestowing on it a climate pleasing to limes.

It was all so satisfying that we lingered over dinner an unconscionable time before the fire, after Señor Sánchez and all the other guests had finished and left the room. At last we tore ourselves away from the fire, and traversing the arcade about the patio, we sought shelter in the drawing-room. Here there was no fire, no fireplace, no method of heating provided. The room was well-proportioned, but most indifferently furnished.

We tried to amuse ourselves with old copies of illustrated Mexican magazines. Then we selected the exact portion of a wall that cried out for a baronial fireplace. The manager, a Spaniard of good breeding, was pleased that our choice of a fireplace site accorded precisely with his. "A little blaze is of course desirable in this climate of cool nights," he agreed. "And the proper furniture is ordered," he added, divining our criticisms. "But you know what war does to make delays." At the door he turned and said: "I think Madame should have a hot-water bottle for her bed. I'll send one up now. And tomorrow morning we shall have a fire in the dining-room for breakfast."

Thérèse, who could never bear to be a trouble to anyone, did not demur about the hot-water bottle—she merely thanked the proprietor warmly for his thoughtfulness.

Señor Sánchez appeared out of the shadows to bid us good night. "Tomorrow will be fine," he said with assurance, "for a boat trip on the lake."

"How blessed are the feet of him who bringeth good tidings—" Hoagland murmured appreciatively. And this little descendant of Aztecs had a way of seeming to bless situations.

The morning was as fine as Señor Sánchez had predicted. Sunshine poured molten gold upon the near slopes and distant hills and threw a sparkling radiance on the water of the lake. The highland air made one lift the head and breathe deep.

We breakfasted leisurely near the open fire of mountain logs. The oranges pulled from the hotel-garden trees were not quite ripe and the juice had too much tang; but the ham and eggs were ham and eggs on a brisk morning before a welcome fire.

I recalled that I had a mission to perform for a friend of mine in Memphis. "If you go to Pátzcuaro," she had written, "find a little crippled boy named Manuel Solís, who lives near the railway station. Please let him guide you about, however inexpertly. We took a great fancy to him and adopted him 'spiritually.' " I left the others lingering over a second cup of coffee. On the front veranda I sought Señor Sánchez to get him to take me into the town to find the lad. I approached some boys who were lounging on the edge of the veranda. The one in the largest hat and clean blue overalls caught my attention with his smile. He smiled like an angel, an angel surrounded by natural imps of Satan. There was no sanctimony in the smile, no silly cherubic roguishness—just a pure smile of goodwill, a wish for the other person's happiness.

"I am going out to find a boy named Manuel Solís," I said. "Could you take me to him? Do you know him?"

The other boys began to laugh gleefully. What a joke!

"*Yo soy Manuel Solís, señor,*" the one in the big hat said, his smile now lighting up his whole face. If the boy was not pure white, he had no more than a sixteenth of Indian blood. His eyes were gray, his eyebrows light-brown.

"No," I said doubtfully. The coincidence was too pat. "He lives near the railway station."

"*Sí, sí. Yo soy Manuel Solís.*" The boy slipped from the edge of the veranda and stood on the ground.

"No," I insisted, and then appealed to the other boys. "Is he?"

"*Sí, sí!*" they shouted in unison. "*Es verdad. Es Manuel Solís.*"

"I have a letter—" The boy took a step forward. His leg was sadly twisted, and the limp was marked. This was unquestionably the Manuel Solís my friend had written about. I showed him the name signed to the letter—"Jenny Gardner."

"*Sí, sí!* Señora Gardner! I have many letters from her and a picture of her *casa,* with snow."

I invited Manuel Solís to be an assistant guide to Señor Sánchez. When Thérèse and the men came out I introduced him.

"He looks like an angel in overalls," Thérèse said promptly as he took off his enormous straw hat. His hair was brown and fine in texture and it had been combed.

"He is the friend of Señora Gardner in Memphis," I said. "His mother is a widow and lives near the railway station and takes in washing. His father was a rural schoolteacher and was murdered by

Indians in the mountains of Guerrero." I knew all this from the letter.

One of the inquisitive boys began searching in a tattered Spanish-English pocket dictionary for a word.

Manuel Solís smiled apologetically, and said in Spanish, "If I had one of those books I could learn English more quickly."

Dr. Hoagland was struck with a sudden thought and excused himself. In a flash he was back with a little red book in his hand—a present for Manuel Solís.

The boy's face brightened, and he held the book in his two hands for a moment in ecstatic half-belief. As he moved into a shaft of intense sunlight, his yellowish straw hat was like an oversized halo in a stained-glass window. An expression of deep thoughtfulness came over his face as he debated on the first Spanish word he would look up to learn its English equivalent. Wagus and I stood on either side of him, and watched him turn the thin pages to the B's. His finger went down a page and up the other page and stopped. He impressed the word on his mind, murmured it to himself, holding his right forefinger there, while a black-eyed urchin crowded close, took a look, nodded his head, and sniggered. Wagus and I bent to see and noted the line which had arrested the moving finger. Then Wagus gently took the book from Manuel Solís's hand. He stared in surprise, grinned, and held the page to my eye, his fingernail marking the place.

"Is *this* the word you wanted?" he asked Manuel Solís.

"*Sí,*" said the boy quite naturally.

The Spanish word was *burdel*. After the comma came the English "brothel."

Of all the thousands of words to interest him, why did the child want to know "brothel"? Just above it lay *buqueteatro,* which means "showboat," something gay and romantic. And above that *buque,* just ordinary "boat," the most significant word on the lake after "fish." And above that was *bunuelo,* "bun, pancake, fritter," a thing most natural to interest a growing boy. But *burdel* was the word of words he chose.

"Do you know what it means?" Wagus asked.

"*Sí,*" Manuel Solís said again most naturally. "There is one not far from where I live. I have taken tourists there."

So, it was doubtless professional, not personal, interest that had led him to the word. As a good guide, the twelve-year-old had to know what men wanted to see in his town by night as well as by day.

Whatever the reason for his interest in the brothel, whether he himself went no farther than a commanding knock on the portal or whether he went inside and even sipped beer to beguile the time of waiting for his client, one thing seemed certain—the lad was untouched by whatever he had seen or known. For him there was nothing in the word "brothel" to fear or shy away from. Whatever happened in life—going to confession or visiting a brothel, going to school or flying a kite, the ripening of corn or the outbreak of a volcano—all were merely manifestations of human destiny. And everything was to be taken with good heart: his father's murder, his own ill-set broken leg.

Here was a lad who was not a pipe for fortune's finger to play jigs and dirges upon at will. He responded to life as a whole, and by some strange dispensation he seemed to divine that only attitude of mind made things good or bad, and so he chose to make things good. And I could conceive of his going completely through life's cycle impervious in spirit to buffets and vicissitudes, and making his smiling passage a momentary benediction as he limped past.

Manuel Solís, holding his dictionary tenderly, sat in the front seat of the car with Señor Sánchez and me, and on the way to the boat landing I gave him a brief lesson in English. He reciprocated by giving me one in politeness.

"Whenever anyone gives you something, as *el Señor* Doctor Hoagland gave you *el diccionario,* you must say, "Thank you very much."

Manuel Solís thanked me for the advice. "And, señor," he said politely after a pause, as if teaching me manners for teaching him manners, "when one gives you anything and he thanks you, you should say, *"De nada"*—"It is nothing.""

We arrived at the cluster of rude piers, where large rowboats and small motorboats lay moored awaiting custom. Several of the boatmen stood up and called out ingratiatingly. Two started forward to press us with invitation. And then I saw behind them all the one I wanted. He sat in his outboard motor boat regarding us quietly. In the strong sunlight his Indian face was like a high-lighted bronze mask. It was a sturdy, dignified, and melancholy face. Somehow, strangely I knew this fellow. He turned his head to the side and I was without doubt. There was no mistaking that profile, the sculptural cut of that nose and chin. But he had grown younger. This fellow was hardly twenty. I caught his eye, and his expression did not change. He did not seek to be chosen, but he would like to be, if it required no demonstrable effort on his part.

"There's the fellow," I said to Señor Sánchez, "in the back. I know him. He's an old friend."

Señor Sánchez looked at me uncertainly. "Señor?" he questioned.

"That very fellow is in my studio in the woods at home. He has a net in his hand, a stout pole over his shoulder. He is going fishing with a brother. Lake Pátzcuaro is behind the pair, just like this." I indicated the expanse of water, and appealed to Thérèse. She confirmed my claim.

"Why, of course," she said, "he might easily have been the model —the same profile, the same expression, the same shoulders."

"It's the best poster the National Railways ever got out," I said.

Señor Sánchez smiled and nodded to the fellow. Deftly the youth manipulated the boat up to the pier. His shoulders were as good as the man's in the poster. Señor Sánchez asked the price of the boat. "Give him whatever he asks," I said. The price seemed more than moderate.

"*Como se llama Usted?*" I asked.

"Preciliano, señor." He did not add, "*a sus ordenes,*" but said simply, "Preciliano, señor." His voice was low and melodious.

"Did anyone ever paint your picture—or make a drawing of you?"

He shook his head negatively and smiled slowly. "No, señor." Then he said in Spanish, "But one day an artist from Mexico City painted my two cousins."

"Are they fishermen?"

"Sometimes they fish."

"Surely," I said to Thérèse and the others, "they are the ones in the poster. At any rate I know now they are authentic Tarascan and not a studio creation."

Gravely Preciliano steadied the boat as we got in, and gravely he started the motor.

Manuel Solís sat close to Preciliano, intently remarking the process of starting. He might have been any little sunburned American boy off for a picnic in a great straw hat.

The motor behaved creditably, and we were ready to venture anywhere within the thirty-mile circumference. We let Señor Sánchez and Preciliano make the suggestions and then I consulted Manuel Solís.

As we adjusted ourselves comfortably to the board seats, we gave ourselves over to the worship of the Sunday morning. Because it was Sunday there was no activity of fishing boats. As far as we could see, the area of aquamarine was our domain. The sky was an azure tent pegged down beyond the encircling mountains. Again we noted that remarkable clarity in the atmosphere that made the sharply etched hills look like designs cut out and pasted on a vibrant light-blue background. Where the land was fertile between the rocks, lime and lemon trees held their orderly stations right down to the phalanxes of spearlike water reeds.

A fish passed close to our boat, slicing the green-blue surface with the silver blade of a fin, and then it dived among the roots of some exotic water orchids. The whirling blades of motor churned the water to make a gold-flecked trail behind us, luminous and transitory, like a comet's tail. The sun began to warm us through and through. Thérèse took off her coat and Preciliano his jacket. There was no sound whatever except that of the humble motor propelling us over the glassy surface and making it possible for Preciliano to rest his rowing arms. No one desired to talk. It was all tranquil and exciting. Even the two or three new villas set in orchards on the slopes of the receding mainland looked peaceful and unobtrusive, despite the indifferent taste in architectural style.

The sea-loving Joseph Conrad once said that only a thousand miles from land could one come in contact with his own soul. But here no more than one mile from land there was a strange exhilaration of escape, as if one had shaken off the problems of this earthly world at the pier. Gliding over this flat, jewel-bright floor, set so high in Mexico's geography, one could feel a delicious sense of peace. Looking up, Dr. Hoagland broke the silence by observing, "And what a fine place the middle of this lake might be for writing down the language of the stars."

The three Mexicans, in monosyllabic conference, made a new decision, and we turned again toward the mainland to follow the shore. Occasionally we passed fishermen's huts, with great seines spread out to dry and looking like gigantic silver spider webs spun over the dark-gray rocks. We plowed through a congregation of slender aquatic plants that resembled the ghostly Indian pipes of Maine, but they might have been translucent periscopes from a thousand Lilliputian submarines hiding in the coves. One lone fisherman was fishing from a canoe, dug out at some former time with infinite patience from a massive log. "Evidently, unexpected guests for Sunday dinner have turned up," Señor Sánchez said, "and he must piece out the meal."

We rounded a rocky peninsula that looked like a group of seals piled on each other to sun themselves. We drew up in a cove, and disembarked at a little settlement with a population of seventeen souls. Despite his limp, Manuel Solís led the way up a zigzag path between rock walls and organ cacti. As we climbed we became aware that we were accompanied by a silent reception committee of three diminutive female figures in long dresses that reached to the ground. They looked like an unfamiliar race of pygmies, but though they were pot-bellied, they were rather pretty, with plump cheeks and orange-brown complexions. The girls were in stair-step ages, and they held up the front of their bright cotton skirts like ladies as they scrambled up the path.

At the top of the hill stood a little stone church, ancient and dilapidated, where services were held three or four times a year. Through frames of fantastic slabs of cactus, joined together like linked crabs and forming an auxiliary fence about the diminutive churchyard, we could catch vistas of the lake. From the height of this cacti-studded balcony, the water was more mauve than aquamarine, and it seemed to be lighted from within its own depths rather than from the high sun above.

When I turned from one framed view to another, I noticed Preciliano seated in meditation on the jagged rock wall, with thrusting arms of cacti making a kind of arch above him. "Wait," I said, and got out my Leica. If I had been taking time exposures instead of snapshots, I believe he could have sat motionless for an hour. He was a perfect model. He posed with his hat on, with it off, looking

down, looking up. Whichever way he sat or looked, whether grave
or half-smiling, there were evidenced those deeply ingrained qualities of dignity and inherent melancholy. His features and his figure
mutely invited not a photographer, but a sculptor who fashioned
men out of marble or bronze.

Preciliano was pure Indian, full-blooded Tarascan. These Tarascans traced their historical inheritance back to eighteen kings who
had ruled before Caltzontzin. Long before the Spaniards came they
had been a sedentary people who planted and fished. The repose
and strength and philosophy of his tribal ancestors were there in
the brow and the mouth and the jaw of the boy, but more especially
in the imponderable spirit that emanated from him.

Preciliano had never left his native state. He had been no farther
from Pátzcuaro than Morelia. His education had been only primary, and that most sketchy. Did he have ambition? It was hard
to judge. Would he always be a boatman? Well, if he ended his
days here on the shores of this lake, knowing the world only from
a single window, there were ten thousand worse fates that might
befall a man. Here life was rooted and concentrated. Living was
as cheap as it was simple. Corn and fruits grew plentifully, and
the lake, like the widow's cruse, held abundance of fine-flavored
fish. By night or day there was beauty to be had for the trouble
of remarking it. Instead of going out into the hot struggles of the
world's affairs, one could stay here cool and serene, and let odds
and ends of the world come to Pátzcuaro.

I turned from the Indian to take some snaps of Manuel Solís.
With him, it was not the same. He did not so completely belong to
the lake region. When he grew up, he could, if he chose, find a
welcoming niche in Mexico City. If chance should set him in New
York or Paris or Buenos Aires, he might feel quite at home in no
time. But all the stuff that blew together to make the Tarascan
Preciliano came out of this clear water, these abiding rocks, this
fertile soil, these mountain trees, and the drifting dust of extinct
volcanoes aeons old.

At a cry of delight from Manuel Solís, I looked up to see a
white heron pass over the little church tower and become for one
instant a living weathervane against the sky's blue. Then as we
started to return to the boat, the little girls, who had remained like

mute supernumeraries in a play, shyly presented Thérèse with wild
flowers they had plucked from among the rocks. Gathering up
their ground-length skirts, they swiftly picked their way down the
rough path in front of us, as if to herald our approach.

When the children turned at a side path to the right, we followed.
There through the trees and thick shrubs was an open space before a hut. Some women, dressed in precisely the same style as the
little girls, were boiling a savory mess in a pot. Drying fish nets
spread on the bushes looked like snares with cowering greenish
animals caught and awaiting the cooking. The women were as
plump and well nourished as the children, and not at all unfriendly
at our intrusion. When we gave the little girls coins for candies,
Manuel Solís tried to make them say, "Thank you very much," in
English. But they only clamped their lips together and made a giggling sound. I said, *"De nada,"* very politely, and Manuel Solís was
pleased. At Preciliano's request, the women began to demonstrate
the intricate process of rigging up a *mariposa* net. Suddenly, looking beyond me to the lake, Manuel Solís shouted gleefully, *"Mariposa! Mariposa!"*

Around a bend came a dugout canoe with gauzy white wings
extending some eight or nine feet on either side of the edges. But
the wings were not sails to catch the wind, they were nets to catch
fish. The outfit in motion looked like some incredible and marvelous
new creature akin to the moth family. These butterfly nets are
peculiar to Lake Pátzcuaro, and one of its most picturesque features. But they are rapidly falling into disuse as more modern methods of fishing are being adopted. The nets are sewed onto bent
pliable, bamboolike frames, which are gathered in at the middle,
something like an inflated pair of water wings, and curved upward
in a graceful concave. As the net is dipped first to left and then
to right, the fish are scooped up in the shallow bowls.

We watched the dugout with the spread butterfly wings glide by
like a dream boat, all grace and glittering transparency, making
music of motion. With what poetic tools could a man ply a mundane trade if art was rooted in his being! Though I had never heard
of *mariposa* nets being used in China and Japan, they were just the
sort of thing to adorn an idealized Oriental landscape.

As we crossed the lake headed for the Island of Janitzio, hovering clouds dropped purplish shadows like rugs on the smooth parquet. Except for one lone little boat with a man and a woman rowing arduously, we again had the lake for a private pleasure ground. The couple's craft was piled so high with chairs, *petates*, utensils that it looked as if they were moving all their household goods. Preciliano said they must be moving, and Manuel Solís added the word *"Indubitablemente."*

"What long words children use in Mexico!" I said to Señor Sánchez. "No American boy of eleven would use 'indubitably,' and in Spanish it is even longer."

"Yes, señor. Mexican children seem to take to big words quite naturally. My own kids often surprise me. Only the other evening in Chapultepec Park, one of my little girls got lost and when we found her she said—in Spanish, of course—'Papa, I was completely disorientated.'"

We nodded and smiled at the couple who were taking their goods from one island to another. They smiled back and pulled even more vigorously at the oars. Their faces were strained and wet with the sweat of exertion.

"Aren't you grateful for the outboard motor, Preciliano?" I said.

He raised his eyes and smiled a slow smile. "It is a gift direct from Heaven, señor."

2. ISLAND OF "JANITZIO"

The island of Janitzio basked like a contented cat in the June perfection of highland weather. Though the inhabitants existed by the grace of fish, the island was oddly named "Cornsilk," which in Tarascan is *janitzio* or *xanicho*. In close-packed moorings near the rocks the fishing boats idled. But in their Sunday leisure they maintained their pungent aroma. The pendent seines, too, gave off the scent of their trade as the sun sucked out their moisture. But the smell was memory-stirring, not repulsive. The harbor smelt faintly like a certain wind-swept fishing village in Brittany.

As stone houses climbed the steep hillside, they made patches of henna and beige against the gray of rock and the vital green of fertile pockets. Cobblestoned streets wound up to a village church. In a high cemetery surrounding the church lay the simple graves of the island dead, with a view fit for entombed gods. Still higher, crowning the volcano-shaped island, stood the colossal statue of the Michoacán's most famous son. Morelos's mortal remains lay in Mexico City, but to honor him in his native state, President Cárdenas had commissioned this statue to be constructed by a revolutionary sculptor. What the artist had done was to put the ruthlessness of the Soviet into the gesture of the patriot-priest. There towered the thick Morelos, his head wrapped in a kerchief, his right fist raised—not in Christly benediction, but in Soviet defiance at opposition. This was a man of vengeance, not Morelos the compassionate reformer. The presence of the great dough-colored monstrosity made a crashing discord in the ineffable harmony of Pátzcuaro. It was General Cárdenas's good intention gone wrong.

From the water level of the harbor, Janitzio was like some fantastic opera house viewed from the musicians' pit. Picturesque tiers of boxes and balconies and galleries rose above one another in distorted, haphazard arrangement. And flung out over railings were trailing geraniums and fish nets like tarnished gilt.

We disembarked, and paused in the vine-embowered loggia of a café-shop where souvenirs and handmade garments were sold. Five of us had cold beer. Preciliano preferred his unchilled and took his bottle away to join some fellow boatmen near the landing stage. Manuel Solís took Coca-Cola. When Thérèse selected some useful aprons embroidered in Tarascan designs, Manuel Solís settled on the price with the kindly shopwoman. It was like a limping angel pretending to haggle with a sweet-faced nun.

To prevent Manuel Solís from attempting the climb, we suggested that he and Preciliano order lunch here and eat while we make the ascent.

As we began the climb through the twisting streets, it was a tour through a town of make-believe—an island enchanted like that one in *The Tempest,* though much more densely populated. Señor Sánchez was our guiding Prospero. The main street was so narrow that two donkey carts could scarcely have passed each other without locking wheels. Neighbors across the street from each other seemed hardly more than a serape's length apart. All the house doors were open, and the people were as little private as bees in glass hives.

Just within a doorway a demure girl, kneeling over a brazier as if at some devotional rite, was hand-clapping tortillas, the silver bangles on her slender wrists making a tinkling musical accompaniment. In another house a baby was being swung to sleep in a hammock, its mother singing a lullaby in Tarascan. In yet another, an entire family sat in the semigloom listening to a youth plucking the heart out of a guitar.

At a twist in the road, a small triangle of space had been turned into a leafy grape arbor. Under its dappled shade, before the door of their cottage, a barefooted man lay relaxed on the stones, his dark head in his wife's red-skirted lap. She was combing his coal-black hair. At another small open space where the street turned again, two boys were painting a small boat green. And where the street made a bend in a different direction, a group of young chaps, dressed for Sunday with wide straw hats, were standing about a great net hanging from a house on a higher level, and mending and reinforcing the edges.

As we moved upward among kaleidoscopic visions of daily life, four tots scrambled down a precipitous side street and barred our way, offering to sing songs in Tarascan. The two little girls looked to be about six years old, the boys about four or five. They all had chubby cheeks and bright black eyes. We put them off gently, and they were not persistent, though they bided their time, and followed us discreetly at a distance.

The climb grew steeper, until at last we were entirely above the house roofs. Stone benches had been set at intervals to rest leg muscles and to ease pumping hearts or merely to provide a belvedere for the prospect. When the children looked up and saw we had paused, they made a fresh assault, leaping up the steps like young goats and arriving so out of breath that they could hardly articulate their repeated offers of serenade. At last we consented to be sung to while we rested. The children grouped themselves for the choral with grave expressions. Though the smaller boy was still so out of breath that he could make only a kind of windy wail through the first lines, the others attacked the song with vigor. But they too did a little gasping before they finished the first stanza.

Over the hillside, between lake and sky, the Tarascan tongue rang out in shrill childish piping. The children's expressions were so inflexible and unemotional that we could not tell what the song was about—whether it was a tale of high adventure or a nursery rhyme. Preciliano, who knew Tarascan, had remained below, and Señor Sánchez professed no knowledge whatever of Indian dialects. When the children were through, they broke off abruptly and their faces became more expressionless than ever. The song seemed to have no thought-out ending, no conclusion. The singers simply stopped dead short, as if someone had lifted the lever of a phonograph while a record was being played. We asked for another song. But their repertory of pure Tarascan seemed exhausted with the first one, for in the second, phrases in Spanish about a horse and a moon crept in. The two boys could not carry a tune or remember the words, and the girls had to sing loudly to drown out the male dissonance. At the end of the second song they stood like images awaiting a mechanical signal. When we dropped ten centavo pieces into the little hands, they turned abruptly and scampered down the path in pairs.

At the last resting-stage, perched like an eagle's nest on a jutting rock, we paused for another look at the view. From this height the lake had become like a piece of lacquer ware in mauve and grayish jade.

"Here where the people live daily life in such a refinement of beauty," Thérèse remarked, "it is no wonder that primitive mysticism is ingrained in some of them."

As we made the last lap to the island's crown I thought of the first book printed in the Western Heimsphere. It was called in Spanish *"Escala spiritual para llegar al cielo,"* and in the original Latin, *"Scala paradisi."* It was printed by Juan Pablos on the press Charles V had sent to Mexico in 1535. It seemed a strange choice for the first book to be printed in the New World. It was a treatise on ascetic mysticism written in the fifth century by a Greek monk named John Climacus, who was abbot of the monasteries on Mount Sinai. Another John had translated it into Spanish, a Dominican monk named Juan de la Magdalena. But the narrow spiritual steps to Heaven had not been to the taste of the lusty breed of sixteenth-century Spaniards. They had not crossed the ocean to learn to negotiate the way to Heaven by rules of self-abnegation.

We had come to the top of Janitzio. Where one might have expected a miniature crater, there was a grassy flat on which rested the great granite base of Morelos's monument. A door opened into the hem of his concrete robe. We entered the illuminated hollow body. Iron stairs wound like some weird anatomical ribbing from the floor to the dizzying top. The inner walls were splashed with colors as vivid as the insides of a slaughtered steer. Like the Stations of the Cross, the life of Morelos was depicted in spiraling murals, beginning at his impromptu birth behind a stranger's door, and rising to his apotheosis somewhere in the vast dimness high above.

Faintly we could see two figures moving about near the top like microbes, but making a reverberating clatter on the iron treads with their heavy shoes.

"Here schoolchildren come for lessons in history," Señor Sánchez said, indicating the dramatic pictures on the walls. None of us had a desire for further climbing. We knew this period of Mexican history rather well. We were all admirers of Morelos, but we resented the sculptor's distortion of the man's ideals, even though there was no offense in the painter's murals.

Outside I patted a stone of the great base. "No," I said, "it's too solid. I doubt if an earthquake could do it. But perhaps with all that ironwork inside, lightning might do the blessed job some day."

At the edge of the café-shop Preciliano stood waiting, like a statue carved from cedarwood. He smiled a welcoming smile without showing his teeth or breaking the sculptural outlines of his lips, but Manuel Solís's lips were wreathed in a smile as he rose from the luncheon table.

Out on the sparkling lake again, I thought of a remark the young Darwin had made in Chile, with a strong exclamation point. "What a difference climate can make in the enjoyment of life!" And here in this high altitude, where the air was fresh and invigorating, the sun full of tender warmth, this sample of the thing called climate was as perfect as one could conceive. The only word for it all was "delightful." But not in the sense of a "chaos of delight," as Darwin had used it, but more like the distillation of delight. The islands, the silhouettes of mountains, the clear azure sky, the plane of green-blue water, were not islands, mountains, sky, water, but more the spiritual embodiment of these things. It was easy to look in any direction and say that Deity is here, there, everywhere. "Days like this," as Darwin said, "almost repaid one for the trouble of living."

And as we drew near to the shore of the mainland again, the good earth smell of a fresh-plowed field mingled with scent of lime and orange blossoms, and I knew that for me Lake Pátzcuaro held an attraction that was unsurpassed in Mexico.

3. WORKERS IN THE VINEYARD

A down-at-heel outboard motor boat was just pulling away from the landing-stage. A white man at the control smiled and waved in a surprised but familiar way. It seemed he and Señor Sánchez were acquainted. He pointed to the piled boxes in the boat with satisfaction. "The books are here!" His voice rang out with a kind of joyous satisfaction.

"Good luck," answered Señor Sánchez.

The man waved again and we all waved back. Books? A boatload of books? I wondered.

"Books?" I said aloud in question.

"The Gospel of Saint John in Tarascan." We all looked interested. Señor Sánchez went on to explain. "He is a good man. His name is Mr. Maxwell Lathrop. He and his wife are missionaries. They live in a primitive village at the other end of the lake. They have learned Tarascan, and Mr. Lathrop wrote a Tarascan primer. Now he has translated the Book of Saint John into Tarascan. I was in Pátzcuaro with some tourists the day he sent the manuscript to Mexico City to be printed. My clients were from his home town in the States, and they were much surprised to find him here. They tried to joke him about his missionary work. But he was too happy about his translation to mind."

I thought of calling out to stop him. But it was dinnertime and we were hungry. I knew he must be one of the "Wycliff translators," as they called themselves. I had met their leader, Cameron Townsend, in the capital, and knew of the good work they were doing. These American missionaries were learning the Indian dialects and translating sections of the New Testament and teaching the natives to read it. Four centuries after Bishop Quiroga, missionaries were still coming to Michoacán. These new ones, who called themselves after the man who first translated the Bible into English, came in the humblest fashion and set up their abode in only the most primitive places and endured incredible hardships to spread the doctrine of love and salvation. General Cárdenas had given their work his blessing after he had made a thorough examination of it, and he had often tried to make their burdens easier when he could.

"How long has Lathrop been living here?" I asked Señor Sánchez.

Señor Sánchez relayed the question to Preciliano. "About six years, I think."

He and his wife and two small children had been living these years among the natives in a remote lake village, ministering to them, curing Indian baby sores with sulphur ointment, teaching men to read both Spanish and Tarascan, and preaching the Gospel to them. They had had a most difficult time at first, for the Indians were suspicious and the Catholic priests from Pátzcuaro not inclined to be friendly. One young fellow had threatened the lives of the missionaries. But he was made a friend when Mr. Lathrop came to his rescue after he had been gored by an ox, and nursed him back to life.

Señor Sánchez said that one old Indian had been uncommonly receptive to the Lathrops' teaching. He had become like a saint in kindness, and had visions. And one day last Christmas he announced to his family that it was to be his last day in this earthly world. He was so radiant that the people said it was like a light shining directly on him. His family tried to joke when he dressed himself in his fiesta clothes, pink blouse and white trousers, and wide blue sash.

All afternoon he sat in front of his hut and admonished the villagers "to take the road of God" while they lived, so that they would go to Heaven, as he was going before another morning dawned. He shook hands good-bye with each visitor; but he looked so healthy they said, no, he would not die. When they were all gone, he sat down to his customary evening meal of tortillas. When he had finished, he told his wife, "Now I am going to Heaven to

be with *El Señor Jesucristo,* just as it was told me in my dream."
He lay down on his mat in the corner in his fiesta clothes and
went to sleep. In the morning they found him smiling and dead.

And now Missionary Lathrop was off with a boatload of copies
of the Gospel of Saint John in Tarascan to distribute among the
primitive folk so that they themselves could read of *El Señor* in
their native tongue. Well, surely there could be no harm in that.
And at least the Indians, who are most intuitive in sensing real
goodness of heart, might come to believe in the brotherly love of
some *norteamericanos.* For obviously these missionaries endured
privations for no other reward than the imponderable blessing of
Heaven and the satisfaction of making poor people's lives a little
brighter. I began to think of it the other way around. "If the white
man can go and live happily among Indians in the backwoods,
why could not an Indian come and endure life in the United
States—for at least a year?" I said, as if thinking aloud.

And Thérèse, remembering our country place in Alabama, where
we had such need of strong arms like those of Preciliano, looked
toward the lemon groves and then at the boatman. She began thinking out loud herself. "Do you suppose Preciliano would come to
the States to help us on our place—for a year?"

"Do you think he would like it, and could be happy with us?"
I said to Señor Sánchez.

We had left the States not only without gardener, but without a
cook—so we thought of Preciliano as being able to help at everything. He might even learn to cook. The Chinese made excellent
cooks. Perhaps the Mexicans— And we liked beans, and I raised
an abundance of them—we could eat beans cooked the Mexican
way.

"Señor Sánchez," Thérèse said, "do you think Preciliano could
learn to cook?" She had come to trust his judgment implicitly.

Señor Sánchez cast one steady look at Preciliano, who was intent on making a smooth landing at the pier. Then he turned back
to Thérèse, and said with gentle finality, "No, madam." And we
knew that Preciliano could never learn to cook.

"Perhaps he knows only boats and fishing," I put in dubiously.
"Perhaps he would have no aptitude for digging in the earth,
either."

"But," Thérèse persisted, "he could learn to take care of a garden, couldn't he?"

"Yes, madam," said Señor Sánchez promptly, "he could learn to do that." And we knew Preciliano could learn to be a gardener.

"Do you know anything about gardening, Preciliano?" I put the question directly.

He hesitated. "I handle boats—but I have cousins who tend gardens and others who are farmers."

"Do you think you could learn to plant and cultivate?"

He made the *quien-sabe?* gesture of his people. "I am strong. I can dig a ditch well. I like flowers."

I explained the idea that had come simultaneously to us. "If I can get you a passport into the United States, would you consider coming back with the Señora and me? To help us on our place, to work the vegetables and do the chores? You would have a little house to yourself. My wife and I would teach you English. You would promise to stay one year. After that, you would choose to do what you pleased."

To our surprise, Preciliano's face brightened at the prospect of an adventure in *Los Estados Unidos*. "Yes, I would come, if you could get me there."

For one joyous moment we began to see our labor problem settled: the garden planted, the little orchard tended, and all the odd jobs and chores, which I had so little time for, done. The advantages would be mutual—we hoped—and we would teach Preciliano to speak English.

Though at first thought we were fired with the possibility of having so steadfast a worker as Preciliano gave promise of being, on second thought we were aware of the difficulties and problems of his adjustment to such a different way of life. Whom would he play with? What would his amusement be, besides the moving pictures? Would he gain, or would he lose? Here he was a most perfect embodiment of his environment. He belonged in this landscape and graced it with such a peculiar rightness.

As we stood on the shore, I explained carefully, while other boatmen gathered about as if to offer counsel, that I was not rich, not a businessman or a mine-owner, but merely a college professor, with a nice house and a garden and an orchard and twenty acres of woods. He would not expect high wages, but he would get a trip to *Los Estados Unidos* and learn English and be able to command a better salary when he returned to Mexico. He would have his own two-roomed cottage with a veranda and climbing roses and a private shower bath just for himself, and he would learn to drive my car.

The boatmen began to murmur appreciatively—*"Baño privato"* . . . *"casa privata"* . . . *"flores"* . . . *"automóvil."*

There was no doubt about it—any of the others looked as if he would jump at the chance. If there had been no international red tape about entering the country, and if we had been driving right back to the States now in our car, I believe Preciliano would have come immediately.

As we settled for the boat trip, Preciliano stood there in a kind of unbelief, his smooth lips clamped in a wondering smile.

What we had said only half-seriously had been taken seemingly at full value. Then the thought of getting him into the country and the responsibility of keeping his Indian temperament content for a year almost seemed to overweigh the luxury of a hired man. "Let fate decide the issue as it will," I said to Thérèse. "If it is right for him and for us, it will come about. And if it isn't, it won't."

Whatever was to come of the idea, the offer and the thought that we had chosen him of all other Mexicans seemed to give Preciliano an unwonted pleasure. And because we had made him like himself better, he liked us.

Preciliano promised to think the matter over carefully that evening and to come for a talk with us at the hotel in the morning.

4. THE JAIL VERANDA AND THE NUN

The town of Pátzcuaro lies on the low foothills less than a mile from the lake's margin. It is ancient, shabby, picturesque, and more interesting than any town in the United States between Richmond and San Francisco. The breath of history rises from the façades, the portals, the numerous antique fountains. Pátzcuaro was the summer seat of Tarascan kings when the conquistadors arrived.

Founded by Quiroga as a Spanish town four centuries ago, it is a sleepy place of some nine thousand souls. Because of the uneven

nature of the terrain it seems casually laid out, with churches
terminating cobbled ·streets that amble toward the hills. The two
larger plazas are only a block apart. Many of the one-story houses
have projecting roofs supported by carved beams, so that one may
promenade under a kind of half-shelter. On the Plaza Grande the
portals and the thick masonry columns of the arcades make evocative and shifting patterns with the sun's collaboration. Here and
there remain a few seignorial mansions with lush green patios. At
398 Allende Street still stands the building that was the residence
of Pátzcuaro's first governor, who was himself a son of the last
Tarascan king. In the place where the Counts of Menocal lived
stands an odd and massive statue known as El Gigante. On a prominent corner is the building that was known as the College of San
Nicolás, which Quiroga created in 1540. Now it has become a Museum of Popular Arts. At the top of Calle Portugal in the little
church of La Compañía de Jesús, the venerable ashes of the Bishop
repose in an urn locked within a modern steel safe.

Pátzcuaro invites strolling, and we gave the afternoon over to
it, poking into this or that as fancy directed. Despite the ambu-
lating Sunday citizens, there was a strange atmosphere, as if the
inhabitants had once fled because of some calamity of natural forces,
and that on their return they had not quite readjusted themselves, or
finished cleaning up their town. The great expanse of the main
plaza with the ancient beech and ash trees looked untended.

On one side of the plaza, where Indians from the mountain and
lake villages spread their wares on Fridays, there were series of impromptu outdoor eating-places, where spicy concoctions were cooking under the sun in a variety of primitive and modern arrangements. Across the plaza under the arcades were spread the wares
of the permanent merchants, a mass of imported glass and native
pottery, great piles of hammered copper vessels, cutlery, fishing
gear, serapes, huaraches, flattish Chinese-looking hats, and hand-
carved chocolate-frothers the color of nutmeg. One establishment
sold high-class leather goods and handsome saddles. This leather
shop was owned by a Spaniard, whose face was the only local white
one to be seen for blocks.

We made the circuit of the rectangular Plaza Grande, and as we
completed it we came again upon the most attractive girl we had

seen in Mexico. She was a mestiza of fourteen or fifteen, who was taking the air with a male relative, perhaps her father, perhaps an uncle. They were sitting on one of the benches. He was eating a *taco* and leaning over so that the juice did not spill on him. The girl held a cup of hot chocolate in her hand, but was not drinking. We had passed her before and we were curious to see if she was as luminous as Thérèse and I thought when we first saw her. She saw us coming and looked pleased, because she knew she was admired. Her relative did not seem conscious of our interest.

Sitting still, alert, on the bench, she gave a kind of radiance to the afternoon. Her eyes were large and sparkling, a glowing greenish-gray in color. Her red unrouged lips were parted in a half-smile. Her olive complexion was as smooth as unblemished ivory. Her brown hair was wrapped in discreet, well-disciplined braids around her shapely head. She was not dressed in the red-and-black wool skirts and embroidered blouses of the Indian women. Her dress was of soft green stuff made after a simple pattern from a modern fashion magazine.

As we passed, the whole figure was intensely alive, like a bird poised for flight. There was something innately dramatic in the way she sat and moved her head. She looked us directly in the eye, and in that moment she seemed to see in us the possible agents of her escape into the life she needed and to which she belonged. Her eyes said so clearly that she was ready for other sights. She was as obviously not the natural product of her environment as Preciliano was so absolutely the product of his. If the girl had sprung up and said, "May I go with you strangers into another sphere?" I would not have been surprised. But after that one direct and revealing look, she smiled and turned away and stared into the grassy park and the veiled future. Her chaperon munched on his sandwich and paid us no heed. When we had passed, Wagus said, "With the breaks, there might sit the future Ann Sheridan of Mexico."

Perhaps. Certainly she had the beauty, the figure, the inner fire. Did she have nerve enough to make her way, if she escaped? Did she have any education? But the great Rachel had no education; she was a street gamin selling fried potatoes for a living before she became an actress. And this girl was cared for and wore shoes. She was no barefooted waif like the Pericholi of Lima, who rose to be the viceroy's favorite and South America's most glamorous stage star.

We passed on wondering. We would never know the name of the possessor of the prettiest face in Mexico. But we would always remember the effulgent beauty, which would most likely remain fresh and unspoiled in a metropolitan atmosphere with all the appurtenances of modern luxury.

At the corner we turned for a last look. The girl returned it with a flashing radiance. Then she bent to drink her chocolate.

"Oh well," I said aloud, "her prison is a goodly enough one. To be incarcerated in provincial Pátzcuaro carries blessings. And she will doubtless escape when time is as ripe as she is."

At the mention of the word "prison," Señor Sánchez pointed to the upper gallery of a corner building whose walls were calcimined bright-blue. There men in shirt sleeves were taking their ease, some playing checkers, some drinking cold drinks, some leaning over the balustrade and chatting with friends standing in the street below. Except that the men were poorly dressed and some of them unshaven, the atmosphere of the scene recalled the upper veranda of the old Royal Yacht Club in Bermuda. But this, Señor Sánchez insisted, was the jail. What a pleasant place in which to serve one's penal term, here on the Plaza Grande with the prime view of town life and the illusion of utter freedom! For with no hindering bars whatever, one could step over the balustrade, lock his legs about a rounded wooden pillar, and slide to liberty like a fireman answering to a night alarm.

"Look!" said Wagus. "What kind of monkey business goes on?"

A man with bristling black mustachios was drawing a small basket up very carefully by a thick twine. The rebozo-draped woman below was sending something up to him. A love letter? A file? A rose? A revolver? It might have been anything. But it turned out to be nothing more lethal or sentimental than a mug of hot chocolate bought at a near-by booth.

"What's to prevent a fellow from sliding down a post at night, making love to his girl under the beech trees, and then climbing back up to prison?" Wagus wanted to know.

Señor Sánchez smiled. "Probably nothing, though such a practice would be frowned on. And the man serving time would have to be back at dawn in any case to begin the work of cleaning the streets. Prisoners here are the street-cleaners. When there is a dearth of prisoners, the policemen rout up some derelicts, who are promptly sentenced to clean the street—unless, of course, they have a few spare pesos to buy off the law."

From the clubby jail we wandered circuitously along the cobble-stoned streets and then uphill until we came to what was to have been the great cathedral of Michoacán. Quiroga had conceived it on grandiose lines, and Pope Julian III had given his sanction for its erection in 1550. The site the Bishop chose was that on which a pagan temple had stood as a center of Tarascan religious activity. Quiroga began the cathedral to serve the twenty-eight Spanish families who had established residence in Pátzcuaro and the thirty thousand Indians of the vicinity, who had been wont to worship grim graven idols.

From a psychological viewpoint he had doubtless chosen well, but from a physical standpoint the situation was not good, for the ground beneath seemed to resent the religious change and protested by shifting and throwing stones out of line. Against the advice of engineers, Quiroga insisted that the cathedral should be here. But only one-fifth of the building was ever completed, because the episcopal see was moved to Valladolid before the edifice was well under way. The bell-tower looked lopped off because it was unfinished. The brown façade was pierced with a great wheel window, and the four sainted authors of the Gospels stood large as life in their sculptured niches.

The churchyard was full of Indians coming and going in their Sunday best. The women wore pleated wool skirts of black-and-red with embroidered blouses. A few girls wore the rich China Poblano costume, with maroon-colored petticoats ornamented with gilt fringe, satin vests embroidered in gold thread, silk sashes tied behind with gilt fringe, and a silk handkerchief crossing the neck. Within the edifice a service was in progress, and the interior was crowded with dark-skinned figures on their knees.

Political leaders had maintained that Catholicism kept the people in ignorance and that if they were denied the pap of religious ceremony, they would soon forget it. And for a period of some years under Calles, there had been only bootlegged services in Mexico. But the interim had not weaned the masses from the Church. Seemingly they had returned famished for the word of grace, for the assurance that *El Señor* and *La Madre Santísima* had not abandoned them. On some of their dark faces was a visible awareness of a miracle of faith in their own persons. If the flaming candles, the images of the saints, words murmured in the confessional box, and harmless drops of holy water served as anodynes in their hard mortal life, then they should have their portion of spiritual food, in whatever form was most palatable to them. Where one Indian might go to kneel before the aggressive statue of Morelos, surely a hundred would come to worship before the maize-paste image of *Nuestra Madre Santísima de la Salud.*

Quiroga himself had ordered this image of the Virgin to be made by artisans in a lake village and brought by dugout canoe to Pátzcuaro. In consecrating it he had bestowed upon the statue divine powers of healing; and the Indians attributed the Bishop's own phenomenal vigor and long life span of ninety-five years to the efficacy of this Virgin of Health. For four centuries Indians have made pilgrimages from remote regions to pray for health or for the recovery of loved ones too ill to travel. Metaphysical faith has been proved to possess more curative power than witch doctors' brews and incantations. But like the good Bishop Quiroga, who prudently and invariably established a hospital upon founding a town, General Cárdenas, who was still more of a realistic than a religious humanitarian, had provided Pátzcuaro with a modern hospital for the poor.

From the church we went to see this hospital, which had formerly been a convent. Its façade was as unrevealing as any of those Spanish-Moorish structures which turn their backs to the street and save all their charm and grace for the patio. And the lobby where we waited permission for a visit was markedly uncolonial and unconventual. The walls were not enshrined with majolica images, but plastered with posters as blatant as comic strips. Instead of pictures of the bleeding heart of Jesus, which might move novices to an ecstasy of pity, there were cartoons revealing the perforating ravishes of typhoid germs on human intestines, to move citizens to obey the laws of sanitation. The menace of bacteria was there for the illiterate to read in frightening manifestations. The lugubrious finish of a brain-sick syphilitic was luridly depicted. The sad and tragic downfall of the drunkard was dramatized in primary colors.

In the 1530's Bishop Quiroga had found excessive drunkenness among the Indians of Pátzcuaro. Today there is little evidence of drunkenness. Cárdenas, the teetotaler, put a blight on the sot's false joy by ordering a series of cartoons depicting the evils of alcohol to be set up in every bar and pulque shop. Many a potential drunkard has been checked in his downward path by staring into a picture of delirium tremens as he downed his tequila. With the pictorial representation of hollow-eyed, hungry little ones awaiting their drunken sire's return—with pockets empty, but a belly full of pulque—many an impressionable fellow departs after his first drink.

The cartoons are a law of the municipality. The same kind of cartoons, depicting the evils of improper sanitation or casual expectoration, are displayed in schools. Adults as well as children are made aware in signs they can understand that much of the suffering of the world is needless and self-inflicted. No longer should a gullible populace believe that rheumatism and malaria and smallpox are caused by evil spirits.

We were shaking our heads over the catastrophe that might ensue from the wanton spitting of a tubercular when swinging doors were thrown open and a swish of voluminous skirts made us turn. A tall fair-complexioned nun stood there regarding us with appraising gray eyes. I was unprepared for the black robes and starched white headdress. I knew that for one to appear on the street in the garb of a monk or the veil of a nun was forbidden by law. But of course a nun might wear the costume of her order withindoors, just as a priest wears his vestments at service.

When Señor Sánchez had presented me as a friend of Mexico, and I had introduced Dr. Hoagland as a specialist of the Rockefeller Institute, the Sister informed us that she was the directress of the hospital. She was a brisk, bright-eyed woman in the early sixties, and in her mien there was an air of natural authority. We all made a mass effort to be ingratiating. The nun regarded us with a noncommittal smile. Then she offered to do us the honor of conducting us through her establishment herself.

A renovated Mexican convent makes a most agreeable hospital. All the patients' rooms gave on the rectangular patio, where flowers bloomed along graveled walks converging to a tiled fountain. The nun gave an order to a plain-faced young nurse who wore a uniform of light-blue with the flowing white headdress of a Sister. The nurse passed the word on to an oldish male attendant, who bent and twisted a metal rod. Jets of water rose from the fountain and turned into iridescent spray. We murmured admiration and proceeded. A beamed arcade with fluted columns and cool yellow-tiled pavement encircled the main patio. A recuperating patient was walking up and down to regain his strength. In a ward with ten spotless beds, there were only three bed patients. One was trussed up with a bad foot injury.

"You haven't many patients," I said to the directress.

"We take such good care of them that they mend quickly," she answered with a twinkle in her eye.

The patients smiled. The accompanying nurse suppressed a giggle.

"They all think I am very stern," the nun said. "I won't stand for any nonsense, for any slipshod business. I fuss at them day and night. I'm afraid I fuss too much and the nurses and the patients talk about me behind my back—but our patients get well."

The young nurse put her hand to her opened mouth as if to suppress a protesting denial and an affirmation in the same breath. The nun gave an affectionate pat on the foot of the bed where the man with the injured leg lay, and then turned and led the procession to the operating-rooms. She took her position in the center of the first operating-room and gave orders to the nurse. "Open this cabinet, and that—and that—and that—and that. Let the doctor see for himself."

Dr. Hoagland was obviously impressed. He reeled off names of medicines; he noted the surgical instruments, the bandages, the anesthetic masks. He looked up and said to us, "I tell you this is really something." Then to the nun, "The equipment is excellent."

The Sister smiled with appreciation and with an assurance that was not smugness. She drew some keys from the folds of her skirt and handed them to the nurse, who unlocked the cabinets containing the morphia. Hoagland leaned forward inspecting the labels.

"Everything that is needed. It really is astonishing for this little village. The very latest in everything."

The nun and Hoagland began a fast conversation larded with pharmaceutical terms.

"How does it happen, señora," I made so bold as to inquire, "that a nun is so versed in knowledge of the apothecary?"

The Sister smiled a smile that was like an answer to a challenge. "That is simple, in my case. I have not always been a nun. I did not enter the order until I was forty. As you see, I am considerably past that now. But my father owned the leading pharmacy in Morelia. Our apartments were on the floor above, and as a little girl I developed an interest in curative agencies after a healing of my pet pussy cat. I spent all my spare time among the drugs and the powders, and watched the pharmacists make up compounds and fill prescriptions. I would fetch the jars and boxes for them, and I learned the names and the formulas. I was adept, and read text-books, and became quite knowledgeable—and I think helpful in times of need or epidemics."

"Did you study nursing?"

"When a young lady I got experience in nursing at summer house parties on the haciendas of family friends. There were no doctors for the peons and little or nothing provided in the way of medicants. The hacendados—even the good-in-heart—seemed to have a curious notion that the Creator in His providence had planned for humble folk not to be sick. They used to say that a bad bruise from a steer's horn or a gash from a machete are soon healed by rest and natural vigor. They let the fevers rage at will—and if the patient died, well"—she shrugged—"he would have been little good if he had lived." She paused, and then, assuring herself of our sympathetic interest, she proceeded.

"I thought differently—that something more was needed than an old crone's ignorant nursing. So I took my satchel with me on house parties, and while the others danced, I often prescribed. I taught some peon wives the rudiments of nursing. I found more satisfaction in that than in the frivolity of the sons and daughters of planters." She made a gesture of spreading out her palms in summation of her brief life story, and moved toward the door.

"You did not marry?" I ventured.

For a moment she debated with herself as to why I had asked that conventional question. Then she smiled, but not defensively. "I did not marry. I kept house for my widower father. When he died, instead of running the business—which I believe I could have done successfully—I sold it, and entered an order. And here you find me today, running this little hospital."

"And doing a most excellent job, obviously," Hoagland said.

Barely acknowledging the compliment, she motioned to Thérèse to precede her through the open door into the adjoining room. This was to be another X-ray room and the very latest and finest type of machine was to be installed here. "When the profits warrant," the directress said. "The next profits are earmarked for this."

"Profits?" Wagus said. "From a charity hospital?"

"Profits from the theater, I mean."

Then we got the straight of it. To make this hospital, equip it, and run it, General Cárdenas had metamorphosed an old Augustinian convent down the street into a modern motion-picture house. It belonged to the municipality. The profits from the theater went to support the hospital. The pesos the citizens paid for entertainment went not into private pockets, but into the general welfare fund.

"Like the enlightened Norwegians," I said. "In Bergen, the municipality owns all the picture theaters and returns the profits to the citizens in manifold benefits."

As the white headdress nodded acknowledgment of my comment, and the nun's fingers imperceptibly touched the long black-and-silver rosary, I said in mingled admiration and question: "And Cárdenas did all this? How splendid! What a wise and good man he is!" I knew the Church had no great love for Cárdenas, who made it quite clear to the world at large that he was not a communicant.

The fire in her eyes cooled and her mouth set slightly. She merely murmured a charged "h-mm."

"But without Cárdenas and the moving-picture house you would not have this hospital," I suggested gently.

"That is true," she admitted.

"Then why don't you like him?" I asked, very careful to smile. She knew I was baiting her.

"Like him?" she said, with a cautious hint of a smile. "The Scriptures tell us we must like all God's creatures."

"But don't you think he is really a good man—even if he doesn't go to church?"

She looked at me steadily for a moment. Then she answered: "God sends his rain alike on the just and on the unjust.—Shall we see the rest of the establishment?"

We all laughed and walked out into the gallery along the patio. But we did not have time to visit the women's and children's wards in the back patio. As we began to make our farewells, the directress gave one more order to the nurse, and reaching into the folds of her black skirt, she drew out another bunch of keys. The nurse scurried into the office and returned with a fountain pen and a photographic print of the patio with the fountain playing. Resting the picture on the flat marble ledge of the balustrade, the nun inscribed it in a flourishing hand: *"Dedicamos al Sr. Hudson Strode como un recuerdo de su visita a este Hospital.*

Junio 27 de 1943

M. Magdalena Padilla

And under the signature she repeated the initials M.M. and encircled the monogram in a cloud of swirls.

Mary Magdalen. So that was the name she had chosen for herself from among the female saints. Had her hair been her special pride, and hence a deep-felt sacrifice in the shaving? From her gray-blue eyes it might have been golden once. Was it because of the Magdalen's box of precious ointment? Could she have known a carnal sin like her name saint? I doubted it—still, there was a remarkable spirit of independence about the woman. If her heart had instructed her, she might have defied conventions and canons. One thing was certain: She was in her right place now, managing a hospital with crisp efficiency in an ancient town that lay under a burden of worn-out traditions. She served Cárdenas's good purposes as well as she did the Lord's. Despite doctrinaire disagreement, it was obvious that the nun and the unbeliever worked well together in a complementary fashion.

Taking a last look about, at the order, the cleanliness, the solidity of the walls, the inspiriting play of water in the fountain, I once again expressed my admiration.

"'Except Jehovah build the house
They labor in vain that build it,'"

I quoted. "It is patent that Jehovah had a hand in this."

Sister Magdalena smiled at the aptness of the compliment. Then I added, "Deity has seemed to bless the work of our friend Cárdenas."

Sister Magdalena was unprepared for my postscript. She narrowed her eyes slightly, fingered the cross on her breast, and said succinctly, "God often moves in a mysterious way—"

5. GREAT-GREAT-GRANDDAUGHTER OF A NOBLE

From the hospital run by the white woman, Señor Sánchez took us to an atelier run by a dark-skinned woman who held her head even higher, and whose manner was quite as impressive, if a little less gracious. She came from a scion of Spanish grandees. Her great-great-grandfather was an eighteenth-century count who had taken an Indian girl to wife. The house we stopped at had been inherited. Because the wheat fields and the mines had passed into other hands long ago, the woman had set up a workshop for lacquer ware and filled her drawing-room with showcases. This being Sunday, the workshop was not in operation. But half-grudgingly, as if she were stooping to do aliens a favor, the proprietress permitted us to enter. At first sight of her I immediately thought of Paxinou, the Greek actress, in her role of Pilar in *For Whom the Bell Tolls*. There was the proud carriage, the amused scorn, the good-looking homeliness. Perhaps the darker duskiness of complexion made the eyes of the Mexican woman more smoldering, if with less reason or purpose than those of Paxinou's Pilar.

Through a reception vestibule we stepped into a patio that was so thickly embowered in foliage that you could not squeeze along the narrowed paths without some exotic branch reaching out to clutch at your sleeve or to whisper against your ear. Green was the overwhelming predominant note—green in every shade, from a dank and waxy blackish green to the ethereal green of a plant I had never known.

"Up there on the roof at the back we do our work," the woman said, indicating a flight of narrow stone stairs. "Part of the roof is covered—for rainy hours. The workers do better in the open air. Those at the edges can look down into the garden to rest their eyes. The others can look off to the mountains. I have ten girls. They are all expert—the best the town affords. No men. I want no men about. Men are troublesome to manage. Some of them have ambition, and that is tiresome, for in time they would try to run the shop." She thrust out her chin against masculine opposition. "The girls are very clever. I have taught them the best traditions of lacquer-making. I pay good wages. I give them an appetizing lunch, and they like to work here. Would you care to see some of our products?" She turned, and led the way diagonally down one of the jungle-thick paths to the room that had once been the drawing-room.

"A considerable sense of self-importance," Thérèse commented sotto voce as the woman entered her showroom like a grande dame become businesswoman—or was it a businesswoman simulating the grande dame?

With a gesture that was both executive and elegant, she threw open some solid blinds and let the light stream in through iron-barred grillwork. Where divans once stood were now showcases full of lacquer ware. The woman took her position behind the longest showcase like a presiding deity unimpressed with the reactions of human beings of any category. While we bent to admire this piece and that, she held her head in the clouds.

Señor Sánchez remarked that I was in Mexico for the third time, gathering material for a history of the nation I was writing. The woman's chin lifted a trifle more. She looked at me over the show-case top with a cool scrutiny. Then with a gesture of not believing anything much would come of it, she reached under a shelf and brought out two slim paper-bound brochures. "If you are really writing a book about this land, these may be of some service to you. This, a brief but accurate history of the town. This, notations on my family and my workshop." She handed the books over the show-case. "They were prepared by men of distinction from the University of Mexico. With my compliments, señor."

"Señor Strode is himself a professor in a university in the United States," Señor Sánchez hastened to inform her.

The woman regarded me again, elevated her eyebrows, and made a slight and noncommittal bow. "In that case he should be able to appreciate the better the information in these pages."

"You flatter me, señora. *Mil gracias,*" I thanked her with a studied bow and a hint of a grin.

She acknowledged the bow, and commented on the grin with a slight drooping of her right eyelid.

Wagus had discovered two stunning cigarette boxes in magenta lacquer and asked the price. The woman took up one of the boxes, casually opened it, as if to call attention to the creamy inside and the superior workmanship of the hinges.

"How much?" Wagus asked.

As if touching on imponderables, the proprietress called the figure.

"How much for the two?"

The woman named precisely double the price of one.

"But for two would I not get a discount?" Wagus insisted.

The muscles at the corner of the woman's mouth tightened with perceptible scorn. "There is one price on each piece. The price does not change—by the pair, or by the hundred." The dusky descendant of a Castilian nobleman revealed by her inflection that even the mention of money was hardly seemly where it concerned a work of art created in her atelier. To haggle was utterly degrading.

Wagus was not in the least put out of countenance. He renounced the imminent transaction by setting both the boxes back with cavalier emphasis. No bargain, no trade, with Wagus.

Thérèse and I both had fixed our eyes on two identical cigarette boxes in a rich oyster-white lacquer. They were smartly and immaculately unadorned and as smooth in texture as a gardenia petal. We knew instantly that they belonged on a certain Swedish table in our living-room. The price was high for Mexico, but small for a shop like Jensen's in New York, where they might happily have found themselves.

"I trust you do not mind making a sale on Sunday," I suggested, though I noted no sign of demurring. As she shrugged philosophically, I added quickly, "We have come a long way, and this is our only opportunity to possess such treasures."

She appreciated my tact and tore off a sheet of the newspaper she had already reached for. Wrapping the boxes neatly, she tied them with twine expertly and economically.

When Hoagland decided to buy the boxes Wagus had declined, the proprietress cast a slanting glance at Wagus, who got even by adjusting his pince-nez and peering closely, pretending to detect a defect on the bottom of one of the boxes.

We all turned when we saw Señor Sánchez bowing ceremoniously toward the doorway. A bent and withered old woman stood there, looking like a wrinkled twist of tobacco wrapped in a lavender shroud. Squinting as if her eyesight was not of the best, she emerged into the room like a disembodied spirit.

"*Mia madre, la Señora de la* This *de la* That," the woman announced. We bowed. The old lady raised her bent head, looked toward us, and bowed gravely as we murmured "How do you do?"

"These people are Americans," Señor Sánchez said, in a manner to suggest that he hoped we honored the house by our presence.

"I have seen Americans before," the old lady said. Then with a gesture of smoothing back her unkempt mane of white hair that looked tempest-tossed on this still afternoon, she added graciously, "You are welcome." But she did not add *"Esta casa es sua."*

"Would you permit the visitors to see your wonderful kitchen, señora?" Señor Sánchez asked ingratiatingly. "They are sincerely interested in all phases of Mexican life." Although he addressed the old lady, he ended by raising his eyebrows questioningly toward her daughter.

The daughter turned toward Thérèse. "Would you care to see the kitchen, señora?"

"Very much—if it's convenient."

"It is convenient, of course, if you so desire, señora," she said, almost ceremoniously.

We went along the roofed gallery that traversed the south side of the patio. Technically the patio stopped where there was no more soil, where the tiled floor of the kitchen began. But the yellow-flowered vines and the white-blossoming shrubs spilled over into the kitchen area. The fourth wall did not exist—it was absent, like the fourth wall of a stage set. It was like those modern Swedish rooms where one wall is of glass to bring the out-of-doors withindoors, except that here there was no glass whatever, and the patio with its color and its perfume flowed into the room.

It was a kitchen for a fairy tale or a romantic opera. The stove and

the oven were of blue-and-orange tile, built into the north wall—
more like a shrine than a place for cooking. Utensils of hammered
brass and platters of beaten silver caught and reflected the dappled
light sifting through the greenery. There was an orderly array of
ceramic jars and old bateas, ruby-colored goblets, and antique
painted chests with wrought-silver locks. And hanging in the vaguely
defined boundary between patio and kitchen were two bird cages,
one with two canaries and the other with a single Mexican mockingbird.

As if in our honor, the old lady put her face close to the canaries
and made sipping sounds. The pair burst into song and then the
gray *sinsontli* outdid the yellow birds in volume and sweetness.

Admiration came very easily. When Thérèse stood silently remarking an ancient lacquer bowl, the old lady nodded and murmured, *"Trabajan con cariño."* She meant that the persons who had
made all these things worked with affection. The joy of creation was
a veritable trademark of authenticity. In each piece there seemed to
be a harmonious marriage of utility and beauty, of necessity and
grace.

Looking at the mestizo faces of the mother and daughter and the
taste of their kitchen and the wares of daily use, it occurred to me
how agreeable, after all, was the fusion of the Spanish with the Indian. Whatever had been introduced from Spain had taken on a
Mexican flavor. And Spain had given so much more to the Mexican
heritage than most commentators seem willing to admit. The Indians had learned glassblowing and leatherwork from the Spaniards.
They had not known an upright loom until the Spaniards came.
They had never seen a potter's wheel. They had no wool, no iron,
no steel. Of course, before the arrival of the Europeans they already
possessed the materials, the eyes, and the aptitude to do wonders with
precious stones and with hummingbird feathers, and the secrets of
lacquer were well known to those who lived along the Pacific coast.
The Indians were natural artisans who would produce something
worth while if allowed to work leisurely, and they have never been
the absolute imitators the Chinese artisans can be today. They trans-
form their models into shapes closer to their own heart's desire. The
Indian imprint seems invariably left on every adoption from the
Spanish.

As Thérèse called our attention to a platter decorated inside and out with stylized deer and wild flowers, the proprietress began to believe in our sincerity and thawed. "Done with affection—" she echoed her mother—"as I see you do observe."

"Here, it must be like working in the Garden of Eden," Wagus said, glancing toward the patio.

The proprietress smiled. "Yes, for the pure joy of working, and of course for the livelihood—but without serpents—or men." She laughed as Paxinou laughed for Pilar. "But in Mexico we don't distort production into an ideal of existence, as we hear Americans do. Craftwork is not labor in the American sense, but pleasure."

"And when the work is enjoyed, as it is here, the worker is more than doubly paid," Hoagland said sententiously, but meaning it.

She looked as if such a sentiment seemed strange indeed coming from an American.

"How long can you keep it up?" I asked. "Your way of producing art?"

The woman suddenly seemed to lose her arrogance in her speculation of the future. "Who can say? As the world seems to be going —the way of man with a machine can change overnight, as the way of man with man changes within a generation. With the demand for more and more production—particularly the demand from your countrymen—even Mexicans, who should know better, are turning from art to shoddy."

We offered no defense, for we had seen enough of the recent wholesale buying in Mexico to realize the menace. We began making our *adióses*. The old lady, as well as her daughter, accompanied us through the patio to the street door. The daughter continued the train of thought we had started her on.

"I do not even know if I shall keep this house after my mother's passing. And I do not much care. I went into business so that she might continue to live out her life in her own house, which had come to her through her ancestors."

I turned to the old lady. "So this is your house? You are really *la propriedora?*"

La Señora de la This de la That nodded her head, straightened her bent neck, and visibly became several inches taller. *"Sí, señor,"* she said gravely. *"Yo soy la propriedora."*

The five of us shook hands with the two of them. As I raised the old lady's wrinkled dry hand to my lips, I caught an exchange of glances between the daughter and Señor Sánchez. It was not about the hand-kissing. I think it concerned a commission on sales.

Driving away, I wondered about the commonwealth of the future in Mexico. What would it be? Obviously not white. Not predominantly Indian, either. The pure whites in Mexico would disappear with the centuries, the pure Indians would disappear. Mexico was to be a mestizo country, with the blood of one race saying one thing and the blood of another race saying something different. The fusion would vary in each man—sometimes the best elements would surge to the top, sometimes the worst. There was bound to be some secret warfare going on within breasts, which might occasionally break out in neurotic paralysis or violent action.

In the last hundred years it was obvious how the significance of the mestizo had increased. It was only necessary to thumb through the histories to realize how many heroes, leaders, artists, the mestizos had furnished the commonwealth. One thing was certain: One should have only sympathy with the Mexican for his problem in reconciling racial values at odds with each other.

At the edge of town Señor Sánchez turned into the new automobile road that winds among boulders high to a belvedere on the Cerro del Estribo. Much of the way looked raw and red from the wounds of recent construction work, but wild flowers and new soft grasses did what they could to hide the scars. Before the belvedere a spacious terrace spread itself in a half-circle to the edge of a precipice. Far beneath, the lake lay tranquil in the apricot light of late afternoon. In the outlines of the hills and the mountains, there was again that striking similitude to a Japanese print, where everything is sharply defined and nothing is superfluous to the composition. Directly across was the island of Janitzio in miniature, its white statue no larger now than a heroic ivory chessman. The sun had just disappeared behind the flame-tinted rim of the west. Birds made their last daytime communications as the evening came on delicately, like music from muted strings. The water of the lake turned to the color of moonstone. A single boat glided across its surface like a black-enameled beetle creeping on satin damask.

The bell from the great church began to ring, sending a faint silvery music out over the lake and up the hills and down the hills.

When the overtones and the echoes merged into the twilight, we prepared to leave. At the fringes of Pátzcuaro, Indians squatting before their huts took on the atmosphere of evening, and their faces and clothes blurred against the adobe walls. Indians are a lonesome-looking people, even when several are gathered together. There is an inherent brooding quality about them. But in a phrase of Steinbeck, they do not "carry little clouds of apprehension about them, as American bankers" do. Without the nervous restlessness of ambition, they would sleep well, with good digestions of their rude and simple fare. Relaxed, they breathed in the cooling air of evening, and then began going withindoors, seemingly with quiet hearts and minds untouched by the turmoil of the great outer world. At a corner where our car turned into the road that led to the Vasco de Quiroga, two Indians youths were entertaining a group by singing a *corrido,* a folk song, in a minor key. It was about a man who never more knew happiness after he forswore his rural upbringing for the city's glittering fleshpots.

I thought of Thoreau and his own computation of his blessings. "I am startled that God can make me so rich," he wrote, "even with my own cheap stores. It needs but a few wisps of straw in the sun, some small word dropped, or that has lain long silent in some books." In one respect these people who had little or no profit from words in a printed book went even beyond Thoreau. In the book of nature they instinctively knew something that Thoreau had to learn the hard way, by renouncing civilization.

6. RETURN BY TZINTZUNTZAN

The next morning at eight we were awaked with a telegram that made it seem expedient to return straight off to Mexico City. It was too bad to have our trip cut short, but the three days had been uncommonly rich.

When we had breakfasted and our luggage had been sent down, we thought again of Preciliano. He was to have come last evening. We talked with the clerk. It seems he had come, but the clerk had thought he was asking for another American couple who had just left Pátzcuaro before dinner and had told the fellow that we had gone. The clerk sent a messenger on a bicycle to find him and bring him to us. The messenger turned up with another Preciliano, not ours in any sense. Apparently the name was not as uncommon as we had supposed. Señor Sánchez and I drove to the piers to explain. But the other boatmen said that our Preciliano had gone off on an all-day excursion, since he had heard that we had left. Back at the hotel I wrote a note to him and the clerk assured me he would explain everything. And there in the doorway was Manuel Solís smiling his angelic smile under the great straw hat. He had brought a picture of the Gardners' house in Memphis taken after a heavy snowfall. He promised to give our farewells and apologies to Preciliano.

"It just wasn't to be," I said to Thérèse.

"At least there's nothing to do about it now," she said. "Perhaps you can get back to see Preciliano after talking with the Embassy about getting him into the States."

"But shouldn't you be in school on a Monday?" Wagus was saying to Manuel Solís.

"It doesn't make much difference," the boy said. "The teacher won't get mad. There are so many pupils who don't have regular seats that she is glad when some stay home. And I have this." He held up the little red dictionary and smiled disarmingly.

The clerk who had come to the door with us said: "He hardly ever goes to school. He's always hanging about here waiting for tourists. He had no trouble at all in picking up Ann Sheridan. He was the only guide she would let come near her. She gave him a hundred pesos when she left, and kissed him good-bye."

It was hard for a twelve-year-old kid who found Ann Sheridan an easy pick-up and who could make money by merely smiling and walking about with sympathetic people in the sunshine—it was hard to shut himself up in an overcrowded schoolroom to prepare himself for a future. But still I was about to offer grave admonitions on the necessity of school for a bright boy who wanted to get on in the world. Then I remembered Blake's scorn for all formal education.

> But to go to school in a summer morn
> O! it drives all joy away. . . .

How can the bird that is born for joy
Sit in a cage and sing?
How can a child when fears annoy
But droop his tender wing
And forget his youthful spring?

I halted my fatherly admonitions in mid-sentence. By what right did I presume to spoil the boy's morning by scolding? Let Manuel Solís pick his education where he would, according to his mood. There were too many people in the world with too much ambition, but only one with a smile like Manuel Solís.

"I'll tell Señora Gardner that you are in health and prosperity, and that the beauteous movie star Ann Sheridan says you are her favorite guide in Mexico."

The expression on Manuel Solís's face made even more luminous our last view of Pátzcuaro, which already held all the beauty that a Mexican morning could draw from the gold-filtered sunshine.

The last lap of the encircling journey from Quiroga to Quiroga did not wander, at any point, more than a morning's walk from the lakeside. Most of it followed a way beaten by historic feet before the conquistadors. Between Pátzcuaro and Quiroga lay the ancient capital of the Tarascan nation. It is called Tzintzuntzan—a name, in print or on the lips, to stir the imagination of a Coleridge. In its native tongue it means "Place of Hummingbirds." The name's onomatopoeia suggests the tremulous darting of the gem-colored creatures that once haunted this region as plentifully as bees.

Today Tzintzuntzan is only a small village. No more are the garments of foremost citizens fashioned out of hummingbird feathers. There is not a trace of the pre-Spanish glory where the last of the Tarascan kings, Caltzontzin, ended his rule in 1528. Caltzontzin had made friendly overtures to the white men, and while being entertained in Mexico City he had been converted and baptized. The Christly doctrine of brotherly love was not hard for him to understand and to accept. In 1526, on Caltzontzin's invitation, a Franciscan friar, Martín de Jesús, established a Christian institution in Tzintzuntzan. By his pious goodness this man of God won the peoples' confidence. All was going harmoniously when the notorious Nuño de Guzmán came gold-lusting in 1528. This most hateful of the conquistadors ruined the good work of the Franciscan. Treacherously seizing Caltzontzin, he had him tortured publicly to extort from him the hiding-places of treasure. Finally, in frustrated fury, he ordered the Indian king dragged behind a horse over a stony way. When Caltzontzin's superhuman endurance survived even this cruelty, he was finally burned alive. Before the perfidy and savagery of the white men the Indians fled into hiding, lived in the mountains, took to drunkenness, and turned back to their renounced gods.

Five years later, in 1533, Quiroga arrived to bring order out of chaos, and here at Tzintzuntzan he began his experiments in Christian socialism. It was here he built his first provincial hospital and began to minister to the ailing. Here he poured balm on distressed spirits, and taught the doctrines of co-operation, fraternity, cleanliness, and the disgrace of indolence and greed. He encouraged the natives in their planting and in their handicrafts. Gradually Indians from the far corners of Michoacán began to flock to Tzintzuntzan to observe, and to ask for help in their own districts. They saw that this Spaniard practiced what he preached. As Sholem Asch says of Saint Paul, Quiroga preached with his own fingers the moral of labor, believing that "the word of the Messiah was not something at which a man should earn his bread" without also doing something more practical. So the Bishop acted as a kind of foreman to the various handicraft activities of the villages. For himself, he lived most simply. His only indulgence was books, and he managed to amass a library of some six hundred volumes. His books were the only things of value he had to bequeath at his death.

In 1539, at Tzintzuntzan, Quiroga began the construction of a cathedral dedicated to Saint Francis. But before a year was passed, he decided to make his headquarters at Pátzcuaro. Both Indians and Spaniards who had settled at Tzintzuntzan so strongly opposed the change that they raised an armed force to prevent it. The intransigent Quiroga, however, moved his seat just the same. As Pátzcuaro grew in importance, Tzintzuntzan declined. Today one pauses at the village only to glance within the ancient church and hear the bell struck in the atrium.

Where the king's palace once stood, at the highest point on the slope leading up from the lake, now stands the church and the centuries-old convent. There is nothing remarkable about the smallish church except a large oil painting of the "Descent from the Cross," which some claim to be a veritable Titian. It is well done, but we could not believe that Titian himself had put a single brush stroke on the canvas.

All the beauty lay out of doors in the mellowed atrium, where the gnarled olive trees and ancient cedars basked in the gold-beaten light of midmorning. Though no hummingbirds shot their iridescence about the shrubbery, Mexican mockingbirds were full of song, concealed behind their leafy choir screen. They sang as they did when Quiroga heard them, when he planted his first olive tree, and as the eighteen sequent Tarascan kings had heard them. It was well for the breed that the *sinsontlis'* glory lay in their throats rather than in their plumage. The dazzling varicolored coats of the hummingbirds had brought their near-extinction, as Joseph's famous coat had all but ruined him.

From a heavy beam between trees that made a kind of pagoda halfway from the street gate to the church door hung a great bell, the color of dull platinum. A teen-aged boy who had joined us took hold of the rope and pulled with such reverential gentleness that when the clapper touched the inner surface, it was like a butterfly kiss. The purest sound conceivable came from metal on metal. It was the quintessence of lovely liquid sound. It came clear and moving like a sustained note in a Gregorian chant. Seeing our entranced delight, the boy struck the bell again, and yet again, with great delicacy and discretion.

"The bell was made and put here in 1748," the boy said, giving his information softly, as if not to impair the holy vibrations. "When it was finished, it was found to be too large and heavy to be set aloft in the church tower. So they put it in here in the yard."

Was it the separateness of the bell from the church, uncontaminated by ritual and theology, that made the overtones of such exquisite clarity? Was it the perfection of the day, the ideal composition of the thing called weather, that made the sound transporting?

"The Indians gave all their jewels and their silver ornaments," the boy said, "to get the most beautiful bell that could be made."

But more than treasured gifts or any earth-wrought agencies had gone into the casting. For this tone was hardly a thing contrived by mere physics. It suggested a metaphysical creation, as if men had offered the purer portions of their hearts, and poured their hope of salvation in with the molten metal.

At a nod, the boy increased the volume of the sound—until the whole atrium seemed filled with heavenly echoes. We stood like pilgrims at some spring of healing waters, drinking in the sound.

One would think the dying would ask to be brought here. What could be better for marking a man's passage into bliss—the bliss of oblivion or eternity, of nothing or everything—than the tolling of this bell? What music for the abysmal end of man, or for a transcendental new beginning!

As we drove away, the music of Tzintzuntzan's bell fell softly in sweet cadence on our ears. I knew that in the treasure house of memory, where one collects sounds as well as sights, its tone was recorded forever in a special inner sanctum. I knew that in the midst of the brassy clangor of what is called modern living, I might sometimes hear its gentle harmony.

VI

To Puebla

There are a good many enchantments in this world of God.

—GRAÇA ARANHA

1. THE WAY OF BRIGANDS AND OLD CHURCHES

THE CITY OF PUEBLA is like a bullfight in that a person cannot gauge how he is going to react to it until he is in its presence. The experiences of others won't help much in advance. The visitor knows that Puebla is the fourth city of Mexico in population and a commercial center, strongly Catholic, Spanish, and conservative. He knows that it is famous for its tile and majolica, as well as its churches and battles, and that it claims to be the most aristocratic of Mexican towns. But to judge the effect of its atmosphere he has to sense it in person. Whatever the reaction to Puebla, the eighty-four-mile drive over the mountains from Mexico City has all the excitement it is reputed to have as one of the world's spectacular highways.

A European friend of mine of superior perception and taste, whose advice about travel in Mexico had proved good through many years, had said: "One day is all you need in Puebla. The hotels are among the dreariest in the land. It is not worth a night's spending unless you are a guest of a colonial family that lives in the old style."

We decided to give Puebla the once-over before settling down for a sojourn. We engaged a comfortable car with an educated Mayan chauffeur from Yucatán who had married a Milwaukee girl. We invited Patricia Minnegerode to come with us. She was a friend from twenty years ago whom we had run into in the capital. Her Catholic faith, her sensitivity, and her ten years in Europe, where her husband, Colonel Fitzhugh Lee Minnegerode, was a correspondent for the *New York Times,* made her just the right companion for a day in Puebla.

The highway is built of nonskid volcanic stone, and though it is skillfully banked, there is thrill in the hairpin turns where the car skirts the brink of abysmal barrancas. The road climbs to a height of more than ten thousand feet to cross the continental divide, and to the right are the two volcanoes of the Warrior and the Sleeping Lady towering seven thousand feet higher. This morning, however, we had to take the map's and the chauffeur's word for them, for the risen sun had not yet dissolved the night's mist. But the atmosphere about the car was clear and we could look straight up and straight down into dizzying heights and depths. Some mountain flanks were covered with pine trees and enlivened by golden masses of acacias. Others were mere stupendous slabs of naked porphyry. The wild chaos of forest and stone had that same strange and savage beauty which had filled the rugged men of Cortés with instinctive dread and had touched the young heart of the Belgian Princess Carlota with a queer foreboding.

Just beyond the highest point—ten thousand four hundred and eighty-five feet—we entered the old bandit country. For centuries the crossroads hamlet called Rio Frio was a notorious rogues' nest. In this neighborhood travelers between Vera Cruz and the capital were frequently robbed of their possessions and sometimes their lives. There was little or no redress. The marauders escaped into rocky defiles, and no officers of the law dared pursue them until the 1870's, when Porfirio Díaz created his famous rurales and turned highwaymen into mounted police. Terrifying tales are still recounted of the depredations of the brigands. Sometimes they would take the coach horses and leave the passengers twiddling their thumbs or wringing their hands in the horseless vehicles. Occasionally they would kidnap maidens and deflower them. But generally their booty aim was only gold and silver coin. When there was not enough money to satisfy them, they would often take jewelry.

One famous story is told of a British bride and groom who arrived in the early days of the Republic. They were unlucky enough to have the public stagecoach in which they were passengers held up three times between Cholula and Rio Frio. The first set of bandits took their money. The next lot made off with their jewelry and their luggage. The third gang, out of temper to find them already plucked, lined them all up on the roadside—the English, the Spanish, the Mexican, male and female—and stripped them to their last garment. Then, with malicious humor, they commanded the naked coachmen to their high stations, and the naked passengers to their seats, and gave orders to drive on and not to stop until they reached the next inn. There sat the blushing English bride and her furious groom among the other nude men and women, all strangers to each other, without so much as a lace handkerchief to cover their nakedness. Shivering in the wintry mountain air, they drove on for five embarrassing hours to the next station. At the hostelry, the host and his guests gasped in incredulous astonishment as the half-frozen passengers without benefit of fig leaf staggered out of the coach more naked than the exiles from Eden.

Today the old bandit hangout of Rio Frio has become the Mexican equivalent of a congregation of hot-dog stands. One buys a sizzling hot *taco,* or tortilla sandwich, to fortify himself before or after the drive over the ridge. Itinerant guitarists and jukeboxes make noisy music. Thérèse and Pat and the chauffeur were content to stay in the car, but I got out to have a coffee without milk. It tasted like lye boiled in branch water. One bitter mouthful was enough for me. I set the cup down in renunciation. The servitor behind the counter gave me such a cutthroat scowl that I had a good idea of his grandfather's profession—and his grandmother's, too.

At San Martín Texmelucán, the branch road to the left leads to Tlaxcala, the capital of the state of that name, fourteen miles off the main highway. Little visited, and shrunk in population to three thousand from the thirty thousand Cortés found there in September 1519, the town is rich in history. In a letter to the Spanish Emperor, Cortés compared Tlaxcala favorably with Granada, declaring it "larger, stronger, and more populous than the Moorish City at the time of the Conquest, and quite as well built." Here Cortés made the dicker with the old Tlascalan ruler to join forces with the white men against their powerful Aztec enemy. Here the first Christian church in the continent was established, and four Tlascalan chiefs were baptized into the Catholic faith, and blessings were laid upon their Indian arms, with which they were to slaughter other Indians. This reconstructed Church of San Francisco still stands on a terrace just above the plaza, and on its worn pulpit one may read: "Here the Holy Evangel had its beginning in this new world."

About half a mile north of the plaza, set dramatically on a hill, stands one of the loveliest churches in the hemisphere. It is called the Sanctuary of Ocotlán. Its twin white towers and dazzling white façade, fancifully Churrigueresque and charming in the extreme, stand out spectacularly against the red hexagonal tiles of the outer walls. The great door faces west so that the congregation looks upon the snow-topped volcanoes when emerging from the church. Within, the extravagantly carved chapel of the Virgin is like an illuminated grotto of ice and gold in shadowy woods. The richly detailed work was done by an Indian sculptor named Francisco Miguel. For twenty-five years, in an ecstasy of devotion, he labored to produce one of the most graceful treasures of ecclesiastical art. The shrine is a favored spot of the occasional Americans who slip away into semiretirement in Tlaxcala when they want a quiet, as well as a quick, divorce.

Back on the Puebla Highway, ten miles beyond Texmelucán lies a memorable village called Huejotzingo, after the knotgrass that abounded in the fields. In the stagecoach days, horses were changed here, and, like Rio Frio, it was a favorite holdup place. To us it seemed to be an allegorical town, with the market or Vanity Fair on one side of the highway and an acre of the Kingdom of Heaven on the other.

In the shaded plaza the spreading market was a mass of humanity, bargaining among worldly pots and gewgaws, gulping hard cider and gossip, extracting fun and forgetfulness in the way of the world. Across the street, up an embankment and through a gate, one could step straight out of the material world into felicity. Within the walls the mellowed atrium of the old Franciscan church lay under a spell of peace. The babble from the market became no more than a pleasant hum of bees. At intervals around the walls, half-shaded by ancient trees, were alcoves or prayer stations for meditation, and each dedicated to a different Apostle. "It is," Patricia said as we paused to savor the tranquillity, "as if Saint Francis himself had put his special blessing on the place."

This Franciscan church and convent were among the earliest constructed in New Spain, and they were dedicated to Saint Michael the Archangel. The enormous carved doors of the church were closed, as if forever, and we doubted if we could get inside. But the chauffeur found the caretaker working his little vegetable patch in the back of the grounds. Beatifically smiling, he came forth, wiping his hands on black-cotton trousers. He was a thin, ascetic-looking man, and he wore a faded pink shirt. By his attitude and expression, despite his modern garments, he was like some Franciscan Brother that time had by-passed and left here as guardian. Through a side door he led us into an atmosphere musty with age and tradition. The odor was not unpleasant; it was compounded of old leather, candle wax, worn stone, and rose geranium.

Along the corridors were primitive "white" murals, painted by some of the very first Franciscans to reach the new world. In the architecture and decoration of the church there was an odd synthesis of the Spanish and the Indian, with a touch of Chinese lacquer work out of the Philippines. The refectory and the ovens for baking bread seemed as unchanged as if the Brothers might be returning any day, to take up their life of prayer and ministration. The rows of white-washed cells were so designed that on Saint Francis's day, the fourth of October, a beam of sunlight would pass through the windows at either end along the length of the central corridor. This shaft of sun-shine the Brothers looked to as if it were a direct inspiration from Heaven to guide them in the next year's work.

Out in the patio, pink geraniums climbed ancient pillars to the second story and a twisted orange tree in one corner still bore fruit. There was a peculiar sweetness in the atmosphere.

"Often," said the sacristan, "I take a book from the old library and here in the patio in the late afternoon when I am sure no visitors will come, I open the pages and read the life of some saint. There is much companionship and consolation to be got from books written by good men. It was Saint Paul who said, 'For whatsoever things were written aforetime were written for our learning, that we through patience and comfort of the scriptures may have hope.' "

In the library had been preserved many old volumes bound in parchment as well as leather. "Even then," I said, "and perhaps more than now, books were a refuge from the men of action who go about making a mess of the world."

"The Franciscans, you know," Pat said, "followed in the wake of conflict, asking nothing for themselves, possessing nothing, and only offering peace to troubled hearts."

Back in the atrium Thérèse and Pat seemed unwilling to emerge from the quietude. The peace that the early Franciscans held in their hearts—that peace which was not of this world—still pervaded the place like an active element. And there was a lingering elation, like the consciousness of eternal loving-kindness. Was this timeless good the reality, and the world's folly across the way the illusion? We had hardly expected to encounter mysticism in a roadside town called Huejotzingo. I thought of Dostoevsky, the humanitarian, and his foreboding about the direction of civilization in the comparatively slow-paced year of 1880:

They have science, but in science there is nothing but what is the object of sense. The spiritual world, the higher part of man's being, is rejected altogether, dismissed with a sort of triumph, even with hatred. The world has proclaimed the reign of freedom, especially of late, but what do we see in this freedom of theirs? Nothing but slavery and self-destruction! For the world says: "You have desires and so satisfy them, for you have the same rights as the most rich and powerful. Don't be afraid of satisfying them, and even multiply your desires." That is the doctrine of the modern world. In that they see freedom. And what follows from this right of multiplication of desires? In the rich, isolation and spiritual suicide; in the poor, envy and murder; for they have been given rights, but have not been shown the means of satisfying their wants. They maintain that the world is getting more and more united, more and more bound together in brotherly community, as it overcomes distance and sets thoughts flying through the air.

How ironically prophetic! The thoughts flying through the air in 1943 from any quarter of the globe were more full of discord and recrimination than unbrotherly mankind had ever known. Forces of science were channeled into blind massacre and ruthless devastation, and radio's prime function was to stir up vengeance. To stray into this walled churchyard of peace and love was a welcome respite from the immediate too-muchness of modernity.

The chauffeur began to regard us strangely, with wonder rather than impatience. I said, "We must get along."

Thérèse and Pat began to plan to come again, bring a box lunch, and spend a whole day in the atrium. Next Wednesday was the first day Thérèse was free from doing necessary things with me, and Wednesday was settled on. Then as we moved to the gate and the world, Pat suddenly remembered that she was playing cards with

King Carol and Madame Lupescu at Coyoacán on Wednesday. How could she have forgotten? The lure of Vanity Fair won out. The appointment was left vague, and we drifted out of the sanctuary back into the market place, where Indians were crowding gleefully around a free-for-all dog fight. As peripatetic serape-sellers assailed us from three sides, we got in the car and drove on to the Holy City of Cholula.

From a distance, the towers and domes, bright with glazed tile, glittered like something out of an Arabian Nights' tale. For the size of the town and the population there are more churches than in any other place in the world. When the Spaniards arrived, Cholula, the great commercial emporium of the central plateau, was still venerated as a religious center. Pagan temples had been erected to every conceivable deity, including the benign god Quetzalcoatl. Soldiers of Cortés claimed to have counted four hundred individual towers when they first marched upon the city. To stamp out paganism, the Christians had in time attempted to build a church on the site of every heathen temple they tore down. Modern guidebooks claim a Christian church for every day in the year. But our chauffeur said there were no more than two hundred, and that that was just about one church for each family in Cholula. Through the years, Puebla, eight miles away, had drawn most of the citizens. Cortés said he had found twenty thousand houses within the city walls and twenty thousand more outside. But today there is no more than an under-brush of Indian huts, with a forest of churches.

The Spaniard went to endless labor and trouble to hide the great pyramid and temple of Quetzalcoatl under earth and then on top of the stupendous mass to build a Christian edifice in honor of the Virgin of the Remedies. The pyramid, which is now no more than a hill grown over with trees and occasional shrubs, is wider at the base than the Pyramid to the Sun at Teotihuacán. One must climb uninteresting steps to reach the uninspired structure at the top, and enter a tunnel in the hill to reach the pagan temple buried within. We did neither. We chose only one church to enter, the Capilla Real, adjoining the large Church of San Francisco. This chapel is extraordinary because of its forty-odd domes and its countless columns within. It is more like a Mohammedan mosque in Kairouan than a Christian church in Mexico. Sunlight poured from the skylight towers that are like hectagonal nipples on the outer breasts of the domes. Not a single human worshiper was in the building, but birds were swooping among the columns as if they were tree trunks, and ducking before the high altar, and singing resounding choruses of bird praise that reverberated against the concavities of the domes. With the spirit of the convent at Huejotzingo still upon her, and moved by the chorus of bird song, Patricia knelt to say a little prayer.

It was hard to believe that in pre-Cortés days six thousand human victims were sacrificed annually at Cholula to satisfy the Indian gods' blood lust. Some of Cortés's men turned pale and vomited when, on their arrival, they beheld the savage ritual of priests' slitting living human breasts and tearing out the beating hearts in ecstasy. Yet it was here that the Spaniards themselves committed the wholesale massacre of Cholulans, when they feared an ambush and slaughtered "between 3,000 and 6,000 of their hosts." But all the blood that had soaked into the ground of Cholula had not made the unkempt plaza rich in vegetation. It was sun-baked and uninviting. Only one person did we see cross it—a young man who was breaking the law by appearing in the open in the habiliments of a priest. He caught me staring at him, grinned sheepishly, and pulled up his skirts to reveal his trousers underneath. He held his skirts up around his middle to be technically within the law, and dropped them in the doorway of one of the minor dead and empty churches.

2. CITY OF THE ANGELS

Eight miles beyond lay Puebla de Los Angeles. When the Spaniards found Cholula an active city dating far beyond historical record, Puebla was no more than an unmarked spot on the plain. Ten years after the fall of Tenochtitlán, the Spaniards created Puebla as a strategic center between Vera Cruz and the capital. According to one legend, the precise site was selected by two angels who appeared in a dream to a Franciscan friar named Julian Garcés. The supernatural beings carried surveyors' rods and lines, and pointed the way to what is now Puebla. The powers in Mexico City recognized the sagacity of the choice, and work was begun on the eve of Archangel

Michael's day in 1531. The town was named in honor of the sur-
veying angels.

According to the chronicles of Fray Toribio de Benavente on the
sixteenth of April 1532, forty Spanish families came to settle in the
newly laid-out city. The first buildings were erected by "eight thousand Tlaxcalan Indians, who arrived singing and dancing and playing upon their musical instruments." But for all the metaphysical aid
of angel surveyors and a troop of musical Indians at its origin, Puebla
did not seem simpatico to us on first impression. Its pavements and
its eastern hills palpitate with the history of famous sieges. It was
ever a stronghold of Catholicism (often spoken of as "the Rome of
Mexico"). Its townspeople pride themselves on their old mansions.
Some of its façades fairly blossom with tile. But its streets were narrow and formal, and the cathedral was turned the wrong way. It was
difficult to get a good look at anything.

The guidebooks say Puebla is famous for its fine food. "Excellent"
was the printed word for the place we stopped for luncheon. A man
friend of Pat's, who had lived twenty years in Mexico, had said,
"Positively, it's the only place to eat, even though it looks like a bar."
But an American friend of ours, a seasoned world traveler and a
Mexican enthusiast, had written "awful food!" in pencil in the margin of the guidebook she had lent us, as well as "terrible!" by the
name of the best hotel, reputed to have "an exquisite cuisine in the
midst of eighteenth-century aristocratic splendor." From the minute
we were placed at a corner table of the restaurant near the front, we
were plagued by persistent newsboys, male and female lottery-ticket
sellers, itinerant venders of objects in onyx, and a pestiferous set of
beggars of diverse categories.

Thérèse and I ordered the famous *mole poblano,* "for which Puebla
is celebrated throughout the Republic." Pat was more prudent; she
stuck to the *arroz con pollo.* The principal ingredients of the *mole*
were chocolate and chili. It was blackish-brown and had a rich,
heavy odor. But it was not for our palates or stomach lining. We
tried to pick out the slices of turkey breast and remove as much of
the sauce as possible. But it was still too fiery and sickish, and we
gave up and ordered chilled papaya, something as safe as refreshing,
and that could not be ruined in the kitchen.

Hovering about us like kibitzers over a bridge table stood three wavers of flimsy strips of lottery tickets, mumbling of *fortuna*. At last, when an evil-looking old female beggar joined the group and began to snivel, I rose from my chair. With a stern expression and cold emphasis I said: "No, no, no! To all of you. Go, *por favor*. Go with God! But go! Not *mañana. Inmediatamente!* Stand not upon the order of your going. But go, *instantáneamente!*" The old woman bandied vicious eyes with me for a moment. But with the others, she departed, shaking the dust of us from her draggletailed skirt. I was not as upset as Lady Macbeth at the banquet, but the effect of my speech was something the same. Still, it was the only time I ever felt forced to be rude to peddlers or beggars in Mexico. "Let's go do penance for my manners," I said, "in the cathedral across the plaza."

We did not cross directly through the Plaza de la Constitución, but wound our way under the *portales* which surround three sides. The chief commodities sold here seemed to be sweetmeats and candied yams, onyx knickknacks in a thousand shapes, and puppet dolls dangling from strings. The tile was so emphatically the queen of manufactured products that industrialists had presented the plaza with seats in green-and-lavender tile gaudily advertising their brands of cigarettes and mineral water.

In October 1847, this plaza had been the scene of a strange siege. After the battle of Cerro Gordo, in which the American troops defeated Santa Anna, General William J. Worth had left in Puebla eighteen hundred sick and wounded soldiers to be guarded by Colonel Thomas Childs and five hundred men. Fearing trouble in the naturally hostile city, Colonel Childs made a barricaded encampment in the plaza and brought a quantity of cattle and sheep for precaution against starvation. When the main part of the American army had proceeded over the mountains toward the capital, Mexican soldiers attacked the invaders in the square. For thirty days they kept up artillery fire, shot rifles from the housetops, and attacked with bayonets down the converging streets. The whole city watched the fight with interest, wagers were made, church bells clanged excitedly day and night. At last, after thirty days of holding out in the very center of an enemy town, Colonel Childs was rescued by reinforcements from Vera Cruz.

The church bells had apparently never stopped ringing—at least in one part of the city or another—and we approached the cathedral to the noise of pealing bells. The massive cathedral turns its side instead of its face to the plaza. But it is no great matter, for the façade is not inspired, and the atrium is nothing but arid flagstone. The cornerstone had been laid in 1562, two years before Shakespeare was born and some decades before any Englishman set foot in Virginia. The edifice was declared completed on April 18, 1649. In the bell-tower, the largest of the eighteen bells, which weighs nine tons, was set in place in 1729. In spite of the authentic antiquity, strangely the cathedral has not taken on the patina that comes with age.

The famous interior seemed to us a conglomeration of magnificence, gloom, and bad taste. There is some beautiful carving in the choir loft, but one hardly sees it for the lavish display of gilded pillars, onyx altars, and marble statuary. Amid so much ostentation the series of enormous barred metal gates before the lateral chapels were superbly impressive in their chaste dignity.

"How far is all this pretentious grandeur," we said, "from the pervading spirituality of the little church and monastery at Huejotzingo!" Pat, the Catholic, quite agreed, and she did not even ask to see the shrine behind the bishop's choir which treasured a reputed thorn from Christ's crown when he was crucified.

Though the grandiose cathedral seemed as disharmonious as the chocolate and chili concoction called *mole poblano,* the opulent little Rosary Chapel in the Church of Santo Domingo was as lovely as a Mozart opera. The design and decoration had been created and executed by concordant minds. The lavish use of gold leaf and polychrome was all of one style. In the midst of golden fruits and multicolored garlands, ethereal angels blew silvery trumpets and made a joyful noise unto the Lord. Strange mythological beasts with pastel hides lay down contentedly together. Birds and flowers, saints and animals, dappled light and candle glow, were all mere varied tributes of a God of love and joy. There was no gloom, no lack, no wounded Jesus to darken the spirits. Though this seventeenth-century chapel to the Virgin was the antithesis of Franciscan simplicity, it was as honest as it was gorgeous. To look at it rejoiced the heart like an Easter hymn.

Another piece of Puebla architecture that suggests frozen music is the seventeenth-century Casa del Alfeñique. Its lyrical walls are of rose lava and blue-and-white majolica squares, topped with gay

Churrigueresque adornments in white stone like the frosting on a wedding cake. Its sixteen charming little balconies have iron balustrades so delicate and fine that they look as if they might have been spun by gigantic spiders. This ancient mansion, which is still in excellent preservation, served as a guest house for viceroys in colonial days. Dignitaries fresh from Spain paused here on the arduous trip from Vera Cruz to the capital and gathered strength for the more hazardous stretch over the great mountain wall. No house in Mexico has been the scene of better balls and parties, for the Creoles were determined to make a memorable first impression on the Spanish noblemen and their haughty retinues. Now the Sugar Paste House has been transformed into a state museum. The upper floors have been refurnished like a seignorial dwelling of the colonial period, from the crimson-brocaded drawing-room to the picturesque authentic kitchen.

We passed up the famous clandestine Convent of Santa Monica, though we paused before the private house at 18 Poniente No. 103 that disguises the entrance. Only in 1935, decades after the Juárez law that made convents unlawful in Mexico, was it discovered that this order of nuns had gone literally underground, taking their paintings, brocaded vestments, and embroideries with them. There are thirty-nine rooms reached by various trapdoors and hidden stairs. A secret passage leads to a near-by church. In seclusion, for seventy-eight years the nuns carried on, earning their living by making embroideries that were somehow smuggled out and sold. To keep the order going, novices were admitted as the old ladies died. The secret was disclosed by a servant in the private house who quarreled with her mistress. The state, to which all ecclesiastical property belongs by law, turned the place into a museum and brought the effects of two other unearthed bootleg convents to put on exhibition in Santa Monica.

Instead of visiting the convent, we went to one of the noted tile factories. They, too, do not look like what they are. Their fronts are those of private houses. The Uriarte tile factories have remained in the possession of the same families for generations, and visitors stroll about the public rooms, the patios, and the back gardens much like guests at a party. The Uriarte drawing-rooms have been turned into showrooms and its arcades into ateliers for the artisans, who sit

in a long row applying the different colors. Like a garden house at
the back of the courtyard are the great ovens for the firing. The pieces
are laid on a long paddle something like that used by an old-time
French baker, and shoved into the fiery furnace by a man dressed in
baker's white.

At the far side of the patio are the huge vats of clay and the pot-
ters' whirring wheels. A melancholy-looking young Spaniard with
long delicate fingers paused in his work of modeling a fruit bowl
and deftly turned out a diminutive vase, a pitcher, and a mug. Nodding to each of us in turn, he indicated for whom they were intended.
It was a customary courteous gesture, and for the courtesy one left
money at his elbow to augment the four pesos—eighty cents—daily
wage he received for master craftsmanship.

We had seen enough of Puebla close up and were ready to drive
to the forts crowning the summit of hills east of the city. We did not
stop to see the twenty thousand old manuscripts at the library that
claims to be the third oldest in the continent. Nor did we pause as
we passed the great modern school, built in 1932, where a map of
Mexico is spread out of doors in acres of colored tile, to stimulate
interest in geography. We drove straight beyond the town up to the
site where on the fifth of May in 1862 intrepid Mexicans repulsed
the invading troops of Napoleon III and gave to the country a national holiday and to every town in the land a street name, Cinco de
Mayo.

Under the five-o'clock sun the city lay like a Persian garden, with
domes the polished yellow of squash flowers, and towers like white-
and-green tuberoses. Terra-cotta roofs and lines of treetops were like
turned earth and hedgerows. Patches of blue majolica were like beds
of ageratum. Far in the distance behind the city to the west, Popocatepetl and Ixtacihuatl shimmered like piled diamond dust in the
brilliance of the sun. To the north rose the jagged slabs of Malinzin,
and to the east the climactic cone of Orizaba. All the volcanoes were
in the clear, and all but one were luminous with snow. We had not
considered Puebla deserving of its angelic appellation. But from this
distance we felt differently. It must have been on such an afternoon
and from this height that the churchmen decided that the new-
planned town was worthy of being named for the angels.

VII

Oaxaca

And if there be such a thing as historical memory in us, it is
not strange that the sweetest moment in any life, pleasant or
dreary, should be when Nature draws near to it, and taking
up her neglected instrument plays a fragment of some ancient
melody, long unheard on the earth.

—W. H. HUDSON

I. THE ROUTE OF THE THREE VOLCANOES

SAYS THE BEST GUIDEBOOK, published in 1938, "The night train which
carries sleepers leaves Mexico City Mondays, Wednesdays, and
Fridays and arrives at Oaxaca at 8:10 A.M." It tells that the railroad
is narrow-gauge, but it does not reveal that the sleeper berths are
sliced off short for Mexican-sized patrons. When Ike Myers from
Memphis visited Oaxaca in the late 30's with David Cohn, the Mis-
sissippi writer, they went by the overnight train. It was not so bad
for Myers, because he measures five feet six.

But Cohn, who is six feet three, found he could not possibly get
his rangy frame into the contracted berth space except by thrusting
his jackknifed knees into the everyman's territory of the aisle and
making a triangular hurdle for passers-by to negotiate. After some
tortured hours of honest effort at adjustment, he folded his blanket,
and stole into the malodorous second-class coach. There, bolt upright
on the stiff wooden seats, he passed the night hours among the curious Indians, who roused themselves out of their serapes or stopped
suckling their young to peer incredulously at the strange white giant
in their midst.

Since Myers had flown down from Memphis merely on a businessman's breather in this mid-July of 1943, he did not have the time
to motor over the just completed stretch of Pan-American Highway
from Mexico City to Oaxaca, so we booked seats on the regular
morning plane.

There are mockers who look at you accusingly when they learn
that you are not traveling "like the people," and demand, "How can

you really *see* Mexico if you don't travel second-class?" When they learn that you fly expeditiously in cool comfort instead of in prolonged perspiring discomfort, they curl their lips as if they had uncovered an impostor.

"What can you *see* from an airplane?" the resentful train travelers had scoffed often enough. This July morning we saw at close range a cluster of three volcanoes, the most magnificent specimens in the Northern continent. I had seen them before in various aspects from the ground and from the air, but never had I been so close to them. They flashed upon the visual faculties in rapid succession like electric volts of beauty. At 8:45 the plane rose from the earth toward the unblemished azure of the Mexican sky. In twenty minutes we were passing over the stretched-out splendor of Ixtacihuatl. In five more minutes we were as close to Popocatepetl as a plane could approach safely; and in another ten minutes there was the climactic peak of Orizaba, refulgent under the golden sun. The White Lady, with the fantastic name Ixtacihuatl, lay in eternal siesta, like some pale Norse goddess shrouded in snow-white samite and sprinkled with diamond dust. The glittering Popo had defied death for centuries, and now from time to time it would breathe out a warning sulphurous smoke like an old dragon dying. Only a few weeks before, a party of venturesome Europeans had met a ghastly fate by taking liberties with the snow-crowned Popo. To give his guests a rare treat and let them glimpse hell-fire at the source, a titled host had flown his plane directly over the gaping crater. Popo had sucked the plane and all its sensation-seeking passengers down into its brimstone maw. The witless mystagogue and the ladies and gentlemen with him paid dearly for nosing into the mysteries of a smoldering volcano.

At exactly half-past nine the best view of Orizaba was to be had. Citlaltepetl, "The Mountain of the Star," as the Indians called Orizaba, rises from the tropical earth nearer heaven than any volcano on the continent. Serene in its pride of place, it is the first of the three volcanoes to catch the rays of the sun rising out of the Atlantic. Its thick cone, encased in tons of unmelting snow, looked as smooth as the white-marble flank of some archangel chiseled by Michelangelo. Every high mountain, according to an old French saying, is a sermon which directs the human soul to Heaven, and a peak, as

Lamartine observed, gives point to the sermon. The dullest clod could not but be impressed by this glittering masterpiece of creation. Rising eighteen thousand seven hundred feet, it yet surpassed other peaks in grandeur, more by its classical form than by its height. With its snow whiter than swan's-down or a gardenia petal, it reflected such illumination from the sun that it seemed to rival the source of light in brilliance. As the plane passed, a cloud flung itself like a garland against the dazzling white-marble dome, as if to prevent man from looking too long on beauty unbearably refulgent.

Within a few minutes our eyes had been enriched by an essence of beauty that a thousand railway journeys in Mexico could not equal in their sum of delights. We had been fortunate to behold the three chief jewels in Mexico's treasure house in a brief quarter of an hour. Often they were veiled by mist, and particularly in the summer season. But beauty is inherently evanescent in any case. Climaxes cannot be continuous. One cannot look at the same scene for hours on end and remain in a state of exaltation. There must be an element of freshness and surprise in the impact.

When the volcanoes disappeared, we settled back in our seats under their spell and rested our eyes. The rest of the way to Oaxaca lay above mountains that looked rough and forbidding, without any spectacular sights. A fuzz of trees covered the mountainsides like a green mold. The occasional patches of yellow-green cornfields and the naked outlines of mud-house villages suggested tiny floating islands in the grand tumbling sea of forest trees. A train crawled like a black snake toward the south—the direction in which we were headed. Had the winged plane been an eagle, it might have swooped down and carried the thing off wriggling in its talons.

From the upper air, the Valley of Oaxaca, encircled by a ring of verdant hills, resembles an amphitheater of jadite. At the foot of one curve of it lies the town called Oaxaca, the capital of the state with the same name, which means "Covered with Calabash" or "The Place with Gourds." The surrounding mountains are of gentle contour, protective rather than awe-inspiring. The tones of green range from dark jade to pale willow. Lavender-green shadows mark the ravines. The radiance of midmorning sun lay like a glory upon the valley. It gave the earth a kind of pastoral serenity. In selecting the

ennobling title which the King of Spain bestowed upon him, Hernán
Cortés had asked to be called El Marqués del Valle de Oaxaca. If the
conquistador of conquistadors could only have conquered his own
compulsion to explore and have settled on his vast Oaxacan estates,
including threescore towns, his last years might have been graciously
contenting. Instead, he had continued to venture and seek, to squab-
ble and be rebuffed, at last to die of a bitter heart back in Spain before he was old in years.

In pre-Cortésian centuries, this green jewel of a valley, which
Cortés renounced for the glitter of false El Dorados, had nurtured
a culture that was responsible for the temples of Mitla and gold-
smiths of Monte Albán. The city had been the birthplace of the boy
child whose name was to be the best known of all Mexicans in the
world capitals at the end of the nineteenth century—Porfirio Díaz.
Among these hills, the great patriot Benito Juárez had tended sheep
as an unlettered Indian lad while dreaming vague dreams of democracy.

2. MUNICIPAL HEART

The inhabitants of Oaxaca dwell in a fertile and salubrious climate.
At a mile above the level of the sea, they are neither plagued with
extremes of heat nor do they know the sorrows of winter. The ther-
mometer never varies more than 13° Fahrenheit. The average temperature stands at that perfect for mankind, 70°. Rainfall can be de-
pended upon, and is abundant, yet discreet. Occasionally to make
the Oaxaqueños more thankful for their daily blessing, nature has
sent earthquakes to trouble the ground. To meet nature's challenge,
the builders have made their walls doubly thick. So one gets an immediate impression that Oaxaca is a town of heavy stone and rein-
forced masonry. But in the Moorish manner, towers and domes rise
to break the monotony of flat roofs and earth-hugging houses. The
general color tone of Oaxaca is green, just as in Morelia it is pink,
because in Oaxaca the stone of the regional quarries is greenish.

Green and thick-walled, the city is very old, and Spanish and
colonial in flavor. In the 1480's, about the time Cortés was born in
Spain, Aztec warriors of Montezuma's Emperor uncle founded the
town, because of gold deposits discovered near by. By a decree of
Charles V, Oaxaca was declared a *ciudad* on July 6, 1529, in the very

same edict that created Hernán Cortés Marqués del Valle de Oaxaca. Its growth was rapid. Already by 1532, according to an old chronicle, there resided in Oaxaca, besides the thousands of Indians, "five hundred Castilian families of pure blood, without an African, a Jew, or a Turk among them."

In Oaxaca today, more than in any other town or city of Mexico, life centers about the plaza. The focus is really a double plaza, or a plaza and a brief alameda, with the cathedral dominating one side of one and one side of the other. But it is not the venerable edifice, begun in 1553, that attracts. It is the dark-green laurel trees planted three centuries ago and the faded green *portales,* noble in design and rich in shade. There are abundant benches under the trees and hundreds of tables on the sidewalks of the cafés. From a seat at a café table, you have a panoramic view more interesting and colorful, if less sophisticated, than from any boulevard of Paris. The atmosphere is amiable, and relaxed, with none of that tension in the street crowd that is found in Mexico City. Indians of two tribes, Zapotec and Mixtec, circulate among the arcaded shops or sit in contented ease on the stone benches under the laurels that rise to a height of sixty feet. The faces and hands of some have been baked to the rich color of cinnamon by the heat of thousands of afternoons of working under the sun. A few of them carry folded across their shoulders the famous white-and-blue serapes of the district.

Deep in the shadows of the *portales* are the stations of the scribes, who write letters at the hesitant dictation of the illiterate. From the expressions on the dark faces intent on the effort of forming sentences, one can often tell when the letter is of love or longing, of reproach, or begging extension of credit. With faces as noncommittal as a talking-machine record at rest, the scribe sets down the proposal of marriage, the expression of sympathy over the death of a parent, or the tale of woe about agricultural mishaps.

Peripatetic bootblacks seek custom and enjoy their novitiate in meeting the ways of the world. Itinerant peddlers pass with trays of notions, and flower girls, with baskets of blossoms. Sepia-colored soldiers go by in twos or threes, their uniforms the dusty gray-green of the native stone of Oaxaca. Their eyes follow the full-skirted flower girls or those with short skirts going home from their work in a ceramic factory or an office. The limousine of the governor stops before the governor's mansion that extends the length of a block. A humble cortege, following with lighted candles the man-borne casket of a child, passes into the cathedral. Men showing off in the open-air shooting gallery do not pause in their aiming and firing to glance at the funeral procession. An ancient victoria, minus the rubber tires, passes with an aristocratic old lady, her white hair as elaborately coifed as if she were on her way to be presented to Maximilian and Carlota.

Down upon the slow-moving procession of daily life, the cathedral clock, rusty in its ancient mechanism, drops the announcement of quarter-hours. But the Oaxaqueños pay it little heed. They move more by the sun and the moon and their own internal regulator of the value and necessity of time.

Most of the sight-seeing that needs to be done in Oaxaca on foot or by car can well be accomplished in a day. But you can sit at a side-walk table for hours on end, day after day, and varied sights will come of themselves into your range of vision, just as you observe a Mardi Gras parade in New Orleans from an iron-grilled gallery.

It was Charles Flandrau who pointed out the analogy of the Mexican plaza to an English garden party: "And one meets and speaks with just as many strangers as one does at an English garden party. But in the Mexican plaza or park each person feels he is both host and guests." Nowhere in Mexico does this seem more true than in the municipal heart of Oaxaca. You are continually meeting peo-ple. A Mexican army officer is introduced and joins you in a ver-mouth. When he goes, a poet or a representative of Palmolive Soap takes his place, or you are invited to join a group of mining engi-neers on a spree.

But there is one disturbing element not found in an English garden party, or even in the Mexican towns of Taxco or Morelia or San Miguel de Allende. It is the clocklike interruption of sociable beg-gars. There are a half-dozen who make the rounds within an hour. One is a blind girl, who knows the territory so well that she saunters freely among the tables, without a child or a dog to lead her. She is under twenty and wears her rebozo like a turban in the Biblical fashion. Her features are good except for the blank eyes, which are the color of Malaga grapes. You give her money, and within an hour she is back, with her cupped palm making a shadow athwart the table, as if collecting tribute for the privilege of sitting at the tables.

Another beggar, a man, is more spectacular. He is thin and dramatically dark, with Spanish rather than Indian features. He squirms his way about on his palms and his bottom, for he has no legs. They have been cut off at the rump. He moves like some strange denizen of the deep that is out of its element on sandy earth, but determined to overcome natural laws and survive. His rear end is encased in thick leather, so that he will not wear the meager buttocks completely to the bone. Though the legless man moves in jerks and writhings, he makes the circuit of the *portales* and the shaded walks of the alameda with as much timeliness as the blind girl with her two good legs and sure-footed tread.

Neither begged, I was told by one of my newly made acquaintances, because they were forced by necessity. They begged for the sociability of the act. The town fathers had repeatedly offered the repulsive fellow a comfortable pension if he would remain in seclusion at home. But he had firmly declined the municipality's offer again and again. "What fun would I have if I stayed like a rat in a dark hole?" he pleaded. "Who would come to see me? How would I hear the news of the world? I am yet alive, and while I breathe I must mingle with my fellows. Each day's business is an adventure with me. I am a sorry sight, yes. I know I make genteel people shudder. But am I not an asset to their morale? They look at me and give thanks to God they are not in my legless case, no matter what their misfortune. No, no! So long as I can wriggle on my hands and my butt, I intend to enjoy the companionship of the plaza. When I can no longer navigate on my own power, kill me. But don't pension me, for the love of Christ, and shut me away from the world."

3. FACTORY IN A GARDEN

"Oaxaca," declared another new friend sitting at a sidewalk café table with us, "is composed of ninety per cent weather, nine per cent gossip, and one per cent business."

Although the city is the commercial center of a large territory, the visitor has little awareness of business activity. But since at the table with us was a man who had flown down from Boston to do some wholesale buying under the guidance of his Swiss associate from Mexico City, Myers and I went with them to observe the what's-what of Oaxaca's one per cent. The businessmen hailed a topless taxi and we drove to the "factory district" at the edge of the town.

In the midst of an avenue of trees the car stopped before a long one-story building with thick walls painted a dusty pink. Through the enormous doorway we passed into a reception hall and then into a room proportioned like a state ballroom. Here samples and merchandise for sale were piled on tables and stacked in shelves. Hundreds of serapes; thousands of tablecloths; bathrobes and dressing-gowns by the gross. The Bostonian and the Swiss made swift appraisals and began ordering two hundred of these, three hundred of those, a thousand of the serviettes. American manufacturers could not get the materials or the workmen, so wholesalers flew from Boston to buy table linen and embroidered blouses from Oaxaca. There was no salesmanship, no bargaining, virtually no hesitation about selection. The soft-voiced manager of the showroom named the price, the Swiss and the Bostonian looked at each other and said: "Five hundred, perhaps?—Well, let's make it seven hundred and fifty."

While the buying was in progress and Myers looked on, I went to see the workers at the assembly lines. A barefooted Indian boy with the tail of his pink-cotton shirt knotted jauntily in front directed me out the great arched back door of the reception hall. Then he made a sweeping gesture toward the garden and left me to explore for myself. The place was like Eden in abundance of fruit and fragrance. Green-gold globes weighted the branches of the grapefruit trees. Limes and lemons and oranges made up in numbers for the size they never could attain. The refreshing sharp perfume of citrus fruits mingled with the heavy fragrance of mango and gardenia. In the shade of crinkled flame-colored crepe myrtles Indian girls were doing embroidery. They wore white-muslin blouses and bright-colored cotton skirts. Two had stopped their work to drink from blue tumblers at the flowing fountain.

I wandered until I came to a series of long low wooden pavilions. From within emerged the pleasant muted whir of shifting shuttles, of wooden pedals pushed and released. There, like musicians before harps or organs, sat young men before looms weaving cotton or linen or wool. They wore nothing except white-duck trousers and small straw hats with upcurving brims. Their lithe and muscular backs were the color of wet copper. They worked steadily, with beautiful dexterity and without strain. They would glance at a drawing of the pattern they were to follow, as a symphony conductor might glance at a musical score he knew well. Each man wove his stuff according to his own artistic interpretation of the pattern. And each foot of cloth came out with a bit of the youth himself woven into the texture and the design. To the sounds the weavers made with levers and pedals, birds in hanging wooden cages sang impromptu flutelike obligatos.

I thought of a glowing line Graça Aranha had written about listening to "the lovely joyful music formed by the noises of toil—always the same light manual work, humble and sweet, without the shrill scream of steam"—and it did not seem sentimental here. I thought, too, of the noise of an American factory with its breathtaking machinery and great black belts crackling over the bright wheels. There the tense, stereotyped workers had no more to do with the result than a man who turns the electric switch to heat the eggs in a chicken incubator. These Mexicans working al fresco, unstained by coal smoke, took a special joy in work because they were more than automatons. By the tightness or the looseness of a handful of threads, by running an extra line of orange or blue, they were their own masters within limits. I saw one of the older men regarding a square of cloth he had just finished with peculiar satisfaction, as a spider might admire an intricate web spun from its own insides.

I turned from the looms and the rows of copper-colored backs and started through the garden. Under an avocado tree I paused to watch the girls smiling and chatting as they bent over their embroidery in a setting more like a scene in a romantic opera than in a real workaday world. How long, I wondered again, would it be before civilization would give the deathblow to this simple manifestation of culture?

Myers came out on the veranda to get me. "I have just made all the expenses of my trip," he said. "I've bought five thousand little dusters, which I shall sell to a department store in Memphis. They'll be delivered in time for the Christmas trade."

The Boston buyer had virtually cleaned out the Oaxacan manufacturer's stock on hand and for months to come. The manager, who was naturally gratified at the day's phenomenal business, wore an oddly puzzled expression. He did not bow us out in the really grand manner, because he was of newly risen middle class and his family had never lived in a mansion like this. But he shook hands with each of us, and as he did so, he murmured the conventional *"Esta casa es sua."*

If the house wasn't, I thought, almost everything in it was now. The manager's last look implied that this thought had just hit him between the eyes.

"Now what are the Mexicans going to do for tablecloths and blankets?" I said as we drove away from the factory.

"That's something for them to begin thinking about," said the Boston merchant blithely, making notes for the next day's buying.

4. PRIVATE BATH AND HISTORIC NAMES

Instead of staying at the old hotel on the plaza (atmospheric with faded grandeur) we had all gone to the recently opened Ruiz, because of more surety of creature comforts. Here were plenty of rooms with private baths. But having a bath of one's own in Mexico does not preclude hazards. The first morning, when I was half-shaved, the water from the faucets suddenly stopped dead in its tracks. No swearing, no shaking the pipes, could coax another drop. To complete the shaving job I used half of the pint of gaseous mineral water left in a bottle. That afternoon, when I stepped blithely into the tub and turned on the shower, only empty dry gasping sounds emerged. I twisted hot and cold faucets as far open as they would go and was mocked for my zeal.

The summoned bellboy informed me that the city turned on the water only for certain intervals during the day, at which times the citizens were supposed to make all their ablutions and pull the toilet chains. The finances of the waterworks system were in a sad case. Funds had been misappropriated. Graft was at the bottom of it all. The sanitary-engineering job had not been so well done either. The boy shook his head sadly, murmured, *"Quien sabe?"* and recommended patience. One could not be too whimsical about bathing.

It was all very complicated. I never got the straight of it. My luck in gambling on the water was almost persistently bad. It seemed we were invariably off on a trip or lounging in the plaza when the water ran plentifully. And twice I was caught a mass of soapsuds and had to dip up water from the toilet bowl and use the tumbler for a shower.

"But at least," said another new-made Oaxacan friend, "the hot water and cold water now come out where they should. When the hotel was first opened, it was discovered that the plumber had got his signals mixed. Boiling water came up in the bowl of the toilet and down from the shower. There was cold water only for the tub, and nothing but wind from the laboratory faucets. If old Porfirio Díaz had been President for another quarter-century, we Mexicans might have become really proficient in plumbing."

It seemed remarkable that from the two small cities of Morelia and Oaxaca had come the greater proportion of famous names of Mexican history. The towns were approximately the same size, the guidebooks putting each of them as low as thirty thousand in population and neither larger than forty thousand. Morelia was the birthplace of José Maria Morelos and Agustín de Iturbide, while the careers of Miguel Hidalgo and Lázaro Cárdenas were closely associated with the city. From Oaxaca had come the two outstanding Mexicans of the last half of the nineteenth century: Benito Juárez and Porfirio Díaz.

Though the visitor is never shown anything that does honor to the memory of Díaz, who ruled Mexico for thirty-odd years, a statue of Juárez dominates the beautiful hillside park that looks down on the city from the north. And in recent years the house in which Juárez lived as a servant to a friar has been reconstructed and turned into a liberal shrine.

The theft of a sheep was the turning-point in Juárez's career, and the course of Mexican history was marked by the event. This pure-blooded Zapotec Indian was born in the Oaxacan village of San Pablo Guelatao. Left an orphan at four, he was reared by his father's brother, who could not afford to give him schooling. "Since my parents left me no patrimony," Juárez wrote, "and my uncle lived by his own labor, I had to work in the fields as soon as I reached the use of reason." Until he was twelve he tended sheep on the mountain-sides about a lovely lake called "The Enchanted."

In the year 1818, on a Wednesday, September 16, the date fated shortly to become Mexico's Independence Day because of Father Hidalgo's *Grito de Dolores,* some muleteers journeying by from Oaxaca stole one of Juárez's sheep. Spurred by the fear of his uncle's fury and desiring to make something more of himself than a shepherd, he resolved to go to Oaxaca, where an older sister was a cook in the house of an Italian merchant. With nothing but his palm-leaf rain cape for luggage, the lad walked the forty-two miles to the capital, and passed the first milestone on his great career. The Italian family fed him and got a Franciscan friar to keep him as a kind of servant apprentice. In a little house four minutes' walk from the plaza this Antonio Salanueva resided, and made his living by binding books. Benito helped him with his trade, besides doing the chores. In return the Franciscan taught the boy how to read and write. His aptitude was so remarkable that soon the friar was teaching him Spanish grammar and arithmetic. Within three years young Benito had entered the Seminary of Oaxaca, where his classmates made sport of his country ways. When the time came to take up the study of theology, the friar discovered the strong will of his ward, who was to be a future President of Mexico. The young man scorned religious dogma and begged to study jurisprudence. In January 1834, the Indian was admitted to the bar. Shortly after, he married the daughter of the Italian merchant. And at forty-one he became governor of the state at a time when Mexico was a violent hotbed of struggle between conservative and liberal forces. Despite the vicissitudes and exile and hairbreadth escapes from death that came into the fabric of his life, Juárez became the foremost Mexican liberal of his time. It was he who dispossessed the Roman Catholic Church of its rich holdings, and he whose dogged will rid the country of the French domination.

"The blows which I suffered," he wrote, "and which I saw inflicted almost daily upon unprotected persons who complained against the arbitrary action of the privileged classes consorting with civil authority, proved to me beyond doubt that society would never be happy so long as the latter groups continued to exist. . . . I was confirmed in my proposition of working constantly to destroy the doleful power of the privileged classes."

In the reconstructed little house of the Franciscan there are few

relics of the former houseboy. And the fact that Juárez may have
used a certain pen or have worn a certain hat seems somehow un-
stirring. Of all the material objects associated with his corporeality
the one I would like to have seen preserved under glass was the
palm-leaf rain cape in which the shepherd boy made his fateful
flight. But the palm leaves had become moldy dust long before
Benito's dark brow was wreathed with enduring laurel.

When I left the house where the genius was incubated, I knew
there was no need to inquire for a memorial to the other Oaxacan
boy who became world-famous. The revolutionaries after 1910 had
seen to it that Porfirio Díaz was discredited, for the radical democrat
had turned into a conservative after he got in power. Born twenty-
two years after Juárez, in a third-class inn run by his parents, and
left fatherless at three, the mestizo Díaz, with half Mixtec blood,
knew poverty almost as bitter as the full-blooded Zapotec. In some
respects their careers were parallel. As a lad Díaz was resourceful at
making his living while going to school. He too was intended for
the priesthood, and he too turned to the law. He studied civil rights
under Juárez himself. Just as he finished his studies, the turbulence
of the time turned him to soldiering. He became one of the most
valorous fighters Mexico has known, rising to be brigadier general
early in his thirties, and winning strategic battles for Juárez.

At length the Oaxaca compatriots became enemies, and Díaz ran
for the Presidency against Juárez, who had already held two terms
of office. When Díaz finally became President himself, he did not
relinquish his power for thirty-five years. Mexico made phenomenal
material progress under his administration, but the masses were
neglected. Díaz, who had been born of the people, proved to have
no interest in them. Only the handful of the Mexican upper classes
mourned his death in France in 1915. Laid to rest in the Paris cemetery of Montparnasse, he has as his only monument an urn filled
with the Oaxacan earth from which he sprung.

5. CORNERS IN ANTIQUITY

After the Maya temples in Yucatán and Chiapas and the Toltec
pyramids of Teotihuacán, the most impressive ruins in Mexico are

those of Mitla, some twenty-five miles southeast of Oaxaca. The three businessmen and I hired a car for the trip.

Six miles from Oaxaca on the road to the templed fortress we stopped at the village called Santa María del Tule to see one of the wonders of the world. In a corner of the churchyard of Saint Mary of the Bulrushes stands a gigantic cypress tree estimated to be some fifteen hundred years old. It reaches to a height of a hundred and sixty-five feet, and four feet from the base its circumference measures a hundred and sixty feet. Cortés and most of his troop rested under its spreading shade on their ill-fated journey to Honduras. At the turn of the nineteenth century, Baron von Humboldt came to pay his respects to this venerable organic monument, and he carved his immortal name in the gray-green bark. Today a printed sign warns the tourist not to do likewise. Where the great naturalist honored the tree, the incision of a lesser name would profane it. Almost a hundred persons with backs to the bole and shoulder to shoulder could encircle the tree like a broad-banded finger ring. Cottages might be erected under the branches, with their spread of a hundred and forty feet. Lovers could hide themselves from the world's eye in the mossy dells between the swollen roots. That morning, tots under school age were using it for a playhouse, clambering up and down the root ridges with innocent intimacy, unimpressed by the fabulous quality of something that had been like a cradle to them and their ancestors.

In the little village three manifestations of modernity had sprung up within sight of the great antiquity. One was the terminus of a streetcar line within fifty yards of the tree. The other two were a federal school and a co-operative mill for grinding corn. Across the dusty empty space as large as that of the green plaza of Oaxaca, an electric mill was doing work in three minutes that would have taken a woman three days to do. A line of some forty girls and women with wide fat baskets on their heads and deep tall baskets in their hands were lined up, waiting their turn to have the corn kernels crushed into meal. It was a nice composition for an artist. The short part of the line was in the shade of the crude stucco portico, the longer hind part stretched out into the white sunlight, which made brilliant the blues and reds of the women's full cotton skirts and the variegated dyes of their baskets.

The mill was operated only one day a week, but it was enough to grind the corn for the entire region's tortillas. The words Molina Cooperativa were painted in simple letters across the front of the low white building. Here was a leap of centuries out of the primitive ways. Until literally only yesterday, and as far back in the decipherable records as mankind in Mexico went, the females of the species had endured a laborious process in preparing the raw corn. They had boiled it in lime to make the husk easy to remove and then ground it by hand with a stone pestle in a stone bowl. It was the woman's lot to spend a goodly part of every day squatting over the implements for corn-grinding. The larger her brood of offspring, the more arduous her task, until the older girls were big enough to help with the work. But now, even in remote districts, girls were going to school until they were twelve years old, and they could not be as much help to the mothers as they were before the Government decided to make the Indians literate. So a co-operative mill, in which all the peasants held shares, was almost necessary after the federal school next door came to take up the children's time. One manifestation of civilization brings on another.

"El Arbol del Tule" has seen more changes in the ways of men within the last decade than in all its twenty-five centuries of continuous living. But the humankind who still take siestas on the cool couches of its bark alcoves still cling to many old ways. Though the household meal is ground in the new electrical manner, the tortillas are cooked over a fire on a flat sheet of metal in the shape of flat pancakes, just as they were long before the first white man observed the process.

In the corn-colored one-room Escuela Federal, a host of black-eyed urchins were being taught to read and write. There would be little danger in the future that some Juárez might miss greatness by lack of literacy. The children were being taught the meaning of patriotism too, and as we entered the building they were piping a hymn to their fatherland. At the conclusion of the singing they did a march, faintly like the conga, with their right foot stamping the rhythmic punctuation of a savage drumbeat. As they passed a Mexican flag stuck in a hole in the floor, they jerked their hands in angular salutes. Some of the kids were as grim-jawed as strikers on picket, but others wore the impish expressions of monkeys and grinned at us slyly, as if to say, "Education is diverting in its way, but not to be taken seriously."

The teacher in charge, a short middle-aged mestizo of good physique and earnest heart, took his job as if he had been a missionary called by God. There were lines of worry and perplexity between his eyes, as if it were not easy to instill diligence in the pursuit of learning into his charges. His assistant, too, seemed a bit perplexed. She was a skinny, milk-white girl with fluffy gold hair and pale-blue eyes. She was dressed in unadorned black cotton, the skirt so short that her knees were showing, as well as inch-wide runs in her black-cotton hose. (The salaries of teachers, I knew, were sometimes less than twenty dollars a month in some small places.) She stood looking like an anemic angel fagged by her journey to earth, but singing hosannas shrilly with the dark-skinned imps to make them feel she was at one with them.

As we made our adieus and thanked the principal for his courtesy in permitting the interruption, I asked him about his vocation. His answer was simple. Times were hard, good jobs were scarce, he was fond of children, and he had himself completed the sixth grade of school—so he had become a teacher. He smiled and made a deprecating gesture toward his assembled charges. "You see, though I often feel inadequate, señor, it is hardly necessary to hold a degree from the university to instruct these little ones."

The line of patient women bearing baskets had shortened. Those whose corn had been turned into warm spicy-smelling meal were walking away fast in every direction to prepare the midday meal. We drank some unchilled bottled beer at a place near the church and went on our journey to the temples. The way lay along fields of alfalfa and corn, and through three Zapotec villages. This was all Indian country, and the inhabitants had the quiet assurance of Indians. It was only in the revolutions that they lost it. And here in this pleasant valley there were always ripened fruits to be picked direct from the trees to sweeten the bitterness of life.

The ruins lie on an eminence beyond the village of San Pablo Mitla, whose mud houses are hidden behind fences of organ cactus, wild figs and oleanders. Strangely, after the green valley, the site around the ruins is nothing but sun-parched earth, bare flanks of

hills, and a stingy stream devoid of shade. The sun glares upon a
sand-colored monotone, where in a past age these four ruined palaces
were the center of an advanced culture. The ruins are remarkable
for the stone mosaic work, the arabesques and geometric designs,
and the monolithic pillars of porphyry, three feet in diameter, without capital or pedestal, which once supported palace roofs. The deep-
red color of some of the inner walls still remains. Beneath the palace,
reached by narrow stone stairs with unduly high risers, are the tombs.
With lighted tapers in hand we descended into the narrow subterranean passages that once sepulchered the high in estate. The businessman from Boston, who had studied engineering, was mightily
impressed with all that had been accomplished without metallic
tools.

What a contrast this represented in the degree of culture the
Zapotecs had reached, as compared to that of Indians of the islands
in the Gulf that Columbus and Amerigo Vespuccius first beheld.
Early in the sixteenth century Johannes Schöner had written in
Luculentissima descriptio in Latin as follows: "In America are wild
and savage men of handsome stature. . . . People of both masculine
and feminine sex go about not otherwise than as their mothers bore
them. . . . They lack iron and other metals. . . . They have no
king, but live in their liberty . . . they observe no law, nor have in
their marriages any legitimate compact of the bed; their life is there-
fore entirely voluptuous. . . . They make no sacrifices, nor have
they a place or a house in which to make speeches."

Men that built palaces like this did not go about naked, and certainly they had rulers, for only those of the high category had lived
within these well-constructed walls. They must have observed strict
and ceremonious laws. And from numerous courtyard terraces, as
well as within the larger walls, they could have made speeches to
multitudes. These folk of Mitla were not as simple as Rousseau's
noble savages or the free wild men of Johannes Schöner. There must
have been austerity in the character of the breed of men who created
Mitla. The ordered geometric beauty could not have been executed
by a people who lived an entirely voluptuous life, or who had been
devitalized by self-indulgence.

But except for the beautiful patterns of the mosaic work, I did not
care much for Mitla. I could get little feeling of life ever having been

lived here, whereas in Chichen Itzá and Uxmal every turn of a corner is stirring to the imagination. Ghosts come in troops at Chichen Itzá, but here not a ghost could I call up, at least not in the middle of a July day. The hot suns of centuries had preserved the ruins so that they are still in as good a state of preservation as when the conquistadors came first upon them. But direct sunshine is not flattering to Mitla. The scene cries out for a softening of moonlight. I resolved if I ever came to Mitla again it would be by the light of the moon.

6. THE STIRRUP SERVANT

A gentleman to whom I had a letter of introduction came to call and drove us out to the ruins of Monte Albán. Señor C.'s family had lived for many generations in the state of Oaxaca. Before the Revolution they had been well-to-do, and both he and his brother had been educated at the University of Wisconsin. He was as knowledgeable as he was stimulating in conversation, but he knew little more about the mystery of Monte Albán than the guidebooks.

The ruins have a splendid situation on top of a hill, with the best view you can obtain of the Valley of Oaxaca unless you take to the air. Beauty lies all about the citadel, but the ruins themselves—great earthen mounds out of which emerge partially restored pyramids, surrounding a vast courtyard—hold little more than hints of former splendor. Various civilizations have passed here. Archaeologists set 500 B.C. as perhaps the earliest date of the foundations. The chief value of Monte Albán lies in the subterranean tombs. Only in 1931 did the famous archaeologist Dr. Alfonso Caso of the National University make his rich discovery. In Tomb No. 7 he unearthed the bones of nine Mixtec priests or nobles who had tried to take their wealth with them on their migration into the mysterious world beyond. Besides the funeral urns, there was jewelry of exquisite workmanship, which we were to see later in the glass cases of the museum. Other tombs were opened in 1937 and 1938 and more treasure brought up into the light.

The guard allowed us to descend into a now empty tomb, where the walls had retained the freshness of its bright-colored frescoes to a remarkable degree. Then we climbed the northern pyramid's great staircase, which is one hundred and fifty feet wide, to the top of the eighty-feet-high platform. There we stood looking down among the ruins and out over the verdant valley to the encircling mountains. The Mixtecs had chosen well the site for their temple. Both for protection and for scenic view, the position was superlative. Standing at the edge of the platform and letting my eyes roam the cyclorama, I thought of Spengler's definition of "home" for classical man: "Home for him was what he could see from the citadel of his native town, and no more. All that lay beyond the visual range of this political atom was alien, and hostile to boot; beyond that narrow range, fear set in at once, and hence the appalling bitterness with which these petty towns strove to destroy one another." The Mixtecs of Monte Albán had fought the Zapotecs of Mitla for centuries. Then, long after the templed cities of both lay in ruins, they had joined forces again to fight the common enemy, the Aztec. Afterward they became leagued together against the white man. Today they mingle amicably on the streets of Oaxaca, and they quarrel neither more nor less than do men of one family.

We came down one high step and sat leaning against the top stone riser. Though our host had a thousand times remarked his native land from the height of Monte Albán, he too sat without speaking.

Myers broke the silence gently with a verse from the poet Jeffers, who had found small satisfaction in his contacts with his fellows.

"The beauty of things was born before eyes and sufficient to itself;
    the heart-breaking beauty
Will remain when there is no heart to break for it."

After a pause, our Mexican friend pointed down toward the courtyard within the four pyramids. "My boyish heart was broken right there," he said, with a reminiscent grin.

When a boy our host had come here with his brother to meet other yearling conspirators and plan a revolution of their own while Pancho Villa and Carranza were sweeping down from the north toward Mexico City.

"Many boys of the upper classes were as revolutionary as they come," he said. "We often met in secret with the peon youths. We were to take over our fathers' haciendas, and the peons were to live with us like brothers—though, of course, somehow, we were to be jefes. The thought of surprising Uncle Claude with blazing guns on the next hacienda, and running him off his own property, gave us a thrill. We could hardly wait to scare the daylights out of our Aunt Juliana, who was stingy with dulces. We would march upon her— she was a widow and defenseless, except for her twenty-odd servants—and force her to prepare the very best sweets, with plenty of fruit and sugar, and enough for a whole army of kids.

"With our Christmas money, we bought some sombreros almost as big as Zapata's. We were very proud of those hats. On special nights, we would slip out after the family had gone to bed and hold meetings with other young sons of hacendados. They would gather together their peon playmates, and we would make plans for assault and attack and for distribution of land. Our parents could not understand why we were so sleepy and listless the next day. They called in the doctor to prescribe tonics. The peons would beat their sons, who dropped asleep at their tasks.

"One night, just before we were to launch our concerted assault on our relatives in the name of liberty and freedom, we held a meeting here. There was a half-moon, and we were full of solemnity and importance as we discussed strategy. Then, in our midst, Pablo Pacheco, our father's stirrup servant, our idol and devoted friend, suddenly, almost as if by magic, appeared.

"Though we did not know it, Pablo had had an eye on us for some weeks. But as if nothing were amiss, he had gone on training us in marksmanship and riding. He had been like a nurse and a tutor to my brother and me, and we thought him the most wonderful fellow in the world. However, we had not dared to take him into our confidence, because we feared his loyalty to our father would come before everything else with him. He had let us go on with our conspiracies and said nothing, amused to see how far we would go. Then he proved perfidious and broke our hearts. That night when he appeared here, he pretended to be a *revolucionario* too. He himself would lead the gallant band of muchachos, defenders of liberty. He flattered us like puppies, and said in time we might become the most fierce and famous fighters in the Revolution. In these days, boys in the north, he said, were rising to be high officers in no time. We might all get to be generals.

"Turning to the peasant boys, he asked had not Pancho Villa and Emiliano Zapata been the poorest of peons and were they not now the most famous soldiers in Mexico? The thought made them wild with anticipation. One peon youngster began to speak of cutting out our father's tripe and feeding it to his favorite pig. The announcement sobered us somewhat, and started an argument. Pablo stopped it adroitly. He picked up a goat's horn from the ground and flipped it into the air to catch our attention. Then he set it at some paces on a mound, and casually drawing out his shining pistol, he shattered the horn in the pale moonlight. The word of a man who could shoot like that was more than law. When he said, 'Let's get some sleep now and meet tomorrow at midnight,' we followed him down the hill as if he were the Pied Piper. He put the others on the roads that led to their estates, and marched us home, singing to us softly in his magnificent baritone voice.

"We slept until noon the next day, and when we awoke we were greeted with astounding news. We were leaving that very afternoon for Vera Cruz to take the boat for New Orleans. Our father was sending us to boarding school in the States. He said it looked as if Mexico was in for a desperate time. It was safer to have children out of the country. Our trunks had already been packed while we dreamed of conquest.

"We were too flabbergasted to protest. But it was difficult to restrain the bitter tears. We knew Pablo Pacheco had turned informer. Our youthful hearts were broken, and black with disillusion. The crisis, however, passed with well-bred decorum, for Pablo kept out of sight. But the coals of fire that were heaped upon our rebellious heads were almost too overwhelming. Uncle Claude rode over on his fine Arabian stallion to say good-bye, accompanied by his stirrup servant. He presented us each with two purses full of American money—to buy ourselves, among other things, proper hats such as young American gentlemen wore. Aunt Juliana drove over in her lumbering carriage and brought enough rich dulces to give us stomach-aches for a month. Only at the last, at the station, did Pablo appear. He had the face to sing us a farewell song, accompanying himself on the guitar that he could pluck better than anyone on earth. As he embraced me, I hissed in his ear 'Traidor!' He kissed me on the cheek and cooed 'Mi general!'

"As the train pulled out, the careers of two future generals of Mexico were nipped in the bud. We did not return for three years."

"And so you missed the Revolution?"

"All of it. It passed over Oaxaca with less rury of destruction and bloodshed than it did in the north. We were out of the beaten track. The big land divisions did not come until much later, under Cárdenas. In the end, I got cheated out of my patrimony without having the fun of fighting to defend it, or tossing it about to the peons in a lordly gesture."

A light drizzle of rain began to fall. We thought it wise to climb down before the stairs got slippery.

"And Pablo Pacheco?" I said as we got up and stretched our legs.

"Ah, Pablo! He ended as you might expect—with his handsome throat slit from ear to ear by a woman, one of the hundreds he maddened with jealousy. She begged him to return—her lily flower, she called him, her love, her white ram—on any terms, even to bring the new girl, for she had bought a bed big enough for three. When he would not come back, not even to sing her one good-bye song, she sought him and cut his throat with a butcher knife while he was sleeping off a hangover under a willow tree."

We paused halfway down the staircase for a last view of the valley that was partly in shadowy mist, partly in sun.

"But Pablo was the most wonderful stirrup servant in all Mexico. He was a he-man plus. He was a tall Indian, with just enough Spanish blood to season him and give him dark-auburn hair. He was as handsome as a hero in a cloak-and-dagger romance, but very real flesh and blood."

"What was his *real* job?"

"He held the stirrup when my father mounted, and rode at his side."

We laughed. "A kind of body servant."

"And a bodyguard. There was extraordinary power in his muscles, and he was lightning-quick and accurate with a gun. Those he could not conquer by his beguiling ways might have their bones cracked. If stronger measures were necessary, Pablo could send a bullet through precisely the center of whatever bodily organ he chose for the coup de grâce. He sat a horse magnificently, and dressed superbly. He spent all his wages on his clothes. Once he spent three months' wages on a white sombrero loaded with silver embroidery. It was so elegant, however, that he hardly dared to wear it when out with my father. I often wondered why my father was not jealous, because Pablo made so much more an impressive spectacle than he. But my father adored him, and twice he saved my father's life from brigands. I can tell you those stirrup servants always 'put out their chest' for the master."

We had reached the ground, and my eye was caught by some hieroglyphics on a wall before which lay objects in stone. As I moved over toward them for a glance, I asked, "Were stirrup servants common to all the gentry?"

"In this district they were. A Spanish colonial hangover that a century of republicanism had not blotted out. The stirrup servant served two purposes: to protect the life and limb of the master on the highway and in the tavern, and to be his emissary and decoy in the pursuit of venery. Up to a quarter-century ago, gentlemen still made an art of illicit romance, as Englishmen did in the eighteenth century. Men of Spanish blood escaped the stuffy Victorian household morality that came in with the nineteenth century.

"Stirrup servants were selected for their sex appeal and musical talents, as well as for their marksmanship and punch of fist. They did the serenading—a gentleman could not properly serenade a girl of the people. They did the preliminary courting, and made the rendezvous. The master finished the job. It was all ordered in a kind of back-street Chaucerian courtliness. The girls knew they were to be deceived in the end—that they would have to take the middle-aged master for the lusty servant. Stirrup servants were the personal love scouts of the time. They were far too elegant ever to be vulgarly called 'pimps.' And the thought of immorality did not enter the civilized picture—any more than it did in the days when the Indians created images like those objects and set them up in their temples for the world to see what made the world go on."

Señor C. motioned to a row of sleek and monstrous phalluses carved out of greenish stone. They had been unearthed and laid at the base of the wall with the hieroglyphics, waiting to be classified and either left here, or sent to a museum. "The cult of sex belonged to the primitive Indian heritage, as well as that of the cultivated Spanish. But now in this present age, the formulas of its pursuit have become as crude as jukeboxes. The refinements of stirrup servants have passed forever—gone with the wind, like the landed gentry."

"I don't think you have become reconciled to the achievements of the Revolution—and the work of Cárdenas," I said questioningly.

A cloud passed over Señor C.'s face. "Cárdenas took the little watch to pieces—but he was not able to put it together again."

Being an admirer of Cárdenas, whatever his mistakes, I might have launched into a stout defense. But there was no use to start an argument. I did venture to say, with some gentleness: "But the watch was very old, wasn't it? Its mechanism was worn and rusty, and it did need cleaning badly, didn't it? The job is too complicated to finish in a short six-year period."

Señor C. gave me a long look, shrugged, and then with a smile decided to let it pass.

"Was all your land taken from you?" Myers asked. "Did you keep the hacienda house?"

"Virtually all—and we have let the house go to pot. It lost its whole point and significance when the land about it was confiscated. The great house on a hacienda had a practical function. The weighing, the sorting, the curing, the packing, the storing, the management and administration, all went on there. Without the products of the field, without cattle and horses, without sufficient laborers, the house has no reason. The hacienda was created for making a living. There never were country houses here as in Great Britain, where wealthy families lived because they preferred to. In Mexico one never has to go to the country or to summer resorts to escape the heat, as you do in the United States. All the Mexican cities except Vera Cruz and Mérida lie high above the sea, where the climate is mild or cool. As far as temperature goes, a Mexican is quite comfortable in his town dwelling, in the sanctity of his own patio."

While we were talking, twilight, which lasts only a few minutes in southern Mexico, had come. The guardian of the ruins came up to ask if we would let him ride back with us. We left the pyramids, the mounds, and the tombs of undivulged treasure to the night.

As we drove down the winding road from the citadel, a flock of white milk goats came leaping down the side of a little ravine and rushed to a trough where girls were drawing water for their last drink of the day. We passed some square houses of dried mud, where dwelt the families that owned the goats. I recalled that some Mexican traveler of the past had been deeply impressed that they did not crumble. He had written: "That these little squarish mud-heaps endure for centuries after centuries, while Greek marble tumbles asunder, and cathedrals totter, is the wonder. But then, the naked human hand with a bit of new soft mud is quicker than time, and defies the centuries."

The humble houses lined the roadway of the valley. Temples up on the hill had disintegrated to mounds of earth and stone stairs and fragments of grotesque picture writing. Only the retrieved jewelry, safe in the museum, and the phalluses that remained stanch in all weathers, spoke in positive accents through time.

Though the gentleman had shown us great courtesy in driving us out to Monte Albán, and though we entertained him at dinner and at apéritifs on the plaza, though we had several mutual friends, and though he seemed to like us, he did not invite us to his home. I had hoped to glimpse family life in Oaxaca. I had wanted to see what provincial society was like. But only rarely does the most flourishing or most intimate letter of introduction get the stranger through the portals of a Mexican home.

A spot of mango juice proved to be the key that opened one of the great Oaxacan doors for me.

7. WITHIN THE DOORS

A young Mexican with blue eyes, fair wavy hair, and aristocratic features had introduced himself to me as a friend of my cousin from New Orleans, who had been to Oaxaca a fortnight before with her daughter. It was this chap who took me within one of the fortress-walled private mansions, if not into Oaxacan society, because of the spot of mango juice. He had been born in Morelia of Spanish parents, and he now lived in Oaxaca, where his brother-in-law was manager of a mica mining concern. The young man was bored and looked eagerly for contacts with foreigners. There was no society and no future here, he said. He was merely marking time—for what he did not know. And he was faced with the necessity of making his own living. His patrimony had vanished when his father's estate in Michoacán had been expropriated. He had even begun to study for the priesthood—it had been long since Mexico had had a white bishop, he said—but he couldn't stick it. At present he was reduced to keeping accounts in his brother-in-law's concern—a most uninspiring task.

It was a bit surprising to find a young man of twenty-one in 1943 resentful at being asked to earn his own bread. Apparently work seemed as unfitting to him as it had to the young Creole aristocrats in the halcyon days of Díaz. If he had not possessed pride in such degree, and the high wide brow of a scholar, I daresay he could have pursued the career of a gigolo with success. For he was quite good-looking, and my cousin had written that he was a divine dancer. He spoke French and English as well as he did Castilian Spanish. Besides ingratiating manners, he had a bright, if cynical, wit. But he seemed a lost young man, whose pseudo-salvation would doubtless come only if he married an heiress of one of the new industrialists, whom he despised.

He had dropped in after dinner, about nine-thirty, to see if he could be of any service, and he found me concerned about an ugly spot on my coat.

"But come," he said, "we can easily remedy that. My sister has a bottle of American cleaning fluid—'Mufti,' it is called. If you would walk to our house."

"Mufti in Oaxaca! Wonderful." So I excused myself to Myers and our two businessmen friends, and said we were going to get some Mufti.

The man from Boston had had just enough Spanish brandy to find the situation highly diverting. "That's a fine new name for it—'mufti'!" He winked a ribald eye, and grinned mockingly. "Better than anything we ever thought up to call it at college. Is 'mufti' Alabama slang or Zapotec? Throw a pebble at my window when you come back, and I'll unlock the hotel door."

There is no more night life in Oaxaca than there is in Morelia. At ten o'clock the plaza was as quiet as a graveyard. The few people who lingered on the benches or at the sidewalk café tables sat as if lost in meditation and undesirous of speech. On the Avenida de Independencia we turned left and went down the faintly lighted street between the rows of stout-walled dwellings with the great doors so tightly shut that not a ray of light escaped through a crack.

The heavy blinds at the windows were drawn, too, behind the iron grills. I thought of what D. H. Lawrence had said: "Whoever gets into the house or patio must go through these big doors. There is no other entrance, not even a needle's eye. The windows to the street are heavily barred. Each house is its own small fortress."

At a door studded with metal spikes we paused while the young man reached into his pocket for a key. Not a weighty foot-long key that should have gone with such a door, but a key to a Yale-lock that had been fitted into the door within the door. Out of the gloom of the street we entered the gloom of a great vestibule leading into a patio of paving stones edged with green planting. One pale electric bulb glowed in an ancient lamp, but it gave little more light than the incandescence of the stars in the fretwork of the blue-black ceiling of the sky.

I could discern no sound except that of our own feet treading softly on the tiled floor. Where were the family, the children, the servants? I paused to listen and to peer into the shadows. "Do come in. Let us go this way," the young man said most hospitably. We turned left along the semidark patio and entered a room whose windows would have looked upon the street if they had not been blacked out with solid wooden blinds. An unshaded electric-light bulb dangled from the high ceiling. The furniture was sparse and undistinguished, and there were no rugs on the floor.

A door opened, and a good-looking, middle-sized man in white trousers and open-necked sport shirt came in, with a book in his hand. I was introduced to the brother-in-law, the mica-company manager. He was as unaffectedly gracious as a Spanish gentleman is supposed to be. He made me feel quite at home on the stiff, uncomfortable divan. He was not fair-haired like the younger man. His hair was glossy black, his eyes gray, and his complexion white, but healthy-looking. He had been reading José Rubén Romero's story of the poetic scamp Pito Pérez. "Or rereading it," as he said. "It is as amusing and shrewd as it is bitter. And though I would have little patience with the no-good vagabond in real life, I can enjoy his wit and his similes in fiction."

The young man returned with a veritable bottle of Mufti and a clean rag of fine linen. I took off my coat. We went briskly to work. The spot disappeared with celerity.

"It would be felicitous, would it not," said the brother-in-law, regarding the process, "if we had some cosmic elixir with which we could rub out the spots of daily annoyance so neatly? Well, we do have something that helps." He went to fetch a bottle of brandy.

There were only three glasses on the tray he brought back. I knew I would not get to see his wife. One rarely sees a Mexican woman in her home. Those under forty are more than likely to be pregnant, and unlike Americans, Latin American ladies do not appear at parties or in public within a month, or even four, of the event.

"Tell me, what is society like in Oaxaca?" I asked, savoring the Fundador 1904 with appreciation. The brothers-in-law instinctively cast speaking glances at each other. Then the young man raised his eyes toward heaven. The head of the house smiled philosophically. "First, let me tell you this—against the general opinion both here and abroad," he said, "the Mexican is far more of what you call a family man than you might believe. This may not be true in the capital, but in the other cities I have found it so. Outside Mexico City, you know, there is virtually no night life. We go sometimes to the movies, and once or twice a year we dine at our friends' houses and they with us. The governor's receptions are dreary beyond belief. The occasional dances are stiff and stuffy."

"The most pretentious new people go about now!" the younger man put it deploringly.

"The ever recurring fiestas are fine for the Indians and the uninitiated, but they hold little novelty for us. For the politicians or those scheming to get into politics or for those who have passionate social convictions, there are the men's clubs and the sidewalk-café conversation. But for the rest of us there are only the inner walls of our own homes and the growth of the children and the struggle to make money to educate them properly, whatever that may mean. The day of the well-bred white man and his traditions is about done in Mexico. Only those souls interested in uplift, political power, or graft find living exciting in Mexico today. The rest of us merely carry on, or find a little zest in being obstinate about giving in to the new ways. Though we are in active business, spiritually we have retired within the seclusion of our patios. I remain coolly conservative, but without the faintest hope. I am too intelligent to beat my head against a tidal wave. But I refuse to join in the popular chorus singing paeans to the new age of the common man."

It was my cue to listen, not to argue. And I was impressed by the man's detachment and lack of passion.

"As places go, though, mind you," he said as he rose to fill my little glass, "Oaxaca is more pleasant to live in than many another provincial town might be. At least there is a breath of a once-rich heritage here that stirs memories, in the midst of the bourgeois dullness. But if I may be so bold, when one compares the attractions of Oaxaca with a town of forty thousand in one of your great states—Nebraska—for instance, well—" he gave a shrug that was both eloquent and apologetic.

The hotel door was locked when I got back. I rang, and an old Indian let me in. The door of the second-floor room of the man from Boston was open when I went by. "Back already? The mufti must have been disappointing." He laughed gleefully.

"On the contrary." I touched the lapel of my coat. "See, I am now spotless."

8. STRANGE FRUIT AND PRICELESS TREASURE

Though tourists may sit all around the cathedral at different cafés and look at its exterior from every angle, few go inside. Begun in 1553, its construction proceeded at a leisurely pace for a century and three-quarters. It was completed in 1730, two years before the birth of George Washington. Like most Mexican churches, it has endured pillage as well as bombardment. Not all the sculptured saints in their niches could prevent the pilfering of the paintings, the silver, the ornaments. And the interior architecturally has no remarkable distinction.

The visitor of only one day, however, is invariably taken to see the Church of Santo Domingo, a few minutes' walk to the north, on the Plaza del Rosaria. Many enthusiasts consider its interior the most splendid in all Mexico. The edifice was erected by the Dominicans and is the crowning temporal glory of their order in the Western Hemisphere. It was begun in 1575 on no more than a silken shoestring—two and a half pesos, according to tradition. But during the century of construction, the building fund swelled to a dozen million pesos. To behold the massive brown walls of the exterior one would not suspect the elaboration of detail and the extraordinary fancy within.

The outside, defensive against mundane calamities such as earthquake shocks or cannon fire, is merely a strongbox to safeguard the jewelry within. But here, too, stout walls and holy prayers have not been proof against military vandals. Here, too, pictures were torn from their frames and used for tarpaulins; the silver and gold of the high altar was melted to fit into thieving officers' pockets; the exquisite carved wood of the choir was split up to make bivouac fires. But the chief splendor, which lies overhead, has remained largely undefiled. There in the decoration of the barrel-arched ceiling, the baroque reaches its climax in Mexico. The entire ceiling is covered with sculpture in high relief, heavy with multicolored enamel and gold leaf. The busts of hundreds of saints hang like strange fruit amid the weighty grape clusters. The walls ooze with the same sort of painted and bespangled figures. Though the plastic designs are fantastic, the colors are as soft as the polychrome angel fish—with pearl-pink, turquoise, and pale-gold predominating. In the dim cathedral illumination, one has the feeling of entering a mammoth cave of bizarre stalactites.

In the most ornate chapel, the decoration takes the form of a genealogical tree with a heavenly hierarchy branching out into noted Dominican Brothers. It is as strange as an Alice-in-Wonderland creation, with the saints' faces peering out among the vine leaves and enchained by loops of pale-pink tubes, which reminded Aldous Huxley of nothing so much as coils of tripe. Despite the century of devoted labor of hundreds of sculptors up on dizzying scaffolds, the gorgeous effect is hardly conducive to spiritualizing the thought. The labyrinth of wonders above is distracting.

Yet the Church of Santo Domingo is indubitably something not to be missed as a tourist attraction. And there might be a temporal blessing for the seeker who paused to read the inscription at the left of the entrance penned by worldly-wise, devout King Solomon. There under a statue of a blinded Virgin of Sorrows are two supplicating verses of King Solomon which may be as serviceable today for contemporary Gentiles as they were for ancient Hebrews at the dedication of the great Temple.

Oh Lord! Most High God! Look upon this thy temple with clement eyes. Hearken to the supplications which we make thee and which thy children will make thee in the succession of time when, laden with their offerings and their tears, they come to implore thy pardon for their sins, to lament their misfortune, to pray for rain for their crops, to invoke thy aid against plague and hunger in the days of thy just punishment.

When strangers from far countries come hither attracted by the greatness of thy name; when those who doubt, those who falter, and those who suffer enter this holy place, hear them, Lord; shower upon them thy kindness and thy mercy.

The church itself continues to draw in the faithful and the curious like the seine cast on the right side of the ship. But the vast monastery adjoining the church, which once housed the Dominican Brothers, is now used for a military prison. The change in the category of inmates is significant of some of the differences in Mexico since the days of Juárez. But the prisoners can still watch the swallows building their mud nests on the stone ledges just as the friars did, and listen to the mockingbirds singing the same notes by moonlight. They can hear the prim steps of donkeys on the cobblestones in late afternoons and the swish of rush brooms cleaning the sidewalks in the early morning. From the prison windows they can no longer see religious processions, for these are forbidden by law. But they can catch glimpses of Indians going to the market with their craftwork and their produce—to sell green glazed pottery or mangoes perhaps, and to buy salt or a machete. For despite the changes in political thought and ecclesiastical dominance, life's routine goes on in Oaxaca much in its wonted way, soft-voiced, and without any high-tensioned activity.

The pervading quality of restfulness that belongs to Oaxaca extends into the museum. There is not enough to tire one with looking, and everything is happily arranged. Its great upper chamber, shaped like a small ballroom, contains the stirring mementos brought forth from Tomb No. 7 at Monte Albán. In this spacious room there are no crude idols with their hideous, obscene faces, no fragments of primitive weapons and elemental cooking utensils over which some people go into an ecstasy. Here are clues to a culture that knew refinements. Here is evidence of artists of delicate perception and invention, men who saw beauty in their mind's eye and who had the skill to execute it in precious metal. In case after case jewelry and artifacts bear evidence of a people of superior taste. There are elaborate necklaces wrought of gold and sea shells, pearls, and jade. There are breastplates set with amethysts, and sophisticated masks and tiger heads and most intricate filigree work studded with turquoises. There are cups fashioned of silver and copper, and exquisitely chaste bowls of quartz. There is a rock-crystal chalice so lovely one wishes Keats might have seen it, for it starts speculations on the quality of what human mouth touched its lip and what dark fingers caressed its grace.

But the people who created these things for their use and their adornment remain yet a mystery. They had disappeared centuries before the Spaniards came to Mexico. Happily they had hidden their treasure so skillfully that it was not brought out from the tombs until the 1930's. Cortés's fortune-hunters did not find the precious cache to melt down or tear to pieces for the intrinsic value. And because these objects under glass were saturated with antiquity and mystery as well as beauty, their value was a hundred thousand times the worth of the raw materials.

Besides the two major attractions of the Church of Santo Domingo and the State Museum and the lesser one of the house of Juárez's youth, there was a fourth triple-starred sight we never got around to seeing. It lay within a few minutes' walk of the plaza cafés, and again and again we purposed to visit it. But just when we would rise from our seat under an arch of the *portales,* some new person would turn up—an archaeologist, a lawyer, a young Mexican army officer who had been stationed in a puma-prowling hinterland—and we would order another beer, or coffee, or lime sherbet, and plan for mañana. As far as the Church of La Soledad went, mañana never came for us. The postponement was disrespectful, for within the edifice resides the patroness of the state of Oaxaca —the southern rival of the famous Virgin of Guadalupe. This Lady of Solitude is locally reputed to have powers as miraculous as those of her northern prototype, and she is only a few years younger.

According to the story, in 1543 a strange donkey with a long box strapped to its back appeared in the midst of a mule train on its way to Guatemala from Vera Cruz. At the very spot where the church now stands, not far from the railway station, the donkey dropped dead. In the box was found a sweet-faced image with a label that read "Our Lady of Solitude at the Foot of the Cross." After consultation and meditation the wise bishop declared a fiesta in her honor. And ever since, the eighteenth of December has been celebrated as the most blessed day in the Oaxacan year.

Indians from the farthest reaches of the spreading state come to the capital to pay homage to their patroness, and to make merry with much eating and drinking and continuous band music. As recently as 1909, the lonely Virgin, who wears black encrusted in pearls and brilliants, was crowned with a golden diadem that cost one hundred and fifty thousand pesos. Like a queen of flesh and blood, she has ladies in waiting who dress and attend her. Formerly they were nuns of noble lineage. Now they are impoverished aristocrats, whose fortunes went with the winds of revolution. Each night, so I was told, two of these local ladies in waiting attend the Mother of Christ to the privacy of her own little room, and there disrobe her and lay her to rest. For their pains they receive a special blessing of consolation.

Instead of stirring on pilgrim feet, we sat beguiled by the slow-moving pageantry of the streets and thinking each hour anew how delightful an institution is the plaza. Its contribution to the charm of a town and to the happiness of the citizenry can hardly be overestimated. It is a blessed oasis in a wearisome desert of daily living. Here is beneficent shade from the sun's too-muchness. Here the world and his wife mingle without sense of protocol or privilege. The legless beggar and the palsied old marqués leaning on a gold-headed stick fit concordantly into the same composition. The ragamuffin bootblack and the smartly dressed young lady back from her four years in the Baltimore convent take the same sort of seat at this outdoor concert hall, where the band plays every night. Indians traveled from afar roll up in their blankets and use the plaza for a hotel. Old women squatting at the curb, cooking piquant stews over braziers, make restaurants for the humble out of it. Young lovers use it for rendezvous. College boys preparing for examinations make it a study hall. To little children from every category of home life, it is a common nursery.

A mestizo countryman guides a pair of yoked white oxen with a slender pole and soft commands right through the motor traffic. Indians in white pajama suits make transitory streaks like chalk marks as they move along the faded green walls. A barefoot Indian woman passes bearing an unruffled turkeycock upside down. She walks noiselessly on tiny bare feet that no kilometers of walking on hard roads through the centuries seem able to spoil. Oaxaca, you say again to yourself or aloud, seems so right in tone and quality. With all the multifarious, multicolored life in the plaza, the tempo is as slow-paced as the mood is harmonious. And you realize how agreeable you find the Spanish culture, with its inherited Moorish strain superimposed on an Indian foundation. Here it seems to have special flavor and body, like good wine of a good year from a good region. Oaxaca is a town you regret to leave, and one you resolve to return to and to bring persons of whom you are fond to see and to taste of its quality.

Sitting in contentment in my last hours in the plaza, a line of the German poet Rainer Maria Rilke seemed peculiarly pertinent to this town of southern Mexico: "We, of this earth and this today, are not for a moment hedged by the world of time, nor bound within it: we are incessantly flowing over and over to those who preceded us and to those who apparently come after us."

VIII

The Isthmus of Tehuantepec

If you have traveled at all you are bound to have noticed (unless you are an incurable pessimist) how often one plays in better luck than one really deserves.

—JOSEPH HENRY JACKSON

1. THE WOMEN OF JUCHITÁN

As WE FLEW UP and away from this ringed Valley of Oaxaca, it was like being magnetized out of a magic circle. Within an hour we had left the mountains completely behind us, and were sailing over the tropical flatlands of the Isthmus of Tehuantepec. To the south and west lay the gray-blue slab of the Pacific, with humped islands looking like porpoises sunning themselves on the surface of the sea. Directly beneath stretched the miles of concrete runways of the largest landing-field in Latin America. From the air it looked something like the crossbarred crust of a mammoth green-apple pie. This Ixtepec field was still in the process of construction, and some of the gigantic hangars had not yet been started. With the largest near-by town totaling no more than sixteen thousand population, the only answer to "Why here?" was "Defense of the Northern continent." The United States was putting up the money for its construction.

When we got out of the plane, Señor Garza, the youngish red-haired airport manager, explained how everything at the airport was temporary during the construction. "We are daily expecting a new station wagon to transport the passengers. But now we'll have to ride this antique bus. Hope it makes it. We may have to walk a mile or two."

My first question was about a man named Wilbur Barker of the town of Tehuantepec. "I saw Barker in Ixtepec this morning," the official said. "Maybe he's still here."

The road lay through a kind of mannersome jungle, with deep grass, palm trees, and wild castor-oil bushes. Here and there were clearings where the castor-oil plants were cultivated for commercial purposes. Corn was growing in scratch-plowed *milpas*. A layer of jungle, then a layer of rudely cultivated acreage, then adobe houses much the color of the occupants' complexions. Each house had its loggia or dirt-floor veranda with hanging cans of flowers, and hammocks invariably occupied. Before the houses naked children played. Men, young and old, walked about clad only in white-cotton trousers.

"The men till the fields on some days," Garza said. "On others they hunt or fish. When fiestas come, they go to town. Most of the families own their own land. These people have always been free. The hacienda has never been significant in the Isthmus. There are no vast-rich plantation-owners. Individual wealth is negligible. In the towns even, only two or three Syrian merchants could be called wealthy."

From the slow jogging bus, we could see that these Indians were better-looking in feature and physique than others in Mexico. And there was something intimately idyllic in the simple scenes of family life. Here was evidence of an ambitionless enjoyment of being alive and of working only for the necessaries of existence.

We came into Ixtepec by the new military camp. The neat, well-screened buildings were set in groves of coconut palms. We crossed the network of railroad tracks and drew up at the Pan-American Airways office, which occupied the front of the Hotel Rasgado. Like a pilaster between the two open double doors of the office stood a tall man with gray hair and blue eyes and a firm, prosperous belly. "That's Barker now," the airport manager said.

I straightway introduced myself and Myers, gave him greetings from Señor Corres Innes of Oaxaca, and asked if he could put us up for a few days in Tehuantepec.

It was not entirely convenient, because his wife was here in Ixtepec visiting their married daughter. But even so, Barker made a quick decision—we would all take tomorrow afternoon's train. The lodging in Tehuantepec settled for tomorrow, we entered the hotel to get ourselves settled for today. Yes, the sad-eyed young manager said, he had received the telegram about our reservations, but, alas! the place was full. All eighteen rooms were occupied. Since the Rasgado was the only decent hotel in the district, the engineers working at the airport had just about filled it as permanent guests. At our look of dismay, the melancholy manager recalled there was one very small single room. He escorted us to see the room at the end of a passage on the upper floor.

The Rasgado was advertised as strictly modern, and it had only recently been done over. Each room had a shower blocked off with a concrete wall in one corner. To Americans, Mexicans sometimes are unaccountably perverse about comfort. They often seem to go to great trouble to make things inconvenient. The manager pointed proudly to the tiny electric bulb way up in the center of the high ceiling. "The switch?" I asked, looking along the wall near the entrance. He promptly demonstrated by leaping on the bed with his feet straddling the pillow and reaching up to a button halfway up the wall.

"But why up there?"

He shrugged indifferently and half-smiled.

I turned to Myers. "If a Mexican woman ever occupied this room, she would have to call the manager every time she turned on and off the light," I said.

"Maybe that's why it's stuck up there," Myers said with a wink. The manager smiled appreciatively. He understood no English.

I was reassured to remark that the screen door to the room was intact and adequate; for this was potentially fever country. There were no windows. The light came from a two-foot opening all along the top of the wall under the eaves. This arrangement kept out the sun and let in the breeze. "But look!" I said. "There are no screens up there." The outside opening was completely screenless. "Mosquitoes can enter in battalions—and buzzards and eagles, if they have a mind to."

The manager had vanished like a disinterested ghost. Myers and I grinned at each other blankly. There was no use to ask the whys or to inquire into the thought processes that led to such halfway precautions. At least the shower let down cold water when you pulled a chain, and the commode flushed, even though the water compartment wouldn't fill up again unless you called a chambermaid, who conjured or cajoled it in some way. "One shouldn't ask for everything in the tropics," Myers said nobly.

We would have to occupy the room in relays. Since Myers was

not siesta-minded, I would take a siesta now while he rested in one of the wicker chairs in the Pan-American office. Then he would sleep the first part of the night in the bed, and I the latter part. We divided the quinine, and Myers left. I swallowed a capsule, stripped, flopped on the bed naked, and in profuse tropical sweat dropped pleasantly off to sleep.

The occupants of Room 11 were still indulging in siesta when I came out at four o'clock to join Myers. They were spread all over the corridor floor space before the open door. One man lay on the narrow bed within the room. Two men lay on strips of matting on the floor at his feet. Three others had spread their matting strips so solidly between the door and the balustrade that ran around the square of the patio that no one could possibly pass that way to get to the stairs leading to the ground floor. All the men outside lay flat on their backs, their beige-colored bay windows rising like the rounded sand piles children construct on sea beaches. They were all clad only in rayon shorts, each pair of some shade of pink. Two of the men were awake, and fanning themselves listlessly with little palm-leaf fans. Six sombreros were stacked outside the door. "Politician's bodyguard?" I asked the manager, whom I met on the stair landing.

"No. Economy," he said morosely. "One hires the room, the others bring their matting."

"A splendid scheme in this time of room scarcity," I said, determining to buy a piece of matting myself to use while Myers slept in the bed his part of the night.

Myers professed to have dozed comfortably in the big wicker chair. And since he was an American businessman, he could not have felt right about taking off his clothes and lying down in the daytime.

The traffic manager announced he was preparing to accompany us to Juchitán, a town famous for its colorful women, fifteen kilometers away. He was a bright, personable young man whom I liked at once. His name was Joaquín Piña. He looked to be about twenty-two. We found out later that he was not quite eighteen. But he had an air of responsibility and serious purpose. He spoke good English, for he had been brought up in Texas and finished high school there. He had returned to Mexico only the year before.

Piña had sent a messenger, he said, to engage the only good car for hire that Ixtepec possessed.

As I turned to get a drink at the cooler, the messenger came back. He spoke in low tones to Piña. Piña informed us regretfully that the driver was drunk and in bed with his girl. "Shall we wait?"

"How long will he be?" I asked.

He smiled. *"Quien sabe?"*

"As a Mexican, you might guess."

He smiled again. "Mexicans vary. *Quien sabe?"*

"Suppose we send again and ask him point-blank."

We sent. The messenger returned without definitive news or optimism and again spoke in low tones to Piña.

"The driver says he is still drunk, and he can't tell when he's drunk. But he will come sooner or later."

"Even if he has done with amour, he will doubtless still be drunk," Myers said. "I don't like the idea of driving with a drunk Mexican on a bad road. It's often adventurous enough driving with a sober one on a good road."

Piña bethought himself desperately. "There is one other fellow. But his car is so ancient it just barely holds together. Still, he himself doesn't drink, and he's too told to visit his sweetheart in mid-afternoon. Shall we risk him?"

"By all means."

When the teetotaler's car arrived, it was veritably a museum piece among jalopies, but the driver-owner looked steady and kindly. We engaged him and left immediately.

The recent heavy rains had happily settled the dust, but there were some ugly mudholes in the road. The driver negotiated them with rare good judgment. The land was mostly flattish, with castor-oil plants, sugar cane, corn, beans, and coconut palms here and there. All the adobe houses had loggias with hammocks, like those we had remarked coming from the airport. And here, too, naked boys were everywhere. Many of the boys apparently remained naked until puberty. Sometimes their nakedness was moderated, or accentuated, by short buttonless shirts of pink or green that stopped just above the navel, so that their shoulders and upper backs and a part of their chests were covered, but nothing else. No one seemed to be doing anything in particular. In the two villages we passed householders sat before their flat-surfaced houses in low chairs made of cowhide, with commodious curving backs and graceful arms that recalled the chairs of Pompeii. At one place a group of girls were gathered about a well filling their water jars. They were good-looking, and all wore the colorful costume of the region. Two of them had light-brown hair, and their complexion was light-olive.

Just within the town limits of Juchitán we ran into a procession of maidens bearing long wax tapers in the left hand and carrying spikes of tuberoses in the other. The tapers were lighted, though it was five o'clock on a summer's afternoon. "A funeral," Piña said as the car slowed down. Six of the young women were carrying a coffin made of white boards. There was no sadness in their faces, only a kind of serene dignity. It was almost as if they were rehearsing a scene from a drama and knew that their playfellow would rise smiling at the end of the journey. A fine misty rain began to fall as we crept slowly alongside the cortege. Tapers flickered, but did not go out. The starched lace flounces of the skirts skimmed the dirt of the street gracefully, and the white-lace headdresses flowed down their backs like frothy cascades. When the mist became a gentle rain, the maidens did not change their pace. One taper went out when a huge drop made a direct hit on the moving flame. The procession vanished down a side street, as if the whole spectacle had been a dream.

At a corner of the plaza we got out of the car. While we were debating whether to put on raincoats, the drizzle stopped. An oldish woman with cropped gray hair and a vigorous figure approached us with a smile, and made a halfway gesture of an upturned palm. Piña said something to her in a tone that was not unkind. She merely nodded and went her way. "She's faintly touched in the head," he explained.

Under the columned arcades facing the square walked the stately women of Juchitán. We gazed with delight as we remembered what brought strangers to the Isthmus. There is nothing historically noteworthy in the Isthmus of Tehuantepec—no famous battlegrounds, no outstanding churches, no great haciendas, no primitive ruins. There is not a single hotel that might attract tourists—in fact, most of them repel. The roads are not only inferior, but impassable in the wetter spells. The only attraction, besides the tropical scenery, is the women. One goes to the Isthmus to look at the beautiful Tehuanas. In the narrow hundred-mile strip of land that keeps the Pacific from joining the Gulf of Mexico, there is more feminine beauty than in whole states of Mexico together. The Tehuanas bear only casual resemblance to the other women of Mexico. As a rule, Indian women, despite whatever virtues they may possess, are squat in body and flattish-faced. The Tehuanas are considerably taller, and lighter in complexion. They have profiles; their noses have distinction and shape. The original native dress is by far the most eye-catching of all the costumes of Mexico. Only in the highlands of Guatemala is there anything of comparable picturesqueness north of the Panama Canal.

In their daily affairs most of the women still wear the flounced floor-length skirt and a loose blouse, square-necked and sleeveless. The blouse is called a huipil, and under it is worn nothing at all. The high breasts are allowed to take care of themselves. The women walk superbly, their heads held like floating banners. All the movement is from the waist down. The hips and legs move with an assured gliding motion, as if they were aware they are bearing aloft a torso a sculptor might use for a model. Their posture comes from generations of ancestors bearing water jars and rush-woven trays of fruit on their heads. And from early childhood the girls have practice in the art of walking.

None of the huipils and the skirts were of the same color, but they all seemed inspired by the colors of tropical fruits: lemon, melon-green, the red of pomegranate, the purplish shades of guavas or figs. Orange huipils were embroidered in red; orchid huipils, in saffron. The skirts were generally of a solid color, yards and yards of gathered cotton cloth, with deep flounces of cream-colored lace. The one color the olive-skinned Tehuanas seemed to avoid was light-blue. Perhaps they do not want to compete with the tropical sky, or they know that blue is better for blondes.

A few women wore chained necklaces fashioned of American gold coins, inherited from the great trading days when Salina Cruz on the Pacific was a flourishing port. The fall of the gold or silver chains divided the bosom and accentuated the thinly concealed contours of prideful breasts. Not a woman in sight wore a

ALL TAXCO LIES ON HILLS.

THE MAGUEY IS PERHAPS THE MOST TYPICAL PLANT OF MEXICO.

THE CROSS IS IN EVIDENCE IN THE MOST HUMBLE VILLAGE.

STRODE

WATER CARRIER.

MARIPOSA FISH NET AND DUGOUT CANOE, LAKE PATZCUARO.

STRODE

MEXICAN TOURIST ASSOCIATION

WHAT HIGH SIGNIFICANCE LAY IN THE CREATION OF THESE STRANGE TEMPLE SCULPTURES?

J. GUZMAN

CACTI BEFORE THE PYRAMIDAL TEMPLE.

THE FAMOUS GIANT AHUEHUETE TREE IN THE CHURCHYARD OF
SANTA MARIA DEL TULE.

ZAPOTEC CHILDREN PLAYED AT THE ROOTS OF THIS FAMOUS TREE IN SANTA MARIA DEL TULE.
OAXACA, CENTURIES BEFORE CORTES'S ARMY RESTED IN ITS SHADE.

STRODE

OLD MAN OF JUCHITAN.

A BEAUTY OF JUCHITAN IN THE ISTHMUS OF TEHUANTEPEC DRESSED FOR A
PARTY AND WEARING THE TRADITIONAL HUIPIL GRANDEE.

LUIS MARQUEZ

DIEGO RIVERA READING ON THE STAIRS OF HIS GARDEN MUSEUM.

CHUCHO SOLARZANO, NOTED BULLFIGHTER OF UPPERCRUST SOCIETY WITH
HIS ELEVEN MONTHS OLD SON AND HEIR.

THE CHILDREN OF THE ISLAND FISHERMEN OF LAKE PATZCUARO ARE WELL-
NOURISHED AND SELF-POSSESSED.

FLOWER GIRL PADDLING HER CANOE AT XOCHIMILCO.

THIS PURE BLOODED TARASCAN INDIAN NAMED PRECILIANO IS A BOATMAN
ON LAKE PATZCUARO.

hat. Nor did any wrap their shapely heads in drab-colored rebozos, as other Indian women did. They piled their abundant hair high and wound ribbons among the coronet braids.

We stood there on the corner of the plaza for some minutes watching the women passing under the arcades. The Doric severity of the façades made an excellent setting for the women's romantic costumes. There was repose as well as grace in their walk, and a kind of eternity in their movements, a timelessness as well as immediate purpose.

Though they belonged to the tribe of Zapotec, these women seemed as unlike their kin in Oaxaca across the mountains as if they were a separate tribe. Piña said that they themselves believed in the legends of their superior prehistoric antecedents. Some commenators, however, attribute a portion of their beauty to fair-haired Austrian soldiers who were stationed in the region during the French intervention under Maximilian. There is another theory: When the gold rush was on in California after '49, the fortune-hunters who took ship from New York or New Orleans to Puerto Mexico and crossed the Isthmus to Salina Cruz would beguile the time of waiting for a ship to take them to California by making love to the native girls. Most of them forgot their promises, and never returned to the Madame Butterflies and little Troubles. Whatever is the truth, the Tehuanas's distinction in pulchritude, costume, and spirit has been maintained largely because of the Isthmus's prolonged isolation.

"But look, the women are barefooted!" I noticed for the first time the bare feet preceding the swish of skirts.

Piña laughed. "Like the peafowl. Don't look at their feet. It makes them self-conscious. In shoes they don't walk so seductively."

"The businessmen of the Isthmus are women," Piña was saying as we crossed the street to the market. "The women possess the stalls in the market and they preside over most of the shops. They crowd the trains going to Puerto Mexico on the Atlantic for wares and supplies. They do business on the way, selling melons and tortillas to passengers. They do not care for what might be called traveling dress. So they wear these same flowing skirts and huipils. Though they never wear hats, they wind fresh ribbons in their hair for travel. A passenger coach on an Isthmus train is like a kaleidoscope. Sometimes mothers take all the children under fare age with them, including babies at the breast. Often the women spend a week buying from the wholesalers or bartering at the docks. Sometimes they bring all their purchases back on the train with them: bolts of cloth, jars of cosmetics, saucepans, skillets. The aisles of the coaches are often impassable because of the piles of merchandise."

In the pillared market of Juchitán the women reigned over the stalls like queens in their own provinces. Whether they sold sausage or scent, fish or filigree lace, their bearing was marked by dignity. Some two hundred stalls, and there was only one lone male concessionaire among them.

"Let's buy something from the poor male," I said.

"What?"

"Whatever he sells."

He happened to sell not hardware or men's clothing, but little cake rings called *roscas*. The man's cakes were protected by glass cases. The neighboring women's bakery products were exposed to the flies. The cakes were perfectly browned and crisp and just half the size of the conventional doughnut. I took one and bit into it gingerly. It tasted something like hard-baked Swedish coffeecake, not too sweet, and of excellent consistency. It was delicious. I bought a small bagful.

I wondered about the male stallkeeper. "Perhaps he is a widower and inherited the business from his wife," Piña surmised. "Or perhaps he is just keeping it for her while she is buying at Puerto Mexico."

"Let's have some coffee to go with the *roscas*," I said.

We went into a café opening off one corner of the market. A tall woman in a black skirt and a scarlet huipil embroidered in black greeted us. A ruby ribbon was wound among her coronet braids. The woman was luxuriantly beautiful in the way Maxine Elliott was in her prime. The eyes were large and luminous, the profile sculptural, the complexion deep-cream color. "Be seated," she said graciously. "I will prepare fresh coffee." She disappeared into the kitchen, her voluminous black skirt swirling about her.

"But she's magnificent," I said as we sat down at a table covered with sea-green oilcloth.

"Think so? Look there, then." Piña touched me lightly on the shoulder and pointed to an iron-grilled window that opened on a narrow side street. The wall opposite had been washed in some chalky cream paint and seemed waiting for a muralist. A slim woman in apricot silk appeared. Long amethyst earrings hung from her ears. Gold gleamed about her neck. A fringed scarf of orchid-colored chiffon was caught in her slightly crooked arm. She wore gilt-leather shoes heavily studded with stones like topazes. Directly in our range of vision she stopped and turned to speak imperiously to someone behind her whom we could not see. She must have heard our combined breaths of admiration, for she gave the window one quick glance, registered a kind of haughty indifference, turned, and moved out of sight toward her rendezvous.

"Evidently she's going to a party," Piña said. "She's top upper-crust. She wears shoes in the afternoon. But she must walk, because Juchitán has no cars or carriages."

"Or sedan chairs, alas! to match her costume," I said.

"No gondolas, either," Myers said. "It's a pity."

The hostess of the restaurant—like a great lady acting as serving maid—brought in the cups of steaming coffee and a plate for the *roscas*. She stood regarding us for a moment with mild curiosity, and then, rearranging a straying curl over her ear, moved with easy grace back into her kitchen.

"Where is her man? Where are all the men?" I asked Piña.

He smiled and shrugged. "Perhaps still in the fields. Perhaps lounging at home, or perhaps already taking an evening dip in the river. Perhaps she has no husband. There have always been many more women than men in this province. The men are said to feel their inferiority here, and sometimes deliberately drink themselves to death. Look now—"

In the place where the vision of elegance had been framed, another woman passed holding her reeling shrimp of a husband executively by the arm. He was drunk and in somewhat obstinate mood, but she was propelling him, and murmuring *"desgracio"* between her teeth.

"Yet, strangely, when sober," Piña said, "for all his inferiority feeling, the man is the master of the house and the woman presumes to do his bidding. And if he marries a girl who is not virgin and keeps her, she becomes like his slave. But now with education coming thick and fast, how long will all this be?"

The word "education" reminded me that I wanted to see the school. We made our adieus to the hostess, thanking her for her hospitality as if she had been the chatelaine of a manor house.

As we walked diagonally through the main plaza, we passed an inferior bust of Mexico's greatest Indian patriot, Juárez, a man of the same Zapotec blood as these people.

"They should have done better by their hero," I said, indicating the cheap commonplace replica.

"The people here don't feel the need of man-made art," Piña said. "History holds small meaning to the Isthmus folk. The Revolution here fell flat. No one cared a hang about it. The people merely smiled at the passionate orators who came from the north to stir them up. They had never been hungry. The industrious had always owned their own land. They had no political convictions. They merely wondered what all the spouting and shooting were about."

The secondary school was built in an agreeable functional style of architecture and quite extensive, three stories high, spreading about a great courtyard. There were music rooms and basketball courts, and toilets that flushed and were kept clean. The school seemed about as well equipped as any high school in a town of the same size in the United States, except for a deficiency in library books. But reading, I reflected, is not a pastime of the lulling tropics. I had never yet seen an occupant of a hammock in any tropical land holding a book. Books may be essential diversions for Scandinavians in their long winters, but not in the Isthmus of Tehuantepec, where the only season is summer.

"Who is responsible for this imposing school building?" I asked.

"Cárdenas, of course," Piña said, and smiled. "He's responsible for almost everything except the churches."

The loveliest girl in Mexico came gliding like a phantom along the sidewalk. She bore a raffia basket of pale fruits in her right hand. To balance herself she held the left hand out in the air, the fingers slightly curved, in a gesture that looked like the beginning of a wave to a beloved friend. We watched her coming—the embodiment of shy virginal beauty, a young gazelle in grace. Her huipil was of pale-yellow and the small breasts accentuated the pattern of silver-colored embroidery. The long skirt was a faded orange, and her bare toes twinkled along the pavement as she walked. The creamy complexion was as smooth as rose petals and her red lips were slightly parted with haste or wonderment. She looked as if she might be emerging into the stream of life for the first time, hesitant, afraid, and yet under a compulsion to move swiftly, like the brook meeting the river.

"She is Miranda," I said. "She is the ethereal creature of *The Tempest.*"

I caught Piña by the arm. "Stop her! Ask her if she would let me take her picture."

"Señorita!" Piña called. The girl hesitated, and gradually brought herself to a stop and turned to him with startled wonder. Piña approached and ingratiatingly asked the favor.

She stood poised for a moment in modest doubt. Her free-waving arm dropped to her side. Then a flame of dismay seemed to dart through her, as when a doe gazelle hears an unfamiliar sound in the bush. She blushed and became more lovely. Looking as if she might burst into tears at the momentousness of such a proposal, she debated with herself for a moment and then said: "No, no, I'm afraid not. Thank you very much." As she fled, her back was tense against the arrows of our admiring gaze. Without once looking around, she swiftly swerved down the first street to the left, as if to throw pursuers off the trail, and vanished.

Of course we did not follow her, but once again later in the afternoon we met her suddenly face to face on another street. She was returning home, her basket empty. This time there was no need to hold out a left hand for balance or to steady herself against the breeze created by her own swift motion. But her hand went protectively to her heart and she stopped stock-still, trembling like a doe surprised by hounds she thought she had completely thrown off the scent.

"Our vision of loveliness," I said, and half-got the Leica ready. But like a flash the girl darted up an alleyway of almond trees.

"The girls of Juchitán," said Piña, "are delightfully innocent. But they are not ignorant. They know they must keep their virginity. Since there are almost two women to a man here, there are plenty of virgins to go around. Almost never do the firecrackers fail to go off."

"Firecrackers?" Myers repeated, as if not sure of the word.

"On the wedding night. When the groom finally retires with his bride after the nuptial festivities, the guests linger on for the verdict. When he throws the first firecracker out the bedroom window into the night, it is a signal that all is well. The consummation has proved the girl virgin."

"And if she isn't?" I asked.

"No fireworks. But an outraged groom, who hounds the bride with questions of who? who? who? He may beat her into confession. Then he delivers her back to her parents as damaged goods, and they close their doors in mourning. Sometimes if she's not all she should be, a fellow will set off the cracker just the same, to save his own face. And sometimes he will pronounce her virgin when he finds her deflowered simply because he loves her so much. When there are no fireworks and the girl is sent home, she becomes an object of scorn, though often she is pitied."

We had turned a corner and were approaching the church. Piña went on with his discourse. "Do you remember that oldish woman with the cropped gray hair near where we stopped the car? Well, no firecrackers went off the night she was married. Her family, too, threw her out. Though she never became a whore, men treated her like one. Happily, she became a harmless lunatic. Now she's in the sixties. She developed a half-cracked wit. People laugh at her and are friendly. Whenever there's a wedding, she's always hanging about for some of the refreshments, and when the firecrackers go off, she whoops with joy."

The main church of Juchitán, built in the severe style of the Franciscans, was not impressive. But the sexton, taking the air in a high-backed chair set against the wall, was unforgettable. He was a superb old man with white hair and a narrow white beard as soft as cornsilk. He was both handsome and ascetic-looking, with highbred Spanish features and nut-brown skin. He was dressed in immaculate white and wore white sandals. He suggested a thin and un-self-conscious Rabindranath Tagore. Piña nodded to him and asked permission to enter.

The doors were open, and we stepped into the dusky coolness. While there was no service in progress, there were six worshipers, all seated on the third row from the back—three on each side of the aisle. The three on the left side were boys in their middle teens; the three across the aisle were girls in their early teens. "The lambs on the right and the kids on the left," I said sotto voce. When they were aware of our presence, the girls dropped to their knees and inclined their heads. They wore the *huipil grandes*. The *huipil grande* is that elaborate headdress of starched lace that ripples over the shoulders and down the back like a diadem of white peacock feathers. It is usually worn only on festive occasions, but often it is used for churchgoing in lieu of a headkerchief or a scarf.

The boys just sat and exchanged glances with each other and then looked out of the corners of their eyes at the girls. One girl's *huipil grande* twisted slowly in the direction of the boys. Suddenly an ill-suppressed titter burst forth, and she quickly dropped her head in a prayerful attitude.

"I don't believe the Juchitán girls are quite so innocent as you think," I said to Piña.

The sniggering became infectious. Two of the girls put their hands discreetly over their mouths. The boys gave up pretense and frankly turned away from the altar and the saints in the niches and cut their eyes at the girls.

"Evidently they are supposed to be readying themselves for communion or confirmation," Piña whispered.

"Sacred or profane?" I ventured.

The beautiful old man with the white beard came in with the dignity of a heavenly guard. He leaned over the girls, and spoke quietly. The girls flushed guiltily. The boys did not wait for their reproof. Before the old man could reach them they had grabbed their hats and scooted, without making the proper genuflexions. As the girls went out with heads demurely lowered, like novices in procession, the old man looked toward the altar and shook his head and muttered something that might have signified, "Father, forgive them, even if they know what they do. They are young and awakening, and it is summer."

Strolling away from the church, we became aware of the pleasant quietness of the town. There was no toot of an automobile, no grind of industrial wheels, no factory whistle announcing the hour for labor to come or to go. And this felicity of absent noise was continuous daily. There were doubtless radios in some of the houses, but we heard none breaking the peace. I thought of the simple foreigner who asked in all innocence: "To what glorious temple are Americans going when they hurry so?"

Juchitán was urban in design and pastoral in feeling. Most of the houses opened directly on the street, but the streets were lined with almond trees. And some had gateways where one could see into the patios of flowering shrubs. Here and there the rows of pastel houses were broken by very small plazas, which the inmates of the surrounding houses used as a communal garden.

Before one of the doorways on such a diminutive plaza, a pretty woman had set her low cowhide chair in the shade. She had a basket of sewing at her side. Her huipil was white-embroidered and her skirt a rich pomegranate-red. Her hair was not braided, but hung in chestnut waves about her shoulders. Before her stood a handsome male wearing nothing but a pair of lobster-pink shorts and sandals. He measured up to the Juchitán women in physical attraction. He had a strong jaw like a Basque. His legs and torso were as impressive as those of a Hawaiian surf-rider. His skin was the glistening sunburned shade of a lifeguard.

The man was eating a bunch of grapes and playfully teasing his wife by pretending to feed her like a parent bird and then popping the grape into his own mouth. She would laugh when she missed a grape, and threaten to jab him with her needle. Throwing himself at her feet, he leaned his head imperiously back in her lap, almost upsetting the sewing basket. He reached up, offered her a grape, and let her have it, brushing the tips of his fingers caressingly over her lips. Then he shut his eyes and pretended to go into a profound sleep. She laughed indulgently, as she might at a little boy's prank, and went on with her sewing.

"Idyllic as Paradise," Myers said, as we moved on.

"If you're sure there's marrying and giving in marriage in Paradise," I amended. "Why not idyllic as Juchitán?"

"Precisely. And look there!"

Around the corner from the house of the handsome mated couple, a gate in the wall was open, and just within the gateway framed by two almond trees laden with glistening green nuts, an old beardless man dressed in white knelt before a frame and was doing something with hanks of red wool. His hands moved lovingly at their task. On his face was an expression of preoccupied contentment.

These folk of Juchitán seemed to hold a special peace in their hearts, I was thinking. The leaven of disturbing ambition was absent, like the mechanical noises. The citizens had few contacts with the outside world to make them discontented by false comparisons. In this region of moderate fruitfulness of field and vine, a kind of serene quietude lay upon the land. And what if all their tomorrows would be like the present? Would the lack of progress be so tragic?

Soon the approaching Pan-American Highway would bring new contacts, and the jingle of tourist money, more trade. Doubtless in a few years the women would lay by their huipils and assume stereotyped mail-order-house garments. We were seeing the end of something—something that only this little corner of the world had preserved.

When we got back to the Plaza Mayor the businesswomen were closing their shops and leaving the market. Some bore on their heads, in trays or shallow baskets, the food for the evening meal. We watched the procession of stately figures and shifting colors against the Doric façade.

"Now the women who cannot afford a maid go to cook supper for their families," Piña said. He indicated the white benches in the plaza occupied by men in slack suits. "The men will wait here until they think supper is ready. Then they will go home. After supper they will come back and sit again until they feel the call to make love. This is their community club. The bachelors and the young boys will remain until very late, talking about it. A group of them may go courting after midnight—serenading their respective inamoratas with a *gallo,* going from house to house in succession."

"A *gallo?*" queried Myers.

"Literally 'a cock.'—A *gallo* is a serenade after midnight, after first cockcrow. Those who can sing or play an instrument are lucky. If a man has no voice or no skill in music, he must hire musicians.

Music in the night is part of the Tehuana culture. The women run the businesses, but the men still have to run after them. Businesswomen here guard their womanliness tenderly. They are not like your brisk, emancipated businesswomen in New York. They are too wise to renounce their femininity. They are aware that the high breasts under the bright blouses remain their best stock in trade. Business is not allowed to interfere with romance in Juchitán."

2. IXTEPEC BY NIGHT AND DAY

That night back in Ixtepec we dined well enough in a drab restaurant facing the railroad tracks. We had fish fresh from the Pacific, stewed rabbit, fried chicken, rice, and tomatoes, with thick slices of luscious pineapple for dessert. The price per person was forty-odd cents.

When we left the restaurant at nine the sidewalks seemed more crowded than they had been at eight, for news had got around that the four-o'clock train from Puerto Mexico might be turning up at any time now. The curb and the street glowed with charcoal braziers and burning sticks under impromptu stoves made of broken bricks. The atmosphere reeked of hot grease. The businesswomen mothers waiting for the train were preparing a last meal of the day for their sleepy youngsters, some of whom toddled perilously among the legs of pedestrians and the strolling soldiers from the military barracks.

The felicitous absence of crowding and noise in Juchitán was sharply contrasted in Ixtepec. The town seemed in ceaseless hubbub and motion. A distraught engine on a siding kept up an agitated screeching, apparently for no reason whatever. In all the cheap little eat shops, where the customers were served standing, loud-mouthed entertainment blared from radios. Since there was no station toilet in this chief railroad center of the Isthmus, women were continually on the march with urgent youngsters to the shadow of marooned boxcars. Sometimes matrons without pretense or the excuse of clamoring children would saunter with grave dignity to the semishelter of a boxcar, and raise their billowy skirts and squat in one well-synchronized and graceful gesture.

The mile-long street of Ixtepec that ran at a right angle to the tracks and ended at the station invariably became a promenade after nine. The townspeople turned out to walk up and down the middle of the narrow, ugly street as contentedly as if it had been the luxurious Calle Florida in Buenos Aires at five in the afternoon. Everyone was bareheaded except the soldiers, and everyone said *adiós*. Instead of saying "Good evening" or "How do you do?" they all said "Good-bye"—"God be with you." In Ixtepec, *adiós* is both a greeting and a farewell. And since you passed the same persons again and again, you blessed and were blessed a hundred times during the nightly promenade. Since a blessing is a wish for the other person's happiness, perhaps the best thing that can be said about Ixtepec is that the citizens walk up and down the streets blessing each other between nine and eleven. Their voices were soft and their murmurings musical, and it was very agreeable to hear them commending each other to God, though some of the young men could hardly be said to have a holy expression in their eyes as they passed some particularly nubile feminine form.

At eleven o'clock, the four o'clock train had not yet arrived. The fires in the braziers had turned to ash. The children were asleep in heaps on the sidewalks. The businesswomen sat heavy-eyed on spread strips of cloth, waiting with absorbed Indian patience. In the pale street illumination that fell flickeringly on their bright-colored skirts and huipils, the night sidewalks looked as if littered with trampled chrysanthemums that had been scattered in a noon carnival.

There was still no other room vacant in the hotel, so I prepared to sit up the first part of the night. But Piña did a most self-sacrificing thing. He persuaded a young engineer in Number 6 to occupy his own bed in a private house down the street, so that Myers could have the engineer's room. Piña adamantly refused to accept money for his own night's lodging elsewhere. He was as secretive about the place as he was reassuring about his comfort. As I undressed in the dark, so as not to attract the mosquitoes or the buzzards, I got a clairvoyant vision of the young man stretched out on the Pan-American counter, and I prayed he wouldn't roll off and crack his skull. The next morning he was quite sound, and as cheerful as usual, though he was vague about where or how he had passed the night.

We spent a goodly part of the morning avoiding the direct rays of the sun and drinking Canada Dry Pale Ale with the juice of green limes squeezed into it. At eleven o'clock I had an appointment with General Joaquín Amaro, the commandant of the army of the Isthmus. I knew that he had one good eye and one glass eye and that he wore an earring when he first came into political prominence in the capital as President Pascual Ortiz Rubio's Secretary of War. In the province he came from, the wearing of one earring was said to signify vengeance to be done. When his one earring was laid aside, people said, "Amaro has got his father's killer." The General, who was noted for his fierce and ruthless fighting and for preferring the floor to the bed for sleeping, took to the amenities of Spanish culture with alacrity when he became a Cabinet officer. He also achieved such an astounding reputation for facility in languages that a book by an American, published in 1932, proclaimed that Amaro had mastered French, English, German, and Russian all within two years. I was especially curious about this almost legendary Indian soldier of the Revolution, because he was currently so admired by the reactionaries, and I knew that he had once made a sensational attack in print on some of the more liberal policies of President Cárdenas.

When the General received me informally in a smallish sitting-room, my eye immediately caught the piles of books on a long table. Noting some French titles, I thought his linguistic reputation might be true. But he himself quickly disabused me. French was really his only foreign language. English, he claimed, he neither spoke nor read.

Amaro was under medium height, powerfully built, and very well proportioned. The day before he had celebrated his fiftieth birthday in bed with laryngitis. Despite his indisposition, he looked extremely virile. He was dressed in elegant white-doeskin trousers and a sport shirt of champagne-colored silk, cut very full and with long sleeves ending in cuffs that came to his fingers. His swarthy Indian face was handsome and his dark-brown glass eye was such a remarkable success that I was doubtful which eye was which.

I was rather disappointed to find the General seemingly little interested in the reforms for which the Revolution was supposed to have been fought. But his face lighted up with pleasure when I spoke of the esteem and affection with which a prominent Spanish family of Oaxaca had spoken of him.

It had been gracious of General Amaro to receive me in his convalescence and I was grateful. I understood the prudence of Cárdenas —after he had become Minister of Defense in 1943—in sending Amaro to the remote Isthmus, where his great abilities could be so well utilized far from the ferment of politics.

About three-thirty in the afternoon, when waves of heat were shimmering on the asphalt streets, Myers and I dropped in to call on the Guasti brothers, the leading wholesale grocers of the district. The younger had married a daughter of Wilbur Barker. The Guastis were blue-eyed blonds of north-Italian stock. Forty years ago, as their parents were on their way to California, they had paused at Salina Cruz for the birthing of the elder. Since business opportunities looked good in the thriving port, their father had decided to remain. Their uncle had gone on to Los Angeles and had become the wine-maker whose trade name of Guasti is known across the continent. Both these Guasti boys had been educated at military school and college in the States, but had returned to the Isthmus and their father's business.

We had just begun our conversation when an Indian girl arrived bearing a tray with cups and saucers and a pot of hot coffee nestling under a padded tea cozy. Every afternoon at half-past three their wives alternately sent coffee. They insisted that we join them and sent the maid back home for more coffee. As the temperature was steaming hot outside, we regarded the idea of hot coffee dubiously. "But," the elder brother said, "it stimulates you so that you forget the heat. And you don't perspire as much as when you drink long cold drinks."

I recalled that I had drunk coffee on hot afternoons in Brazil and that I had sipped it in the souks of Biskra at the edge of the Sahara with pleasant relief. So I encouraged Myers to fall to. The coffee was black and very strong, and right enough, we immediately felt fortified to endure the blistering sun and the lateness of the four o'clock train.

Later that afternoon the spanking-new station wagon of the airline arrived before the door of the airways office. It had just been unloaded at the depot and serviced. "It works fine," said the at-

tendant who had gone to fetch it. "This is something more like,"
Piña said proudfully. "Would you like to christen the car, so to speak,
by taking the first ride?"

I was delighted, though there seemed no place in Ixtepec to drive
except the mile length of the one principal street. "Can we go to the
river?" I suggested.

"Almost," he said. We turned down a side street, which was bordered with organ cacti, their green pipes bristling with a multitude
of silver stilettos. These were the fence walls surrounding the cottages
of the poor. Through the gatelike openings we could see women
ironing bright-colored garments on ironing-boards set up in the yard.

When the road became indefinable, we left the station wagon
and walked to a little promontory with a cluster of trees. Three
youths in military uniform were huddled together and peering
down obliquely at the river. They looked a bit self-conscious as we
approached. Down on the bank a woman was slipping out of her
huipil, pulling it over her head. Piña and I stood apart from the
soldiers, like another group of elders spying upon Susanna at the
bath. Ingeniously the woman slipped her skirt up her bare torso and
gracefully tossed it onto the bank as she stooped under the water.
Piña and I strolled down the slope to the lower bank, as if to get a
better view of the declining sun, but really to get a better view of
the bather without seeming to be interested. The reflection of the
flaming disk slashed the surface of the river like a livid lash on a
brown back. A lone man appeared some twenty yards beyond us
and, sitting on a rock, took off his clothes. He too slid into the water
modestlike, with the briefest display of nakedness, and began to
swim out to the flame-colored streak. The woman did not swim,
but stood up to her breasts in water and laved herself with cupped
hands, keeping her back to the shore.

"In the early mornings the river here is full of men and women,"
Piña said.

"They seem to do it very modestly."

"Oh yes," Piña said. "The men and women bathe in separate
groups, but in full sight of each other. All over twelve enter the
water in a kind of crouching position, and when they stand up out
of the water, both sexes make gestures of hiding themselves with

their hands. The men who are long enough hide themselves between their own legs."

As the woman's bath seemed about to terminate, I got my Leica ready. Just as she stood up knee-deep in water and turned to come out, I snapped the picture. Only in the after-moment as she reached for her skirt did I realize how lovely in figure she was. "The Tehuanas, who are always painted in their flowing finery," I said, "are the only women in Mexico—to judge by the hideous squat females of the famous painters—who are worth painting in the raw."

3. AND SO TO BED IN TEHUANTEPEC

When Barker arrived at six-fifteen to accompany us to the station, he carried a large paper sack of something which he handled as tenderly as if it might be gold dust. We were lucky, he said—the train was only two and a half hours late today. As we reached the crowded platform we heard its whistle. We pushed through the multicolored jam until Barker stopped before a short, good-looking, middle-aged Indian woman who wore the costume of her people. "This is my wife," Barker said simply by way of introduction.

I was unprepared for Señora Barker. I had thought of her as Mexican, but not as full-blooded Indian. Barker introduced his daughters, who had come to see their mother off. One was the wife of the younger Guasti. The other daughter was unmarried. They were both attractive mestizas, and the only women on the platform not in Tehuana costume. Their quiet American-style clothes were in excellent taste, but they looked oddly out of place among the swirling colors of the flowing skirts and huipils.

In the coach Myer and I rode backward, facing Barker and his wife. Barker's six feet two made him tower in Tehuantepec, even when he sat, and in the whole coach his were the only pair of blue eyes. Beside the big white alien, little Señora Barker, in her orange huipil and rust-red skirt, sat very erect, with the dignity of a princess. She was too self-consciously poised to be demure. Her features were delicately molded, and her eyes were full of knowledge. She cast one resigned glance at the full paper bag on her husband's knees and then looked out the window. Her husband was interrupting her visit to her daughter to take her back home to cook for us. I felt that she had a right to be resentful.

Barker continued to hold the bag with both hands as tenderly as if it contained an objet d'art retrieved from a tomb at Monte Albán. "Pancakes tomorrow for breakfast," he said with a gleam in his eye as he gave the bag a pat. "Real American pancakes. My wife makes 'em as good as you've ever eaten. A Scotchman—of all people—taught her to make pancakes over thirty years ago, before we were married. She cooked on the ranch where he and I were comanagers. When he left for another part of Mexico, he planned to lure her away, but I fooled him—I married her. She was the most beautiful thing you've ever seen. I'll show you her picture. I was completely mad about her."

I glanced with concern at Señora Barker. She returned my glance momentarily, but there was no comment on her husband's remarks in her eyes. She turned to gaze out the window at the fields of flax.

"She doesn't understand English," her husband said. "She speaks Spanish, though, as well as her native Zapotec. She's a full-blooded Zapotec. We've been married thirty years. I've never regretted my marriage."

As dusk fell swiftly an attendant turned on the weak lights in the coach. "It's good we're traveling first-class," Barker said with a wink. "When the engine needs refueling, the second-class passengers have to help." He looked out into the dusk. "But we'll have to walk home in the dark."

"Can't we take a taxi?"

His laugh was like a little snort. "There's no such thing as a taxi in the town of Tehuantepec."

"How far do you live from the station?"

"Less than a mile."

Myers glanced at the suitcases up in the rack.

"We're lucky not to be arriving in a cloudburst," Barker said. "We had a few earlier in the week, just as the train got in. This country! Oh me, oh my!"

"But you must like it. You've lived here forty years. It must have something."

"Well—" Barker gave an expansive shrug as the engine began to shriek warnings of arrival. It slowed down and crawled toward the

station. Barker stood up, handed his wife the precious bag of pancake flour, and began reaching for the suitcases. "Here we are. Welcome to Tehuantepec!"

But we did not have to carry our own luggage. A tobacco-colored
oldster and two youths boarded the train before it came to a stop
and took charge of the bags. Outside, it was night already, and for
the benefit of the teeming humanity pouring out of the coaches onto
the platform the stationmaster had lighted one kerosene lamp. In
the west a new moon was like a slit in a dark-blue paper screen.
Beyond the station the engine's headlight shot a stream of light down
the tracks where millions of buttercups were blossoming between
the crossties and along the shallow railroad embankment. The light
was like a stream of liquid gold, and illumined the parallel dirt
road we had to traverse. By the illumination of the silver curve in
the sky and the hosts of buttercups along the tracks, we proceeded
due west into the town. The rocky road rose and fell, with loose
stones and sudden depressions to be negotiated. When the little
houses of stone or white mud cut off the beam of the headlight, we
trod with caution. We came into the town and passed the dim-lit elevated plaza on the left and the empty market with its columns and
shadows on the right.

Before the Barker wall gate we paused, and he rang the bell. "The
Pan-American Highway is coming here right by my house," Barker
said. "In fact, this southwest corner of my wall must be lopped off
to give the road the proper width. They are going to buy me the
property next door to make up for it."

When the gate swung open, a woman who looked strikingly like
his wife, but ten years older, appeared. She mumbled a greeting,
received from Barker's hand the bag of flour, and scurried away.
The patio was bathed in soft moonshine. We paused to admire.
Shadows of palm trees lay along the paved courtyard. In the back
middle distance a young girl seemed to be making ritualistic gestures,
her right arm moving to right and left in graceful strokes. A large
basket sat at her feet and a brazier of glowing coals. She was ironing
clothes in the dim moonlight.

A strange metallic cry in the shadow of a flowering shrub made
me start. Something like a baby ostrich ran out on swift but awk-
ward legs to greet us. Then, recognizing strangers, he hurried away

on his hinged stilts. "That's Tony, the night bird," Barker explained. "He's rounding up the mosquitoes and insects, so we won't be plagued. I'll show you to your room."

The girl stopped her ironing, rushed into the kitchen and then back across the patio. She bore a stubby oil lamp in each hand like an extrawise virgin. Then, almost as swiftly as if she had merely rubbed one of the lamps Aladdin-fashion, she was back bearing ewers of water.

The beamed-ceiling bedroom was huge, with four double beds and several wardrobes. Through the iron bars on the street window the pale moonlight sifted gently onto one of the beds. I chose that one, while Myers took the bed with the crucifix above it. In looking for a place to hang my coat I opened one of the vast wardrobes. Seven long skirts and huipils and lace headdresses hung there, like the relics of Bluebeard's seven wives. I opened another wardrobe door and was confronted by a row of white duck trousers and a couple of young men's coats. I draped my own coat on a chair back. "I'm afraid some of the family have had to give up their room," I said to Myers, who was making his ablutions at the washstand. "But if the guests would all sleep in this one room this caravanserai could accommodate eight persons."

"Listen! What's that?" Myers said.

Out in the rocky street there was a creaking sound of wooden wheels and of heavy animal hoofs on the hard surface. At a command, the sounds ceased. Our luggage had arrived by oxcart.

A remarkably good-looking chap clad only in white duck trousers appeared in the doorway with our two bags. Barker followed him in. "This is my son," he said. "He is called Willie. He is sixteen."

The youth set the bags down and smiled broadly. He had beautiful teeth as well as eyes. We each shook hands with him and thanked him. He said, "De nada," smiled again, and disappeared.

When we came out on the veranda, Barker had poured the V-8 vegetable juice cocktails from his last can. The veranda was divided into two unequal sections. The smaller and back portion served as vestibule or boudoir to the two bedrooms. Built-in seats filled the wall space, and in the corner by the patio balustrade stood a round table with one high-backed settle and two straight chairs. The

larger and front section of the veranda gave off the drawing-room
and served as Barker's business office. Here were ranged in shelves
along the walls Zapotec idols and images, authentic and fake, in
jadite, terra cotta, and native stone. Barker's desk, strewn with papers,
was set diagonally across the far corner. A magazine stand with the
six latest copies of *Fortune* stood by his high-backed chair. Within
reaching distance of his desk was the dial of a radio. A soft grass
hammock, where Barker took his siestas, swung invitingly.

With cocktail in hand, I stretched out in the hammock and
breathed in the night air, fragrant with the odor of angel trumpets
and herbs and something like tea olive. A faint coolness had come
with the evening and brought out the odors. One small oil lamp set
on a corner of the desk made the gray-green idols against the wall
look like weird slabs of bas-relief. Across the sunken palm-shadowed
patio was the open dining-room with columns, and the kitchen and
the storeroom. The dining-room cabinets and table were almost
obliterated by bales of medicinal grasses to be weighed and graded
and exported to a drug firm in New Jersey, where they would be
processed into a specific for fever.

Just as I sighed audibly and ostentatiously with content, Barker
began bewailing the incapacity of the radio and the lack of war news
and swing music. "The confounded electric-light plant went out of
commission three months ago, and the authorities haven't got it
fixed yet. The demand for graft is too steep. They pretend they can't
get the equipment from Mexico City. But it's graft. In the capital
the big fellows are holding out for too much, and won't leave enough
for the little politicians here. And I sit here night after night, and
can't find out what our boys are doing to the damned Japs and the
Germans. I nearly go crazy. No radio to listen to and no electric
light to read by. Nothing to do but go to bed at first dark—and at
sixty going to bed isn't what it might be." He laughed the laugh
that accompanies such a remark, and reached over and viciously
twisted the radio dial in frustrated desire.

I said impolitely: "Thank God for the breakdown of the power
plant. I'm enjoying this lamplight and this blessed quietness."

And Myers said: "Peace. It's wonderful."

"Well, I'm relieved," Barker said tactfully. "I thought you fellows
would have a fit without the radio. I'd go crazy down here if I

didn't hear some English on the radio. No one here speaks anything but Spanish and Zapotec."

"But your family. Your sons and daughters?"

"They don't know two words of English."

"What?" I blurted out. "You haven't taught them English in all these years?"

Barker shrugged in the Mexican way. "They didn't seem much interested. But I am teaching English now three days a week in the Catholic school. Me and all those nuns."

"Are Catholic schools allowed?" Myers asked.

"Oh, yes, if they swear not to teach religion. They're everywhere, and they are a damned sight better here than these communist Federal schools, where some of the ignoramuses teach the kids to sass their elders. They actually say the parents are not to be obeyed, because all comrades are equal, old and young, parent and child. I took my children out of the Federal schools and put them under the nuns and paid tuition for them. The nuns know grammar and speak good Spanish. They teach the kids manners and discipline, too. I'm no Catholic, understand. It's all a mass of superstition to me. I was raised a Presbyterian. These saints and holy pictures you'll see all over my house belong to my wife and my sister-in-law."

"Your sister-in-law?"

"She's the one coming across the patio now with our supper. She's been with us ever since we were married—over thirty years. She helped raise all five of my children. My wife nursed them at the regular hours when they were babies, but my sister-in-law took care of them. In Mexico, when a woman does not marry, they say the old maid stayed unmarried to dress the saints in the church. My sister-in-law stayed unmarried to dress my kids. Now she cooks and cleans and does whatever is necessary. I don't know what we'd do without her. She's no trouble at all, doesn't even care whether she has a bed. Like most Indians, she can drop down on a blanket and sleep quite contentedly anywhere. My children adore her."

Again I noticed how the sister-in-law was a replica of Señora Barker ten years hence. Their features were almost precisely the same, and apparently they were the same height and the same weight. But the aura was entirely different. There was none of the queenly dignity in the sister-in-law as she brought the platters to the table almost on the run. The pretty slant-eyed girl that looked like a Balinese trotted behind her with a grace so natural that it seemed like a movement in a ballet. The expression on the face of this second kitchen maid and laundress was that of a radiant smiling mask. She served the dishes in a style all her own. She stood in one spot with her back to the balustrade and leaned halfway across the table.

"Isn't Señora Barker coming?" I said, hesitating to begin to eat.

"No, she'd rather eat in the kitchen."

"And your son?"

"He'd rather eat rice and beans with his mother in the kitchen."

We fell to the hot tortillas, the frijoles, and the scrambled eggs with an appetite. When the huge slices of watermelon came, Barker said: "You see we're just picnicking tonight, getting in so late. Tomorrow we'll feast on pancakes for breakfast and lobster for dinner."

After the watermelon was served the girl went back to her ironing by moonlight. The night bird darted here and there making its ghostly squawking noise as it snapped at insects among the shadows.

"Tony is our Flit gun," Barker said. "He gets his own living. He doesn't like our food. We never feed him a crumb. But he's contented—even when the gate is open, he never ventures into the street or tries to escape. He hunts all night and sleeps all day. I guess you fellows could do with a bit of sleep yourselves."

When we were ready to make our arrangements for the night, Barker indicated glazed chamber pots with yellow asters and blue forget-me-nots stationed under each of the four double beds. But we preferred to make a pilgrimage to the W.C., each holding a stubby oil lamp with a circular handle, through which we crooked a forefinger. We passed under trellises of coral vine and between green wooden bins containing horned lizards. Barker had collected these rare and deadly poisonous reptiles for a zoo in the States. He raised one lid and stirred up the sluggish creatures with a stick. They were big fellows, about two feet long. Their baleful eyes shone in the lamp flame like polished black jewels, and their welted and scaly hides looked tougher than rhinoceros armor. As they began undulating over one another, I thought of Othello's line: "Or keep it as a cistern for foul toads To knot and gender in."

"These are magnificent specimens," Barker was saying. "I should get a good price for them. The beauties are no trouble. They sleep almost all the time. They need little nourishment. Once a week I feed them a beaten-up egg yolk. They'd make nice pets if they weren't so poisonous." He half-lifted one affectionately with his stick. The creature opened his jaws menacingly with slow fury. Then he dropped back on the heap of his slow-squirming comrades. Barker closed the lid and we moved on under the trellis of coral vines.

"Here's the bath first, and next the W.C."

By the three lamp flames we examined the bath. The tub was a double square of smooth concrete with rounded edges. One half was full of clear dark water. Barker explained that you sat in the empty side on the three-legged stool and dipped the water from the full side with the lacquered calabash and sloshed it over your soaped body. A servant poured the cold water into the open container from outside through a concealed tunnel. The whole scheme looked as refreshing as original—but somehow more akin to Pompeii or Japan than the Western Hemisphere.

"Where do you get your drinking water?" Myers asked.

"From a clean part of the river. It's brought in five-gallon kerosene tins on burroback every morning, thirty centavos a day—six American cents a day for the family's drinking, cooking, and bath water."

"And this is the W.C.!" Barker opened a screened door with a yard length of bright-green calico strung across its middle, like the swinging half-doors of an old-fashioned saloon. By our three lamps' illumination we inspected and were instructed. A conventional toilet bowl with a mahogany seat stood in its quiet corner. But there was no water container at the back, at the side, or above, no chain or gadget for flushing, no water to flush. A roll of toilet paper, however, was there properly on its rack.

"Please don't put any toilet paper in the toilet," Barker admonished.

"No?" said Myers, in some astonishment.

"No, drop it here." Barker indicated a nail keg enameled in blackish green with hand-painted calla lilies decorating the front. The keg had a top of galvanized tin painted a rich henna color. "There is no city sewerage system. Ours is a private arrangement.

After you are done, the girl will come with a pitcher of water and flush the toilet. But paper would clog the works. Put it in this container." With his sandal toe he lightly touched the tin top of the painted nail keg. "When it's full, it is taken out and burned."

Later, after Myers and I had made our arrangements for the night, we lingered for a few minutes on the veranda.

The sister-in-law and the slant-eyed damsel brought a great double-size canvas cot out into the center of the patio, set it up securely, and placed a heap of pillows on it.

"On moonlit nights, I sleep in shorts," Barker said. "On black nights, 'starko,' as the British say."

The moonlight was almost gone now, and without benefit of the guttering candle on the ironing-board, it would have been difficult to tell whether the *patron* wore trunks or let the night breeze refresh his body thoroughly.

Barker explained his original nocturnal habits. "I sleep here in the open the first part of the night, until the coolness comes, say at 1 A.M. Then I go to my hammock on the veranda, where I stay until about half-past four. Just before dawn I go to my bed in the bedroom. I find I can rest better by this process, and make the most out of the temperature. Besides, the changes break the monotony of the night."

The girl had laid her last ironed garment in the great basket and staggered into the storeroom with the load. She snuffed out the candle and disappeared. We said good night on the bedroom veranda. Barker made his progress through the almost imperceptible palm shadows to his imperial cot. Myers turned in. I remained for a moment looking up at the tropical design fretted in white-gold on the dark-blue marble of the sky. The invisible night bird brushed by my feet, making faint staccato squawks that sounded like noises I once heard come from an excited medium at a séance. I went in, and closed the curtained screen door gently. Myers was already in bed, his eyes turned up to the ivory image on the cross over his head. When I blew out my lamp and slipped into bed, a profound silence hung about the place. There were no passers-by. No village dogs barked. If cats prowled, they did it voicelessly and on noiseless pads.

"Peace—it's wonderful, isn't it, tired businessman?" I said.

"Wonderful." Myers mumbled like a man talking in his sleep

"Though you and I wouldn't want it for a steady diet, it's easy to see there's something that holds Barker to Mexico."

"Yes," I mumbled back. "Three different beds a night. Three women to wait on one man."

4. FOOD AND FAREWELL

Just as breakfast was being brought across the patio, a raggedy countryman with a wisp of a gray beard was admitted at the gate. He approached Barker humbly, hat in hand. It seems he had come from Señora Barker's little farm across the river. There was some question about both the milk goats and the turkeys. Barker was slightly put out. Didn't the man know by now that he didn't have any concern with such matters? He waved him toward the kitchen. "My wife attends to such truck."

His wife was a remarkable manager, he explained to us. She hired and fired the farm workers, decided what was to be planted, and gave the orders about the selling of the goat milk. "The workers respect her, I can tell you—and if they need cussing, she can do it, in both Spanish and Zapoteca. I can't be bothered with petty accounts. Down here the women do that."

Barker divined that I was wondering just what he did do. "I'm too busy with my commission business," he immediately amended. "I'm agent in these parts for a lot of different American products. And I collect idols for sale and specimens for zoos. I entertain men like Covarrubias and Rex Ingram when they are down here painting or gathering material for books. And I'm correspondent for the Associated Press." He pulled out his wallet and showed us his press card. He sighed profoundly. "But nothing much ever happens now. When there was no Panama Canal, the bay at Salina Cruz was jammed with ships of every nation. The steamer cargoes used to be transshipped across the Isthmus to the Atlantic. Money flowed like molasses in June. Those were days! The whole Isthmus swarmed with sailors and traders. All the women wore chains of American five-dollar gold pieces. Now Salina Cruz is a ghost town, gone to rust." He sighed again as the breakfast began with watermelon.

"The warehouses have rotted. No ships, no trade, no tourists, no nothing. Just fishing and sea bathing. Even the bathing is not as it

was. Sharks come close to shore now. The quality of the once famous bawdyhouses has deteriorated shockingly. No more French or
Spanish or even Chinese girls—only the dregs of local talent. The
movie house runs pictures only once a week. The families who were
rich in 1910 curse the Panama Canal, which brought them ruin. But
now there is new hope pounding in their hearts. The Pan-American
Highway is imminent. Motorists will want to stop to look at the
Pacific, to bathe in the surf, to go sail-fishing. The town of Tehuantepec will pick up too when the highway comes through. I'll probably have to do the patriotic thing and turn this place into an exclusive guest house."

"You'd be doing your fellow Americans a real service," I said, as
Myers and I declined a second slice of melon.

With no trouble at all Barker consumed half a good-sized watermelon. "I don't drink coffee or liquor," he said, "but I eat a lot of
fruit."

After the eggs came the pancakes, piled high on a great family-
sized platter, and maple syrup imported from Vermont. "You'll
hurt my wife's feelings if you don't eat more," Barker urged again
and again. And we rose from this July breakfast as full as from a
Thanksgiving dinner.

It was two hours before we were able to rouse ourselves for a
stroll. The morning was far advanced, the sun at prime heat. The
businesswomen of Tehuantepec did not even take the Sunday-
morning rest. The market stayed open throughout the forenoon. It
was not as attractive as the one at Juchitán. It lay a few steps below
street level, and the stone floor was not as clean as it might have
been, so the women got their bare feet dirty. Among the women
merchants and money-changers in the stalls there were three men.
One of the men sold iguanas, those gigantic lizards whose white
meat is considered a delicacy. Another sold melon by the slice. The
third handled toilet articles, with a small display of Yardley's lavender shaving soap in wooden bowls. Barker remembered he was
out of razor blades, and made a purchase. From a dignified old
woman squatting on the pavement I ordered a bouquet of tuberoses
and white gladioli to be sent to our hostess.

A corner made by two streets that edged the plaza had been
blocked off, and men were setting up the framework of an arbor.

It was to be covered with the mountainous pile of palm branches that were being unloaded from a procession of oxcarts. Citizens were sawing timber and hammering just as blithely as if it were eight o'clock of a Monday morning instead of eleven o'clock of a Sunday morning, with a marimba band practicing in the bandstand.

"You should stay for the fiesta Tuesday," Barker said. "The parties are very colorful here. When the marimbas play a *sandunga* even the onlookers get excited. The *sandunga* is the native dance of the Isthmus. And when it is danced to marimba music, it sets you tingling in every nerve and fiber. It has grace and slow fire, but it's not melancholy, like the Argentine tango. It's a dance of courtship. First the girls dance alone with eyes cast down, and the boys dance around them. There is none of that barnyard vulgarity of the Cuban rumba. You have to be native-born to do the *sandunga* well. The dance steps can be learned—it's the inner intensity of feeling that has to be bred in you. Often the young people dance all night, and the old folks join in when they can't stand it any longer. When the aged get very merry and lose control of themselves, it is called 'throwing their gray hairs into the air.'"

As we turned up a steep narrow street a teen-age boy stupidly drunk bumped into me. He was acting smart and silly. One of his companions thought him funny; the two others were embarrassed and were trying to take him out of the public gaze.

"This younger generation of Indians!" snorted Barker. "Oh my, oh my! They make me sick. That kid's ancestors would have fixed him. Before the Spaniards came, drunkenness was not only abhorred, but in the case of a young man it was punishable by death. Adults who became drunk in public lost their property. Only persons who had passed sixty could drink as freely as they wished. Here in Tehuantepec it's the graybeards and the old ladies at the wedding feasts who drink themselves sick. Alcoholic puking is à la mode with the very aged in the Isthmus. But it's frowned on in youngsters. That boy should have his tail beat until he's sober."

We climbed the rocky southern heights of the town for the view. Part of Tehuantepec lay to the north and west, across the river. Each barrio (district) had its own separate church. Despite a sea breeze from the Pacific forty miles away, the heat from the yellowish sunlight was so intense that the churches and the houses seemed to quiver as if made of lemon jelly.

Behind us, at the highest point where we had paused, was a house built of bamboo. The door flap was raised, so that all the stark poverty within was revealed. There was a slung hammock, and something that may have been a cookstove squatted in a corner. Besides a soap-box seat and a rickety table, nothing else was visible except inquisitive hens, pecking about the dirt floor.

While we were looking, the owner—we guessed her to be a widow—returned up the rocky path. She bore on her head a brown jug of water and looked like a figure emerging from the Old Testament. "God knows how far down she had to go to get that water," Barker said as the woman passed us, the lace flounce of her purple skirt just missing the mud puddle before her door.

"How in hell do these women keep their hems clean?" Myers wondered.

Barker laughed. "It's a gift. But you should see the bottoms of their feet at night."

"Don't they wash?"

Barker looked surprised and almost pained. "Don't you know that the Tehuanas are noted for personal cleanliness? They bathe every day. There." He pointed toward the river. "Women, men, and children, every morning in the river—buck naked. At seven o'clock half the town is in the water. There may be a few stragglers left. Do you want to go? It's two miles from here to the river."

But we didn't get to the river. We had really had plenty of noonday sun. "You should have worn a hat," I said to Myers, who was looking a bit dazed as he wiped the perspiration off his sun glasses. He had been *muy hombre* and gone bareheaded like the acclimated Barker. "You're not this rugged in Memphis in July."

On the way home Barker discovered that Myers was a Mason, and he was determined that his lodge brother should see the local hall. So he got the big key and dragged Myers off to the lodge.

I started to write some letters. But the curve of the hammock beguiled me like the serpent in Eden, and I fell. Close by, the night bird was asleep, squatting on the tile under a grinning idol. His chopstick legs, jackknifed at the knees in repose, reared above his head on either side like skis upended. When I dropped into the hammock, Tony opened one eye and gave a weird little whimper. "Go back to sleep, old chap," I said. "I shan't disturb you." The bird shivered his skis and settled down between them back to sleep.

Myers came back looking fagged, but he ate dinner. The boiled lobsters were delicious, with more the flavor of the delicate Swedish crayfish than of the regular Maine crustacean. Barker used an old tomahawk head to crack the shells on the ledge of the balustrade. After we had made a meal of lobster, came the fried chicken, potatoes, rice, eggplant, and tomatoes, followed by fresh pineapple, mangoes, and more watermelon for dessert. The only truly Mexican dish was the stack of *totopos,* those dry waferlike tortillas which are cooked slowly in a deep hole in the ground. *Totopos* are round and flat like tortillas, but twice their diameter and too large to be hand-clapped into shape. In taste, they are inimitable and I think unsurpassed by any bread in Mexico.

Across the patio I saw the sixteen-year-old son William swat a fly in the kitchen. "Why don't we have your son come eat with us?" I suggested.

"Oh, as I told you, he'd rather eat in the kitchen with his mother —and he doesn't speak English, though he's begun to study it this summer."

With an Indian wife and five mestizo children, and with forty years in Mexico, speaking Spanish or Zapotec most of his days, Barker was incorruptibly American. He had enjoyed the seductive leisurely living of Mexico, but he had resisted becoming Mexican. He was among them and yet apart. He was most courteous and diplomatic, and he would give the *abrazo* to any Mexican with professional gusto. But he was still as American as if he had never ventured farther than ten miles from his birthplace on the Ohio River.

Barker had arrived in the days of the refulgent Porfirio Díaz, and had lived through the succeeding revolutions unscathed. "I have been in only one tight place in the revolutionary years," he said, "and that was when a train I was on was stopped by a band of revolutionaries bent on plunder and killing. I had the presence of mind to save my neck by presenting as passport extraordinary a Singer sewing machine invoice, thick with official customs stamps."

When we left the table gorged like boa constrictors, even Myers was not averse to a siesta to sleep it off. He was looking so pale about the gills that I felt sure he had suffered a mild sunstroke for his bravado in defying the law of the tropics that says a stranger must wear a hat in the sun. We waited until the sun was down and then strolled to the plaza to enjoy the marimba concert and watch the people dance on the pavement.

Neither the Señora nor her sister was visible at six o'clock breakfast next morning. The young girl served us coffee and *totopos,* and Barker a slice of watermelon. She did it very cheerfully, though I thought she looked tired about the eyes. When I said good-bye to her and thanked her, I slipped a couple of silver two-peso pieces into her hand. In her astonishment and delight she dropped both coins and they rang out on the pavement of the patio. Barker glanced about as the girl in her pleasurable confusion retrieved the coins. "Four pesos," he murmured. "That's a fortune for her—precisely what my wife pays her a month."

I refrained from expressing astonishment, though Myers and I exchanged a noncommittal glance. Eighty American cents a month for a maid—up before six and still ironing clothes after ten at night. Living in the tropics was even cheaper than I had conceived. But in a short time, when the Pan-American Highway had cut the corner off the Barker drawing-room and rooms for guests had been built on the property next door, and American money left in the Isthmus and minimum-hour laws were passed—well, here too the servant situation would doubtless be drastically changed.

The seven-o'clock air was very fresh as we walked to the station. Cartloads of cut flowers being unloaded at the market as we passed made the morning fragrant. When we got to the station it looked as if we had come to the end of the rainbow. Not that there was a pot of gold, but that the rainbow itself was concentrated in one dazzling lake of color. The businesswomen about to set out for the Atlantic side of the Isthmus were arrayed in all their glory. And they bore purple baskets and red trays of fruits and foods to sell along the way.

The dew-moist buttercups made the railroad track look like a run of molten gold in some celestial smelter. The rising sun turned the flanks of the yoked white oxen to silver and the great solid wheels of the carts to disks of burnished copper. A sea breeze from the west came like a harbinger preceding the train as it whistled for the river bridge at the far end of the town behind us. The wind stirred up the gold-flecked dust where the oxcarts waited, and blew it toward the platform as the women stooped for their baskets, balanced trays on their heads, and gathered their children about them. The rumbling engine seemed to mow down the buttercups, and its mechanical breath swirled the women's flounces. When we said our last adieus, Barker seemed regretful to see us go.

"Remember," he called as the train pulled out, "we have a saying here: 'Once the dust of Tehuantepec has settled on your heart, you will return.'"

IX

San Miguel de Allende

In a few hours that little city had stolen our hearts away.

—JOSÉ VASCONCELOS

I. HISTORIC PLEASURE TOWN

I AWOKE WITH A singing in my ears. For a few moments I went through that curious feeling of not knowing where I was. Then in the dimness—for only slivers of light seeped in at the edges of the rubber window shades—I made out the brass rails of the bed's foot-board. But the train was motionless, and there were no railroad noises whatever. Everything was intently still, except for the sing-ing that came from outside. I lay in a delectable semiconscious state and listened, remembering the first time I had ever heard a night-ingale. It was in Kairouan, the Mohammedans' holy city in Tunisia. I had arrived at midnight by train from Susa, after a sea voyage from Malta, and the serenade took place in the moonlit pepper tree out-side my hotel window. But as I listened now more intently, this bird song in Mexico reminded me of mockingbirds in Alabama. That was what it was—a kind of blending of African nightingale and Southern mockingbird.

I stretched, and felt the buoyant mattress respond to flesh and muscle. I got to my knees and raised the shade. Sunlight streamed in like a golden cascade. Outside, instead of railroad-yard sights, stood a neat adobe cottage with a swept dirt yard. On a branch of a willow tree hung a cage with wooden bars. Within, a black-and-gray bird sang for his own pleasure. I recognized the trim *sinsontli,* which, like the mockingbird, has an extensive repertoire, and can reproduce the notes of any bird it hears.

I recalled that in a town not a hundred miles away, Captain Lyons, the young Englishman, had remarked many of these birds in 1826. He had written: "In passing through the streets many cages of birds are seen suspended within the wooden barred windows, of which the *sinsontli,* or mockingbird, seems to be the favorite. These are very abundant in the surrounding country, yet fifty dollars are considered as by no means a high price for a good singer."

This cage of wooden bars swung in sun-dappled shade instead of within a window, and I doubted that the cottagers had paid more than five dollars for the singer, excellent as he was.

The bird went on with his random song, and I lay back for a moment in the wide, comfortable bed that was both restful and exciting. It was the first time I had ever slept in a real bed on a train. A Mexican friend had lent me his private car. The night express from the capital to Laredo had dropped it off around 3 A.M. at the station called San Miguel de Allende in the state of Guanajuato.

This gem of the colonial period is among the least visited of all the lovely places in Mexico. Although only fifty miles north of Querétaro, the roads are not good for motoring, and in the wet season they are virtually impassable. There is no airplane service, as there is to remote Tuxtla Gutiérrez in Chiapas. The trains both from the Texas border and from Mexico City arrive at the station at doleful hours between two and four in the morning. The town lies some two miles distant from the station, and cab-drivers hardly think a fare worth sitting up for. So for all its reputation among connoisseurs, San Miguel is almost invariably passed over or saved for a future visit.

I had skipped the town three times myself, and for fear that I might pass up his favorite spot in Mexico, my Mexican friend arranged for me to use his private car. It had all seemed to go by magic. I had slept so well that I had not known when the car was detached. Now I lay there in gratitude on top of the covers and stretched out catercornered just to sense fully the pleasure of a luxurious mattress with inner springs on a railway train. A light knock came on my door, and the tall mestizo porter from Michoacán came in with a bright morning smile and a glass of chilled tomato juice on a silver tray.

The car was well staffed with a steward, a cook, and this porter. Since there were three bedrooms available, besides the staff's quarters, I was allowed to bring three friends along. As a sort of escort I had a Mexican army captain, whom I had met at a cocktail party at the Officers Club in the capital. I had found him remarkably knowledgeable, with excellent judgment and a singular lack of prejudice. Though he had gone to a military school in the United States, he was not at all anti-American. I had asked him to accompany me because he was simpatico and because he had a great and understanding love for Mexico. He was unusually tall for a Mexican—six feet—and more heavily built than lean. Though I certainly did not anticipate trouble on such a highly civilized trip, it had occurred to me how useful this Captain might prove in a fight. His name was Victor Esperón y Urbina.

The other two men I asked to come were also both chosen because of their fondness for Mexico. One was an American nonsectarian missionary, Cameron Townsend, the head of those Wycliff translators who translated the New Testament into various dialects and taught the Indians to read in remote hinterlands. The other fellow was Jess Wagus, the young Spanish instructor from Iowa who had gone with Thérèse and me on the motor trip to Michoacán. Captain Esperón had a room to himself and shared a connecting bath with me. Townsend and Wagus had a room together and shared a bath with the steward. It was a rather oddly assorted but strangely harmonious company—bound together by a deep regard for Mexico.

As I drank the tomato juice served at the bedside in the English manner of "a cup of tea and one thin slice of bread and butter to get you through the affair of bathing and shaving," I thought of the past pleasant evening, the lingering over the good dinner, and then sitting about the dining-drawing-room table until midnight keeping the conversation to Mexican themes. I had jotted down in my notebook some desultory comments and for a few minutes dallied over the tomato juice remembering.

"Americans," Captain Esperón had said significantly, "simply cannot realize our problems. And they cannot know the strangeness or the depth of the Mexican inferiority feeling. You see, our people—I mean the general run—and your people are invariably comparing our things with your things—living standards, wages, clothes, material gadgets—and it puts us at a disadvantage. It makes the Mexican draw into himself and appear much less than he really is.

"You may recall that Lawrence wrote of the 'almost deliberate visionlessness of Mexican eyes.' He spoke of the voice 'that is the inevitable flat resonance of aloofness,' as if to say it is not becoming

to an Indian to know anything. There is enough truth there to make
it difficult to get at Mexico and its truth. And besides, we have fifty
odd languages and dialects, as Mr. Townsend well knows."

Townsend had nodded ruminatingly, for his field workers had
come in contact with most of them. "In your country," Esperón had
continued, "Mr. Roosevelt gave his chimney talks over the radio and
everybody in the United States could understand him—even the
blacks in the piney woods. So it is all easier for you.

"The inferiority feeling that the Spaniards deliberately created in
the Indians is a part of this so-called mystery of Mexico. No one can
tell you the truth about Mexico. You have to have the perception to
sense it."

"Yes," I said to myself as I finished the tomato juice, "you have
to sense it. There's no use trying to sum up Mexico. The answer is
neither in what's said nor in what's done."

As I went through the unwonted pleasure of a shower on a motionless sleeping car, a bit of Mexican poetry came to my mind, and
I recited it to a drenching of cold water after hot.

> "O incongruous Mexico, dolorous and gay,
> Sonorous as bronze, fragile as glass,
>
> Made up of melody, of hates and joy,
> Of stubborn prejudice, of boundless energy,
>
> Of doubtful elegance and of glaring red,
> O Mexico! with your bleeding Spanish heart."

The author, Torres Bodet, knew his native Mexico as well as any-
body, not because he was an intellectual or a man-of-the-world diplomat, but because he had the sensibilities of a poet. "Incongruous" was
his best single word for it.

All through breakfast sang the *sinsontli,* as if bursting with joy at
the day's perfection. As we ate, we indulged in a pooled refresher
course in the pertinent history. We had come to the Cradle of Independence. Here in San Miguel was born the struggle for freedom
from Spain. It was the home town of the chief begetter, a young
Creole army captain named Ignacio Allende. Handsome and well-
to-do, he was one of the founders of the Society for the Study of Fine
Arts—an innocent name for the refined study of conspiracy. Allende

had the vision in 1809, and helped form a secret independence league with the object of throwing off the Spanish yoke. Like most revolutions, this movement began among the intellectual upper classes. To avoid suspicion, the patriots met at fiestas in their own homes. They talked conspiracy over chocolate cups and wineglasses. The movement spread to neighboring towns, where branch groups began to study the "fine arts."

By 1810, the society at Querétaro, fifty miles away, had assumed the leadership. There, among the conspirators were the corregidor himself and his wife, Josefa Ortiz Domínguez, who became the heroine of the Independence. Father Miguel Hidalgo, the progressive priest at Dolores in Guanajuato, was in sympathy with the movement and often attended meetings in Querétaro. Allende and his fellow townsman, Juan Aldama, had spread their underground propaganda as far away as Mexico City and Puebla. The plan was to seize the wealthy Spaniards and officers in the towns, nationalize their property, and declare Mexico's independence of the Spain then dominated by Napoleon. The revolt was to be launched in December of 1810. But a traitor within the ranks betrayed the plot before it was fully ripened. The wife of the corregidor in Querétaro discovered the betrayal through eavesdropping on informers calling on her husband. By tapping with a stick on the floor of her upper bedroom to a waiting servant in a room beneath, Señora Ortiz Domínguez sent a warning to Captain Allende at San Miguel that all was discovered.

The young man rushed to Dolores for consultation with Father Hidalgo. The priest realized that their only recourse now, to save their own lives and the movement, was to act immediately. So at dawn on Sunday of September 16, Father Hidalgo uttered his famous *Grito:* "Long live Our Lady of Guadalupe! Long live Independence!" With fifteen of the workmen from his little co-operative silk and pottery factories and sixty-odd men freed from jail, Father Hidalgo marched to war, under the banner of the Indian Virgin of Guadalupe. The revolution was loosed. There was no turning back. Recruits were gathered along the way. In San Miguel late that evening, Captain Allende arrested all the Spaniards, shut them up in a convent, and proceeded to win over the dragoons of the Spanish regiment. Because of the priest's seniority of years and knowledge,

Allende insisted that Father Hidalgo be made leader. The extraordinary title of Captain General of America was bestowed upon the parish cura. Allende was elevated to the rank of lieutenant general.

For the first months the revolution prospered. Yet, despite early victories everywhere, Father Hidalgo did not have good judgment in military affairs, and whenever he refused to follow Allende's advice he met with disaster. Divided in opinion as to strategy and procedure, the leaders fell. On March 21, 1812, both were captured through treachery. The trials took place in Chihuahua. The gallant young Allende was executed on June 26, being forced to turn his back like a traitor to the firing squad. Hidalgo's life was not dispatched until a month later, after the ceremony of unfrocking by the Church. Both the brown-haired head and the white were severed from their respective bodies and sent to Guanajuato. Here, as gruesome souvenirs, they hung in iron-barred cages for a full decade. In 1823, after Iturbide's successful rebellion and the establishment of independence, the weather-blackened skulls of the old priest and the young soldier were reassembled with their bodies and laid to rest in the cathedral of Mexico City with solemn ceremony. In 1926, their remains were removed to the Monument of Independence in the Paseo de la Reforma, where only the foremost heroes of Mexico abide.

The *sinsontli* was still singing in its cage when we took the rattle-trap of a taxi that had been patiently waiting for custom since half-past six. Though the morning was more than two hours past seven, it had the quality of exaltation Pippa sang about as she passed along the dew-bespangled countryside of Italy. On either side the broad road to the town, the semitropical scenery shimmered with morning freshness. A bloom seemed to lie upon the neat cottages of the humble, sitting so contentedly among their green vegetable plots. To the east, the north, and the south one could lift up one's eyes and draw strength from the towering hills. It was a splendid part of earth, and the season was midway between sowing and reaping.

Like the Biblical city on the hill whose light could not be hid, San Miguel was built on a slope of the Cerro de Montezuma. A great water jet of a spring that rose on the crest of the mountain irrigated the gardens that spilled down the inclines. Flagstoned paths and staircases wound like countless rivulets among parterres of flowers belonging to the villas. The tall tranquil trees took on a golden sheen, the spires and domes, a mellow glow.

The town had celebrated its four-hundredth anniversary in 1941. Founded by a Franciscan friar who called himself Juan de San Miguel, the town had been named for Saint Michael the Great. In the middle of the nineteenth century, its name had been changed officially to San Miguel de Allende, in honor of the local hero. During the seventeenth and eighteenth centuries it had been a nobles' pleasure town. Families who made their fortune from Guanajuato's silver, but who did not like to live close to the smell of labor, removed here to enjoy the fruits of mining in an atmosphere of Eden. The town is chock-full of seignorial mansions with beautiful old doorways and spacious courtyards.

The house of a Senator to whom I had a letter was typical—three stories of harmonious eighteenth-century architecture, with two upper galleries completely embracing a square patio, and hundreds of potted plants in porcelain jars lining the ledges of the balustrades between the arches. But as an untypical note, a dozen snow-white cats lay sunning themselves decoratively on the ledges of the second gallery's balustrades.

"I suppose you have discovered," said the genial Senator, whom we caught before he had got to the barbershop for a shave, "that in a Spanish-Mexican house, the patio is another room—generally the best room. It brings the heavens into the house by night and by day, a successive variety of sunlight and cloud and moonshine. It has been so here in this room for two hundred years."

I looked up at the azure canopy, and then at the flowerpots and the cats. "I trust," I said, "that Heaven also blesses you with servants to water all these plants and feed the cats—in these times."

The Senator smiled. "So far—it goes not bad. But even here we learn there are changes going on in the social order. And you see I am a Senator and attend the Assembly in the capital—and I hear things, and—I espouse the liberal cause." He shrugged his shoulders. "How long a mozo will prefer to earn an easy living watering flowers instead of working in a mine or a factory, who can say?" He smiled again and rubbed a forefinger across the day-old stubble of his jaws. "If my lack of a shave is not offensive, may I be your guide for an hour or so?—Where shall we go first?"

We strolled to the lane called the Street of the Cradle of Allende, where the patriot took his first breath on January 21, 1779, while the success of the American Revolution still hung in the balance. Over the door of the birthplace is a Latin inscription which says, "Here was born one who is known everywhere." But Ignacio Allende is not as well known to the world as his fellow townsmen would like to think. If he had not been the victim of treacheries, and if his rebellion had succeeded as Iturbide's did a decade later, he would have a much wider fame than he owns today. But whereas Father Hidalgo is revered as an old gentleman with white hair, Allende, who did not live as long as Jesus, remains the young Mexican's ideal of a gallant hero.

"While Ignacio was growing up," said the Senator as we walked to the main square, "his family got richer, and this house here on the plaza was his home at the time of the conspiracy." The ground floor had become a corner apothecary shop, but we rang at the great door behind the shop on the street facing the church. A humpty-dumpty little man, hardly five feet high, admitted us, trying to conceal a sniffling head cold behind a brown handkerchief. He was the present owner of the Allende house and the proprietor of the drugstore. The patio reeked of iodoform and mustard and a mélange of medicinal odors. I got the impression that all the purges and plasters sold in the shop were brewed or concocted in the household. Preceding us, with a kind of toddling run like that of Josephine Hull playing the whimsical murderess in *Arsenic and Old Lace,* the druggist led the way to stairs that ascended from the patio to the upper floor. Halfway up the flight he paused to blow his nose three times, as if heralding our approach. But at the portal of the drawing-room he drew himself up to his full four feet eleven, maneuvered his rotundity through the doorjamb, and, fluttering a plump little hand, ushered us into the room where the Society for the Study of Fine Arts held its meetings.

I looked in all four directions of the beautifully proportioned room. There was not a vestige of Allende, not a hint of the aristocratic tradition. Yards and yards of starched lace curtains hung from gilt rings over the windows and trailed the floor—the kind of lace curtains in high vogue with Irish immigrants who graduated from Boston shanties at the turn of the century. The furniture was flamboyant in gilt, and the plaster ornaments might have been won in paddle games at a street carnival. To cover my disappointment, I walked to one of the windows, clutched my way perilously through the masses of stiff lace, took a deep breath, and gazed upon the pleasant plaza on which Allende must have looked a thousand times.

"Why, in Heaven's name," I said quietly to the Senator, who followed me, "does not the municipality buy this house? The drawing-room could be redone with authentic furniture of 1800, if none of Allende's original pieces could be found."

"It has been talked of," said the Senator blandly, and we began thanking the druggist for his courtesy. The little man ducked and bowed, blew his nose three snorts at the head of the stairs, and shook his head apologetically. "This cold, this cold," he murmured sadly.

As we came down into the patio, the gases and fumes of doses being mixed or cooked rose with overpowering persuasion. "I should think all these smells would rout a whole army of cold germs," I said sotto voce to Esperón. "I feel positively polluted with antiseptic."

"You mean polluted with the atmosphere of that room," Esperón said shrewdly. "I had an eye on you."

"Well, you must admit it's a smelly commentary on the change in taste between 1810 and 1943."

"Ah, but you see the family of Allende no longer lives here." His look explained his commentary.

The town's exterior had not remained wholly a museum piece, any more than Allende's drawing-room. The plaza church had had its face done over in a Gothic approximation by a celebrated Indian architect named Ceferino Gutiérrez, some years after the death of the hero. The architect was a pure-blooded Indian entirely without education or technical training, and he had to impart his plans and ideas to his workmen by making drawings in the sand with a stick. He had an extraordinary gift for estimating stress of materials and an indigenous dramatic, as well as poetic, sense. He would take his conception of a style like the Gothic and use it after his own fashion.

His genius for folk architecture, however, was not up to the advanced culture of a Gothic cathedral; hence the strangeness of the design. The façade was not right, but it was interesting, and in no sense offensive. In many parts of the town, the architecture of San

Miguel de Allende has been touched by the crude brilliance of Ceferino Gutiérrez. He liked to do daring, original things like building
the dome of La Concepción with a two-storied drum. If Gutiérrez
had been trained in architectural design as a young man, he might
well have proved to be one of the most significant architects in
Mexico. Since he never traveled, his fame is local; but he is another
one of the examples of remarkable ability found in unlettered Indians throughout Mexican history.

I had observed so many hundreds of churches in Mexico in my
various visits that I had little desire to examine in detail those in
San Miguel. On the whole they were attractive, but none of them
were of such distinction as to make us ecstatic. What did impress
us all was the innovation of neatly printed admonitions posted in the
vestibules above holy-water fonts. Apparently the priests in the Ora-
torio de San Felipe had had difficulty in keeping the attention of
male communicants because of the style of short skirts. There in bold
black lettering for the women to read as they blessed themselves at
the font, was this notice:

> To the temple you should go
> with dress honest and long.
> Do not be guilty of serving the Devil.

In another church the trouble had been not skirts, but pets and pro-
miscuous expectoration. A plea read:

> Do not bring dogs to the temple,
> since God lives in it.
> Do not spit on the floor
> and you will set a good example!

Whereas the tone of these injunctions smacked obviously of the
present day, there was an inscription on another church door that
attested to a more cultivated spirit and phraseology in the past. I read
the gracious precept aloud:

> Punctuality is the virtue of saints, the courtesy of
> kings, the duty of gentlemen, the need of men of
> business, and the custom of men of sound judgment.

"You and I were both for the Revolution," I said to Esperón, "but
now there is something gone with it that I could wish back again."

2. WITH THE ARTISTS

The telegraph company of Mexico had obviously not been imbued with the spirit of punctuality urged by former church fathers in San Miguel. The "extrarapid" telegram I had sent to Stirling Dickinson yesterday from Mexico City had not yet been delivered when we sought him out. Through mutual friends, Dickinson and I had exchanged letters about Mexican roads, and he had advised me some weeks earlier not to try to reach San Miguel from Morelia by automobile. I had never met the man, but I was eager to see the new art school he and Felipe del Pomar had established.

Dickinson proved to be a brisk, lithe young man with blond coloring and a Princeton degree. His home was in Chicago. He looked as thoroughly and alertly American as the casually elegant Peruvian-born Felipe del Pomar looked the Latin American patrician.

"Obviously a fountain pen," Esperón said of Del Pomar.

"A fountain pen?"

"A Mexican expression for bluebloods—we use blue ink in our fountain pens here."

The two men were glad to show us about their layout. It was something to be proud of.

Though up to 1940 it was only the exceptional tourist who had heard of San Miguel de Allende—it is not even mentioned in Frances Toor's comprehensive *Motorist Guide to Mexico* (1938)—artists began to drift here after 1935. In 1938 Pomar and Dickinson joined forces and founded an art school. The expressed aim was to further the development of an indigenous American art and bring together artists and students from the various republics of the Americas. The founders gave the school an imposing name: Escuela Universitaria de Bellas Artes. Pomar furnished most of the money and Dickinson got the students—about half of them coming from Illinois in the first four seasons. Both of them taught classes in painting, and by 1942 nine new instructors had been added to the faculty—among them the distinguished Mexican artist Rufino Tamayo, who teaches in the summer term.

The Mexican Government had believed in Felipe del Pomar's vision and had made the new school a generous grant. The former

Convent of Las Monjas was remodeled carefully in a manner to preserve the glories of its colonial architecture. Commodious studios,
offices, a dining-hall, a kitchen, a shop, and living-quarters for the
faculty were arranged. The students study modern art in a gentle
atmosphere of Old World beauty. Besides courses in painting, those
in sculpture, fresco, weaving, ceramics, architecture, and languages
are offered. Two pleasant new hotels have been built in the town to
accommodate the students, as well as take care of the sweep of tourist traffic that is sure to come when the projected highway to Querétaro is constructed. Some of the students live at the Ranch, which is
one of the most attractive features of the school.

A few miles from the town, high in the hills and extending over
a hundred fertile acres, the Ranch is like a combination of country
club, gentleman's estate, and dormitory. The gardens and orchards
supply fresh vegetables and fruits the year round. There is a tennis
court, and even a *frontón* for playing jai alai, doubtless inspired by
the Havana-born Señora del Pomar, who is the niece of the Cuban
diplomat Marques Sterling. At the bottom of a series of lawn terraces, at the very edge of an enchanting wooded ravine is a modern
swimming pool. Students who do not live at the Ranch use it as a
recreation club. The group that does live there are like both guests
and hosts at a hacienda house party.

For his own dwelling Pomar has reconstructed a colonial house
on the highest road directly above the town. His balconies face the
setting sun and the domes and towers of the town below. The focal
point of the gardens is a great majolica fountain, which reflects cascades of blossoms. Tiers of planting fan outward up the hill in in-
creasingly wide arcs. Pomar's studio is apart from the main house
and higher up in the garden; and in one of the rooms Tamayo
painted while his own house was being constructed across the street.

The stone walls and partitions of the modern house the Tamayos
were building were already erected. One could stand in what was to
be the drawing-room and look out of the great long window that
extended the length of it and see what would be seen through plate
glass when the building was completed. From the site there was a
steep drop to the rooftops below, which were so drenched in flame-
colored bougainvillea that the property seemed to rise like a promontory above a turbulent sunset sea. And far down and away lay

the pattern of the town's center, with the creamy domes of churches like mounds of winter butter. The house was to be spacious and to have an abundance of clear light, so essential to a painter. It would cost just three thousand dollars to build, Tamayo said, including architect, stones, flooring, glass, plumbing for two bathrooms—everything. I made an estimate in terms of United States construction—certainly not less than twelve thousand.

"And for the land," said Señora Tamayo, "we paid a hundred dollars."

I did not gasp, but asked about taxes.

"Two and a half pesos, every other month," Tamayo replied.

"Fifty cents bimonthly?" I repeated to make quite sure. "Three dollars a year for taxes?"

"Right," said Tamayo, nodding his handsome Indian head, and smiling with the corners of his mouth down.

"Just that," said Señora Tamayo, her eyes sparkling with humor and gratitude to Providence.

But how can you "uplift the downtrodden masses" on such taxes as these? I wanted to ask. (I knew that Tamayo was an avowed sympathizer with the Marxists.) How can you raise the living standards of the poor on such wages for construction? But I refrained from indelicate questions and said, "You are blessed indeed," and looked away from the view and back to husband and wife. I noted the texture of skin—the rich brownish tones of his, the rich cream of hers. I remarked the moody, smoldering quality of the man's honest eyes. I turned to the radiance of his lady's—such frank eyes, full of fun and incorruptible goodwill, always expectant of the best, quite assured of beautiful tomorrows, and exhilarated by the happy now. An excellent woman for this strange man stirred by creative fire, rapt in poetic moods, and moved by the suffering of his brother man.

Señora Tamayo was wearing a peasant costume with sheer muslin blouse and full-gathered skirt of red-and-yellow cotton embroidered in cotton thread. Besides being a charming outfit, it gave her a practical, capable look, as if she could prepare a substantial meal, keep accounts, and cultivate her own kitchen garden as well as play hostess to international friends. She was saying that they would continue to live half the year in New York, where Rufino taught and painted, and the other half-year here.

"Six months of the year in Paradise," I said, taking in the panorama, the atmosphere, and my conception of the completed house. "And apparently for a song," I added as I turned from the window at strange noises and stranger sights.

A procession of mouse-colored donkeys was coming in at the front door. Each bore on its back two large building stones, which it wore like kidney pads. As the burro boys unloaded them, Señora Tamayo gave each beast a caressing word and a pat. "Where it is impossible to get a truck to the mountain quarry," Tamayo said, "transportation by burroback is convenient and cheap. All the stones for this house have been transported by burro. Primitive way to get materials for a modern house, isn't it?"

"Without the burros we could hardly run the school," Señora Tamayo said. "Today we're having a picnic lunch at a mountain shrine—the whole school up the trail on burros. Stirling Dickinson has been engaging animals for days from all the villages about. May we take you?"

I declined without regret. I had no notion of spending half my day with my legs stretched over a donkey. Nor did Esperón relish the sport. And Townsend and Wagus were going off to visit an Indian village some dozen miles away.

We stopped again at Pomar's studio to look at a picture Tamayo had been working on for weeks. It was an ancient woman with an indefinite, triangular brown face and vague, deep-sunken eyes. She sat before a kind of spinning wheel, staring blankly. Her dress was a strange shade of dark-blue, like something from another world. I saw the form Tamayo had created, but I did not know what he was saying. I could not know what was in him that begat that form. I merely beheld the visible productive activity of his waking consciousness. And since I knew the beholder is supposed to see and hear only himself in a work of art, I confessed to some blankness in myself—for this work was only obliquely meaningful to me. As I stood there silently before the picture trying to divine its secret, I recalled Spengler's words: "Men of two different kinds are parted, each in his own spiritual loneliness, by an impassable gulf."

Tamayo was a rebel—I knew that well enough. And I knew he did not fall into the "Mexicanist tendency to indulge in the picturesque." He was looking, he had once said, for pictorial purity without loss of local color. He proclaimed that he was seeking universal principles, working for unity and purity of expression. His themes are neither popular nor national—and yet in some supersubtle way the mood or inner heart of the Mexican people shows forth. Perhaps, as an admirer claimed, this highly sensitized Indian expresses with his intuition and emotion the inexpressible qualities of his people. I understood that art is supposed to rise from folklore and gradually become sophisticated. I wondered if the phantasmagoria of Tamayo's art is perhaps a kind of equivalent for the longings of a people still on the naïve level of culture.

I recalled a gouache of Tamayo's entitled "Harmony in White," where white horses are trotting sportively to music made by a melancholy dough-faced clown, who sits strumming a guitar with his brown fingers. Great sticks of wood lie about. And there are sticks and logs scattered through many of his other pictures, just as he often uses three mandolins or three guitars. I did not ask him what these symbols of scattered sticks and three musical instruments meant to him. I stood there fascinated, gazing at the misty old woman in unearthly blue. I cannot say I was at ease before this picture, but I was intrigued by its other dimensionality, and I could quickly recognize the artist's genius.

At half-past five that afternoon Del Pomar and Tamayo, very spruce in white-doeskin trousers and dark coats, arrived at our private car in the Ranch station wagon to take the Captain and me to Stirling Dickinson's cocktail party. When we stopped to get their wives, the ladies floated out of the Pomar gateway in billowy chiffon evening dresses, with flowers in their hair and jewels twinkling at their ears.

"Oh yes," Señora Tamayo said, laughing, noting the expression on my face. "San Miguel is quite, quite gay. After the dinner for you tonight, we go to a wedding dinner party at ten. So—" her fingers caught at the chiffon of the skirt, held it out, and dropped the filmy stuff as if she were scattering white petals in the dust—"this."

"My, my!" I said, handing her and Señora del Pomar into the

station wagon. "A picnic luncheon on burroback, a cocktail party and two dinners. I had not dreamed social life in this idyllic spot could be so demanding."

She laughed a musical, bantering laugh. "When the season here is over and we are completely fagged, we return to New York to rest up."

Stirling Dickinson's place lay some two miles from the town on a winding, leaf-shadowed road rimmed with low rock walls. The rooftop lay just below the road, and the house followed the contours of a sloping ravine. Through a gate, you descended an oblique stone staircase to a terrace, where you entered a small living-room done in masculine Rembrandt tones. Like a linked chain the house proceeded—a kitchen, two bedrooms, and a bath, all clinging to the sides of the ravine and edged with a balustraded gallery and belvederes with stone benches. It was at once spectacular and intimate. Across the emptiness, on the other loftier side of the barranca, rose an extraordinary three-storied stone ruin.

The cocktail party was in full swing when we arrived. So, happily, no one but the host and a young man from Ohio paid much attention to me, and I could gaze across the void to my heart's content. With its broken rows of platinum-colored arches silhouetted against the dark-green velvet of the slope, it was like some figment of dream architecture, as evocative as a setting for a poetic drama by Maeterlinck.

"It's really a relic of an eighteenth-century mill," Señora Tamayo said, "where the wheat for the nobles' bread was ground."

We stood at the edge of a little belvedere and looked down into the ravine's great V. The whole view had a lyrical quality. A stream, concealed by profuse vegetation, made music playing on the rocks. And as the foliage began to stir with the breeze of late afternoon, I could imagine an orchestra tuning up for an operatic performance. A blue bird, the color of the sky, shot across my range of vision like the warning flash of a conductor's baton. In a moment romantic figures might emerge from behind the stone pillars and burst into a choral. The tinkle of donkey bells from a drove passing on the road above us merged with a tinkle of glass on tin as Dickinson set a tray with cocktails on the white iron table beside us.

Only last month he had completed remodeling the stone cottage he had discovered and bought. The fixtures in the black-and-white tiled bathroom had just been installed. The bath had cost more than he paid for the dilapidated house and the land. For the house as it stood and the land down to the bottom of the barranca, he had paid the sum of ninety dollars. And recently he had bought the view, the ruins and the acres of hillside across the way, he said—for three hundred dollars. He had struck such a golden bargain because San Miguel de Allende is two hundred miles from Mexico City. It is too far for the "millionaire socialist politicians" of the capital to commute, as they do from Cuernavaca.

Guests sat on stone stairs, on balustrades, or stood about in the smallish drawing-room. Captain Esperón and two men students sat with Del Pomar's handsome wife at a painted iron table. A group of girl students gathered about Del Pomar by a pomegranate bush illuminated by the red stars of its own buds. The Tamayos and I took our glasses to a far edge of the gallery and sat on a stone bench facing the ruin. The shadows deepened in the ravine, and the scene took on an even more dream-stuff quality. I thought of what moonlight might do to it.

"San Miguel is a place where one can idle to some purpose," Señora Tamayo said at length.

"It's the only place we have seen in the world where we cared to build a house to call home," Tamayo said. "But we don't idle—we work."

"If it weren't for news of the outside world," his wife said, "one could exist here in a state of grace."

The perfume vials of the flowers in the little narrow garden directly beneath the balustrade seemed to have been unstoppered by the approaching twilight. Fragrance rose like a mist. The sound of a cowbell now came drifting faintly from somewhere across the abyss, like a ghostly overtone. The deep blue of the firmament was being drawn closer to earth, as a tent is pegged down tightly against a windy night. Despite the hum of talk and desultory bursts of laughter behind us, the hour was so mellow it seemed it might dissolve between one's fingers. Tamayo gazed moodily toward the depths of the ravine, where the leafy boughs blanketed the stream. His lady raised her slim white hand from the stone ledge as if to caress some invisible thing in the air.

"Dinner waits. We should go." Señora del Pomar had joined us with invitation and reminder. We turned to make our adieus. Virtually everyone else had already disappeared. The host and the young man from Ohio were on the verge of tidying up. Never before had I been present at a cocktail party and so delightfully oblivious of it.

3. BITS OF TALK AND MUSIC

We dined at a long table in the old refectory of the convent. Captain Esperón sat on the right of Señora del Pomar and I at her left, with Señora Tamayo next me. The hostess, who had tasted dishes in the world's best restaurants, had a skill in cookery which she had been able to impart to the native cooks. The atmosphere was anything but monkish. There were bright lights, and napkins the color of buttercups.

Down at the other end of the table where Pomar and Tamayo and Townsend and Wagus sat the conversation took a serious turn. I saw Tamayo's eyes flash, and he was almost shouting at Pomar. "But, why, why, why?"

"The Indians don't hanker for Communism and the brotherhood of man—they want a piece of land to call their own," Del Pomar said.

"Forty acres and a mule," Wagus put in. "Or the Mexican equivalent—ten acres and a burro."

Tamayo threw up his hands and glanced toward heaven.

I turned back to Señora del Pomar to praise the delicious *haricots verts* fresh from the ranch garden. They had been cooked the French way.

"General Cárdenas gave five thousand budded orange trees to our village," Townsend was saying. "The cacique said the whole town should have them—for he wanted the control, to use them to hold his political power. But we knew we couldn't work on a communistic basis, because one fellow might kill another over an orange. So we gave ten trees to each family by lot, as long as they held out."

Señora Tamayo turned to me, her eyes bright; she did not take radical ideology as passionately as did her husband. "Do you remember when John Reed asked Pancho Villa what he thought of socialism? The General echoed the word: 'Socialism—what is it? Is it a thing? I see it only in books, and I do not read much.'"

We laughed, and Esperón across from me said: "Villa had no intellectual theories, but he knew Mexicans. He said the only thing to do with soldiers in times of peace is to put them to work. An idle soldier is always thinking of fighting or getting into mischief."

The salad came—perfectly ripened, perfectly textured avocado, with French dressing such as one gets in Paris.

"Villa could hardly read," Esperón went on, "but he sensed that Mexico's redemption would come through schools. He had a passion for schoolhouses, and in towns where he passed a crowd of children playing, he would say: 'There were a lot of children on such and such a street. We'll build a school there.'"

"Did not one of your best writers say that highways teach the language better than schools?" I said.

"It's true that we need roads and more roads," Esperón said. "It is hard to say which are more needed. About schools—you know in the army I get all around—when rural schools are started up in a school-less section, the attendance is always large at first. Kids trudge for miles. The district officials virtually command the parents to send them. But no matter how ardent the teacher's endeavor to interest and instruct, attendance soon falls off. Many a poor man has explained humbly to me that it is more essential to cultivate the soil than to cultivate boys and girls, more imperative for kids to get something into their stomachs than into their heads. Children are needed at home to scratch in the earth to get food. It's lack of machines, as well as lack of roads and schools, that holds Mexico back."

At the other end of the table they were asking Townsend about his work as a teacher. The two conversations began to merge. We stopped talking to listen to the missionary.

He was saying in his soft-spoken way that he despised scientists who use humanity as a laboratory instrument in their research, but think nothing of men's actual welfare. "So I cannot admire priests who seek only to inject dogma while leaving the people in economic, intellectual, and moral stagnation. I have no interest in the propagation of a sect. I am not an ordained minister. I give the people the simple Bible, and I am having portions of it translated into all the Indian languages."

He told how the students from his linguistic institute went into the remote regions and lived the life of the village peoples. "Only those who have some sympathy with their customs can really teach the Indians," Townsend said. "Many people told us that the Indians did not want to be stirred out of their drabness. And of course some of their misery is due to their own shiftlessness, but far more is due to forces beyond their control."

Tamayo nodded his dark head in agreement at the last statement.

"So I not only desired to see portions of the New Testament of brotherly love translated and published in all of the Indian languages, but I wanted to have a small part in the Indians' economic progress. I wanted to help get drinking water piped into villages and to see vegetables planted to supplement the tortilla-beans-pulque diet. In some places, we exterminated a pest of ants; in others, we started a pottery industry. In some, we persuaded families to whitewash their huts inside and out as an incentive to cleanliness. We teach simple sanitation practices. We make an effort to reduce drunkenness. The Department of Rural Education has made us grants of books and provided chalk and blackboards for the schools. It ordered an edition of an Aztec primer I formulated for use in towns where Aztec is the predominant tongue. Doctors have been sent into districts where no honest medical treatment has ever been known. So," he finished, as if having talked too much, "these are some of the objectives, and the results have been gratifying."

"Don't your workers find it difficult to make contact, to be taken in by the Indians?" Del Pomar asked.

"Sometimes it is quite difficult. Often the students meet with serious hostility, and it takes courage to face it. Remote, uncivilized people are generally suspicious. Our workers have to learn to conquer that suspicion. When they've learned that, they understand the fundamental principle of diplomacy—if you respect others and treat them well, they'll treat you well and respect you."

The dessert, a frozen pudding, was served. Tamayo wanted to know if the Mexican Government had been co-operative to Townsend's work.

"Most co-operative. You see, we began the work when General Cárdenas was President, and—" Townsend paused and smiled— "you can't fool General Cárdenas. He knows when a motive is sincere and worth while. He was, and still is, marvelously helpful."

They had all listened attentively to Mr. Townsend, and the mention of Cárdenas's sanction set the seal of approval on the mission. For Cárdenas happened to be admired by all present.

"It seems to me," I began, to keep the subject going, "that Cárdenas's leaning toward socialism grows out of brotherly love and compassion. With many another down here socialism seems purely a will to power. Doesn't your theoretical socialist desiring power want to take the Indians and recast them according to his theories of what's good for them? I wonder if the people themselves like that."

"Lombardo Toledano would have Mexico bear the stamp of his ideas—everybody fit into the world of his vision." I turned. The young man from Ohio had come up to the table with a message for Del Pomar, had stopped to listen to the talk, and now put in his say.

"The socialist can be quite tyrannical," Wagus said. "And if the masses rule, won't you find about as much oppression?"

"And far more confusion?" murmured Señora del Pomar.

Del Pomar said: "The will to power is pretty terrific in these times —as terrific in the worker and in the industrialist as in the politician. The world has never had more complete dictators than Hitler and Stalin."

"Cárdenas was certainly no dictator," I said.

"By no means," Townsend said. "He is a pacifist, really. He was a youthful revolutionist, but he really does not believe in revolution by force."

"He doesn't believe that propaganda-stirred hatred is the proper way for securing peace," Esperón said. "I have heard him say often that there is no reason why men can't learn to love each other."

"And I heard him say once, quite casually," Townsend said, "that material bigness is not the same as the majesty of honest achievement."

"You can talk all the socialism or democracy you want," said Señora del Pomar, making a move to rise, "but it will be a long time before the peasant forgets the old proverb: 'Though we are all of the same clay, a jug is not a vase.'"

Music from the distant wedding feast had been drifting through the open windows for some time. Our hosts were already late. The

student from Ohio delivered his message to Pomar. We all got up.
Talks are never finished in Mexico anyhow; conclusions are never
reached.

Star shadow lay upon the shrubbery of the patio and traced the
outlines of the galleries' great arches just as in decades past, when
women under vows trod the pavement in devout meditation. The
flowing evening dresses of the ladies brushed by the obscured doors
of former nuns' cells. Transitory time was seeing a variety of strange
mutations in the world. If the clay of life would always be the same
clay, would the jugs all become vases, or would there be merely one
universal stereotyped model of jug?

After Wagus and Townsend had gone to bed near midnight,
Esperón and I came out on the car's observation vestibule to take
a last breath of the fresh night air. Not far off there was guitar
music, and male voices singing. We went down the steps and followed the sound to the station. There, outside the door of the empty
waiting-room, two young guitarists were wasting their talents on the
atmosphere. They wore enormous straw sombreros that curled up
around the edges, and over their left shoulders lay folded serapes of
brown-and-white wool. One youth was seated on a small upended
box. He sang tenor, with his eyes tight closed, throwing back his
head as a hound does when he howls. But his voice was not unpleasant, and he sang with plaintive energy.

The other lad, who stood with one foot resting lightly on the edge
of the box, looked better-fed, and as he sang he thrust his chest out
like an operatic singer, and drew down his chin. There was not
another listener in sight. When we paused before them, the troubadours did not in any way change their technique or their volume.
They sang a *corrido* about a bear hunt in the hills, and they were
in sympathy with the poor bear, who was so valiant in his efforts to
escape from the cruel hunters. They sang about a village church
bell calling, calling on a Sunday morning. They sang about a poor
peasant forced into the Revolution against his will:

> "You ask me why I am still a rebel?
> Well, the revolution is like a hurricane—
> If you're in it, you are not a man,
> You're a dead leaf, blown by the wind."

Whatever they sang about—a bear, a church bell, or a man—each had a universal value, each was just as important in the scheme of things as the other. A mountain, a sunset, a snake, a desirable girl, all got the same emphasis. Everything was a creation of God and so deserved respect; and apparently, because the singers had themselves known trouble, they had compassion for all created things, animate and inanimate.

After some minutes, they paused to rest and we gave them applause. The standing fellow removed his right foot from the edge of the box and shifted his position. The one seated relaxed his hands and his neck.

Esperón began requesting certain pieces, the old favorites sung by the various armies of the Revolution. The boys nodded after each request. They seemed to know them all. The cockroach marching song of Villa, *"La Cucaracha,"* had lost none of its vigor and animality after three decades. But the best rendition the troubadors gave was of *"Valentina,"* perhaps because Zapata was their hero.

> "Valentina, Valentina, dead-drunk I lie at your feet.
> If they are going to kill me tomorrow
> They might as well kill me now."

I glanced within the dim-lit waiting-room and saw it was a quarter past midnight. Evidently the youths were waiting for the two-thirty train from Laredo, which was to pick up our car and drop us off at Querétaro. "We'd better give them some money and get along," I said to Esperón.

"If you don't know 'Tears of My Heart,' I want you to hear it for a last one. It's a prime favorite at *gallos*. The boys have probably sung it a thousand times. That's the way they make their living— serenading at night for swains who themselves have no voice."

The troubadours were delighted with the request. We moved closer to them. The seated fellow moved an inch over on his box so that his companion could put his foot more firmly on the edge. He plucked at his strings with a passionate despair, and his face, with the tight-shut eyes, became a mask of desperate longing.

> "Of what value is life
> If I cannot be your sweetheart?
> Why do I love you so much?
> Why, why do I love you with such blindness?"

His comrade moved back a little, and the faint light from the waiting-room door reached the boy's face. I caught Esperón's arm questioningly. But there was no doubt about it—the boy was blind.

We thanked the singers and gave them some money. I had to reach down and catch hold of the blind boy's hand to put the paper note in it. He passed it on to his companion in a manner of perfect trust in one's friend. We said *"Buenas noches"* and strolled back to the car. "Well, Providence was kind to give him some musical talent," I said.

"Yes. In Mexico it will always get him food and shelter."

The amiable porter, who was still up, brought us a glass of cool beer for a nightcap.

"The Revolution *was* like a hurricane, as the song tells, wasn't it?" I said. "And many of the men like driven leaves."

"Men fought and killed each other without the foggiest idea of why they were doing it. They would change sides without the slightest compunction, often merely to be with the winners and looters. Both sides had propagandists writing of sacred principles. And both sides destroyed property merely for the satisfaction of destruction. Yet of course the Revolution had to come.

"I myself have seen things since the Revolution which you wouldn't believe. One day I saw a man sitting on the roadside in so dismal a mood I stopped my horse and asked if I could do anything for him. He shook his head with a terrible apathy. 'The boss wanted me to leave my place,' he said, 'where I had once worked for him. To make me go, first he killed my horse. Then he killed my ox. And now he has had my wife killed, when I walked to the village to buy something to eat. Thank God we had no children.' I saw this with my own eyes and heard it with my own ears."

The Captain's great dark eyes dilated with indignation and pity. Then his taut fingers relaxed around the glass. "Anyone who loves Mexico," he said quietly, "stays with his heart broken."

We drank our beer. Esperón went on speaking, as if thinking out loud. "It was bad to have to have the Revolution. Gunfire is not good for Mexicans. It brings out something terrible in them. It frightens me to see the way Indians react to shooting. As soon as a soldier hears a shot he gets excited—the most humble one gets terribly excited and sometimes starts yelling. But the Revolution had to come, though thousands upon thousands were slaughtered unnecessarily. The peon himself did not mind walking into a pistol. He had nothing to lose by death, he said." Esperón got up from the table. "Shall we turn in?"

"Well, this little town where the first revolution was conceived seems delightfully at rest now," I said. "Even the *sinsontli* is asleep. It's a charming place. I hope it doesn't change too much—too soon. I'd rather like to bring my wife and live here for a year or so."

"It seems like a supergood place to retire to," Esperón said, "or to rest up in—or write a book in—or where a fellow might paint some pictures."

"Mexico's coming along," I said, getting up and stretching. "Don't you feel more hopeful about it?"

"Oh God, yes! But there will be ups and downs. Cárdenas got it on the right track. But he saw the reverse side of the medal. He knew he couldn't get things adjusted in his own short term. He had human beings to deal with—it's a job for generations. Civilization is a tricky thing. I believe Confucius was about right. He said the final test of a civilization is the human product—whether it produces a good son, a good husband, a good brother, a good friend."

"Say a good individual, who is careful not to hurt another's feelings?"

"Exactly." He smiled and drained his glass standing. *"Hasta mañana."*

"Buenas noches."

X

Querétaro

Equality is to be found only in the spiritual dignity of man.

—DOSTOEVSKY

I. TO THE GLORY OF GOD AND MAN

THE CITY OF QUERÉTARO is doubly notable: for its magnificent eighteenth-century aqueduct and for the execution of Maximilian in 1867. The pale Austrian's death before a firing squad looms out of the chronicles as emphatically as the grandeur of five miles of linked and lofty arches that march across the plain bringing water from the mountains. Today's view of the massive masonry of the aqueduct still draws the attention like a magnet. And one's imagination returns again and again, historically, to the fate of the inept Emperor, whose dramatic end settled forever the question of foreign-sponsored monarchies in the Western Hemisphere.

Like the town of San Miguel de Allende, Querétaro (population, thirty-five thousand) is opulent in atmosphere. In fact, it deservedly ranks high among the half-dozen best colonial cities in Mexico. The district round about is enriched with deep and fertile soil, excellent for crops and stock-raising, and men still dig fortunes out of the neighboring mines. But where San Miguel was a residential pleasure town, since the sixteenth century Querétaro has been a trading and business center. Yet its active churches are proportionately more abundant and elaborate than those of any Mexican city except Puebla, and its sometime great houses retain their splendid symmetry and their Old World patina, even if they are now inhabited by owners of the textile mills or agents for automobiles.

As we breakfasted, bronze bells tempered with silver swung back and forth in the belfries, calling communicants to mass. Our car had been dropped off at a spot conveniently distant from the station, so that we could look from the windows to the opalescent domes and towers of majolica that reflected the full glory of the Sunday morning sun. Townsend and Wagus did not tarry over breakfast, but went off to visit an Indian village in the more mountainous region to the north.

When Esperón and I left the car and approached the station along the tracks, three teen-age boys, an old man, and two rebozo-draped women emerged to meet us like a reception committee. The left hand of each was outstretched. At first I thought they might be beggars, despite their respectable dress. But objects resting on their outstretched palms glinted in the sun like multicolored fireflies. On neat squares of dull black paper lay polished opals of various shades and sizes. These persons were venders offering precious stones for sale. We paused briefly and admired. When Esperón said sotto voce that he knew of a family that trafficked in opals, and where the quality could be assured, I shook my head politely. The peddlers did not try to urge or pursue. They smiled politely and moved aside for us to pass.

Querétaro is the center of the opal-mining region, and many of its citizens draw their daily living from the stones, either as owners of mine property, or miners, or lapidaries, or sales agents. The conquistadors did not add opals to their spoils of conquest, for the first stones were not discovered in Mexico until 1835. Like the fellow who plowed up the volcano Paricutín in 1943, a farmer had struck a vein of opaliferous ore that lay just under the surface of his cornpatch. No mines were systematically worked, however, until 1870, three years after the execution of Maximilian.

Though the main part of the town lay at some distance, we declined a cab. It was too fine a day not to walk. The morning was translucent blue and gold, the July atmosphere fresh as May. As we crossed the little square in front of the station, I thought of the Emperor scenting the June air of that morning on which he was to end his earthly adventure. "I could not have chosen a better day on which to die," he had said smilingly to guards come to escort him to the Hill of Bells.

The way from the station lay along a cobblestoned street, through one of the poorer districts. Already at this morning hour the short blue-green doors of the *pulquerías* were swinging back and forth as swarthy men in big hats went in to swig pulque, the popular intoxicant of the humble.

"The cotton mills may be short of twenty per cent of the laborers tomorrow," Esperón commented. "It's often so on Mondays. But we can't blame pulque on the Spaniards. The Indians made it and knew drunkenness long before Cortés."

The cultivation of maguey from which pulque is made is among the most lucrative businesses of the region. For generations, proprietors of great estates kept their fortunes by fermenting maguey juice into pulque. With the expropriation and dividing up of the haciendas, there has been some decline, for the new small proprietors are encouraged to let the maguey go and to raise proper foodstuffs.

From the *pulquerías* that punctuated every other block came the raucous blare of *noiséolas,* another Mexican name for jukebox, like *traga-diezes,* "swallow-dimes."

"Now *that* importation of modern culture," said Esperón, cavalierly waving a hand toward the noise, "can't be blamed on Spain either. We owe that to you in the United States."

From the window of a private home came a jabbering of human voices on a radio. "And I suppose," I said, "we must take the credit also for this further vulgarization of your way of life."

Esperón grinned in double assent. It was good to be with an alien companion with whom there was such harmony of opinion.

At a street corner we paused to watch two women filling great ollas from a wall hydrant.

"The people drank pulque," Esperón said, remarking the procedure, "because they didn't have good drinking water. Only in the last few years have they had hydrant water in each neighborhood. As you know, more danger lies in Mexican water or milk than in alcoholic pulque. The germs of dysentery of every kind lie in the water, and God knows what-all in the milk. In Mexico, scientific dairying is still virtually nonexistent. And until pure water and clean milk are to be had, a few millions will go on drinking pulque for health's sake as well as pleasure."

We moved aside as a besotted old man staggered out of a joint.

"But pulque is the drink of degradation," Esperón said darkly, "from the beginning of its processing to its conclusive effect. You know how it's made, of course?" He did not wait for me to answer, but went right on.

"My father's cousin owned a pulque ranch, which naturally means fields of cultivated maguey. By moonlight, I think a plantation of maguey is the most beautiful of all growing crops, with its geometric spacing and its silver-green blades sparkling with moonshine. And where part of the acreage is allowed to go to flower, it is extraordinarily lovely by day or night. Each polished green column rises from the heart of the plant to a height of twenty feet, and is crowned with its candelabra of waxy white bells. As far as the eye can see, it's like something out of this world." The Captain heaved a sigh. "But there's no market for the flowers, and to get pulque juice the heart must be carved out of the plant just as the shaft is ready to shoot up into the air. Something like the Persian lamb, you know, that must be ripped from the ewe's womb at the psychological moment for its commercial value. So with the maguey.

"The Indians have an uncanny insight into just the day this birth is to begin. Into the scooped-out place where the flower and stem substance was, liquid begins to flow, and the plant gradually bleeds to death. The white-green heart is stuck on one of the plant's own bayonets—as a sign to the gatherers that there is honey in the bowl. The death process takes as long as two months, and as the plant expires, it pours some five or six quarts of liquid into the cavity every day. Men suck the stuff through a long tube into a pigskin container. Then it is carried to the sheds. From pigskin, the honey water goes into the hairy side of a bull's hide, for fermentation. This process is hastened by adding some pints of rank, yeasty mother of pulque, with potato parings and other garbage, and, believe it or not"—he paused on the cobblestones and pointed with his boot toe at a round of stuff a cur dog had just left—"they often drop in some of this to speed the process."

Esperón made a grimace of disgust and shrugged eloquently. "Naturally, the taste for pulque has to be cultivated."

"But," I said, "isn't pulque supposed to have virtues in vitamins, which the people can't get in a diet of tortillas and beans?"

"That's what the makers claim." He gave me a knowing look. "But you will notice that in the sections where they don't drink it, people thrive just the same."

We had come out of the poorer section into a street with weather-dimmed escutcheons over doorways, and glimpses of cool green patios through grilled gates.

"I notice a lot of them are drinking beer now, and Coca-Cola," I said as we arrived at the edge of the main plaza.

"There is one strong ray of hope," Esperón said. "It takes seven to ten years to get a maguey plantation into production—and the new small holders can't afford to be that patient. They have to eat immediately. When all the great pulque haciendas in the State of Querétaro are broken up, the acres may go into wheat or pasturage.

"And some bright, beautiful day in the future," he added as we hesitated which side of the square to take, "Mexico may be able to furnish good milk and pure drinking water to her people. A small thing to look to, but it would be like a millennium—to live in Mexico without a perpetual threat to the bowels."

The main plaza, called the Jardín Zenea, is the real hub of commerce and sociability. A small band was playing in the kiosk. The benches were moderately well filled with conscripts in gray-green uniform and citizens. Bootblacks were kneeling here and there at their brisk trade. Before the cathedral, dealers in secondhand books had spread their sparse collections. But the plaza was as disappointing to me as Puebla's had been. The glazed tile of the cathedral's tower and dome was more alluring from a distant than on a near view. The interior was not impressive in design or decoration. The church was crowded, but most of the worshipers were women. A boys' choir was singing in full soprano and doing very well. The air was thick with incense. Some of the representations of agonized martyrdom seemed unusually gory.

"Why do Mexicans make their sacred pictures and statues so bloody?" I asked.

"Mexico has been so drenched in blood that an image that was not bleeding like a stuck pig would stir little emotion. The usual moderate drops of blood from the spear-pierced breast would hardly seem worth a passing sigh. Before the Spanish cruelty and the imported bullfight, we have the Aztec inheritance, when the temples were veritable slaughterhouses of the gods, with field days of human sacrifice. And so many personal knives in Mexico get smeared with human gore that the Church has to overdo the bloody wounds to make an impression. The people get an emotional purgation kneeling before a gashed saint. The bloodier he is, the easier their lot to bear."

We turned a corner. I said, "You think the return of the Church's influence is bad for Mexico?"

Esperón stopped on the sidewalk to make himself clear. "Depends. If the Catholic Church came back with a love for the people, that would be fine. But if it is coming back with desire for political power, and stirring up old fanaticism! Mind you, though, if the Catholic Church had not come with the conquistadors, the history of the Indian would have been far more desolating. The Protestant conquerors of your country were infinitely more ruthless. They did not settle among the Indians, as the Catholic Spanish did; they killed them off or pushed them clear out of the way. The Spaniards may have robbed the Indian, and worked him half to death, but they did declare he was a human being with a soul to be saved. For all their brutality and greed, the Spaniards still had an evangelical mission, no matter how much it was mixed with superstition."

We walked on again. "But the priests don't need to fool and scare the people, or resort to such ways to get money. They say that in Guadalajara they once sold printed passports to Heaven for forty pesos. I would hate to estimate the millions of pesos that went out of Mexico to Rome."

"But if the Church had not collected money," I protested, "they could not have built the beautiful things like this before us." We had come to the favorite ecclesiastical building in Querétaro, the Collegiate Convent of Santa Rosa de Viterbo.

"This particular one," Esperón said with a grin, "was erected from goods confiscated from smugglers."

"Even so—however they got it—here it is, and without the Church this fine structure would not have been."

Dating from the seventeenth century, the convent had been reconstructed by that remarkable Creole, Eduardo de Tresguerras, born in Celaya in 1765. This was the last renowned architect of the viceregal period. Like Michelangelo, he was gifted with numerous talents. He was not only an architect and a sculptor, but a painter, an etcher, a wood-carver, a poet, and a musician. A deeply devout man, he was endowed with tremendous energy and drive to express his religious fervor in enduring beauty. When he had finished all his commissions at his home town, Celaya, he came to Querétaro to build afresh, to reconstruct, or to adorn. His best work in Querétaro is to be found in this Church of Santa Rosa, in the Convent of Santa Clara, and in the Federal Palace, with its splendid Spanish-Moorish patio.

Tresguerras took the seventeenth-century structure of Santa Rosa and stamped it with his genius. He did over the cloisters, the dome, the towers. He gave the roof a balustrade, and hung sculptured Saracen heads from the curves of the outer arches of the façade. He tiptilted the roof of the bell-tower in the manner of a Chinese pagoda. The whole exterior effect is daring, but remarkably pleasing. Within, the nave is adorned with elaborate altars in Churrigueresque, lavish with thick gold leaf. The confessionals with their iron grills and gilded arabesques suggest Persia rather than Christendom. Like Shakespeare, Tresguerras made use of any source that stirred his imagination.

In the sacristy, the great mural that fills the head of the room and reveals a strong Murillo influence is perhaps the finest specimen of Tresguerras' painting. It depicts the legend of the Closed Garden, with Saint Rose working among her pupils, and white lambs receiving white roses from the Virgin to be dyed in blood from the Christ's wounds. Where the brilliant Indian Ceferino was obviously groping in San Miguel de Allende, Tresguerras' mature work reveals an assurance, as if he had been commissioned and empowered by Heaven to express his devotional zeal in any radical manner he chose.

"It was Tresguerras," Esperón said, "who turned the head of the eagle backward on his Independence monument in the plaza of Celaya. When asked why, he replied, 'So that the eagle may not see the barbarities committed by our municipal authorities.' He was referring to the City Hall facing the monument with its ugly mediocrity."

Though I had found Querétaro's main plaza disappointing, I was delighted with the little square called the Plaza de la Independencia. Although it lay only two blocks away, the rhythms of the two were very different. There were no hotels, no streetcars, no church. It was like a retreat amid parterres of flowers, with a commodious central fountain, an outlet from the great aqueduct. On one side of the square stood the Municipal Palace, which had been the home of the famous wife of the corregidor, whose three taps on the floor of her bedroom to the waiting janitor beneath sounded the warning to Allende that launched the fight for independence. On the façade there is a description of a climactic moment in Mexican history and a tribute to Josefa Ortiz Domínguez, "the heroine of the Independence."

Near this square Maximilian made his headquarters when the royalist troops were besieged by Juárez's forces. He used to sit on the flat stone curbing of the central fountain and take the sunshine as doom closed about the city and the water supply was cut off by the enemy. This morning girls who had come to fill water jugs lingered. Some sat on the curbing, their skirts spread wide, the dazzle of youth upon them—the tentative way of youth, assuming an obscure indifference.

On a bench by a white-flowering tree we sat down, facing the most charming colonial mansion in Querétaro, with its four great upper windows and its three fluted balconies. It was the sort of house from which one might expect to hear Viennese waltz tunes lilting from music boxes. I imagined the house had belonged to the eighteenth-century Marqués whose statue dominated the square, the gentleman who was the principal donor of the great aqueduct. An inscription on the monument gave the information that the work on the aqueduct was begun the day after Christmas 1726, and the job completed on October 15, 1735. The construction, then, took almost nine years. The inscription stated precisely that the project cost $131,091; of which amount the benevolent Marqués contributed $88,287 out of his own pocket. Considering the length of building time and the five miles of masonry, the cost seems extraordinarily small for so great a work.

"But we Mexicans have always managed to get good value for our money," Esperón said as we hailed a cab to drive us to the city's edge to look at the aqueduct. "By paying next to nothing for labor," he added ironically as we got in.

Near the aqueduct terminal at the highest spot in town is the Church of the Cross, and adjoining it is the convent, which Maximilian's troops used as a barracks during the siege. When Querétaro fell on May 15, 1867, General Mariano Escobedo's troops took possession and used it as their barracks.

Passing the town's high-walled cemetery on the right, we curved down the little hill to flattish country, and there stretching in front before us obliquely was the aqueduct. It was like something conceived by the extravagantly romantic mind of Lord Dunsany. I thought of a single-file procession of toast-colored giants bearing the five-mile-long water trough on their shoulders. Each majestic arch rose to a height of fifty feet and was triumphal in itself. Pictures of earth and sky were set in countless colossal frames. The same scene, with only slight variation, infinitely framed, with sometimes a whitewashed hut, or a man sowing seed, or a group of white goats grazing against a background of emerald and cobalt.

The closer one came, the more impressive was the magnitude. As I surveyed the miles of dark-yellowish brick with its patina of subdued topaz and mellowed amethyst, I thought there was little in Mexico to surpass this aqueduct in memorableness. I thought of Spengler, who had said, "I prefer one Roman aqueduct to all the Roman temples and statues." And it was he who had written: "I would sooner have the fine mind-begotten forms of a fast steamer than all the pickings and stealings of present-day 'arts and crafts,' architecture and painting included." What collections of old Mexican arts and crafts, what series of murals done in the last two decades, could measure up to the impression of the simple grandeur of this project conceived and executed by eighteenth-century engineers?

The road to Mexico City went through and under one of the arches. We stopped the car and got out to stand beneath a massive arch and look up fifty feet to its capstone. There came to me lines of Humboldt in his *Essai politique sur la Nouvelle Espagne*: "Wherever nations are divided into castes, and wherever men do not enjoy the right to private property and work solely for the profit of the community, we shall find canals, roads, aqueducts, pyramids, huge constructions of every kind. But we shall also find that these people, though for thousands of years they may preserve the air of external prosperity, will make practically no advance in moral culture, which is the result of individual liberty."

Well, whatever the lack in moral significance, this aqueduct was not constructed as a sop to one man's vanity or as a supplication to Deity. It was erected for a most practical community purpose—to bring pure water from the uncontaminated mountains to quench men's thirst. What church-builder or library-founder had made a better gesture in behalf of his fellows than the old Marqués?

We drove under the aqueduct, and out a few miles into the countryside up to a slight eminence where we could get the full sweep of panorama. We could see where one end of the aqueduct disappeared into the man-made city and the other vanished into the God-made hills. As we returned, the high uncompromising sun turned the flowing grass of the fields into a green becalmed sea. To the right, a flock of sheep, shepherded by two companionable old men, reflected the sharp silver-arrowed light in all their tight curls. To the left, a young woman sat on the roadside placidly suckling her baby at high noon. Birds, gathered about some golden grain spilled in the road, scattered like a fling of seed as our car bore down upon them. Countryfolk, dressed in their Sabbath best coming home from church, passed under the roadway arch like Lilliputians in Swift's satire.

The aqueduct could not last forever to bring water or to make memorable the landscape; but it would doubtless be there long after these people and their children and their children's children would be above the surface of the earth to pass to and fro beneath it, with different desires pulling them this way and that.

2. CONVENTS AND AN EXECUTION

It is interesting to remark the practical modern uses that converted monasteries and nunneries have been put to in Mexico. Hundreds of former ecclesiastical buildings have been transformed variously into hospitals, labor headquarters, libraries, museums, art schools, and military barracks. Because of the war that was raging in the Eastern Hemisphere and the possibility of an attack either by Japan or by Germany, the Mexican Government decreed one year's compulsory military training for all youths of eighteen. While army posts in numerous sectors were being enlarged and modernized, carpenters, masons, plumbers, electricians, transformed many vacant convents into living-quarters for the youths in training.

As the Convent of the Cross in Querétaro had been used in Maximilian's day to house first his own troops and then the soldiers of General Escobedo, now another convent in the center of the city has been turned into a barracks for new conscripts. Where the sandals of cloistered nuns once trod lightly on the cool corridor stones, now the roughshod heavy feet of soldier boys made harsh reverberations. We arrived just as a group of trainees came clumping down the stone stairs, with the look of girl quarry in their eyes.

It was Sunday and a day of freedom. The great upper rooms were almost empty. In one room of forty cots, a sole occupant lay immobile on top of his bedclothes, fully dressed, no sign of life except in his flicking eyes. As Esperón went down the aisle, the Indian boy remained as still as an image until the Captain was right at his bed. Then he rose and stood trembling, almost like a trapped animal. Esperón spoke pleasantly to him. The boy nodded and muttered. I came up and spoke. His lips widened slightly, but the smile did not quite come. His narrow face, with its small glass-black eyes, was like an ugly bronze mask.

Esperón began talking about his not being out with the others, enjoying the fine weather. At first the boy listened without any sign of agreement or contradiction. His attitude, as he stood upright the way his officers had taught conscripts to stand, was one of humility mingled with painful diffidence. He had been in the army four months, he said, with difficulty. He came from a remote mountainous region in Zacatecas. He had never been more than a few kilometers from his home before the conscription order came. The boy was obviously most uncomfortable in this strange new world: his distrust was mirrored in his obsidian eyes. He was only beginning to understand Spanish now. As he stood rigid at the foot of his cot, careful not to make an unnecessary gesture, he spoke like a child pronouncing words from a primer, and those hardly more than a guttural whisper.

Captain Esperón was very amiable with the boy. He was careful to give his deep voice the gentlest accents, to inspire confidence. Gradually the frozen fear began to thaw.

"But this training will be splendid for you," Esperón was saying. "You will learn to speak Spanish and to read and write. You will see things to remember always. You will find that there are many good people beyond the mountain rims of your district. You will make new friends before long, and go back to your village much more of a man."

"*Sí, señor.*" A smile hovered at the corner of his lips. But he was afraid to give himself away by loosing it.

"You should be out in the plaza with the crowds, listening to the music."

The boy broke his immobility to point to the region of his heart. "But, señor, I have a little heaviness here."

Esperón smiled understandingly. "It's a longing for home. It will pass in the plaza, I assure you."

The twanging of a musical instrument behind us made us turn. A bright-eyed fellow in undershirt and trousers walked down the rows between the beds with a mandolin cradled in his arm. Out of curiosity, he had wandered in from the next dormitory through the great doorway. He was a well-built, lusty youth, with aggressive black hair and an assured manner. He spoke good Spanish. He turned out to be a native of Esperón's own northern province.

"Why the hell aren't you out this afternoon?"

The boy grinned philosophically. He had splendid white teeth that made his mestizo face even handsomer. "I have no money. I see a pretty girl and I cannot even buy her an ice-cream cone, so it is no good. I shall save my pay for next Sunday. This Sunday I do penance—and practice my music." He touched off some chords on his mandolin.

Esperón reached into his pocket and gave the chap a two-peso note. "Get out and enjoy yourself." The youth could accept it with casual grace from a compadre.

I gave a two-peso note to the Indian from Zacatecas—to go to a picture show to make the heaviness in his heart pass. He trembled, and swallowed his "*Muchas gracias.*"

We turned again, for there was a third soldier regarding us with quiet interest. He looked like a kid dressed up in his big soldier brother's clothes, and he seemed to be pure white. If there was Indian blood in him, it was not more than an eighth or a sixteenth. With large gray eyes and an innocent little-boy expression, he was what would be called the appealing type.

"What are *you* doing in the army?" Esperón said, in some amazement.

The boy smiled slowly. Maybe it was a joke, but here he was. "They called me." It was as simple as that.

"How old are you?"

"Eighteen."

"No. You can't be more than fourteen."

"My mother says eighteen."

For all his lamblike expression, there was no homesickness eating at him. His name was Josefat Mendes. He came from near Jacala in Hidalgo. I got him to write his name in my notebook. He had had three years in school. He said he liked the army well enough, and was glad to get some more schooling. He seemed to find life amusing, and he could make out anywhere. He had the aura of a pet that couldn't be spoiled.

"In the Revolution," Esperón said, "they had them as angel-faced and even younger than he looks. Some could just raise their guns, but they shot—and they could kill."

While the other boys were getting ready to go out, I took some pictures of Josefat Mendes with my Leica, on the stairs, against a column, here or there where the light was right. Half-lost in his soldier's outfit, sitting or standing, smiling or grave, he posed with no trace of self-consciousness. He said he did not know his father's profession. His father had disappeared before he was born. His mother had had a hard time. He did not know what occupation he himself would choose. He thought building bridges might be nice, or running an ice-cream shop. But he liked the army for the time being. There was plenty of time to decide.

Josefat Mendes was not as readily communicative as the crippled Manuel Solís at Pátzcuaro, and he did not have the radiance of the younger boy. But somehow he had the same effect of filling one with wishes for his happiness. For all his claim to eighteen years, which we could not believe, he was like a fourteen-year-old you would like to take to the circus or give a pony to. Instead, I gave him some money for the movies and a treat for some of his friends, and told him to study his lessons and write to his mother.

"Well, there's a cross section of our future army," Esperón said as we walked away. "Most likely they'll never get into an actual battle. But this training is fine for them individually, and fine for the nation's morale. As soon as General Cárdenas became Minister of National Defense in the emergency of '41, he began reforming the army—putting shower baths in barracks, seeing that the food was wholesome and well cooked, that the army cots were not uncomfortable, the blankets warm, the youths free of lice, and school lessons heard every day. He made use of the army appropriation to further his educational aims, and to give unfortunates a taste of respectable, if plain, living.

"Here, it's like a boy's boarding school without frills. And they come from every class and condition of society. Many of these chaps had never heard Spanish spoken before, never slept anywhere but on the floor. The Indians are excessively parochial. They look upon anyone who doesn't speak their provincial dialect or live within a morning's walk as an enemy. Now they will learn better. They have never known dental care or seen a doctor or heard of a hygienic law. When they go back home they will be able to carry a message of civilization with them. And if they have a spark of ambition, they may find a way up. Who can foretell the flight of a word?"

There was still time before luncheon to trace the last steps of Maximilian. After the capture of the fever-racked Emperor on the morning of May 15, 1867, he was first incarcerated in the Convent of La Cruz. Later he was moved to the Teresita Convent, which has now been transformed into the offices of the Department of Public Health. There Juárez ordered that the sick man be kept in the dank crpyt, and that his fare be that of the criminal, bread and water. Either for humane reasons, or because he feared that death would overtake the fallen Prince before he could be tried and shot, the commanding officer disobeyed Juárez's order, and had Maximilian brought up to an upper floor, where the Mexican Generals Miguel Miramón and Tomás Mejía were imprisoned.

The Emperor was given more palatable food and allowed to have his physician in attendance. But he was too ill to appear in court for his trial. To make up for this cheating of public curiosity, the citizens of Querétaro and all the encamped victorious soldiers were permitted to pass in line through his sick room day after day to stare upon fallen majesty. Maximilian was in such a weakened condition and of so gentle a natural disposition that few of even the most insensitive had the heart to mock. But his helplessness did not prevent the crowds from pilfering all his last meager possessions, except the black suit he was to die in and the gold pieces he saved under his pillow to give the firing squad.

At the Department of Health Building we tried to find the room where Maximilian had spent his last days, half in delirium, dreaming of exile on the Adriatic and recuperation among friends on his yacht. Until his hour actually came, he had hoped world opinion would sway Juárez to clemency, since the crowned heads of Europe had humbled themselves before the Indian to beg for his life.

There was only a charwoman in the building, doing Sunday cleaning. She looked at us with dull resentment at our intrusion. She did not know any Maximilian, she declared. No one that she knew had been kept here until his execution. She waved a hand toward the right and then vaguely toward the left. If what we said was so, it might have been that room or that room. She couldn't see what difference it made now, if the man was already shot. "Seventy years ago?" She stared at us confusedly, and muttered something unintelligible. Then, seizing her bucket of dirty water, she disappeared through a doorway behind a desk, out of range of such a crackbrained pair.

We retired in complete defeat and went out the door by which Maximilian had left for the final scene. He was feeling a little better that morning of June 19, and he roused himself for his last act. With remarkable grace he greeted his final hour, from the moment he said, "I could not have chosen a better day on which to die" to the moment the rifle bullets plowed into him.

On our way to the Cerro de las Campanas beyond the city, we drove past the Iturbide Theater, where the trial of the three M's, Maximilian, Miramón, and Mejía, had taken place. The Emperor had to be tried by proxy. The aristocratic Miramón and the Indian Mejía had sat side by side on the same bench and received their sentences promptly. (The bench is a prize exhibit in the Federal Palace.) Expert Mexican lawyers defended the Emperor ably, but his fate was considered a foregone conclusion by those who knew Benito Juárez. Yet the vote of the six jurors was divided: three for death, three for banishment. The foreman settled the matter by deciding on the death penalty.

We had noticed flags at half-mast here and there about the town and now remarked particularly the one before the theater. I asked what for. Esperón did not know. But the placard on the wall beneath the flag had the answer. We stopped the cab. The tribute was to commemorate the fifty-first anniversary of the death of Benito Juárez.

"See, the people put their flags at half-mast fifty-one years after Juárez's death," Esperón said. "They know that without him there might not be even a semblance of democracy in Mexico today. But don't think Juárez is the great patriot to all Mexico, as George Washington is to the United States. He is so only to those who support the Revolution and the Constitution of 1917. To priests and many of the old families he is anathema."

In his own day, Juárez was not solidly backed by his own people. For the most part the Indians fought with the white upper classes on the side of the Emperor and the Church. The mixed bloods fought with Juárez. The sensational execution was symbolic. By the Emperor's side stood the white Mexican, General Miramón, and the full-blooded Indian, General Mejía. The firing squad was mestizo.

The Iturbide Theater is famous for more than the signing of Maximilian's death warrant in 1867. Here exactly half a century later the constitutional convention met to draw up the Constitution of 1917. This famous document is the finest that has been yet produced in behalf of the common man in Latin America, and it has served as a model for other republics in their designs to foster liberty and justice.

"The changes aren't coming as fast as the planners and the idealists had hoped," Esperón said as we drove on. "But we have gone a long way since 1917."

At the end of Calle de la Fábricas, we came into a country road. The platinum-green cactus flaunted its coronets of coral-colored fruits, sweet as honey inside the shells. On low stone walls washed garments were spread out to dry. Bees were humming greedily about pomegranate blossoms. Bright-colored birds were copulating on low tree branches. Gilded flies swarmed about something in a ditch. Three colts frisked in a pasture. Noontide intensified the aliveness of nature.

When our car turned to the right, we traversed a flat meadow, and then to the left rose the Hill of Bells. Built over the place where Maximilian met death is a little chapel in brown stone, which the Austrian Government ordered erected in 1901, to replace the three slabs that marked the spots where the three M's fell. The Austrians were rather niggardly in honoring their Hapsburg prince. The project cost only ten thousand dollars and has the earmarks of a thing done out of a sense of duty. The chapel is ordinary, without a hint of inspiration by the architect, and no more impressive than a one-room railway station at a Tirolean village. What a memorable job, I thought, another Tresguerras might have turned out here!

Against the bulk of a crumbling adobe structure where Maximilian had been captured, the three leaders of the imperialist forces took their stand. The Emperor yielded the center place of honor to General Miramón with insistent courtesy. It was his last command. To both the generals he gave a farewell embrace in the Mexican fashion. To the presiding priest, who turned faint at the imminent occurrence, he offered smelling salts. Then he handed each member of the firing squad a gold piece, imploring them to shoot straight, and to spare his face for his family's sake. He made a brief patriotic statement about his sincere love for his adopted country. He took one last look at the towers of Querétaro and the invulnerable beauty of Mexico's blue sky. Then he nodded to the lieutenant to signal his men to shoot.

The rifle shots rang out in the crystal clarity of the morning. Maximilian dropped to his knees and grabbed his face in horror and agony. One bullet had torn out an eye. He fell prone, crying more in despair than accusation, *"Hombres!"* The lieutenant, aghast, commanded the men to shoot again. To the bitter end everything connected with Maximilian's Mexican venture seems to have been bungled.

We turned our backs to the chapel and stood on the terrace. The acres before us had been transformed into a public park and a tree nursery. A painted wooden sign, for all recreation-seekers to read, said in bold black letters, "A people that respects, and causes to be respected, flowers and plants, gives a sign of its culture." In the playing-fields at the foot of the hill on the south side, boys in varicolored shorts were having a lively game of soccer.

I looked off to the city. The distant structures seemed opal-tinted
like a vision in a mirage. "But you are right," Esperón said, when
I hinted at what I saw. "Some of the building stones dug from the
region are full of opaliferous particles."

"Don't forget we want to look for opals."

"But first let's satisfy the inner man. We are already late for
luncheon."

3. SUNDAY SHOPPING

Townsend and Wagus were still away. They had evidently decided to eat beans and tortillas with the Indians. So we ate luncheon without them. After a brief siesta, we set out to look for the
private home where opals were sold.

On Calle del Descanso, at Number 14, we passed the house which
claims to be the original meeting-place of the Society of Fine Arts
that plotted conspiracy. "Perhaps it began here, instead of in Allende's house in San Miguel," Esperón said. "But because Allende
became the military leader and meetings were held at his house,
some people like to think the entire idea originated with him."

On a less distinguished street, where all the conventional one-story
stucco-faced houses touched each other, we found the house number
that corresponded with that in Esperón's address book. We rang
and waited. At last a grave-faced woman appeared at the door. She
was plump like a partridge and dressed in a black skirt and an embroidered blue blouse.

No, *el señor* was not at home.

But did he not own an opal mine, and did he not have opals for
sale?

Yes, he owned and worked a small mine, and occasionally sold
opals.

Could she let us see some?

She hesitated—since her husband was not in. Esperón gave references, introduced me as a *profesór*. At last she said she supposed
she could show us some stones. She knew where they were kept.
Would we be so good as to enter?

Beyond the vestibule was a smallish patio, every square foot thick
with greenery. We were ushered into a little parlor on the left and
invited to be seated. The room was furnished with six highly var-

nished chairs and two small stiff settees of reddish wood. A table in the exact center was covered with an elaborate piece of drawnwork.

The lady of the house disappeared, and returned promptly with two wooden drawers, one on top of the other. She put one on the table, the other on a vacant chair. In one, the opals were spread out on a piece of black velvet. In the other, they were wrapped in numerous little packages of black paper.

The hostess opened wide the blinds, so that we could see better. I had never realized that there were so many varieties of opals. There were fire opals with emerald-green tints on a brilliant red ground, and little flames forking at the center. There were opals like clouds at sunset; and harlequin opals that flickered and flashed, changing from one color to another at the slightest movement. There were some of fiery red set off by a luminous black background. And some were just the ordinary blue and pink opals one buys for little girls whose birthdays come in October.

No, our hostess herself was not born in October.

Yes, she had heard it was considered bad luck for anyone not born in October to wear opals. But she herself was not superstitious. She did not wear opals because she did not care for jewelry.

We turned opals this way and that, took several stones over to the street window. The woman offered us a magnifying glass.

Quietly, patiently, methodically, she undid the black papers, displaying the hidden gems. She gave the price of scores without consulting a price list. Her manner was dignified, slightly constrained. She did not by a hint or a gesture press a sale. She was anything but a voluble woman, and acquiesced only faintly in our admiration.

Had she ever been to the mines with her husband to see the work?

She had been only twice. The matrix was hidden in the reddish-gray rock, she explained. It was very difficult to unloose. Sometimes it required dynamite, which ruined a quantity of stones. Often the volcanic glass surrounding the opals was polished and sold as agates. Opals varied greatly in hardness. The best of them ranked sixth after diamonds in hardness. The hard ones that wouldn't scratch brought the big prices. But some of the softer ones were just as pretty, she thought.

Her face lighted up in remembrance. "My husband took me to

see the opening of a newly discovered vein near the surface a few years ago. It was beautiful beyond description. It dazzled the eyes with every conceivable color. It almost hurt my heart, it was so beautiful. It was like—like blasting the gates of Paradise." She subsided quickly, as if she had let herself go too far.

Three times when she named the price of a stone and I offered a lower figure, she answered quietly, *"Es imposible, señor."* She did not look aggrieved, or raise her eyes to heaven, or flare with indignation. She merely shook her head and murmured, *"Es imposible."* One really did not haggle with a lady in her parlor.

We did not purchase any expensive stones, none of the very hard, enduring kind. But we got some lovely ones. Esperón selected three: for his wife, his sister, and his little daughter. The stone I got for a dinner ring for Thérèse was the size of a robin's egg sliced in half. It was of pinkish white with countless tiny emerald stars irradiating a universe in miniature. I had never seen an opal like it. It would look quite smart and chaste and lovely in a modern setting of Mexican silver.

"I must warn you, señor, that this beautiful stone is not to be banged about. It is not proof against scratches. It should not be worn in the everyday household routine. Where one can wear a diamond without danger in almost any kind of work, opals should be saved for leisure hours."

We got up to leave. We had spent a full hour examining, admiring, selecting opals in the modest little parlor. We knew we had got values at wholesale prices, for she had sold them to us for no more than she would have asked a dealer from Mexico City. Knowledge of good value was doubtless part of the enjoyment.

Now I wanted to buy an old crucifix for a Catholic friend of mine. Esperón said he knew of an antique shop in another private home, so we got a cab, and were let out at a posada that he thought was within a stone's throw.

"This posada was an old stagecoach terminus," Esperón explained, "and still operates as an inn today. But it's purely for lodging; no food is served except to animals."

We stood within the entrance of a barny kind of structure that suggested an old-fashioned livery stable. "This inn," he went on, "is the sort of thing Joseph was looking for in Bethlehem when Mary and he went up to pay their tax money. That's why we call our Christmas parties posadas, and go from house to house asking to be taken in. If you're ever caught hard up in Querétaro, you can get a night's lodgings here for ten centavos, two American pennies, no more. Take a look at the price list."

We stepped up to a blackboard where the prices were neatly printed in white chalk.

Piso de Caballo	.10
Piso de Macho	.10
Piso de Burro	.05
Automóvil	.50
Camión	.50
Posada	.10

I knew the word *piso* really meant floor or apartment. Here, I assumed that *piso de caballo* or *macho* meant the apartment or stall a horse or a he-mule might occupy. Ten centavos for a horse or a mule, and the little burro came in at half-price, a penny a night.

"The prices are reversed from the American way," I said. "Here lodging for an automobile or a truck costs five times as much as for a person."

"But five persons can sleep in the space of an automobile," Esperón said laughing. "You don't think you are getting linen sheets and a mattress for two cents, do you? It's up to you to make yourself comfortable with whatever you bring." Upstairs there were bare windowless rooms, without a stick of furniture or an inch of matting.

Three youngsters had noticed us looking at the price list on the board, and our reaction had excited their curiosity. They stood speculatively at a near distance. One, the color of cinnamon, and another the color of vanilla wafers, were each wearing pink shirts. The third, the tall one, had cheeks of light tan with a few freckles. He was a gangling, gap-toothed kid with pale-green eyes, carroty hair, and a scarecrow flatness to his figure. His skinny frame seemed to have shot beyond the dimensions of his shirt and faded overalls only yesterday, and his wide flopping straw hat was frayed around the edges as if chewed by a donkey. He looked like an overgrown thirteen, touch and go with puberty. I thought of a city Huck Finn, without much of Huck's country sophistication. I could wonder at the boy's paternity, and I suspected bastardy. Perhaps his daddy was a sandy-haired Scot, or maybe a former Western Union boy from Texas. However he may have come into the world, he was obviously enchanted by the curiosities of life.

His eyebrows perpetually raised, he watched me with unabashed, frank interest, as he might a zebra in the plaza. There was no impertinence in his manner, but merely a genial curiosity. Like a mute with keenest hearing, he gazed with ears cocked and eyelids stretched wide, endeavoring to collect some meaning out of my strange language. When I smiled, he smiled. Once I frowned. Caught off guard, he looked perplexed—and then frowned vaguely. I smiled again and he smiled instantly. It was like catching an oblique view of oneself in one of those distorted carnival mirrors. I found him quite as interesting a phenomenon as he found me.

Esperón had discovered from the cinnamon-colored kid that the antique shop was only three doors away from the posada. The boys rushed ahead to have the honor of announcing our coming, as if they had secured custom by their own scouting. They tore up some narrow wooden steps, calling for the proprietor as they went. The tall boy was the last to go up, and he paused in mid-flight to make sure we were following. I grinned. He grinned. Then he made the upper half of the stairs in a couple of leaps, his ragged overall legs flapping in abandon about his ankles.

"A charming chap," I said to Esperón. "Bet he's a bastard."

"Most likely. Paternity among the humble is often highly speculative. Sometimes you hear a mother in the market place upbraid a worrisome youngster with *'Hijo de quien sabe quien,'* as if it was the kid's own fault that he was 'a son of who knows who.' "

The proprietor was in the midst of his dinner. But he was not in the least put out. He was an amiable, refined little man, wearing a beige alpaca coat. He withdrew a chain and pushed open a door leading off a gallery vestibule. To make sure they were not left out, the three boys brushed past us before we could enter.

The room was large, with a high ceiling and two great dust-begrimed windows. It was so crowded with deal tables loaded with knickknacks that we could just squeeze down the aisles single file.

It was as if series of palaces had been cleared of little junk. Heaped on the tables and on shelves was stuff ranging from used Japanese lanterns to altarcloths embroidered in gold, from bronze braziers to cuff links set in seed pearls, from comic broadsides and sheet music to seven-branched candlesticks. One table was laden with old coins and medals, another with photographs and daguerreotypes. Everything bore a film of dust.

The boys kept an eye on us. The two shorter ones with the pink shirts remained watching from the doorway like casual plain-clothes men. But the scarecrow fellow followed my tracks at a respectful distance. He was intensely interested in everything that caught my eye. If I admired a carved wooden fire bellows, he would make note of it. If I picked up and examined a dingy prayer book bound in kidskin that had once been virginal white, he would touch it appreciatively. Everything I took up or touched, he would take in his hands, turn it about, remark its contours and qualities. Objects seemed to take on new values because I had remarked them. I pretended not to notice him, but out of the corner of an eye I could see him watching me intently. If I spoke to the proprietor or Esperón, he seemed carried away by my conversation.

Usually, proprietors chase away street urchins who idle in shops, but not this kindly one. He seemed unaware of these boys' presence, and kept a patient smile on his face as he named the price of this or that.

I spied some seventeenth-century iron spurs embossed in diamond-shaped lozenges of brass, with rowels twice the diameter of a silver dollar. I twirled a rowel appreciatively. The boy picked up another spur and twirled a rowel. I looked at him directly and smiled in greeting, as if I had just now become conscious of him. Startled, he looked embarrassed, and then grinned back.

I selected five spurs, each of distinctive workmanship, and passed on to a table piled with crucifixes. Some were two feet tall, others no more than a couple of inches. The boy looked at me quizzically. An *Americano* interested in these things? He exchanged looks with the kids by the door.

I selected one of dark reddish wood, with a finely carved figure of Christ in old silver. It was a beautiful little object—just the thing for my Catholic friend. And then Esperón boomed out an exclamation. He had found something. He held out a crucifix about seven inches high with round crosspieces; the wood was enameled white. At either end just beyond the pierced hands of the corpus were metal medallions bearing on one side the profile of Maximilian and on the other the profile of Carlota. The girl Empress's narrow crown was set far back on a flowing headdress. Maximilian's beard was strongly emphasized.

"This is something unique," Esperón said. "It must have been struck for a special occasion or as a special gift from the royal couple to someone for a special service."

The proprietor declared he had not seen a duplicate. The man's whole manner bespoke such natural honesty that I felt he was speaking the truth. The price was extremely moderate. I bought it immediately, to keep myself as a souvenir of Querétaro.

"But where do you get all these things?" I asked.

The man's hands made a vague gesture. "Here and there. Rich people sell their houses, or lose them through mortgage or expropriation. Some move away, or go into smaller quarters. Mothers bring basketfuls of trinkets to get cash for a daughter's wedding. I do not go out seeking. People bring things here in handkerchiefs, or in carts. They need money. I cannot refuse to buy."

I bought some old coins and some large coin-shaped medallions. One medallion was half again as large as a silver dollar. On one side of it, in delicate high relief, a Virgin was standing on a projecting rock, her halo in the form of twelve tiny stars. On the other side was an excellent profile likeness of Pope Leo XIII. The piece had been struck in Rome. It had evidently lain in some hidalgo's cabinet and not been fingered much, for a faint green patina had formed on the silver bronze. Another medallion had been so used that the relief was almost flat, the features blurred. A seated Virgin and Child on one side, and Saint Anthony, patron saint of travelers and lost objects, on the other. It had been worn devoutly, for both sides had been smoothed down through the years by contact with human flesh. Most likely it had belonged to a traveler, or a soldier, who needed the triple protection of Saint Anthony, the Virgin, and the Child.

Our hands became blacker with everything we touched. I raised a hand to my nose. It smelt as if it were made of rust and corroded brass. My shadow smelt his hand, and made a slight grimace, as I did.

The boys by the door had grown bored. They shifted their feet. They were nonplussed by the *Americano's* interest in medallions, iron spurs, worm-eaten crucifixes. They themselves were doubtless interested in motorcycles, fountain pens, wrist watches, and various mechanical gadgets. My shadow was more understanding. But there was something I had passed over that won his special admiration. Twice he picked it up and laid it down—each time a few inches nearer to me. It was a small dagger with an ebony handle less than two inches long and a blade only three and a half inches long, but making up in the deadliness of its point and sharp curving blade for its brevity. It could reach the heart of a man all right.

I retraced a few steps, added it to my collection, and nodded my approval of the lad's discrimination. "No more," I said to the proprietor with finality. He wrapped the objects in sheets of old newspapers, announced the sum of my indebtedness without having to use a pencil for addition, and went to get change from another room.

The tall boy set his frayed hat farther on the back of his head, and taking long, silent strides, as if tiptoeing on stilts, went to join his companions. The show was over, and he had enjoyed it; he had shared in the appraisals and purchases. He wanted nothing for himself. I knew that it would be wrong to give him money. He seemed quite indifferent to the minor vanities of life.

We had not exchanged a word. It had been merely a transient companionship in spirit and an adventure in mutual curiosity. At last I decided to risk direct communication. *"Muchas gracias,"* I said to him.

The boy's eyes stretched wider and his mouth opened in surprise, as much as if a burro had suddenly said hello to him. He gave his raggedy overalls a kind of nonchalant twitch. *"Es nada,"* he said gaily, and went loping down the creaking steps.

4. A CAKE AND DEPARTURE

We were late in getting back to the car for dinner, but the steward and the porter were both in good humor, as well as Townsend and Wagus, who had returned with experiences from the hinterland. Tardiness rarely causes irritation among Mexicans or lovers of Mexico.

In the dining-room I stopped, surprised. In the center of the table was an extralarge cake heavily frosted and embossed in red letters. My name was spread across the top in bits of candied cherries. A little card lay at the foot of the cake. Scrawled in ink it said, "To El Señor Profesór from the Cook."

The porter and the steward were standing by to note my reaction. I was touched. I asked to have the cook in to thank him. He was a roly-poly with a round face and a rounder belly. I said I had never seen a more beautiful cake and offered him many times a thousand thanks. His grin made a half-circle.

The cook spoke some English. He had lived for a year once in Tulsa, Oklahoma. "Indians, there, too," he said. "Big, fine Indians, rich, much oil. They ride white ladies about in red automobiles."

"Did you like Tulsa?"

"I like. I like very much—to look. Tall buildings, glass store windows full of everything."

"Why didn't you stay?"

"I no have oil." He chuckled pleasantly. "I feel better here."

We all stood admiring the cake for some minutes before we sat down to dinner. But this creation was too much for me, for us. We should have a child here to enjoy it. A child who has never seen a cake like this—except maybe in a confectioner's window. We needed a child for a proper celebration.

I looked at Esperón. He looked at me. We knew one child in Querétaro by name—no more than a boy, if he did wear a soldier's uniform. Josefat Mendes.

Could we? Would it be proper, permitted? A captain ask a private—less than a private—to dinner?

Esperón put back the chair he had pulled out. "Let's go get him. I'll speak with the commandant." He looked at the steward and the cook. Could the dinner be held back a quarter-hour while we went to fetch a guest?

But, of course. *Como no?* Their pleasure was only to please us. Wagus and Townsend were quite content to wait.

I grabbed my hat, and Esperón, his captain's cap. It had begun to drizzle. But we didn't care and didn't bother to take raincoats. We were lucky to find a taxi waiting on the other side of the station. To the military barracks! Hurry!

We tore down a street so narrow that the taxi almost brushed against the tramcar. Citizens and soldiers were clinging to the rails of trams determined to hold onto their lives.

"The boy has surely eaten by now," I said doubtfully.

"I never saw a boy between fourteen and eighteen who could not eat two suppers," Esperón said reassuringly.

In the ill-lit street before the barracks, the rain was falling steadily. We told the driver to wait, and rushed in. Seeing a strange tall army captain approaching, the sentries snapped to attention and let us through with a flourish. Esperón spoke to the officer of the day, who looked surprised, perplexed, and then acquiescent. He called a soldier to precede and escort us. We crossed the wet paving of the courtyard, jumping the deeper puddles. The soldier bounded up the steps, shouting "Josefat Mendes!"

Loitering youths in the upper corridor became alert with curiosity. "Josefat Mendes?" they repeated, and looked at each other.

"He is wanted," the escort said, rushing on.

"Josefat Mendes," Esperón and I both reiterated. "Do you know where he is? Do you know him?"

"Josefat Mendes?" "I think he is out." "He is gone." "Josefat Mendes went out, but he returned." "No!" "Yes!" "Perhaps." "Let us see." Conscripts scattered in various directions, calling his name.

A group of four joined us. One led the way to a dormitory. "Josefat Mendes!" he yelled. Some boys idling on their beds jumped up to attention.

"Do you know Josefat Mendes?"

"*No, mi capitán.*"

"Do you know Josefat Mendes?"

"*Sí, mi capitán.* But he does not have his bed here. In another room."

Down the corridors rang our original escort's call for Josefat Mendes. He was unaware that he had lost us.

A grave-faced soldier pointed, and offered to lead the way anew. "I know him. He sleeps in there." The other fellows exchanged excited looks. There was some urgency and import in the matter.

Was his mother dying? Was he accused of theft? Had he been left a fortune? Was he to be court-martialed?

Now a score of soldiers trailed behind us through the great arches into another dormitory. Our first escort arrived from another direction. It was his voice that echoed back the cry for Josefat Mendes.

"Does Josefat Mendes sleep in this room?"

"Yes, but he is not here."

"Look in the toilets. Look in the shower room."

The soldier from Esperón's province, the good-looking chap with fine teeth and the mandolin, appeared from the shower room with a towel wrapped about his middle. "Josefat Mendes went out. He did not come back for supper. See? There is where he lives."

He led us down between the rows of beds and stopped before the little table-cabinet that stood at the foot of a certain cot, as similar cabinets stood at the foot of every cot. He pointed to what lay on top: a tin plate with a pile of black beans, stew meat, some tortillas, some boiled cabbage, and a mug of cocoa. Josefat's untouched supper had got cold. These were the only plate and mug visible in the entire dormitory. All the other suppers had been eaten, and the utensils washed and put away.

We stared in silence at the unhappy evidence. No, he could not be in the barracks.

"You see," Esperón commented on the side, "the food these boys get in the army is substantial and fairly well balanced. And note, not a soldier has touched a crumb of Josefat's supper."

"Was it something very important, *mi capitán?*" The boy in the towel spoke.

Esperón looked at him and at me. But before he asked the question he knew that no one but Josefat Mendes would really do. Yet he said half-heartedly, "What are you doing tonight, now, before bedtime?"

The young man showed his white teeth in a grin. "With your money, *mi capitán,* I was able to buy a pretty girl a *tres Marías* this afternoon, and she is meeting me at eight."

"*Tres Marías?*" I queried.

"Three Marys," Esperón said, "is the name of a triple ice-cream cone shaped to hold three blobs, vanilla, chocolate, and strawberry."

If we had not given money to Josefat Mendes, I ruminated, he would be where he should be now.

"What shall we say to Josefat Mendes?" some other boys asked together.

"Tell him—tell him, his new friends—" We both began to feel a little foolish. "Tell him we got permission to take him to a fiesta on a private car at the railway station—and that we were sorry to miss him."

"He will be more than sorry."

As we watched our steps down the slippery stone stairs to the wet courtyard, we knew Josefat could not be as disappointed as we. "You see how it is," Esperón said. "Grownups often get more pleasure doing things for kids than the kids themselves get out of it."

Soldiers scurrying in out of the rain passed us, but none of them was the one we were looking for. We both felt a bit sunk as we got into the taxi.

"*Donde?*" the driver asked.

"Drive slowly to the Jardín Zenea and around it," I suggested. I have ever hated to have my plans go astray. And the kid would have remembered always having dinner in a private car with a big cake like that.

We strained our eyes at the oblique street shadows. Young conscripts lurked in the protection of doorways, but none was the fellow too small for his uniform. We drove slowly around the deserted plaza. Only desultory citizens were streaking across to get out of the rain.

We did not enjoy the excellent dinner with duck as much as we had expected. Even Townsend and Wagus were disappointed. But for the cook's sake we put on a jovial air and made exclamations of delight when he came in to witness the cutting of the cake. Townsend couldn't eat any, because he had some inner discomfort from indulging in too much chili with the Indians. So altogether there were only six big slices gone—three for us in the dining-room and three for those in the kitchen. There was enough cake left to feed a squadron.

After coffee, as we smoked our cigars there sat the great white cake, like a monument to our defeat. We had tried and failed in our efforts to give pleasure and get pleasure by giving.

"It seems a waste to take it back to Mexico City," Esperón said.

"Do you think it would hurt the cook's feelings," I hinted, "if we took him half of it?"

"I can't tell you how much a cake meant to me when I was in military school in the States."

We called the cook. He gave the gesture his blessing. We halved the cake and put the full half in a pasteboard box.

It was now nine-fifteen by the station clock. The barracks' lights were on until nine forty-five.

The rain had almost stopped. Again we were lucky in finding a lone waiting cab. We drove swiftly to the barracks. I bore the cake, since it seemed a bit irregular for a captain to be bringing a conscript such a gift.

We did not go up. The officer of the day sent for Josefat Mendes. While we waited, he and Esperón exchanged comments on the state of the war in Europe, and twice he glanced quizzically at the box I held with such care.

The soldier returned without him. Josefat Mendes was still out— his supper was untouched, the messenger said.

"Here is a present for him," I said. "Please put it in the middle of his cot, and tell him to give you a big slice of it when he comes in. Be careful. Don't slip on the pavement."

I turned to the officer of the day. "Josefat Mendes is out late," I said, casually.

"Sí, señor."

"He seems very young. I hope he hasn't got into trouble."

"Quien sabe?" The man smiled philosophically. "He's a soldier now."

As we returned to the car we felt better since we had left half the cake in the barracks. The rain had stopped, and almost immediately the stars were out, fitfully illuminating the city's silhouettes. Here and there twin towers rose against the background of night sky like double exclamation marks punctuating the municipal plan. Always two towers to a church in Mexico, as if to keep each other company in this unholy world, like nuns who must not go singly, but ever in pairs.

It had been most pleasant to be companioned for some days with this Mexican army officer, and most revealing. Through Captain

Esperón I had a feeling of his country that I might never have got otherwise. We had accepted each other at face value, and he had spoken without reserve. It was not just his knowledgeable comments and his sense of humor that made him such a good companion. Without his kindness of heart and his innate good manners, his other qualities would have counted for so much less.

And what better attributes could a man of any nationality possess than consideration and kindness of heart? I was thinking as I dropped off to sleep the last night I was to spend in the private car. In my half-waking state the problems of Mexico seemed to rise from the valleys or stand out on the sierras like mammoth question marks. So much had already been done. So much was still to do. Many things would doubtless be done the wrong or the wasteful way. But Mexico had a great hope of progress now—and there was really no febrile hurry. In a land so varied and so alien even to segments of itself, there could be few pat answers. As Esperón misquoted, "In life there are no conclusions, only private dirges and occasionally *Te Deums*."

XI

Postwar

THE FIRST POSTWAR year of 1946 saw Mexico advance at an unwonted pace in its growing-up process. The evidence was not so much in notable events as in less spectacular manifestations.

Visitors of 1946 who had known Mexico in prewar years were not entirely convinced that they liked the rapid modernization that was both obviously and stealthily afoot in the Republic. Many of the vivid, sprawling, sociable markets spread out beneath the sun were being supplanted by functional structures of concrete and steel. Random stalls and shacks under haphazard awnings, piled with brilliant serapes and garnished with flowers, were being shunted to the past to make room for orderly showcases, up-to-date fixtures, and washable woodwork. The capital saw the installation of seven new markets built in various parts of the city according to designs of modern small public markets in the United States. Sanitation and refrigeration were superseding the picturesque as well as the unhealthy. Some of the charm, along with some of the unsightliness, of the old-fashioned market was on the way to limbo.

Illiteracy, too, seemed destined to vanish. In January of 1946 President Avila Camacho gave a resplendent new flag to the village of Soledad Etla in the State of Oaxaca, because within one year the four hundred and seventy illiterates of the hamlet's twelve hundred had learned to read and write—the first community in all Mexico to be able to claim one hundred per cent literacy.

The special campaign to wipe out ignorance, instituted by Minister of Education Jaimé Torres Bodet in 1944, was having expansive success under the slogan "Each one teach one." The literate were compelled to teach the illiterate or contribute to a literacy center where groups were taught. By March first each Mexican was required to carry a card proving that he had either taught or been taught or had contributed money to the cause. Soon the day would come, said the newspapers, when illiteracy would be looked upon as a crime in Mexico.

Industrialization was going forward at such a rate that some wondered if the more humble Mexicans would in time become completely ignorant of the useful arts. New local industries were arising and more were being planned, while well-known American firms like Dupont, Goodyear, Celanese Corporation, Crosley Radio, Atlas Cement, and Worthington Pump began to establish or expand factories in Mexico.

In mid-March Antonio Ruiz Galindo, a self-made businessman of forty-eight who had amassed a five-million-dollar fortune from manufacturing steel office furniture, made big news in both labor and capital circles. Near Guadalupe he created a two-million-dollar industrial city designed to raise the living standards of his thousand factory employees. He erected six modern, well-equipped apartment buildings to be rent-free for his workers, who also receive free medical care, free movies, and free lunches. On the factory walls he placed quantities of mirrors, so that the workers might be inspired to keep themselves clean, and he provided a plenitude of showers for their ablutions. In return for this shrewd, paternalistic gesture he asked the Mexican Government to protect his and other infant industries by imposing a customs duty sufficient to enable native products to meet foreign competition.

In July Mexico could rightly take pride in her increased inches in political advancement. For the presidential elections came off with unprecedented order and quiet. Hardly a shot was fired. Soldiers stood guard. Opposing sides did not fight for control of polling booths. Ladies did not throw brickbats or form cordons to restrain voters of the opposition. It was virtually a foregone conclusion that the popular Miguel Alemán, former Secretary of the Interior, backed by the Government and supported by the labor unions, would defeat the scholarly Ezequiel Padilla, former Foreign Secretary. Even most of Dr. Padilla's devoted cohorts were frank to declare the election the most democratic and honest in the Republic's history.

With the advancement in political attitude, industrial development, and literacy, unhappily the year 1946 was marked, as it was in the United States and most regions of the globe, by an alarming inflation. The Government seemed impotent to control black-market activities. The cost of living rocketed. Some food costs had advanced 440 per cent since 1930. The increase in wages lagged far behind.

Women stood long hours in queues to get charcoal for cooking the simple family fare. The price of real estate advanced to absurd figures, and good houses for rent were hard to get at any price. A few took consolation in recalling that inflation came in waves and recessions, and that over a century ago—on February 25, 1842—Madame Calderón de la Barca had written to relatives in the States, "House rent in Mexico City is extremely high; nothing tolerable to be had under two thousand five hundred dollars per annum, unfurnished."

Tourists from the United States were largely blamed for the rise in prices. And as visitors poured into Mexico new hotels were being erected as rapidly as possible, with forethought of an even greater influx of tourist trade when the last stretches of the great Inter-American Highway should be completed to Panamá.

With the cessation of war came a lively interest in providing more entertainment for both citizens and visitors. Symphony concerts and art exhibits flourished along with night clubs, music halls, the jai alai frontón, the race track, and the bullring.

In late March an exhibit of Diego Rivera's collection of primitive figurines and statues made front-page news and was called by some of the critic ethnologists "one of the greatest treasuries of the day." In June Albert Spalding, the American violinist, played with Carlos Chávez and the Mexico Symphony Orchestra. The Sibelius number went over magnificently at an evening concert, and according to one critic the Sunday morning concert was "positively a delirium."

The beauteous Dolores del Rio and the dynamic Arturo de Córdoba held their popularity with the motion-picture fans. Cantínflas, the inimitable music-hall comic, continued to delight capacity audiences with his drolleries, and Augustín Lara's sentimental tunes were played ubiquitously. The intimate College of Love Hour, sponsored on the radio by Glostora Hair Dressing, still appealed to the incorrigibly romantic, while men and women too bashful to declare their love in private spoke boldly into the microphone.

While swains went on hiring *mariachi* singers to serenade their inamoratas at midnight, more and more señoritas laid aside their own guitars to make commercial music on office typewriters.

Baseball became the rage, and many American top-notch players were seduced by the enormous salaries to go south. Plush night clubs like Ciro's and Sans Souci reached a fantastic new high in prices, and yet could not accommodate all who pleaded for admission.

In August an art show, sponsored by President Avila Camacho in the Palace of Fine Arts, exhibited more than four hundred modern paintings by living painters. Of the most famous artists, Orozco and Siqueiros were represented, but not Diego Rivera. Almost everybody else submitted something: among them, Cantú, Merida, Tamayo, Goita, Castellanos, Montenegro, Orozco Romero. According to the critics only one painter revealed the old-time fire. The perennial revolutionary firebrand David Siqueiros exhibited an ugly, fist-smashing self-portrait. To the press he accused his fellow artists of going soft from fat times and tourist dollars—of "leaving the hard road of the social, heroic, and monumental for the path of the exquisite and the snob."

The year 1946 saw the opening of Mexico's new Plaza de Toros, the largest in the world, with seats for forty-eight thousand, just about twice the capacity of the old bullring. In the second week in November the *novillada,* season of young and apprentice matadors, was brought to a close with a benefit fight for a new bright luminary, twenty-one-year-old Joselillo Rodríguez. Formerly a grocery clerk, Little Joe made his debut as a torero in August. His first appearance was so brilliant that the bullfight critics acclaimed him extravagantly. "Here is the *novillero* of the season—of all seasons," one of them wrote. Joselillo was not only a marvel with the cape and the muleta, but so daring that his pants were ripped by a bull's horn in every fight he fought. Some said that this was the reason he shrewdly rented his suits at fifty dollars a performance instead of buying one for several hundred dollars. Scheduled for the winter season of 1946-47 as one of the big attractions, the young man's future loomed brighter than that of any novice in years—he might conceivably earn as much as five million pesos in his lifetime in the ring, if he did not meet an early death.

In the first week of December in a symbolic ceremony before twenty-five hundred guests at the Palace of Fine Arts, outgoing President Avila Camacho draped the official sash of red, white, and green silk about the chest of Miguel Alemán, who thereby became Mexico's chief executive for the next six years. In honor of the inauguration twenty-seven United States Superfortresses flashed their silver wings under the sparkling winter sun high above the capital.

Though a supporter of Miguel Alemán, former President Lázaro Cárdenas, whose life was dedicated to bettering the lot of the under-privileged, did not grace the occasion with his presence. People won-dered if he was too disturbed about the unwholesome economic bal-ances of the country, the food shortages, the augmenting hard lot of the poor since 1941, and the increasing riches of the well-to-do.

But though Cárdenas might question Alemán's choice of a couple of wealthy businessmen and a corporation lawyer for prominent Cabinet posts, he was bound to like the nonpolitical aspect of most of the Cabinet choices. He heartily approved of Alemán's campaign promises to further a prodigious irrigation program to increase agri-cultural production. And he applauded the new President's pro-claimed intention to build up public morality and eradicate the custom known as the *mordida*—"bite," the rake-off—by which cer-tain government and municipal officials coerced money tribute from biggest business to paltry one-man shops. The genial Alemán knew well that his road would not be easy, but he had such a reassuring smile as he assumed office that many of the sufferers said, "It can't be as bad or as hopeless as we think it is."

In the week of the inauguration outgoing President Avila Camacho made a last decision that helped to allay a famous ghost. After much examination and debate antiquarians had positively de-clared that some mysterious bones recently discovered in a crystal casket sealed in the walls of a disused church were those of Hernán Cortés. When the question arose as to what to do with the relics of the great conquistador, President Avila Camacho decreed that they were to be restored to the abandoned church in which they were discovered and that the church be declared a national monument. Thus after four centuries the most famous name ever connected with Mexico was to have his first real monument in the land he had con-quered.

In his first fortnight in office the new President went straight at the Republic's most urgent problem—increased agricultural produc-tion. He proposed laws defining and securing titles for small prop-erty owners, in the hope that the farmers would improve their soil and produce more foodstuff when the land became irrevocably theirs. And he presented Congress with an irrigation program by which fifty million barren acres might be reclaimed and made productive. To handle the great dam-building projects, the power development, the soil improvement, and the colonization of the land, President Alemán created a new Ministry of Hydraulic Resources and earmarked a goodly proportion of the Federal budget for the work.

The new President avowed his special aim was to render Mexico capable of feeding itself and of raising the standards of rural living. But it was obvious that while Miguel Alemán might desire to help the have-nots, he was not going to antagonize big business; rather he would make good use of it by co-operation. And the famous labor leader Vicente Lombardo Toledano, who had already promoted an industry-labor pact barring strikes so that production could be increased, was going completely against the Communist-party line and saying, "Our tactics is that of national unity."

In late December former President Cárdenas left his lime and orange orchards on Lake Pátzcuaro to pay a quiet call on the new President. The press regarded the visit as a benediction pronounced on the new regime.

As 1947 dawned, Mexico on the surface was booming and peaceful. At the beginning of March, President Truman paid a neighborly visit to Mexico's new chief executive, and the capital received him with Latin fanfare. In May, Miguel Alemán returned Harry Truman's visit, and the Americans outdid the Latins in enthusiastic welcome. Alemán's smile and engaging ways won the crowd wherever he went. As a visiting celebrity he was easy to put over with the American public. The climax to Alemán's visit came when, in Spanish, he addressed a joint session of Congress on "The Economy of the Good Neighbor" and announced that Mexico needed money. The Senators and Representatives gave him an ovation and he also got at a low interest rate the several score million dollars he had come to borrow.

The United States press in general seemed to look as favorably on the loan as the public did on Alemán. But *The New Republic* raised a question: Why must the Mexican Government borrow when Mexico refrains from putting a high income tax rate on her moneyed classes, who had even declined to subscribe to a Mexican Victory Bond issue in 1944 because of the paltry 6¾ per cent? The income tax of Mexico had hardly touched the huge profits made during the war, and, besides, tax evasion in Mexico is a notorious scandal. ("In 1944, the Mexican federal income tax represented a mere 4.4 per cent of the national income as compared with our 22 per cent.") For at least 75 per cent of the population, declared *The New Republic,* Mexico's war prosperity had been all but a fraud. Though the national income had almost doubled in six years, the poor were worse off in 1947 than they were in 1940.

Tourists, however, were little concerned with Mexico's economic imbalance and injustices. They flocked across the border all through the winter and spring. Airplanes were booked to capacity for the summer months of 1947. A steady stream of automobiles—some brand-new, some making their perilous last trip—was winding south on the Pan-American Highway to see the sights of Mexico.

With all the real and the pseudo prosperity, amid all the honest new enlightenment and the new-created false values, happily technical science in Mexico has not yet reached the advanced stage of boomeranging to make confusion among man's simple joys. In the small towns and rural districts one could find people who had not lost touch with the earth. Travelers from the States, nurtured on city concrete and gaudy neon lights, might still enjoy the fascination of the primitive in another man's land and delight in antique beauty. There were yet many places where taut-nerved strangers in real need of quiet rhythms could remain in simple comfort for a healing sojourn.

Epilogue

The last time I flew from Mexico's capital, *Te Deums* and symbols of progress were both in my mind. I recalled the cramping little amphibian in which I first approached Yucatán in 1935. Now I was returning to Mérida in a commodious up-to-date plane, and there I was booked for a seat in a giant Stratoclipper which flew at such a height and speed that a constant flow of oxygen was necessary to make breathing normal. I thought of José Vasconcelos' line: "To fight the elements and subdue them to man's will, to utilize them for human ends, what greater incentive can there be for the heroic heart?" And I thought how a flight might be likened to an intellectual hymn to beauty, or a *Te Deum* without words.

There is a special beauty and mystery about a dawn flight. The plane to Mérida took off from the platinum-colored airport in the theatrical glare of floodlights. Then the course through the upper air was feebly illuminated by the greenish glow of a dying moon, three-quarters of its span already spent. Nothing was visible above the earth except the silver wing of the plane and that raveling curve of a moon, reflecting light from the unrisen sun. The sky was murky opal as we traversed the drained bed of Lake Texcoco, its brackish pools pale as if drugged with sleep.

In the eastern distance beyond the reaches of the lake that had known such climactic history, the sky revealed a slender band of turquoise. Then clouds obliterated the blue line like a wash of the sea. Shortly we rose through the vapor and headed for the lemon light that preceded the rising sun. Stray bits of clouds were now sprayed lightly with an essence of gilt. And then dawn touched the snows of Popocatepetl and the Sleeping Lady. Soon the perilous way Cortés came was effulgent with radiance like a path of glory. At six-fifteen the full majesty of the sun appeared, and its alchemy transformed the leaden mountaintops to gold.

Beneath us lay stretches of solid cloud fluff like a cotton field in which stalks and leaves and the soil itself had turned to long staple cotton, like that legendary abundance of the age of the god Quetzalcoatl. Obliquely to the right the crater of Popo was open like the seductive mouth of a carnivorous plant, waiting to close over any venturesome victim. Beyond, in front of us, rose the dazzling cone of Orizaba. And to the left at respectful distance from supremacy, like retainers of an Oriental lord, stood a retinue of small volcanoes long cooled to impotence.

As we approached the port of Vera Cruz all clouds dispersed and the ground was one tropical green. We flew low enough to see coconut palms spread thin parasols over drowsing cattle not yet astir. The moon, which had been green when we left the airfield, had undergone a metamorphosis. Now it was like a lop-sided setting for a ring—a kind of moonstone with a blurred blue figure. We dropped away from the cool upper air and descended to the humid atmosphere of Vera Cruz. Here Cortés had made his first settlement, destroyed his ships, and staked all on the march to Mexico. In the centuries following, Vera Cruz had existed not for itself, but as a gateway to the capital. Few tarried in Vera Cruz except for pressing business. Our plane paid it the respect of a quarter of an hour's halt. Then we took off for the peninsula of Yucatán with its treasury of temples, and from there I would take a Stratoclipper to New Orleans and home.